Properties of Law

Properties of Law is a legal theoretical analysis about modern state law; about sociality, normativity, and plurality as its properties; and what will come after modern state law. The main objective of this study is to offer a legal theoretical recapitulation of modern state law that avoids the fallacies of Legal Positivism. This calls for a relationist approach where law's sociality is related to normativity, and normativity to sociality. Avoiding Legal Positivism's fallacies also includes refraining from extrapolating from modern state law to law in general; replacing Legal Positivism's conceptual universalism with sensitivity to the varieties of law; and acknowledging that law existed before modern state law, that it will exist after modern state law, and that other law exists alongside modern state law. The book concludes with a discussion of the impact of digitalisation on law.

KAARLO TUORI is Professor Emeritus at the Faculty of Law, University of Helsinki, Finland. He has led the Centre of Excellence in European Law and Polity, financed by Academy of Finland, 2008–2013, and has served as a counsellor to the Constitutional Law Committee of Parliament and as a member of the Venice Commission of the Council of Europe (1998–).

CAMBRIDGE
UNIVERSITY PRESS

University Printing House, Cambridge CB2 8BS, United Kingdom

One Liberty Plaza, 20th Floor, New York, NY 10006, USA

477 Williamstown Road, Port Melbourne, VIC 3207, Australia

314–321, 3rd Floor, Plot 3, Splendor Forum, Jasola District Centre, New Delhi – 110025, India

103 Penang Road, #05–06/07, Visioncrest Commercial, Singapore 238467

Cambridge University Press is part of the University of Cambridge.

It furthers the University's mission by disseminating knowledge in the pursuit of education, learning, and research at the highest international levels of excellence.

www.cambridge.org
Information on this title: www.cambridge.org/9781108844727
DOI: 10.1017/9781108953436

First published 2021

A catalogue record for this publication is available from the British Library.

Library of Congress Cataloging-in-Publication Data
Names: Tuori, Kaarlo, author.
Title: Properties of law : modern law and after / Kaarlo Tuori, University of Helsinki.
Description: Cambridge, United Kingdom ; New York, NY : Cambridge University Press, 2021. | Series: Law in context | Includes bibliographical references and index.
Identifiers: LCCN 2021024678 (print) | LCCN 2021024679 (ebook) | ISBN 9781108844727 (hardback) | ISBN 9781108948807 (paperback) | ISBN 9781108953436 (epub)
Subjects: LCSH: Law–Methodology.
Classification: LCC K212 .T86 2021 (print) | LCC K212 (ebook) | DDC 340/.1–dc23
LC record available at https://lccn.loc.gov/2021024678
LC ebook record available at https://lccn.loc.gov/2021024679

ISBN 978-1-108-84472-7 Hardback

Properties of Law

Modern Law and After

KAARLO TUORI
University of Helsinki

CAMBRIDGE
UNIVERSITY PRESS

Brownsword & Goodwin: *Law and the Technologies of the Twenty-First Century: Text and Materials*
Cane & Goudkamp: *Atiyah's Accidents, Compensation and the Law, 9th Edition*
Clarke: *Principles of Property Law*
Clarke & Kohler: *Property Law: Commentary and Materials*
Collins: *The Law of Contract, 4th Edition*
Collins, Ewing & McColgan: *Labour Law, 2nd Edition*
Cowan: *Housing Law and Policy*
Cranston: *Commercial Law from the Nineteenth Century: Law as Backcloth*
Cranston: *Legal Foundations of the Welfare State*
Darian-Smith: *Laws and Societies in Global Contexts: Contemporary Approaches*
Dauvergne: *Making People Illegal: What Globalisation Means for Immigration and Law*
David: *Kinship, Law and Politics: An Anatomy of Belonging*
Davies: *Perspectives on Labour Law, 2nd Edition*
Dembour: *Who Believes in Human Rights?: Reflections on the European Convention*
de Sousa Santos: *Toward a New Legal Common Sense: Law, Globalization, and Emancipation*
Diduck: *Law's Families*
Dupret: *Positive Law from the Muslim World*
Estella: *Legal Foundations of EU Economic Governance*
Fortin: *Children's Rights and the Developing Law, 3rd Edition*
Garnsey: *The Justice of Visual Art: Creative State-Building in Times of Political Transition*
Garton, Probert & Bean: *Moffat's Trusts Law: Text and Materials, 7th Edition*
Ghai & Woodman: *Practising Self-Government: A Comparative Study of Autonomous Regions*
Glover-Thomas: *Reconstructing Mental Health Law and Policy*
Gobert & Punch: *Rethinking Corporate Crime*
Goldman: *Globalisation and the Western Legal Tradition: Recurring Patterns of Law and Authority*
Haack: *Evidence Matters: Science, Proof, and Truth in the Law*
Harlow & Rawlings: *Law and Administration, 4th Edition*
Harris: *An Introduction to Law, 8th Edition*
Harris, Campbell & Halson: *Remedies in Contract and Tort, 2nd Edition*
Harvey: *Seeking Asylum in the UK: Problems and Prospects*
Herring: *Law and the Relational Self*
Hervey & McHale: *European Union Health Law: Themes and Implications*
Hervey & McHale: *Health Law and the European Union*
Holder & Lee: *Environmental Protection, Law and Policy: Text and Materials, 2nd Edition*
Jackson & Summers: *The Internationalisation of Criminal Evidence: Beyond the Common Law and Civil Law Traditions*
Kostakopoulou: *The Future Governance of Citizenship*
Kreiczer-Levy: *Destabilized Property: Property Law in the Sharing Economy*
Kubal: *Immigration and Refugee Law in Russia: Socio-Legal Perspectives*

(continued after the index)

Law in Context

Since 1970, the Law in Context series has been at the forefront of a movement to broaden the study of law. The series is a vehicle for the publication of innovative monographs and texts that treat law and legal phenomena critically in their cultural, social, political, technological, environmental and economic contexts. A contextual approach involves treating legal subjects broadly, using materials from other humanities and social sciences, and from any other discipline that helps to explain the operation in practice of the particular legal field or legal phenomena under investigation. It is intended that this orientation is at once more stimulating and more revealing than the bare exposition of legal rules. The series includes original research monographs, coursebooks and textbooks that foreground contextual approaches and methods. The series includes and welcomes books on the study of law in all its contexts, including domestic legal systems, European and international law, transnational and global legal processes, and comparative law.

Books in the Series

Acosta: *The National versus the Foreigner in South America: 200 Years of Migration and Citizenship Law*
Ali: *Modern Challenges to Islamic Law*
Alyagon Darr: *Plausible Crime Stories: The Legal History of Sexual Offences in Mandate Palestine*
Anderson, Schum & Twining: *Analysis of Evidence, 2nd Edition*
Ashworth: *Sentencing and Criminal Justice, 6th Edition*
Barton & Douglas: *Law and Parenthood*
Baxi, McCrudden & Paliwala: *Law's Ethical, Global and Theoretical Contexts: Essays in Honour of William Twining*
Beecher-Monas: *Evaluating Scientific Evidence: An Interdisciplinary Framework for Intellectual Due Process*
Bell: *French Legal Cultures*
Bercusson: *European Labour Law, 2nd Edition*
Birkinshaw: *European Public Law*
Birkinshaw: *Freedom of Information: The Law, the Practice and the Ideal, 4th Edition*
Blick: *Electrified Democracy*
Broderick & Ferri: *International and European Disability Law and Policy: Text, Cases and Materials*

Contents

Preface

This is an essay in legal theory, not a doctoral thesis. I have tried to keep the footnotes to a minimum and shunned textual footnotes. The essay is, of course, based on extensive reading. In addition to the sources of direct quotations, I have wanted to indicate merely the literature I have most profited from. Yet I have not considered it necessary to identify the sources of all household premises of legal theory and sociology, say, the views and insights of classics such as Hobbes, Bentham, and John Austin or Kant and Weber.

In elaborating my 'reflexion theory' of modern law, I employ two primary methodological tools: the ideal-type method of Georg Jellinek and Max Weber and criticism of Legal Positivism. Criticism of Legal Positivism continues through Parts I–III. Still, this is not a book about other books, but the criticism serves to develop my own ideas. Because I share the basic tenet of modern law's fundamental positivity, my criticism could also be termed internal. I mostly limit my discussion to the Masters of modern Legal Positivism, namely Hans Kelsen and H. L. A. Hart. This I consider sufficient for my purposes: I am not engaged in a wholesale critical presentation of contemporary Legal Positivism. Much of subsequent positivist discussion consists merely of glosses on the oeuvre of the Masters. I deliberately try to avoid getting involved in tribal positivist debates or repetitive positivist criticism of Ronal Dworkin, the favourite straw man of especially the Hartian school.

Legal theorists, too, seem to divide into hedgehogs and foxes. I find my place among the hedgehogs. I am surprised to realise how persistent my interest has been in some fundamental issues of legal theory and sociology, such as the relationship between legal normativity and social facticity, or between legal repression and emancipation. I am also surprised to realise how relevant the authors who impressed me early in my career still are: in addition to Kelsen and Hart, let me only point to Weber, Habermas, Luhmann, and Foucault and – perhaps as my chosen straw man – Schmitt. I had the privilege of having as my professor in constitutional law Paavo Kastari, who had introduced Kelsen to Finnish legal scholars before World War II; who wrote of *The Concept of Law* as early as the 1960s; who loaned me Weber's *Sociology of Law*, with the dedication of the editor of the English edition; who invited Luhmann to Helsinki at a time when nobody in Finnish academia had heard of him, not even the janitors who were ordered to complement Kastari and myself as the audience at Luhmann's lecture on *Der Begriff der Verfassung*; and who circulated photocopies of the proofs of Luhmann's *Rechtssoziologie* in Helsinki - in a shoebox.

After I had finished my *European Constitutionalism*, Hans Lindahl managed to get my thoughts moving again. My foray into European law had taught me the importance of non-state law for legal theory; Hans showed the importance of the phenomenological approach. Hans also facilitated my stay in Stellenbosch at STIAS in 2017 – a highly inspiring academic environment with highly inspiring colleagues, none of them a lawyer or a legal theorist!

My thanks also go to my friends and colleagues who have kindly read and commented on the manuscript of this essay, either as a whole or on individual chapters. Sakari Hänninen and Martti Koskenniemi have tirelessly reminded me of the fact that law is also about power and interests – a fact which from time to time I tend to sidetrack in my predilection for coherence and system-building. Other commentators, too, have greatly contributed to the end result: Ilkka Hiidenheimo, Ari Hirvonen, Juha Karhu, Emilia Korkea-aho, Riikka Koulu, Visa Kurki, Susanna Lindroos-Hovinheimo, Hans-W. Micklitz, and Kaius Tuori. The Law Faculty at Helsinki University have provided me with the infrastructure necessary for completing the project.

The final phase of work with the manuscript coincided with the COVID-19 pandemic. We have stayed in Sysmä, at Mataristo. She has painted in her studio – one of the paintings can be seen on the cover of this book – while I have written in my study or in the summer house. We have missed our children, grandchildren, friends, and colleagues. Still, we have been lucky.

There are many people to whom I would want to dedicate this book. Fortunately, a choice is not necessary: I dedicate the book to all of you.

Prologue

Elusiveness

The Stakes

This is a book about modern state law; about sociality, normativity, and plurality as its properties. Towards the end, it is also about what will come after modern state law. Legal Positivism, with Hans Kelsen and H. L. A. Hart as the undisputed Masters, is the dominant legal-theoretical (self-) description of modern state law. The main objective of this essay is to offer a legal-theoretical recapitulation of modern state law that avoids the fallacies of Legal Positivism. This calls for a relationist approach where law's sociality is related to normativity, and normativity to sociality. I start with sociality (Part I) and then move on to normativity (Part II), but the reverse order might also have been possible and, indeed, equally warranted. Avoiding Legal Positivism's fallacies also includes refraining from extrapolating from modern state law to law in general; replacing Legal Positivism's conceptual universalism with sensitivity to the varieties of law; and acknowledging that law existed before modern state law, that it will exist after modern state law, and that other law exists alongside modern state law. Part III, dealing with plurality, plays a crucial role in exposing the false pretensions of universalising legal theory. Indigenous, religious, and transnational law demonstrate that the distinctions typical of modern state law are not universal properties of law, and that the language of modern state law is not a universal legal language but merely a vernacular.

Part III also points to the shaking of societal presuppositions of modern state law and introduces discussion of the legal consequences of denationalisation (globalisation). The discussion of law after modern state law continues in the Epilogue, where the focus is on another contemporary mega-trend, namely digitalisation. How, exactly, digitalisation will affect law is still shrouded in ambiguity; it depends not only on the vagaries of technological development but also on political decisions: hence, the title *Incertitude*. In discussing the menaces that digitalisation entails to the principles of a democratic *Rechtsstaat*, the Epilogue also overtly indicates that the stakes are not purely intellectual (as if legal theory ever could be a purely intellectual exercise) but the essay is also animated by normative concerns.

The dominance of Legal Positivism has not prevented rival legal-theoretical – or legal-sociological – recapitulations. Their wide array attests to yet another central property of law: evasiveness.

Three Modes of Existence

Law resists encasement by comprehensive theoretical grids, and 'law' is a slippery notion which defies unequivocal definition. It appears that no account of law can do without qualifications and exceptions or be immune to criticism and counterarguments. All definitions of 'law' create a penumbra of uncertainty, and a grey zone is opened in the borderland between law and non-law. Something of arguably legal character is always left over and outside any embracive account of law, while something that really does not fit is included. And what appears pertinent to one aspect of law may seem wholly inadequate to another.

At least three manifestations of and explications for the elusiveness of law exist. First, law possesses diverse modes of existence. Law is about norms, but it is not only about norms; it is also about particular, sociolegal, practices. Law is about social practices, but it is not only about social practices; it is also about norms. Secondly, law is traversed by binary distinctions. Thus, to take an example, law transmits, enhances, and legitimates power – say, political and economic – but law also constrains power – again, say, political and economic. Or, to take another example, law not only determines how we must act and restricts our options; it also creates spheres of autonomy and augments our practical possibilities. Finally, in a fundamental sense, law does not exist as such but only as viewed from a perspective. Law is not the same for lawyers and laymen, for private and public lawyers, or for judges and legal scholars.

Let us start canvassing the backdrop to law's elusiveness from its three modes of existence. Intuitively, both legal laymen and professionals seem to know what they are talking of when they speak of law. Law forms part of the world they take for granted, and knowledge of law forms part of the stock of tacit knowledge with which ordinary members of society orient themselves in their daily life and legal professionals in their professional activities. Yet situations arise where the reference to 'law' appears uncertain and cloudy, and where interlocutors no longer agree on what, exactly, they are speaking of. When asked about the law, in Continental Europe the majority of both laymen and professionals would probably point to statutes and other legislation, while in the USA and England the primary reference would be judicial precedents and the principles these reflect. Although the spontaneous responses presumably differ, they have something in common: they both treat law as a normative phenomenon; as a normative legal order, distinct from the social practices and relationships it addresses.

However, not all societies would share this spontaneous normativism. If members of indigenous peoples in general agreed to talk about something called law, they would most likely not allude to a distinct normative order but, rather, to their way of life, the way things have been done in their community since times of old. Such a response would convey non-comprehension of law as something separate from its substance; law is treated not as distinct from social relationships but as embedded in them, with no autonomous existence. In contrast, under the dominance of modern state law, those who recognise this type of law as their law usually share the spontaneous normativism.

In academic debates, the normativist position has not been as self-evident as it probably is to both legal laymen and professionals. Sociologists, including sociologists of law, tend to shun the idea of a separate normative order and prefer to see in law mere social or psychological facts. If reference in general is made to legal norms, these are not enclosed in an autonomous normative sphere but conceived of as beliefs or expectations with their ontological domicile in the world of Is rather than Ought. In turn, in legal theory positivism has provided the dominant account of modern state law. In a sense, Legal Positivism itself forms part of modern state law. The Grand Masters of Legal Positivism are Hans Kelsen and H. L. A. Hart; indeed, much of the legal-theoretical debate within the positivist school during the last, say, sixty years, is but glosses on their *oeuvre*.[1] Legal Positivism purports to be unwavering in its normativism: in the strict demarcation of legal norms and social facts. Yet even in legal theory the prevalence of the normativist stance, as epitomised by Legal Positivism, has never been uncontested.

Legal Positivism performs two fundamental delineations, both of which are facilitated by characteristic features of modern state law but which, so I will argue, both ultimately founder. Legal normativity is distinguished, first, from the social Is (social facticity) and, secondly, from non-legal normativity such as morality. By the same token, Legal Positivism performs two successive reductions. First, law is reduced to its normative aspect and, secondly, the normative aspect is reduced to its surface level. By no means have the legal positivist delineations or the concomitant reductions gone uncontested. Legal Positivism considers Natural Law a perennial opponent and, indeed, is inclined to label all its opponents natural lawyers. Yet the positivist separation of law and morals has also been criticised by legal theorists who do not subscribe to Natural Law but, rather, seek to elaborate and justify a third-way position; Ronald Dworkin, for instance.[2]

In turn, legal phenomenologists and realists have questioned the normativist reduction and exclusion of the social aspect from law. Legal phenomenologists, inspired by the writings of Edmund Husserl, Martin Heidegger, and Alfred Schütz, have developed conceptual tools to analyse law as it appears in everyday practices; in the lifeworld (*Lebenswelt*) of members of society. By

[1] Especially on the second edition of *Reine Rechtslehre*, 1960, Kelsen, 1967, and on Hart's *The Concept of Law*, Hart, 1961.

[2] Dworkin, 1978, 1986.

contrast, the focus of legal realists has not been so much on lifeworld practices and relationships but, rather, on the behaviour of courts and judges. The general aspiration of both American and Scandinavian realists has been to define law in terms of empirical social and psychological facts, that is, in reference to what courts and judges do or what motivates them to do what they do. For realists, postulating the existence of law as a relatively autonomous normative order is metaphysics pure and simple. Yet, at the same time, they fall into a reductionist trap of their own.

Ultimately, reductionist moves misfire, and the repressed obstinately keeps reappearing. Failures of reductionism are instructive because they tell a legal theorist about the necessity to keep an eye on both the normative and the social side of law. I can be rather brief with realist reductionism. Legal normativity haunts realists in everything they write about courts and judges. If law is defined by reference to the behaviour or mental states of judges, then legal norms are already needed in telling who is a judge. A judge is an institutional fact, which does not exist and cannot be identified without a legal interpretative scheme thrown over empirical reality. Moreover, as many critics, among them Hart,[3] have noted, at least from the perspective of a judge the prediction theory of law cannot work. A judge who invokes the law to support a ruling is not predicting her own behaviour or testing predictions made by others. Clearly, a judge's phenomenological experience involves a dimension of normative constraints and guidance. Finally, the realists' view of even the sociality of law is narrow: it ignores first-order sociolegal practices, and of specialised legal practices it covers only the judicial ones.

Legal positivists conceive of law as a closed and self-contained normative order, whose autonomy – separation from both social facts and non-legal normativity – is guaranteed by its hierarchical structure, topped by a Master Rule, Kelsen's *Grundnorm* (basic norm) or Hart's rule of recognition. All (other) rules of the normative legal order derive their validity from the Master Rule. The Master Rule also provides the criteria for identifying the (other) norms making up the legal order and for distinguishing these from non-legal normativity. Yet, as Kelsen and Hart noted, such an autonomous legal order does not float freely in its non-legal environment or remain absolutely isolated in the sphere of the legal Ought. There are limits to the normativism of Legal Positivism. On some crucial points, legal positivists cannot but acknowledge the relevance of social practices; indeed, the necessity of these for the very existence of law as a normative legal order. Let me pinpoint three issues where the repressed social tends to reappear and where law's social modes of existence call for acknowledgement: the origins and sources of legal norms; the efficacy of law and legal norms as a precondition for validity; and the ambivalent nature of the Master Rule.

[3] Hart, 1959.

Positivism understands all law as positive law; law as posited by human acts. Acts forming the origin of law clearly have their location in social reality. Evidently, autonomous positive law could not exist without legislative acts bringing legal norms into existence. Here the normativist stance of Legal Positivism hints at specialised legal practices; that is, one of law's social modes of existence. Kelsen and Hart note the indispensability of social practices for the existence of law as a normative legal order at another juncture as well. For both of them, validity is the particular ontological mode of law. Validity is defined and assessed by legal-normative criteria. Still, in the account of both Masters of positivism, intra-legal validity has extra-legal, social preconditions. Validity presupposes the efficacy of both the legal order as a whole and the particular norms under examination. And, to be efficacious, legal norms must by and large be complied with by the population and found applicable by the courts. Thus, efficacy intimates both first-order sociolegal practices and judicial practices as an instance of specialised legal practices. The intra-legal chain of validity ends up with the Master Rule – the third critical point where social facticity asserts itself. Hart is rather explicit about the dual nature of the rule of recognition. On the one hand, it is a rule in the sense of social regularity: it denotes how validity is in fact assessed and how valid rules making up the normative legal order are in fact identified in the judicial practices of a particular legal regime. On the other hand, the rule of recognition is a normative rule: judges are obligated to assess validity and identify valid rules by the criteria it indicates. Kelsen's position is more ambiguous: indeed, throughout his long career he had difficulties in making up his mind about the nature of the *Grundnorm*. He even played with a sociological, power-theoretical reading, where the *Grundnorm* is simply reduced to a founding act of a polity or a revolutionary act of constitution-giving, with no preceding legal authorisation or justification. The fundamental ambivalence sticking to the Master Rule explains the never-ending debate among legal positivists as to whether or not the Master Rule is part of the normative legal order or whether it merely constitutes a necessary precondition, in the same vein as the social practices which give rise to particular legal norms and which guarantee the efficacy of those norms. Finally, as Kelsen in particular stresses, law is a coercive normative order, and coercion, with its implication of violence, clearly takes us beyond the normative realm to the field of the social Is.

In sum, legal positivists approach the insight that the normative legal order is not law's only mode of existence. Yet they stop short of conceding that, in addition to its normative side, law displays a social aspect too. In this essay, I will argue that law is about legal norms but it is not only about legal norms; it is also about the social – or, to be more exact, sociolegal – practices without which it could not exist as a normative legal order. If legal norms cannot exist without the contribution of sociolegal practices, neither can sociolegal practices exist without the contribution of legal norms. The normativity of law requires its sociality, and its sociality requires its normativity. Whether law is approached from its normative or social side, a relational approach is needed; an approach where normativity is related to sociality and *vice versa*.

Sociolegal practices come in two types, which play different roles in the kaleidoscopic and constantly shifting whole called law. Looking at law from the perspective of legal norms, first-order sociolegal practices constitute the scene for law's realisation. They include, first, general practices, such as marriage and partnership, in which we engage in our daily life and which make up our common lifeworld (*Lebenswelt*), and, secondly, specialised or expert practices, such as accounting, banking, or doctoring, which require particular knowledge and other qualifications. Law participates in structuring both general and specialised practices and in defining role expectations characteristic of them; roles of, say, a partner, or an accountant, a banker, or a doctor. In first-order sociolegal practices, abstract norms of the normative legal order are transformed into rights, obligations, and legal relationships of particular subjects. The normative legal order takes the shape of a concrete order of behaviour and affects the behaviour of social actors through their legal knowledge. To examine how all this happens and to develop conceptual tools for this purpose is to probe into the sociality of law; to engage in an attempt to specify how and in what sense law exists as and in sociolegal practices.

Law may be indispensable for sociolegal practices, but, still, in a way, it is beside the point. The point of both general lifeworld practices and specialised expert practices lies elsewhere than in law. Law may - and is even expected to - contribute to the point of partnership or banking practices, but the point itself is not related to law. Law remains an auxiliary moment, providing form for social substance. However, among specialised social practices, one group stands out, the very point of which relates to law and which can be called legal practices *sensu stricto*. These are practices which participate in the production and reproduction – in shorthand (re)production – of law. Legislative, judicial, and scholarly practices constitute the main specialised legal practices of modern state law. Correspondingly, law-givers and legislative experts, judges, and legal scholars are the main participants in the legal discourse through which the (re)production of law transpires.

As I shall argue throughout this essay, the normative aspect of law cannot be reduced to its 'visible' surface where it is textually manifested in laws, court rulings, and scholarly standpoints. A normative legal order also possesses subsurface, legal-cultural layers without which surface-level legal texts – legal speech acts – would not make much sense or even come into being. The (re)productive function of specialised legal practices covers not merely the surface of the legal order but extends to legal-cultural supports. Neither do these practices (re)produce merely particular legal norms, enshrined in particular laws and precedents. Specialised legal practices also bring about the order of the legal order, be this order primarily of a formal nature, as is the case with Kelsen's hierarchical *Stufenbau*, or based on substantive values and principles, sedimented into law's cultural layers.

Law possesses three modes of existence which also open three alternative gateways into law for internal and external observers. Law can be approached as a normative legal order, or as first- or second-order sociolegal practices. Evidently, law's modes of existence possess a certain autonomy; otherwise it would make no sense to draw a distinction among them. Yet at issue is merely relative autonomy, to use an expression which to many ears may sound a worn-out platitude. Law's modes of existence are interrelated and interdependent, so that none of them could exist without the support of the others. It is wholly legitimate for a legal theorist to focus a reconstructive enterprise on one mode; say, on law as a normative legal order. Indeed, it may even be necessary to make a choice. What is harder to justify is ignoring the links between the prioritised mode and the others. The normativism of Legal Positivism should not be blamed for privileging law as norms but, rather, for isolating the legal order from law's social modes of existence. Yet, as I shall argue in Part I, positivist accounts themselves prove legal order's reliance on social practices and point to the critical junctures where law's sociality reminds a normativist of its ineradicability.

In turn, the structured character of sociolegal practices testifies to the contribution of legal norms; indeed, without the interpretative scheme provided by legal norms the legal nature of sociolegal practices could not even be identified or the legally relevant features extracted. Furthermore, the very point of specialised legal practices focuses on the normative aspect of law; on the realisation and (re)production of the legal order. In a sense, law's cultural layers create the possibility of specialised legal practices. They provide legal actors with the conceptual, normative and methodological *Vorverständnis* (preconception[s]) without which laws could not be drafted and their coherence guaranteed, reasoned rulings issued, or well-argued legal doctrine elaborated.

Because of their interdependencies, elevating one of the three modes of existence to primordial and defining the others as derivative is a futile enterprise. All turns on the gateway through which we enter law. If we choose the perspective of first-order sociolegal practices, these appear as primordial, with the normative legal order and specialised legal practices seemingly derivative. If, instead, we embark on our theoretical survey of law on the normative side – as we can legitimately do – the normative legal order appears as primordial and the social modes as derivative. And, finally, if we stress that neither the normative legal order nor the legal aspect of first-order sociolegal practices would exist without the contribution of specialised legal practices, we might use those practices as our starting point and, by the same token, label them as primordial. It is to the merit of legal phenomenologists to have brought in the first-person viewpoint of individual and collective social actors, and to have attempted to conceptualise how law functions and is perceived to function in sociolegal practices. Yet to declare these the primordial mode of existence *tout court* does not give credit to law's complicated perspectivism.

How, then, are the interrelations and interdependences between law's modes of existence channelled? A crucial link consists of social and legal actors and their knowledge of law: not only their explicit, discursive, knowledge but also - and even primarily - their social and legal preconceptions, their *Vorverständnis.* Legal actors in the narrow sense of the term are legal professionals as the primary subjects of specialised legal practices. Law stands in the centre of their focus; they are conscious of law's existence even as abstract legal norms; and they possess explicit, discursive, knowledge of the legal order and law's institutional workings, that is, law as specialised legal practices. Indeed, it is possession of such expert knowledge, often enough certified by academic degrees, which in general provides the entrance ticket to specialised legal practices. Yet, when tackling a particular legal task – drafting a law, deliberating a case or composing an article for a law review - legal professionals activate only that part of their legal knowledge which the task at hand calls for. The rest remain in a tacit, practical state, constituting the legal *Vorverständnis* which is also applied in all legal activities, though without legal actors being immediately conscious of this.

The legal knowledge and *Vorverständnis* of social actors participating in first-order sociolegal practices is different. At least in the context of general lifeworld practices, it is probably erroneous even to speak of distinct legal knowledge or *Vorverständnis.* Law is part of an undifferentiated normative cultural horizon of the lifeworld which mainly unfolds its effects unconsciously, through our tacit, practical knowledge and undifferentiated social *Vorverständnis.* A quasi-automatic way of functioning is typical of lifeworld legal normativity and, by the same token, crucial for the realisation of law. Yet situations arise where we become conscious of the presence of law and where the spotlight of our attention zooms in on the legal features of social practices and relationships. Then we cross what can be called the threshold of legal awareness. This mainly occurs when the ordinary course of things is interrupted and legal normativity is deprived of its natural and self-evident character.

Firstly, it may happen that social actors no longer comply with the law in the usual quasi-automatic manner but, from their first-person singular or plural perspective, explicitly pose the question whether or not to respect the law. The reasoning can be of a strategic, moral, or ethical nature. The legendary 'bad man' is engaged in a strategic cost-benefit analysis, weighing the benefits that breaking the law would bring him against the costs in terms of the risk of being caught and the ensuing sanction. Those considering trespassing in the grounds of an animal farm and releasing foxes from their cages are discussing the moral justification of their act of civil disobedience. And a conscientious objector opting for a prison sentence instead of obligatory military service has taken a decision on ethical grounds. Secondly, the threshold of legal awareness is crossed when social actors witness other social actors breaking the law; when they in their everyday lifeworld confront illegality (or a-legality) on the part of other social actors, say, when by chance they come across a mugging in the street or a puzzling instance of a-legality in a shopping mall. Instances of illegality or a-legality – whether based on deliberate instrumental, moral, or ethical reasoning, or not – constitute disturbances in the realisation of law. In the ordinary course of affairs, law is realised in ongoing lifeworld practices, without social actors being aware of law's involvement.

Thirdly, legal norms addressing ordinary citizens do not consist merely of rules of behaviour but even comprise rules of competence. These empower social actors to alter their legal position and even that of other private subjects. In the vast majority of daily contracting practices – say, at the counter of a café or the cash till of a supermarket – law plays its role in the usual unconscious way, through the practical lifeworld knowledge of social actors. Yet, there are contracts – say, renting an apartment or taking an insurance policy – which require explicit attention and where the legal nature of the act is conspicuous. Correspondingly, a social actor making a will heeds – or at least is expected to heed – the legal significance of doing so.

The moment social actors become aware of the legal aspects of their social practices and their lifeworld in general, they also become aware of law's other modes of existence; that is, law as a normative legal order and as secondary legal practices. Those witnessing a mugging realise that criminal law has been broken; that the police are empowered to intervene; and that the perpetrator can be brought before a court. Law stands out from the diffuse socio-cultural normativity of the lifeworld and is recognised as involving expressly enacted norms, as well as specialised legal practices monitoring observance of those norms. In other words, the social actors of sociolegal practices perceive that law possesses three interrelated and interdependent modes of existence.

Binary Distinctions

Law is pervaded by binary distinctions; arguably, binary distinctions are constitutive of law in general and of all its modes of existence in particular. Binary distinctions begin with the delineation of law from non-law. 'Law' and 'non-law' can also be defined in terms of (il)legality and a-legality. '(Il)legality' denotes the spatially, personally, substantively, and temporally defined domain where law's internal binary distinction between legal and illegal is applicable. In turn, 'a-legality' refers to the outside of this domain; to what the law has left unordered, and where the distinction between legal and illegal does not find application.[4]

[4] Lindahl, 2013.

The binary divisions continue with the dimensions of normativity and sociality, and further with internal distinctions within those dimensions. Legal norms are divided into, say, norms of behaviour and competence, primary and secondary rules, and, from a diverse angle, into private and public law, as well as national and international law. Within law's sociality, specialised legal practices have become differentiated from first-order socio-legal practices. Correspondingly, social actors as subjects of first-order socio-legal practices should be kept apart from legal actors of specialised legal practices. In the same way, at the collective level, the legal community in the broad sense, comprising all those subject to a distinct legal regime, should be kept apart from the legal community in the narrow sense, consisting merely of legal professionals. In legal knowledge, discursive knowledge stands out from and against the horizon of practical knowledge; that is, the *Vorverständnis* of social and legal actors. Furthermore, two relevant meta-level comprehensive distinctions add to and reflect law's kaleidoscopic and elusive nature: law's *ratio* (reason) and law's *voluntas* (will) - alluding primarily to the origins of law - and law as institution and medium - alluding primarily to the law's basic orientation.

What is the nature of these distinctions, which may be related but are not equivalent? How should a legal theorist treat them? Are they mutually exclusive, with no possibility of conciliation or interaction? Or, by contrast, are they interdependent, interrelated, and interactive? A legal theorist may approach the distinctions, first, as dichotomies, the parties to which remain strictly separated. This is how Kelsen, for instance, conceived of the relationship between Is and Ought. The domicile of social and psychic facts lies in the world of Is, while the domicile of legal norms lies in the world of Ought, with – so Kelsen argued – an insurmountable wall separating these worlds. Kelsen ends up by negating the social existence of law: his view is both dichotomous and negatory. Yet, as we have already seen, sociality keeps obstinately asserting itself at crucial junctures of Kelsen's Pure Theory.

Another way of treating law's binary distinctions is reduction: one side is reduced to the other or defined in terms of the latter, and denied independent existence. Thus, reduction shakes hands with negation. This is the strategy of legal realists, who propose defining law by reference to, say, the actual or predictable behaviour of judges or the ideology prevailing among them and determining their rulings. However, empiricist reductions have failed: all the definitions proposed by realists include an irreducible normative element. Definitions invoke legal-institutional facts, such as judges, courts, or authorities, which cannot even be identified without reference to legal norms.

A dialectical approach is the main alternative to dichotomies, negations, and reductions. It allows for and even focuses on interdependences, interrelations, and interaction. Instead of 'either / or', the basic assumption is 'both / and'. The reader may not be surprised if I declare adherence to the dialectical programme. How, exactly, the dialectical relations which separate but, by the same token, connect the two poles are shaped varies from one distinction to another; no generally applicable magic formula exists. And the possibility remains that a distinction must be considered to constitute a dichotomy, even an aporia, or that it may turn out to be sham, justifying the reductive move.

The distinction between law and non-law can be drawn from a position both outside and inside law; that is, by an external or an internal observer, a non-participant or a participant. When the legal sociologist Niklas Luhmann demarcates law as a social system from its environment, inhabited by other social systems – such as politics and economy – and by psychic systems, he performs an external distinction. Yet, as Luhmann stresses, distinguishing itself from its environment is also a necessary internal operation of law as a social system.[5] As is the case with many other insights introduced by Luhmann, the idea that law's functioning requires perpetual demarcation from non-law can be adopted without necessarily buying systems theory ballast as a whole.

In first-order sociolegal practices law stands out from the diffuse normativity of the lifeworld every time it breaches the threshold of consciousness; when, for instance, somebody witnessing a mugging exclaims 'but that's against the law!' In specialised legal practices, a judge or a legal scholar draws a borderline between law and non-law whenever taking a position on the legal relevance of a custom or a technical standard or a principle-related interpretative argument. The legislator is not exempt from boundary-drawing, either, but must, for instance, assess whether international or transnational law imposes legal constraints on national legislation; to what extent, say, the jurisprudence of the European Human Rights Court or the Court of Justice of the European Union is law binding on the legislator. A legal theorist must already at least tentatively demarcate law from non-law when defining the object of her reconstruction. Among legal theorists, legal positivists are especially attentive to this necessity in their emphasis on separating legal normativity from both social facticity and non-legal normativity, such as morals.

Kelsen subscribed to Kantian epistemological premises. These entrust our concepts with a constitutive task: our concepts not only facilitate analysis of the object of our research but, in a sense, even constitute that object. For a Kelsenian legal theorist, law is what is captured by the conceptual grid of the Pure Theory. And, correspondingly, Hart's *The Concept of Law*, with its remarkable success in Anglo-Saxon legal academia, has established a conceptual filter which sieves non-law from law. What is not caught by the grid or what has not passed through the sieve remains outside the focus of legal theory. However, such conceptual constitution of law as the object of reconstruction is not a specificity of Legal Positivism or even legal theory; all

[5] Luhmann, 2004.

delineation of law from non-law employs a particular concept of law, be it expressly articulated or – as most often is the case – culled from the *Vorverständnis* of social or legal actors. The definition of 'law' depends on who is engaged in the conscious or unconscious enterprise of delineation; what position she occupies with relation to and within law; and what her ensuing perspective on law is. Law is inherently perspectival. This casts a shadow of doubt over all efforts to arrive at and justify the one correct definition of 'law', and one unequivocal and universally valid criterion for distinguishing law from non-law.

In Luhmann's autopoietic systems theory, social systems are systems of communication, all employing a binary code. The legal system relies on the distinction between legal and illegal, and due to this particular code, law remains closed from and to other social systems, each relying on its respective code. All law hears from other social systems is noise, which can make sense only after having been re-encoded into the language of law. Luhmann's is a dichotomous approach to the distinction between law and non-law, allowing for direct interaction between the two only in exceptional cases. For the purposes of this essay, the most important of these is structural coupling, where one and the same communicative act inserts itself into the communicative network of not one but two social systems; for instance, a legislative act into the legal and political systems or a contract into the legal and economic systems.

Within legal theory, positivists are prone to treat the distinction between law and non-law in a dichotomous manner; Kelsen in the direction of both the social and psychic Is and morals, the Hartian school explicitly in relation to morals but at least implicitly with regard to social facticity too. One of the functions of the Master Rules is to facilitate dichotomous distinctions in both directions. By contrast, this essay tries to follow a mediating programme even in identifying law and in demarcating it from non-law. Such a demarcation is involved in all legal practices, including legal theory, and even in first-order sociolegal practices after breaching the threshold of consciousness. Yet the borderline between law and non-law is of a shifting and porous character, with law and non-law constantly interacting at diverse junctures and in diverse ways, which cannot be compressed into anything resembling the structural couplings which break the isolation of autopoietically functioning social systems. In judicial and legislative practices, the question whether this is law or not cannot be left open but a position must be taken. Particular questions of law and non-law may well be of an 'either / or' character. However, the position is never taken forever or for all legal purposes.

Discussing boundary-drawing between law and non-law is closely linked to discussing law's autonomy. How we treat the delineation of law from non-law determines how we conceive of law's autonomy. Autonomy can be examined in the same directions as the distinction between law and non-law; for instance, in relation to diverse societal fields, such as politics and economy, or to non-legal normativity, such as morals. Furthermore, autonomy is not a property merely of the normative legal order. Of equal importance are specialised legal practices where autonomy takes diverse guises; for instance, professional, relating to the specific qualifications of legal actors; methodological, relating to the particularities of legal reasoning and argumentation; and institutional, relating to, say, the independence of the courts. Corresponding to alternative views of the borderline between law and non-law, autonomy can be depicted, firstly, as closedness or, secondly, as including the possibility of interaction and dialogue; that is, following the logic of either 'either / or' or 'both / and'. Closedness is the choice of Luhmann's sociological and legal positivists' normativist reconstruction of law, while allowing for interaction and dialogue is the approach this essay attempts to pursue.

Although intimately connected to the distinction between law and non-law, autonomy is a wider notion. It also comprises law's autonomy from other law. Legal Positivism does not merely emphasise a legal order's autonomy in relation to the social Is and non-legal normativity; what is also important is autonomy from other legal orders. The Master Rule is expected to guarantee even this aspect of autonomy, which labels the view that Legal Positivism holds of law's plurality.

Within law, the main distinction goes – so this essay argues – between law's sociality and its normativity. Within sociality and normativity respectively, further binary divisions suggest themselves. On the social side, we are already familiar with the division of first-order sociolegal practices and specialised, second-order, legal practices. On the normative side, several distinctions call for attention, each of them addressing a particular aspect or property of the legal order: surface and sub-surface law; primary and secondary rules; rules of behaviour and rules of competence; regulative and constitutive rules; private and public law.

The distinction between the 'visible', textually enshrined surface and the sub-surface layers of law may seem strange and even controversial to lawyers raised under the dominance of the positivist view. Yet, in fact, corresponding divisions have a long pedigree in Western legal thinking. Let me only allude to the ancient Greek distinction between *Nomos* – law as convention – and *Physis* – law as nature, subsequently adopted in Roman law; to the way Natural Law in diverse variations, up to the post–World War II revival, has distinguished between natural and positive law; to how the *ratio scripta* of *ius commune* was distinguished from the *leges propriae* of local customs and positive legislation after the late medieval revival of Roman law; and to how common-law authors, in their polemics against the early legal positivists, such as Thomas Hobbes and Jeremy Bentham, emphasised the importance of *lex non scripta* as a counterweight to *leges scriptae*.

Thus, my reformulation of the age-old distinction finds honourable company. Yet under the prevalence of modern state law it is prone to arouse suspicion and criticism. Questions are likely to abound: Does the distinction between surface and sub-surface law not necessarily imply natural law which has – so the argument goes – irretrievably lost its cultural foundation? Am I not denying the fundamental positivity of modern state law? Am I not violating the separation of law and morals which this type of law, at least, incorporates? Am I not smuggling into modern state law a distinction which may have been apposite in premodern time but which has now lost its justification? By including legal culture in law, am I not throwing the net of legal normativity too far and, by the same token, blurring the borderline between law and non-law? In due course, especially in Part II, I will try to answer these sceptical questions. I will try to show that the expert culture of legal professionals forms an indispensable part of law as a normative legal order, and that law could not even exist or be intelligible in its surface-level textual guise without the support of sub-surface legal culture. Neither would legal professionals be able to engage in their specialised practices: in drafting laws, issuing rulings, or pursuing doctrinal research. Legal norms are never mere surface-level phenomena; they always also incorporate a sub-surface, legal-cultural element. My argument will be that the assumption of a sub-surface level does not inevitably entail the sin of Natural Law or the collapse of law into morals, but can be brought into harmony with the fundamental positivity of modern state law.

The next sub-group of distinctions connects to the functions that particular types of legal rule accomplish within law or with regard to society. Here we encounter Hart's primary and secondary rules, addressing, respectively, ordinary citizens and officials of the legal regime; or, as I would put it, first-order sociolegal practices and specialised legal practices. Turning to another classification, rules of behaviour or regulative rules address behaviour, while rules of competence grant legal subjects the power to alter their own legal position or that of others. This distinction largely overlaps with that between regulatory law and facilitating law; the latter, though, already takes us close to what I will call law's diverse societal orientations. In the distinction between regulative and constitutive rules, constitutive rules fulfil the specific task of giving rise to institutional facts.

Arguably, the general societal vocation of law is to bring about social order; or, as phenomenologists and Luhmannians among legal theorists and sociologists would put it, to manage the double contingency of our mutual expectations. In this fundamental sense, law stands on the side of order and opposes disorder. Yet this does not necessarily make all law inherently conservative. Law not only preserves existing social structures; it can also aim at transforming them and at engendering new structures and practices. Law is not revolutionary but as welfare-state legislation has conspicuously proved, it may well be reformist. Neither is the order that law aspires to produce necessarily imposed from above or outside. Law is often repressive but it can be empowering too. Law may engage social actors in determining the legal framework of their interrelations, as does contract law, for instance. Law may also create spheres of autonomy where social actors may arrange their interrelations as they wish, outside law but protected by law against trespassing. This is the declared purpose of fundamental and human rights as liberty rights. Law is not merely about regulation; it is also about facilitation. Sometimes it might even be about emancipation.

All the above divisions focus on particular legal norms, although they also possess wider implications, as do, say, regulating and facilitating rules. The divisions are partly overlapping, but they differ in the exact functions they assign to the respective norms. It might appear that the distinctions are exclusionary and additive; that the parties to a distinction exclude each other but, by the same token, add something to the properties of law. Yet it may be that the relationship is of a more complex, dialectic, nature; that, at bottom, a distinction may depend on one's point of view so that one and the same rule can be examined as, say, both regulative and constitutive; or that one type of rule cannot exist without the other so that, for instance, rules of behaviour cannot do without rules of competence or primary rules without secondary rules, and *vice versa*.

Other divisions group legal norms into distinct fields for systematising purposes; for ordering the legal order. Comprehensive systematisations have been especially important for German *Rechtswissenschaft* but US debates on the classification of law bear at least some resemblance to the German enterprise. Systematisation has usually relied on two basic divisions: public and private law, and national and international law. In Continental Europe, two factors render fields of law a distinct identity. All fields of law are supposed to possess, first, a distinct object and, secondly, particular *Allgemeine Lehren*; a doctrinal corpus consisting of legal concepts, principles, theories, and methods. This implies that systematising divisions do not cover solely surface-level law but legal culture is involved as well. While bringing about order may be deemed the general societal vocation of law, its general moral vocation – or at least pretension – is to do justice. It may be that diverse fields of law reflect diverse conceptions of justice, for instance, administrative law incorporates distributive justice, private law corrective justice, or European regulative private law, what Hans-W. Micklitz has termed 'access justice'.[6] If we want to probe into the deep culture of a particular field of law, its typical conception of justice is one of the features we might want to excavate.

Below we shall see that traditional divisions of law have run into difficulties: boundaries between fields of law become increasingly blurred and laws are

[6] Micklitz, 2011.

issued which defy unequivocal compartmentalisation, even in respect of private and public law. The very aim of a comprehensive systematisation of a national legal order may seem pointless and futile.

Two major binary distinctions remain, one related to the societal orientations of law and the other to its fundamental sources: between law as institution and medium, on the one hand, and *ratio* and *voluntas* on the other.

The distinction between law as institution and medium was introduced by Jürgen Habermas in *Theorie des kommunikativen Handelns* (1981), his main treatise in social theory, but taken back - rather hurriedly, I would say - in *Faktizität und Geltung* (1992), his major work in legal philosophy.[7] Habermas gave a new social theoretical twist to the debate that twentieth-century legal theorists had waged on law's two basic orientations; the debate on law's bifurcation as we can call it. Many variations of the bifurcation thesis exist. Let me only mention Roscoe Pound, who in his attack on 'administrative absolutism' evoked the contrast between coordinating and subordinating law, a distinction he borrowed from Gustav Radbruch;[8] Lon Fuller, who distinguished law based on reciprocity from law as a form of managerial control;[9] and Dworkin, who buttressed his taking-rights-seriously thesis with the division of principles and policies.[10] Finally, two original thinkers from opposite ends of the ideological spectrum also deserve mention, both mainly interested in law's relation to economy: Evgenij Pashukanis and Friedrich Hayek.

Habermas connects the distinction between law as medium and institution to society's differentiation into System and *Lebenswelt* (the lifeworld). System consists of the action fields of economy and state (administration), both integrated by systemic mechanisms operating behind the backs of social actors. In turn, *Lebenswelt* is the field of everyday sociality, integrated through social actors' communicative, consensual, action. Law as medium is a tool employed by System and closely intertwined with the economic medium of money and the administrative medium of power. Law as medium not only serves systemic integration, but, joining hands with money and administrative power, intervenes in the lifeworld and contributes to its colonisation. By contrast, law as institution strengthens the social structures of *Lebenswelt*; indeed, it forms part of *Lebenswelt*, immersed in the diffuse normativity of everyday sociality and conferring formal sanction on fields of action already informally constituted.

Colonisation of the lifeworld - Habermas' main concern in *Theorie des kommunikativen Handelns* - was supposed to proceed through the increasing intrusion of law as medium into a domain which should be reserved for law as institution. Other versions of the bifurcation thesis express a similar pattern.

[7] Habermas, 1989a, 1996. [8] Pound, 1939. [9] Fuller, 1969, 207–213.
[10] Dworkin, 1978.

One party to the distinction, seen in a favourable light, is endangered by the other, perhaps also accomplishing an important function in law but overstepping its legitimate boundaries. With Dworkin, policies threaten principles; with Radbruch and Pound subordinating law coordinating law; with Fuller, law exercising managerial control law based on reciprocity; and with Hayek, rules of organisation rules of just conduct. Let us dwell somewhat longer on Hayek and Pashukanis, who share with Habermas a social theoretical ambition and present their distinctions in a wider societal setting.

For many bifurcation theorists, public law - in particular administrative law - incarnates the orientation which is feared to menace the favoured aspect of law and therefore calls for relentless vigilance. The claim may even be that administrative law is an illegitimate pretender to the title of law. This was the view of Hayek, who elaborated his distinction with a view to law's relation, not to lifeworld, but economy.[11] For him, the basic task of law is to enable and protect a free market economy. The autonomy that law is expected to guarantee is primarily the autonomy of the marketplace and - at actor level - a market actor, rather than a subject of lifeworld practices and relationships. Guaranteeing autonomy falls to rules of just conduct, which Hayek wanted to keep strictly apart from rules of organisation. Rules of just conduct facilitate individuals' pursuit of their own goals and plans, and establish the general framework for the market economy as a 'spontaneous order'. In contrast, rules of organisation subject individuals to goals imposed from outside; they constrain rather than facilitate autonomy. In Hayek's account, only rules of just conduct were originally called law. Rules of organisation were subsumed under the same concept only after political development, beginning with early modern absolute monarchy, entrusted the same body, the legislature, with the power to issue both types of rule. This has hollowed out the rule-of-law principle and transformed it into a mere demand for legalism. Hayek warned that ever-new public-law rules of organisation, enacted in the name of social justice, will result in establishing a totalitarian planning and command society that will destroy individual freedom.

Ironically enough, with his inclination to shut regulatory public law outside 'proper' law, Hayek shakes hands with Evgenij Pashukanis; a major figure of pre-Stalin Marxist legal theory and an early contributor to the bifurcation debate. Coming from the opposite extreme of the ideological gamut, Pashukanis, in contrast to Hayek, welcomed rather than condemned expansion of instrumentalist, goal-oriented regulation. He contended that the legal contents of what is called administrative law are limited to securing the reciprocal rights of citizens and the administration; the rest is a mixed rag-bag of technical rules and political recipes. Law is needed and can exist only in the context of a potential opposition of interests. If the parties share a

[11] Hayek, 1982.

common goal, rules addressing their relationship are not legal but technical. Accordingly, rules on the liability of a railway operator are legal, while rules designed to ensure frictionless railway traffic are technical. For Pashukanis the Marxist, private law is the original domain of law. The legal form of social relationships derives logically and genetically from relationships of commodity exchange. If Kelsen more or less ignores the contract, Pashukanis elevates it to the *Ur*-form of law. And if for Kelsen law exists only as norms, for Pashukanis law is primarily a form of social relationships, perceived as - or in analogy to - relationships of exchange. Furthermore, reverting to the affinity between Hayek and Pashukanis, both theorists saw law withering away. For Pashukanis, replacing law by technical rules was a vital step on the road towards a communist utopia.[12] By contrast, Hayek experienced the explosive growth of rules of organisation as a nightmarish vision of future totalitarianism.

As is shown by the analyses of Pashukanis, Hayek, and Habermas, bifurcation of law cuts across the modes of existence of law, bearing on and manifested by not only the normative but also the social dimension. In the normative legal order, bifurcation in its diverse guises connects to but does not wholly coincide with the division into private and public law. On the side of public law, constitutional law interacts with society's fundamental moral principles and ethical values, facilitating rather than regulating, and functioning as institution rather than medium. The same goes for the general part of administrative law which establishes the rule-of-law framework for administrative action. The bulk of legislation which reflects the interventionism of the twentieth-century regulatory welfare state and where law is clearly employed as medium falls under what in German classifications is called 'special administrative law'. Yet, especially after the welfare state has exhausted its momentum and entered a phase of retraction, private law, too, has been assigned regulatory tasks, testifying to its use as medium. 'Regulatory private law', reflecting policy and goal orientation, has become a household term particularly among private lawyers specialised in EU law.

As to the social dimension of law, namely law's realisation and (re)production, let me content myself with some tentative generalisations. Law as institution is merged with the everyday lifeworld and its general social practices, which constitute the setting for the realisation of facilitating or coordinating law. Yet, in the distinction between facilitating and regulatory law, not all regulatory law falls under the umbrella of law as medium but law as institution also comprises regulatory law, such as criminal law strengthening the moral texture of the lifeworld. Furthermore, as bifurcation theorists with an economist emphasis have pointed out, framework structuring of the economy through, say, contract law, performs a facilitating and coordinating function rather than a

[12] Pashukanis, (1929) 1978.

regulatory and subordinating one. We should also keep in mind that the economy is not only a Habermasian System, guided by the invisible hand behind the backs of individual actors, but also possesses a lifeworld aspect. Employees or consumers are not mere cogs in System; they are also living out lifeworld roles. Law contributes to the structuring of these roles, thereby manifesting characteristics of law as institution.

The preceding discussion suggests that the parties to the distinctions drawn by bifurcation theorists are not mutually exclusive, and that one and the same set of rules can display features of both sides. Even the division into law as institution and medium is not as clear-cut as may seem at first glance. Still, it tells something important about the range of law and the development of modern state law. Consequently, I would propose sticking to it. Variations in law's orientation have implications for second-order legal practices as well. A great part of regulatory administrative law is produced not by the democratic legislator but by executive and administrative authorities. Regulatory administrative law is the promised land of delegated legislation. Often enough, technical expertise on regulatory issues is considered more pertinent than democratic legitimation. As instances of self-regulation and co-regulation attest, delegation can reach beyond public authorities, to private 'stakeholders', and involve new modes of regulation, blurring the boundary between law and non-law - such as soft law or non-judicial monitoring and enforcement. Regulatory administrative law is also the promised land not only of delegated legislation but also of technolegality, including digitalised law.

Finally, we arrive at the distinction between *ratio* and *voluntas*, which relates more to the general sources of law than to its basic orientations. *Autoritas non veritas facit legem*, claimed Hobbes, the godfather of Legal Positivism. Kelsen, a Master of twentieth-century positivism. agreed. Connected to the strict separation of law and morals, Kelsen emphasised that legislative, law-creating acts are volitional and not cognitive; acts of will but not of cognition. Yet Hobbes and Kelsen, influential as they have been, were mistaken. Inherent in Western law is a perennial tension between *ratio* and *voluntas*. In the history of law, *ratio* and *voluntas*, as well the tension between them, have assumed diverse guises, but not even modern state law, the reference of twentieth-century positivism, can do without the contribution of *ratio*. Fuller once remarked: 'When it is said that law represents the rule of reason, it is appropriate to ask what kind of reason is meant'.[13] Indeed, we should heed Fuller's wise advice and be attentive to the wide variety of meanings assigned to the *ratio* of law.

Law's identification with reason goes back to antiquity. Cicero coined the catchphrase *lex est suprema ratio*, frequently cited in late medieval and early

[13] Fuller, 1969, 5.

modern writings. After the revival of Roman law, jurists called *Corpus juris civilis* written reason, *ratio scripta*. It was considered the foundation of *ius commune* and served as a measure of the rationality of *leges propriae*; that is, local customs and positive legislation. Identifying revived Roman law with law's *ratio* proves that the latter could also have other than natural-law sources. In seventeenth- and eighteenth-century English debates, proponents of common law claimed *ratio* for their side. Yet their *ratio* was of a very different kind from the natural reason of Thomist Natural Law, which also had its proponents. Against the attacks of Hobbes, and later, Bentham, English common-law authors erected the bulwark of a peculiar artificial, diachronic, and communal reason. Within Natural Law, the advent of early modern individualist doctrine entailed an important shift from objective to subjective (to which, as we know, Hobbes made an important contribution); *ratio* retreated from the law-governed universe of Thomist thinking to individual minds and, now, justified individual subjective rights. In eighteenth-century Germany, the *Vernunftrecht* school, with Christian Wolff as the main advocate, followed a geometric model of reasoning (*moro geometrico*) where legal rules were deduced from self-evident axioms; again, law's *ratio* acquired novel features. In turn, German nineteenth-century Conceptual Jurisprudence (*Begriffsjurisprudenz*) vindicated the 'productive' tasks of legal science by law's allegedly logically oriented rationality. This rationality had very little to do with, say, the artificial reason attributed to common law in seventeenth- and eighteenth-century England.

The *voluntas* of law has displayed more stability: positive, enacted, legislation has been its main depository. As long ago as *Antigone*, arbitrary convention – *Nomos* – of the polis stood against the natural order of things – *Physis*. Ever since Greek antiquity, positive law has occupied a legitimate place in the normative hierarchy of Natural Law, as indeed it has in common-law thinking too. Positive law as an embodiment of *voluntas* not only opposes *ratio* in its varying manifestations, as Sophocles depicted the tragedy of Antigone. The *ratio* of Natural Law needs the *voluntas* of positive law for specification and realisation. Under the dominance of positive law, the connection between *voluntas* and *ratio* can also be articulated in terms of the interdependence between law's surface and sub-surface layers. To put it succinctly, the *ratio* sedimented into sub-surface layers imposes constraints on – but, by the same token, creates the very possibility for – the legal practices specialised in (re)producing law. Ignoring the *ratio* of positive law implies reducing the normative legal order to its surface level and neglecting the indispensable presence and contribution of legal culture.

It may appear that fostering *ratio* would fall to judicial and scholarly practices, while legislative practices would constitute the domain of *voluntas*. However, things are not that simple. It would be erroneous to equate law's *voluntas* with irrationality or even a-rationality. Still, distinguishing *voluntas* from *ratio* intimates that the rationality allied with *voluntas* is of a truncated character. In the Kantian division of practical reason, it puts the emphasis on the instrumental, goal-rational dimension and tends to downplay moral and ethical aspects. Through democratic procedures and responsiveness towards civil society and its public sphere, legislative practices may add to law's rationality in the moral and ethical dimensions as well. And, on the other side, at least a residue of decisionism and strategic orientation obstinately sticks to judicial and scholarly practices and injects them with a dose of *voluntas*. What law's *ratio* is may be highly contested, and scholarly debates may be involved in political controversies, even in struggles over political power; think of the political context of the argument between Hobbes and his common-law adversaries in seventeenth-century England. All in all, the distinction between *voluntas* and *ratio* should not be taken as an exclusionary dichotomy, either, but as allowing for dialectical interrelations. *Voluntas* is not devoid of *ratio*, nor *ratio* insulated from *voluntas*.

In a previous study,[14] I have relied on the most celebrated icon of Western law: the image of the Roman goddess *Iustitia*, holding a balance in one hand and a sword in the other, in order to symbolise the foundational aspects of *ratio* and *voluntas*. Yet the symbolism does not work. The balance could well stand for *ratio* but the sword does not really connote the *voluntas* that law embodies or expresses. Rather, the sword is a symbol of the coercion which ultimately guarantees the realisation of law, both *ratio* and *voluntas*. The voluntarism of law should not be confused with coerciveness, although they often go together. This was the case in the heyday of the Westphalian state, when the *voluntas* of law was largely identical with state will as expressed by the state legislator or by state courts; and when the sword of *Iustitia*, too, had passed to the state, the possessor of the Weberian monopoly of legitimate violence. Still, the paths of the *voluntas* of law and the coercion guaranteeing its realisation can also part ways. Post-national developments have shaken the legislative monopoly of the will of the state, and states have mostly accepted this, explicitly or implicitly. By contrast, states have been much more reluctant to relinquish the sword of *Iustitia*. This has resulted in an at least partial institutional separation of the voluntarism and coerciveness of law. Even where legislative or judicial power is wielded by non-state bodies, as can be the case in transnational law, states remain largely responsible for exercising coercion whenever needed for the realisation of law.

Discussing the difference but also the link between *voluntas* and coercion introduces us to the topic of law and power. Will and power are related but not identical. Power is will which possesses particular means – resources – to secure its realisation, even when faced by an opposing will. State will, as expressed by the legislative or judicial speech acts of modern state law, avails itself of coercive machinery. This turns state will into state power. Yet 'state

[14] Tuori, 2011.

will' and 'state power' are but formal abstractions, empty cups filled by the will – the political objectives and programmes – of dominant political forces.

That modern state law is about power is a truism; of course, it is. The contention, often expounded in a critical vein, only becomes interesting after making some tentative heuristic divisions. Not only must we separate different kinds of power in accordance with, for instance, the means by which power holders assert their will; such as political, economic and cultural, or symbolic power. Here also belongs Habermas' division of state power into coercive administrative power and communicative power engendered by democratic law-making which includes not only institutional procedures but also surrounding discourses in civil society and the public sphere.[15] Furthermore, when examining the relations between law and power, we should take law as a process and distinguish among power *on*, *in*, and *by* law. Power *on* law affects law, as it were from the outside, from the societal environment. Power *in* law is the power inherent in law. Power is a social phenomenon, and when discussing power *in* law, we are discussing power intrinsic to law as first- and second-order sociolegal practices. Finally, power *by* law refers, first, to creating, reinforcing, and legitimating societal power positions and relations in diverse fields of society; not only the economy and administration but the lifeworld as well. In addition, not only is law affected by cultural, symbolic, power, but law itself produces symbolic power effects. Law is an agent of symbolic power which tends to impose on the members of society a particular vision of their social world. Yet all criticism of power *by* law should take heed that law not only creates, strengthens, and legitimates power; law also constrains power. Law has the potential to produce not only positive, enhancing, but also negative, restricting, power effects. Constraining power – this is approximately what fundamental rights and the rule of law are about. These fundamental principles of a democratic *Rechtsstaat* bring to the fore the moral and ethical dimension of practical reason, which is easily sidestepped by the primarily instrumental rationality allied with law's *voluntas*.

Perspectivism

Perspectivism further adds to the elusiveness of law. Perspectivism is inherent in law. In a specific sense, there is no law as such but only law as seen by a particular social or legal actor from a particular perspective. What law shows of itself depends on who is watching and where from. Perspectivism *in* law differs from perspectivism *on* law. My focus now is on intrinsic perspectivism, or perspectivism *in* law. The distinction between perspectivism *in* and *on* law may bring to mind Hart's discussion of the internal and external points of view or Luhmann's treatment of *Selbstbeschreibung* and *Fremdbeschreibung*:

[15] Habermas, 1996, 144ff.

observation of law from within the social system of law and from another social system, such as the system of science, where sociology has its domicile. The distinction proposed here is related but not equivalent to these renowned predecessors.

Intrinsic perspectivism is connected to and, at least partly, a consequence of law's multiple modes of existence and binary distinctions. Grasping the varieties of law's perspectivism presupposes taking law in all its three modes of existence; that is, understanding law not only in its guise of a normative legal order but also in and as particular social practices. Perspectivism affects and is expressed by how social and legal actors view the law. Social actors enter the law through the gateway of sociolegal practices. They live out legal normativity as an integral part of general social normativity and through the diverse roles they occupy in their everyday practices. Only when something extraordinary occurs does law stand out from the general normativity operating through social actors' practical knowledge. When this is the case and the threshold of consciousness is breached, social actors' field of vision also covers law as a normative legal order, the realisation of which is guaranteed and which is (re) produced by specialised legal practices. Yet even then the law they see is not the same as the law for the legal actors of specialised legal practices: laymen lack the legal *Vorverständnis* through which legal professionals perceive law.

Social and legal actors are not 'free-floating' observers but situated participants, carrying out particular social and legal roles. The specific perspectivism of sociolegal practices is perspectivism of social roles. Correspondingly, the specific perspectivism of specialised legal practices is perspectivism of legal roles: the perspectivism of the judge, the legal scholar, the legislative expert, and the practising lawyer (the legal counsellor), to list major legal roles of modern state law. Legal actors are aware of the relevance of law's social modes of existence, although perhaps understanding law as a normative legal order is their common default position. Yet, depending on the legal roles legal actors occupy, they also heed the practices embodying law's social dimension. Their roles also impact what position they take on, and how they weigh, law's binary poles, such as law as medium and institution. Let me present a brief and inevitably schematic sketch of the particular perspectivism arguably implied by the main legal roles of modern state law.

The legislative expert, in line with the law-giver, treats law primarily as a means of achieving politically defined societal objectives. In turn, the practising lawyer looks at law through her client's extra-legal interests which she is supposed to promote. Both the legislative expert and the counsellor tend to an instrumentalist view of law. To put the point in terms of speech act theory, they are prone to focus on the extra-legal, perlocutionary effects of legislative and judicial speech acts, and downplay the illocutionary dimension. By contrast, judges privilege the illocutionary dimension, where criteria such as argumentative cogency and normative justifiability hold sway. In a more detailed discussion, the judicial role should be divided into sub-categories, in accordance with the varying functions of courts. In modern state law, the roles of judges in constitutional and ordinary courts, and among the latter supreme and lower courts, may display significant differences. Constitutional and supreme court judges bear a heightened responsibility for maintaining the unity of the law and protecting its sub-surface, legal-cultural, foundations. In turn, in a transnational legal regime such as EU law, different expectations define the roles of European and national judges. Variation in judicial roles entails variation in legal *Vorverständnis*; that is, the way judges conceive of law.

What, then, about legal scholarship, which also belongs to the legal practices specialised in law and its (re)production? What characterises the scholarly perspective on law? Doctrinal researchers – 'legal dogmaticians' – assist other legal actors by providing them with interpretative recommendations and systematising proposals. Scholars' focus is clearly on the illocutionary aspect of legal speech acts; they appraise the normative credentials of laws, court rulings, and their colleagues' positions. Accordingly, the perspective of a doctrinal scholar is closer to that of a judge than a legislator.

Let me repeat the qualification concerning the schematism of my account. Employing the conceptual framework of speech act theory, both the illocutionary and perlocutionary dimensions are present in all legal speech acts, although the emphasis varies. In judicial deliberations and rulings, as well as scholarly recommendations, teleological arguments alluding to perlocutionary effects are also invoked. A further perlocutionary ingredient is added to judicial practices and speech acts by, say, turf wars within the national, or between the national and transnational or even international judiciary. And by no means are scholarly practices free from academic self-enhancement and competition for authority, reputation, posts, and funding. A perlocutionary element is present in scholarly speech acts too. As is the case with the majority of, if not all, binary distinctions within law, the distinction between illocution and perlocution also calls for a mediating approach.

Legal actors are situated with regard not only to particular legal roles but also fields of law, starting from divisions into national and international, and private and public law. Perspectivism of legal fields and corresponding legal disciplines adds to that of legal roles. Often enough not only scholars but also other legal actors, such as practising lawyers, legislative experts, and even judges, specialise in a particular field and develop a professional identity as a private or public lawyer, international lawyer, constitutional lawyer, criminal lawyer, and so on. Fields of law and corresponding legal disciplines are marked by particular concepts, principles, theories, and even methodologies: the ensemble of what Germans call *Allgemeine Lehren*. These impregnate the legal *Vorverständnis* of legal actors specialised in a distinct field. The shaking of law's traditional divisions and the advent of transnational law have perhaps abated the significance of field-specific *Allgemeine Lehren*. Yet legal-cultural particularities following traditional divisions linger on in the *Vorverständnis* of not only national but also transnational lawyers. This is the case despite the fact that, for instance, EU law - in line with transnational law in general - makes little use of these divisions. Many, perhaps the majority of, lawyers have acquired their professional identity within a distinct field of law, have internalised its *Allgemeine Lehren* and tend to share its general view of law; as regards, say, the respective emphasis on law as medium and institution. We may surmise that criminal or family lawyers lay more stress on law as institution, while tax or administrative lawyers are more inclined to treat law as medium. Yet again, though, let us be wary of the pitfalls of generalisation. Every field of law displays features of both orientations, while legal professionals specialised in a field of law - say, international lawyers - do not constitute a homogeneous group. Disagreements within fields of law often reflect divergent views of the import of the poles of law's binary distinctions. In tax law, for instance, how should we weigh policy objectives against legal protection of taxpayers and other rule-of-law requirements?

One major aspect of intrinsic perspectivism remains to be tackled. This relates to a property of law which we have not yet addressed, namely plurality. The perspectivism of legal orders caught even Kelsen's attention. As law's social modes of existence are also affected by and contribute to this variant of perspectivism, 'perspectivism of legal regimes' would actually be a more accurate expression.

Perspectivism in Kelsen's Pure Theory revolves around the notion of the *Grundnorm*. This notion is supposed to capture the fundamental presupposition that makes legal knowledge possible in the first place: legal cognition is premised on the (assumption of the) general validity of the legal order, a validity that ultimately flows from (the assumption of) a hypothetical, transcendental *Grundnorm*. Adopting Kelsen's position, normative claims of legal speech acts are always made by reference to a particular legal order. For Kelsen and his disciples, this means adherence to the respective *Grundnorm*. Present-day Kelsenians find here the explanation for - to cite an example - the divergent views that the Court of Justice of the European Union (CJEU) and national constitutional courts hold of the basis of the validity of EU law. At least legally speaking, judges are granted no option: they are bound to take the perspective of the referential legal order under which they have been established and function.

In his Kantian way, Kelsen is engaged in reconstructing the internal viewpoint of legal actors; the *Vorverständnis* through which legal actors approach the law. Yet he makes two mistakes. First, he depicts legal *Vorverständnis* in exclusively cognitive or epistemological terms; as a doctrine of legal sources which indicates both the grounds of legal validity and where valid law is to be found. Secondly, he treats this doctrine as an a-historical premise. He contends that assuming a *Grundnorm* and the concomitant hierarchical understanding of law is a transcendental presupposition for all legal cognition, irrespective of time and space. *Pace* Kelsen, legal *Vorverständnis* is not transcendentally fixed. Legal actors draw their *Vorverständnis* from the temporally and spatially variable legal-cultural reservoir available to them. Furthermore, legal *Vorverständnis* should not be portrayed in merely cognitive terms; it also comprises a normative orientation, which can be pinned down in legal principles.

In sum, perspectivism of legal orders – or, to be more exact: legal regimes – should be understood in legal-cultural terms. In legal *Vorverständnis*, perspectivism of legal orders meshes up with perspectivism of legal roles and disciplines; they all impact the way legal actors tackle the legal issues they confront in their professional activities within specialised legal practices. Yet, noting the legal-cultural particularities which mark legal actors coming from different legal regimes, possessing different disciplinary identities and occupying different legal roles should not obscure the similarities, the cultural common ground, which facilitate cross-border dialogue and interaction. Legislators, judges, and scholars are all engaged in a joint legal discourse where the contents of the momentary legal order are determined; international, constitutional, and administrative lawyers present divergent readings of EU law but are still able to learn from each other and adopt viewpoints from rival accounts; in spite of diverse referential legal orders, the CJEU and the German Constitutional Court have almost always managed to find a peaceful solution to their conflicts of authority, over, say the issue of *Kompetenz-Kompetenz*; and lawyers coming from legal regimes from opposite ends from the globe or the cultural spectrum can at least perceive that what their interlocutor is talking about is law. All this intimates that legal-cultural differences are not necessarily fault lines but can be bridged by deep-cultural commonalities.

I shall conclude the discussion of law's inherent perspectivism by turning to a legal role we have not yet examined: that of the legal theorist. This role must be defined in order to determine the perspective of this essay.

Legal theory should be distinguished from doctrinal legal research. They both share the peculiar dual citizenship of legal scholarship. Doctrinal research is not only a specialised legal but also a scholarly – Germans would say scientific – practice; it contributes to the ongoing legal discourse on the contents of the law, but it also attempts to nourish that discourse with scholarly rationality. In spite of its academic ambitions and affiliations, legal theory, too, should be included in the expert legal practices specialised in (re)producing law. Diverging from sociologists' external *Fremdbeschreibungen*, legal theory produces internal *Selbstbeschreibungen* of law. Unlike doctrinal research, legal theory is not a participant in the ongoing discourse on the momentary contents of the normative legal order. However, through its 'reflexion theories', as Luhmann's term goes, even legal theory contributes to the overall (re)production of law, occupies a participant's position in and shares the internal perspective on law.

Legal sociologists and political scientists may criticise legal theorists for insulating law and legal discourse; for neglecting the fact that law is about power and interests; for reducing law to *ratio*; and for ignoring - and by the same token legitimating - the *voluntas* which uses law as its medium and the coercion (violence) accompanying that *voluntas*. Legal theorists should be alert to such criticism and heed its cautionary admonitions. Still, openness and responsiveness should work both ways. Legal theorists can remind social-scientific colleagues of the importance not only of power *on* and *by* but also *in* law. They can also point to the power-constraining effects of the law, and to the contribution of legal *Vorverständnis*, informed by the prevailing legal culture, to these effects and to law's functioning in general. I confess to a predilection for flirting with Luhmannian terminology, such as *Selbstbeschreibung* and *Fremdbeschreibung*. However, this does not entail subscribing to Luhmann's views on the mutual closure of social sub-systems in general or legal theory and sociology, as inhabitants of diverse sub-systems, in particular.

In relation to specialised legal practices engaged in the continuous legal discourse on what the law is, legal theory is a meta-level, second-order, legal practice, producing – as a Luhmannian systems theorist would put it – second-order observations. Legal theory, so I would argue, consciously or unconsciously connects to a particular first-order perspective and lends it a reflexive twist. The first-order perspective may be the normatively (illocutionarily) oriented perspective of a judge or a doctrinal scholar, as is the case both in Hart and Kelsen's Legal Positivism and in Dworkin's or Robert Alexy's[16] principle-oriented jurisprudence. But legal theory may also approach law from a legislator- or counsellor-related meta-perspective. The former choice may not be so common but it has animated endeavours in 'legisprudence' or *Gesetzgebungslehre*.[17] In turn, the point of view of a practising lawyer was the main gateway into law for American realists, as it appears to be for their successors in Critical Legal Studies too. As legal phenomenologists have shown, legal theory may even connect to the first-order perspective of social actors, that is, subjects of first-order sociolegal practices.

In a second-order account, a legal theorist may, of course, also attempt to heed all the first-order perspectives or at least as wide a variety of them as possible. The ambition of this essay lies in that direction. Yet not even a legal theorist can attain an Archimedean point where all law's modes of existence, all the parties to its binary distinctions and all its intrinsic perspectives are attended to and accorded equal relevance. Striving for unity, attempting to (re)construct law as a unity, may be inherent in legal theory. Yet unity is bound to remain truncated and biased; all modes of existence of law, all parties to its binary distinctions and all its inherent perspectives cannot receive equal

[16] Alexy, 1989, 2002. [17] Wintgens, 2012.

attention. Law never sheds all its elusiveness, not even for a legal theorist. What a legal theorist is able to see and narrate depends on her *Vorverständnis*, which is susceptible to the same perspectivisms as legal *Vorverständnis* in general. Kelsen's Pure Theory was influenced not only by his chosen perspective of legal cognition (the legal scholar standing for legal actors in general) but also by his background and education in German-oriented public-law culture. For his part, Hart privileged the point of view of a judge. This was probably less due to a conscious decision than to the impact of English common-law culture. Through self-reflexion, a legal scholar can gain awareness of the penchants of her legal *Vorverständnis* and take deliberate perspectival decisions. Such self-reflexion can even be considered, if not a scholarly duty, at least a scholarly virtue. In the following section I shall explicate and justify the fundamental perspectival choice of this essay: adoption of modern state law as my privileged frame of reference.

As advisable as it is for a legal theorist, self-reflexion has its limits. We can never make our legal *Vorverständnis* wholly transparent to ourselves, or make explicit all our tacit, practical, knowledge. In legal scholarship, the Freudian device *Wo Es war, soll Ich werden* is justified, but impossible to live up to completely. My (re)construction of law – my 'reflexion theory' – certainly carries traces from my legal subconscious as a legal theorist with a background in public law and a German-oriented legal culture. For a colleague coming from a different legal culture these traces are bound to be visible even in places which lie beyond the reach of my self-awareness.

Modern State Law

In our era of post-national law, the state has, even in our perception, lost the monopoly in (re)producing law and in guaranteeing its realisation. We are increasingly aware of non-state law, such as transnational, religious, and indigenous law. By the same token, the boundary between not only state and non-state law but also law and non-law appears increasingly fluid and perspectival. Claiming autonomy is a common, though probably not universal, property of law. Awareness of varieties of law has sharpened our sensibility to extra-legal presuppositions for and limits to law's autonomy too. These vary not only synchronically but also diachronically. Historicity, too, is a vital property of law.

Legal historians and anthropologists have drawn attention to pluralist phenomena accompanying even the rise of the Westphalian state and concomitant legal centralisation, and enhanced our sensibility to law's varieties. Scepticism as to the possibility of arriving at a general concept of law seems warranted. A general concept of law may well be a chimera not worth pursuing. Still, so I argue, we need a tentative conceptual starting point which serves to clear our way through the jungle of post-national legality – a conceptual ladder which we might be able to discard after use (to insert the obligatory Wittgenstein reference). We cannot start examining post-national plurality of law before we at least tentatively identify instances of that plurality, drawing tentative borderlines between law and non-law and among instances of law. This we cannot do without recourse to a heuristic conceptual starting point. Neither can we discuss the variation in law's properties without first relating them to an ideal-typical framework. In this essay, I rely on the premise of modern state law, being wholly conscious of the suspicions of Eurocentrism and bias towards Western legal tradition that such a premise is bound to provoke. I have three main arguments to justify my approach.

States no longer hold a monopoly over law (if they ever did). Yet state law can still be considered the dominant type of law - indeed, much of the functioning of present non-state law presupposes its support, for instance in transposing transnational norms into national, 'hard', law and in securing realisation of those norms. Consequently, state law still deserves special attention even if its monopolistic claims cannot be accepted. This is the first argument. Secondly, and perhaps more controversially, state law is not only dominant and widespread but also, in a specific sense, the most developed instance of law. As emphasised by historically and sociologically oriented scholars of law – say, from Savigny through Weber to Luhmann – modern state law has resulted from interrelated processes of differentiation. These include detachment of legal norms from sociolegal practices; of specialised legal practices from first-order sociolegal practices; and of secondary, meta-level, rules from primary rules. Modern state law also facilitates insights into law's realisation and the contribution of social actors' practical knowledge; as well as into law's multi-layered nature and the indispensable role played by legal-cultural layers in the (re)production of legal normativity through specialised legal practices. As a corollary to its high degree of differentiation, modern state law reveals more of law's modes of existence and binary distinctions than other types of law. This also explains why it can serve as a general point of reference in examining the particularities of non-state law, such as transnational law, indigenous law, and religious law.

This is Eurocentrism, but conscious and, I hope, non-evaluative Eurocentrism. I only claim for modern state law the title of the most developed instance of law by the criterion of differentiation; I do not claim that modern state law is 'better' or 'worthier' or 'more just' than other types of law. Nor do I, *pace* Luhmann and some Weber readings, make any assumptions about an evolutionary path which law would follow in an inevitable, law-like manner. 'Modern' implies 'premodern' and 'postmodern', and I may use these terms, too, although I prefer 'post-national' over 'postmodern'. Yet here, too, I want to avoid intimations of evolutionary theory. 'Premodern' and 'postmodern' serve as reminders of the fact that there was law before and will be law after the era of modern state law. Premodern and postmodern (post-national) law share some of the properties of modern law and some not; otherwise we would not call them law and distinguish them from modern law by prefix.

To a certain extent – and here starts my third argument – reliance on the framework of modern state law is not a free but an imposed choice. Law is a profoundly historical phenomenon, although its historicity is not the same at all times and in all places. Even the historicity of law is historical (as are histories of that historicity too). Legal actors, including legal theorists, internalise law's history through the legal culture that informs their *Vorverständnis*; the concepts, principles, theories, and methodologies through and with which they approach the law and tackle their professional tasks. Legal culture includes a legal language which enables dialogue not only among diverse legal practices and disciplines but even across the borders of diverse legal regimes, thus mitigating the impact of law's intrinsic perspectivism. The roots of the legal language which in legal globalisation has conquered ground with the same speed and efficacy as has English as the global vernacular hark partly back to Roman law and even further back in history. Centralisation of law and the dominance gained by state law – developments on which positivist legal theory has bestowed a theoretical expression – have left a deep imprint on legal language and modified premodern concepts to fit in the state-law framework. Exploring post-national legal plurality requires conceptual innovations and recourse to novel concepts. Yet legal language cannot be revised at a stroke. Conceptual innovators, too, are imprisoned in the legal language which imbues their legal *Vorverständnis*; a language they have inherited and which bears traces of a bygone era. The *Vorverständnis* of those of us who have received our legal education and accumulated our legal experience under the auspices of modern state law is still impregnated by the self-evident dominance of this particular type of law. This colours our concepts and reasoning. We can, to a certain degree, gain reflexive awareness of our legal *Vorverständnis*, but we can never make it wholly transparent to ourselves.

Modern state law can, and should, be approached as both type and tokens. Legal theory focuses on type rather than tokens, though it should, of course, be aware of the importance of tokens too. Modern state law, such as I shall present and analyse it, is an ideal type in Max Weber's sense, generalised from tokens, enhancing some of their features and downplaying others, consciously or unconsciously. Legal Positivism is the theory *par excellence* of modern state law. However, in my ideal-typical modern state law I do not recommend buying the whole package of positivist legal theory, in either its Kelsenian or Hartian version. On the contrary, the ideal-typical conceptual framework I have in mind should cancel the positivist reductions with regard to both the sociality of law and the cultural layers of legal normativity. *Pace* Legal Positivism, modern state law does not consist merely of the normative legal order, such as it appears on its surface. My ideal-typical conceptual framework includes the differentiation between and interaction among the three modes of existence of law, namely law as a normative legal order; law as it is embedded in first-order sociolegal practices; and law as it appears in specialised legal practices. And as concerns law as a normative legal order, the framework is premised on the insight that the legal-cultural layers underlying surface-level manifestations are integral elements of law. In sum, my ideal modern state law consists of a full-blown legal regime where the surface-level legal order is supported by legal-cultural layers, and where the legal order is primarily realised in first-order sociolegal practices and (re)produced in specialised legal practices.

I also include in ideal-typical modern state law the institutional setting for specialised legal practices, such as a democratic legislature, an independent judiciary, and law faculties in autonomous universities. Such enrichment implies that ideal-typical modern state law is the law of a democratic *Rechtsstaat*; law that displays democratic origins, adheres to the Enlightenment idea of the self-governance of a *demos*, and protects fundamental rights and rule-of-law principles. In the normative dimension, the constitutional and procedural norms of a democratic *Rechtsstaat* can be shown to imply something like Habermas' ideal discourses. Yet the ideal type of modern state law is not only about norms and their underlying assumptions; it is also about social practices. In the latter dimension, even an ideal-typical depiction of modern state law cannot exclude power *in* law, that is, the fact that legal practices, whether legislative, judicial, or scholarly, also involve power relations and that the force of a better argument is not the only determinant of their outcomes. Not even in an ideal-typical presentation should norms and their underlying assumptions be confused with portrayals of social practices.

Inclusion of norms and practices characteristic of a democratic *Rechtsstaat* implies that I have extracted the distinctive features of the ideal type from a rather limited number of Western legal regimes, setting aside the fact that contemporary states and their legal regimes constitute a rather motley array. This is a conscious choice and the abstractions of the ideal type will be at least partly abandoned towards the end of this essay.

Modern state law is dependent on extra-legal presuppositions. Ideal-typical modern state law is the law of an ideal-typical modern society. Since Max Weber, at least, this has primarily been defined through the emergence and diversification of a (capitalistic) market economy and a centralised, bureaucratic, state; in Habermas' account these constitute System, which is integrated by systemic mechanisms operating behind the backs of social actors. Yet social theorists at least since Karl Polanyi have noted that a market economy and a bureaucratic state must be embedded in social relationships which obey different principles of coordination, engage social actors as autonomous subjects, and invoke – to employ a distinction going back to Friedrich Tönnies – *Gemeinschaft* (community) rather than *Gesellschaft* (a society of formal, impersonal relations). This is what Habermas, in the wake of sociologically oriented phenomenologists, calls *Lebenswelt*. It is also evident that many of the central concepts of modern state law presuppose social actors as autonomous subjects of social relationships; concepts such as 'legal subject', 'legal relationship', 'legal obligation', 'subjective right', 'contract', and 'human rights'. And if the institutional features of a democratic *Rechtsstaat* are included in ideal-typical modern state law, further social pre-assumptions follow; such as the existence of an active civil society and public sphere. What is crucial to note, too, is that the society which modern state law addresses and in which it is embedded is supposed to be circumscribed by state borders. Modern state law relates to a national society, a national bureaucracy (state administration), a national economy, as well as a national lifeworld with a national civil society and public sphere. A further societal precondition relates to the typical textuality of the normativity of modern state law: a particular information and communication infrastructure, based on the printing press.

In exploring the sociality and normativity of law in Parts I and II, I more or less take the framework of modern state law for granted. It also constitutes my point of reference in discussing non-state law in Part III. However, the rise of non-state law intimates a shaking of the extra-legal pre-assumptions of modern state law; such as the paradigm of a national society. In the Epilogue, I will, at a more general level, discuss the uncertain future of legal regimes which have approximately matched the features of ideal-typical modern state law, including the institutional structures of a democratic *Rechtsstaat*. We know that the societal and subjective presuppositions of modern state law are wavering, but we do not yet know exactly where globalisation and digitalisation or – for that matter – climate change are taking us and our law.

Legal Positivism

Arguably, Legal Positivism has been the dominant school in the legal theory of modern state law, rendering a theoretical expression to the spontaneous positivism of the legal actors of specialised legal practices. Yet its dominance has never been uncontested. It has been challenged from the side of both Natural Law and 'third-way' theorists like Dworkin. The very definition of Legal Positivism is controversial: indeed, all proposals will probably arouse objections. Furthermore, although Kelsen and Hart as the Masters of Legal Positivism agreed on many things, they did not agree on everything; they came from diverse legal-cultural backgrounds and possessed diverse perspectival commitments. Most likely, disciples of both Kelsen and Hart will find my treatment of Legal Positivism incorrect or unjustified at least in some places, but not necessarily in the same places.

Accepting the risk of oversimplification and overgeneralisation, I venture to present a summary of the basic tenets of Legal Positivism. Such a summary is indispensable, not only because in a way it wraps up my discussion of the ideal type of modern state law, but also because in the following I approach the properties of law through a criticism of the positions of Legal Positivism.

I share with Legal Positivism the basic starting point that positivity is a defining feature of the normativity of modern state law. However, I will provide an account of law's positivity that differs from the Kelsenian and Hartian schools. Yet my approach could be classified as positivist, too, and my criticism as internal criticism of positivism. I will indicate the main lines of subsequent criticism already in my summary, which I compress into six tenets:

1. positivity of law
2. bracketing of law's sociality
3. non-recognition of law's sub-surface layers
4. separation of law and morals
5. non-recognition of non-state law
6. a black-box view of law's unity and plurality

1. It should not come as a surprise that Legal Positivism claims that all law is positive law: indeed, what else could 'Legal Positivism' connote? Yet it is important to note the specific sense in which Legal Positivism employs the term 'positive'. 'Positive' is equivalent to 'posited', and positive law is law based on human decisions. Positivity comes with voluntarism. In Kelsen's Pure Theory, the contents of the law depend on the capricious *voluntas* of the legislator, and substantive overlaps between legal and moral norms are purely contingent. In Hart's Legal Positivism, judge-made law occupies a more prominent position than in Continental theorising. Yet voluntarism is manifest, for instance, by the emphasis on judicial discretion.

The voluntarist view of positivity makes validity a crucial, if not *the* crucial, problem for legal theory, and 'validity' its central, if not *the* central concept. If positive law can no longer draw its validity from the foundational law it expresses, that is, customary or natural law, where can it draw its obligatory force from? The question is ever more acute because of the intimate link between positivity and the coerciveness of law. If the law could have any content whatsoever, coercion becomes ever more necessary to secure its realisation. Kelsen did not much care for Kant's practical philosophy, but could perhaps have agreed on Kant's definition of the main problem that philosophy of law sets out to solve: how to justify the external coercion that one human being exercises over another.

The mere fact that the law has been posited, that is, decided on, cannot suffice to prove its validity or explain and justify its obligatory force. A contrary view would entail legitimating unbounded arbitrariness and naked power; totalitarianism in legal disguise. Legal positivist after legal positivist, starting from Hobbes, has found the solution in authorisation: in order for posited law to be valid, the law-giver must be properly authorised. Hobbes formulated his suggestion in terms of a hierarchy of power, twentieth-century legal positivists in terms of a hierarchy of norms. Yet legal positivist after legal positivist – again starting from Hobbes – has bumped into the problem of regress: the chain of authorisation inevitably breaks at a certain point. Here Kelsen and Hart introduce their respective Master Rules: the *Grundnorm* and rule of recognition. Still, as I shall argue, insoluble problems remain. Kelsen was never able to explain how a transcendental, Kantian, presupposition for legal cognition can found the validity and obligatory nature of norms created by the volitional acts of the legislator. Hart, too, had difficulty in combining the epistemological and foundational tasks of the rule of recognition.

2. Legal Positivism makes three reductive moves. It reduces law to the normative dimension; it reduces legal normativity to its surface level; and it reduces all law to state law. With Kelsen, excluding law's sociality is a conscious choice which he tried to prop up with philosophical arguments. Hart or his disciples have not shared Kelsen's penchant for ontological ruminations, or his Kantian epistemological predilections. Hartians would probably zealously recuse the normativist label; after all, they take great pride in what they call the social-sources or social-facts thesis; see here a decisive difference from Dworkin's principles jurisprudence; and may even consider the thesis the very defining feature of Legal Positivism. However, Hartians' interest in legal practices (re)producing the law ends with the social-sources thesis, which culminates in characterisation of the rule of recognition as a social rule. Law's realisation enters their focus only as an extra-legal precondition for validity. Indeed, law-creation as an act of will and efficacy as a precondition for validity are two crucial junctures where social reality – the social Is – reminds us of its presence even in Kelsen's Pure Theory. Yet with both Kelsen and Hart sociality, in the guise of creation of law and meeting the requirement for efficacy, remains external to law, even if indispensable for its existence. For legal positivists of both the Kelsenian and Hartian hue, law exists merely as a normative legal order. Paradoxically enough, Dworkin, whom Hartian positivists blame for not perceiving law's social roots, showed much more interest in exploring specialised legal practices; law as a particular type of interpretative social practice.

If we are searching for explicit discussion of and justification for the normativist reduction, our search must be directed to Kelsen. The dichotomy of the (legal) Ought and the (social and psychic) Is forms a central pillar of Kelsen's Pure Theory and a crucial aspect of the alleged purity of this theory. Considering the centrality of this distinction throughout Kelsen's *oeuvre*, it may be surprising how unsure he was of its foundations. Three alternative philosophical explanations run side by side: Kantian epistemological-constructivist; Humean logical; and Neo-Kantian ontological. Yet, as I will argue, they all fail.

3. Legal Positivism's second reductive move is performed within the normative dimension. Legal Positivism reduces the normative legal order to its surface level and excludes legal culture from law; that is, the sub-surface layers which

facilitate but, by the same token, put constraints on the legal speech acts maintaining continuous agitation on law's surface. Indeed, the positivist reconstruction of the normative legal order as a hierarchically structured whole, topped by a Master Rule, could only have been elaborated with a view to surface-level law, and whatever descriptive or explanatory force it ever has had is restricted to that level.

Legal positivists are particularly anxious to deny 'unwritten' principles the status of law. Again, Kelsen makes the point explicitly. He argues that legal principles can only be created but not presupposed by a legal order. The legislator, as well as custom, can be directed by general principles, but these are moral or political and not legal. Kelsen's uni-level normativism is intimately related with his voluntarism. Legal norms result from legislative acts of will, unbounded by any sub-surface principles. Law, meaning the surface-level legal order, can have any contents, as Kelsen never tired of repeating. The Hartian school shares Kelsen's uni-level view of the contents of law, but prefers to discuss it from the perspective of judges. Hart and his followers, at least those who situate themselves in the 'inclusive' and 'incorporationist' camps, have conceded that law can include norms which Dworkin called principles, but only on one condition, namely that they meet the criteria set by the rule of recognition. Related to their judicial voluntarism, Hart and his disciples contend that when judges invoke principles failing the test, they step outside existing law and enter the domain of judicial discretion. Dworkin's hard cases must be solved based on considerations drawn from outside existing law.

So both main variants of twentieth-century Legal Positivism exclude principles from law, except when these are explicitly enshrined in surface-level law. More complicated is to identify the positivist position with regard to conceptual and methodological elements of legal culture. For Kelsen, a vital task of his Pure Theory was to provide the fundamental concepts for describing the positive law of a definite legal community. Kelsen's aspiration was to purge legal concepts of normative substance, thus enabling legal science to focus on its purely cognitive task, as well as of extra-legal references, thus preserving the purity of cognitive legal science even in respect of the social or psychic Is. The Pure Theory pursues structural analysis of positive law by examining legal norms; their elements and interrelations; the legal order as a whole; the relationship between different legal orders; and, finally, the unity of the plurality of positive legal orders. It regards 'legal rule' as the central concept of jurisprudence, while other fundamental concepts include 'sanction', 'delict', 'legal duty', 'legal right', 'legal person', 'legal order' and, last but not least, *Grundnorm*.[18] When presenting his Pure Theory to an American audience, Kelsen stressed its kinship with Anglo-American analytical tradition and its

[18] Kelsen, 1945, 50.

aspiration to adhere to the method of Analytical Jurisprudence even more consistently than Austin and his followers.[19]

Kelsen's conceptual programme aimed at articulating and, by the same token, elaborating the conceptual dimension of legal actors' *Vorverständnis*. Yet, the programme suffers from the same a-historical apriorism which afflicts his view of positive law as a hierarchically structured legal order crowned by the *Grundnorm*. A corresponding criticism can be directed to Anglo-Saxon Analytical Jurisprudence – say, from Bentham and Austin onwards to Hohfeld and his successors – with which both Kelsen and Hart professed an affinity.

The methodological element in legal culture includes a doctrine of legal sources. It is here that Kelsen and Hart come closest to an understanding of a legal culture that primarily works through the practical knowledge - the *Vorverständnis* - of legal actors. Kelsen and Hart treat their Master Rule as a tacitly adopted and applied presupposition for specialised legal practices, although they differ in its more precise characterisation. For Hart, the rule of recognition is not a transcendental presumption in legal cognition – as is the *Grundnorm* for Kelsen – but a social rule which officials of the legal regime follow when identifying applicable norms, and which these officials also experience as normatively binding. In spite of these differences, both of these Master Rules are supposed to play a constitutive but mostly tacitly performed role in specialised legal practices, typical of sub-surface legal culture.

In sum, my claim that Legal Positivism reduces law to its surface level and ignores the sub-surface, legal-cultural layers should be taken with an important caveat. The claim focuses on the normative contents of law and neglect of legal-cultural principles, that is, what I shall call the normative or the principle element in my analytical division of legal culture into conceptual, normative (principle) and methodological dimensions.

4. Separation of law and morals is intimately related to the voluntarist view that legal positivists hold of law's positivity. It is also closely connected to positivists' second reductive move, namely reduction of law's substantive contents to its surface-level expressions. I would even contend that such a uni-level view is a *sine qua non* for defending the thesis of law's separation from morals. How this thesis should be specified and what its implications are is an inexhaustible topic, particularly among Hart's disciples. The smallest common denominator of positivist views appears to be the following: no necessary substantive connections exist between law and morals, but overlaps are of a contingent nature. This formulation should be acceptable to both Kelsenians and Hartians. Yet Hart's much-debated reference in *The Concept of Law* to the minimum content of natural law vindicates a caveat.[20]

[19] Ibid., xvi. [20] Hart, 1961, 193–200.

The separation thesis ensues from the way the Masters of Legal Positivism understand law's positivity and criteria of validity. Kelsen elevates the 'dynamic' principle of authorisation to the main criterion of validity and emphasises the substantively unbounded discretion of the legislator. Law and morals are supposed to constitute two separate norm orders, subject to different *Grundnorms*; law to a dynamic and morals to a static one. We cannot apply them simultaneously as a frame of reference in our assessments but must make a choice. In Kelsen's view, substantive congruences between legal and moral norms are purely accidental, and have no impact whatsoever on the validity of law.

On the Hartian side, the separation thesis has taken many guises. Hart himself related to Bentham and John Austin, the utilitarian predecessors – someone would say founders – of analytical Legal Positivism, and stressed the importance of drawing a distinction between law as it is and as it ought to be. Hart does not deny that morals have exerted a substantive impact on law (and law on morals), but argues that such relations do not establish necessary and conceptually relevant links between the two. The validity of law does not necessarily require its conformity with morals, nor does a moral principle possess legal validity simply as a moral principle. However, as a seeming concession to Dworkin, Hart argued in the celebrated postscript to *The Concept of Law* that the rule of recognition can – but need not – involve not only references to social sources but also moral criteria. Hart's admission of moral yardsticks into the rule of recognition, although on a contingent basis, has spawned a wide-ranging and by now an almost self-perpetuating debate among Anglo-Saxon legal theorists; a debate from which Dworkin – positivists' preferred straw man – retreated at a relatively early stage.[21] Hart's view came to be labelled as 'inclusive positivism'. By contrast, 'exclusive positivists', under the leadership of Joseph Raz, have maintained that moral criteria cannot even contingently be included in the rule of recognition

I shall continue my discussion of the Hartian position in Part II but try to avoid intervening in the rather one-sided dispute between Dworkin and his positivist critics or among the latter between inclusive and exclusive, soft and hard, or incorporationist and non-incorporationist positivists. Fresh insights into the relationship between law and morals require a shift of terrain: cancelling the positivist reductions of law to legal normativity and legal normativity to its surface level. Examining specialised legal practices and the legal discourse interlinking them allows us to discuss claims to normative correctness which legal speech acts raise. In turn, perceiving the multi-layered nature of law as a normative legal order facilitates perceiving the substantive overlap of legal and moral principles.

[21] Dworkin, 2001.

5. Neither Kelsenian nor Hartian positivists are likely to disclaim the separation thesis. By contrast, attributing to Legal Positivism the next tenet of my summary, namely non-recognition of non-state law, may be more controversial, in particular among the Hartian school. In my summary, reduction of law to state law is the third reductive move of Legal Positivism, complementing the reduction of law to its normative dimension and the normative dimension to its surface level.

Legal Positivism is a theoretical expression of state tradition, the legal mindset owing its emergence to the rise of the centralised state. With regard to the particular mixture of *ratio* and *voluntas* in modern state law, positivism privileges the latter. That *voluntas* in law is the *voluntas* of the state is a self-evident, unquestioned and at least partly even unarticulated starting point for both Kelsen and Hart, as is the sanctioning coercive power of the state too. The way Legal Positivism understands the very positivity of law ties it to the state. Kelsen was cautious not to hypostatise state will. Yet he never doubted that the legislative and judicial bodies whose subjective will was transformed into the objective will of law through validation were state organs. Kelsen even presented the somewhat provocative thesis of the identity of state and legal order. He also took for granted *Iustitia*'s need of a sword, implying the sanctioning power of the state.

Hart ousted 'sovereignty' from its key position in English positivist legal theory and showed that not all law is coercive. Hobbes already articulated the hierarchical, step-wise regress of the validity chain as a central problem for legal theory. Instead of Hobbes and Austin's Sovereign, Hart assigned the task of breaking regress to the rule of recognition. Yet by this replacement, Hart did not cut Legal Positivism's ties to the state.

To my knowledge, Kelsen or Hart never explicitly denied the possibility of non-state law in the contemporary world. Apparently, that 'law' means state law was so evident a premise for legal theory that it needed not be spelled out. Both Kelsen and Hart discussed, though only briefly, legal evolution in terms of the differentiation of specialised second-order legal practices or corresponding secondary norms. But in their concise historical or anthropological forays, primitive normativity was not-yet-law; a transitory stage in the emergence of law in the proper sense of the term, rather than a type of law which could coexist with state law as indigenous or tribal law. For Kelsen, the state is equivalent to a centralised legal order, and what transforms a primitive community into a state is centralisation of judicial and administrative functions; the legislative function follows later on. Hart's is the celebrated narrative of the transition from a set of primary rules of behaviour to a developed legal system where the primary rules are complemented by secondary rules of change, adjudication, and recognition. The narrative implies a corresponding detachment of specialised legal practices from first-order sociolegal practices.

Kelsen and Hart did discuss international law but treated it as a variant of state law, as regards both its sources and its substantive scope. Legal Positivism identifies the *voluntas* of international law with the *voluntas* of states. And although Kelsen saw no legal limits to international law's potential substantive scope, he examined international law primarily as interstate law. Neither Kelsen nor Hart hinted at the existence of anything resembling transnational law.

In sum, both Kelsen and Hart elaborated their versions of Legal Positivism in the light of modern state law and did not heed the possible simultaneous existence of non-state law. In recent decades, attempts have not been lacking to show that the legal positivist ideas of the Masters can be applied to instances of non-state law as well. Yet often enough these attempts have foundered at the feature of Legal Positivism, which constitutes the sixth and last tenet in my introductory summary, namely the black-box view of law's plurality.

6. In the relationship between the unity and plurality of law, Legal Positivism's focus is on internal unity. Positivism tends to treat national legal orders as self-contained wholes, insulated in their respective boxes and closed off to each other. They exist in plurality, but plurality is understood as simple diversity; as the mere coexistence of self-contained national legal orders, each subordinated to its particular *Grundnorm* or rule of recognition, without any intimation of interconnections, be they conflictual or cooperative and dialogical. What primarily matters for positivist legal theory is reconstructing and explaining the unity of a single positive national legal order. Plurality is subordinated to unity. This is a solipsist view of plurality; legal plurality as perceived through the black-box model.[22]

The tenets of Legal Positivism are interrelated. The black-box view connects to Legal Positivism's other central premises, such as the three reductive moves: non-recognition of non-state law; focusing on the normative aspect of law and sidestepping sociolegal practices; and, finally, identifying the contents of law with their surface-level expressions. The Westphalian state may have been successful in the policy of legal centralisation, and in suppressing medieval legal pluralism and spontaneous customary law – although in their colonialist and empire-building enterprises major European states were soon confronted with a new type of legal pluralism and customary law. Moreover, the centralising achievements of the largely mythical Westphalian state were limited to surface-level law and the institutions which housed specialised judicial and legislative practices. What it did not achieve – or even pursue – was national compartmentalisation of the legal-cultural underpinnings of surface-level law; it did not annul the legal-cultural transnationalism which was a legacy of late medieval reception of Roman law. No *Grundnorm* or rule of recognition can

[22] I have borrowed the term from Twining, 2000.

identify and delineate the principles, concepts, theories, and methodological devices which provide surface-level law with legal-cultural support. Here the solipsist black-box model has never been able to convey an adequate picture of the plurality of law. Legal-cultural interchange and commonalities, beginning with a basic legal vocabulary originating in Roman law, have always balanced the diversification of national legal orders.

The black-box view stresses the autonomy of national legal orders from other national legal orders. Autonomy implies universal and exclusive authority of the national legal order within its territorially delineated legal space: authority covers all substantive fields of law (universality), and no overlapping, rival claims of authority are recognised (exclusivity). In political theory, the corresponding concept is 'sovereignty': the autonomy of the national legal order and the legal and political sovereignty of the state go hand in hand. The black-box model presupposes that national legal orders reciprocally recognise each other's universal and exclusive claims to authority within the respective state territory: they treat each other as black boxes. Furthermore, the model presupposes agreement on the course of the borderline demarcating the boxes of national legal orders. Border disputes over the exact reach of competing claims to authority arise only sporadically and can be settled by conflict of laws (private international law). Non-state law does not define its jurisdictional claims territorially but either substantively (transnational law) or in personal terms (indigenous and religious law). Under post-national plurality, fundamental conflicts of authority where the very autonomy or identity of at least one of the parties is at stake are not only possible but even likely, as is proved, for example, by the ongoing debate between the ECJ / CJEU and the German Constitutional Court over the competence to define the competence of EU institutions (*Kompetenz-Kompetenz*) or the protection of Member State constitutional identity against (alleged) encroachments by EU law. The black-box model does not possess conceptual tools to articulate fundamental conflicts of authority.

The black-box view can accommodate international law as a variant of state law, although not all legal positivists have been convinced of its credentials as positive law. International law can be understood to be subordinated to its own Master Rule and relegated to regulating the external relations of sovereign states. Thus, it would not disturb the self-containment or the universal and exclusive territorial authority of national legal orders. Still, Kelsen's analysis of the interrelationship of international and national law is much more complex. Kelsen conceived of the reciprocal (non-)relations among national legal orders in accordance with the black-box model as simple diversity. By contrast, his views of the relations between international and national law qualify his black-boxism. As we shall note in Part III, for Kelsen, national and international law are not self-contained and mutually independent but interdependent instances of law.

My discussion with Legal Positivism, in its Kelsenian and Hartian variants, continues throughout this essay. The discussion is not an end in and of itself but serves my purpose of recapitulating the qualifying properties of what has come to be called modern state law: sociality, normativity, and plurality. I shall try to show why the reductions of Legal Positivism should be revoked; why legal scholarship should also attend to law's sociality and not only its normativity; why sub-surface legal-cultural layers and not only the surface level should be included in legal normativity; and that non-state law is also law, although different from state law. I shall also demonstrate how post-national plurality has dealt the final death blow to the black-box model and requires acknowledgement of instances of non-state law and conceiving of the relations among instances of law in terms of interlegality and pluralism, instead of the simple diversity of the black-box template.

In addition to questioning the basic tenets of Legal Positivism, my other central methodological device is to relate my discussion to ideal-typical modern state law. As children of Western legal culture we easily identify law in general with modern (Western) state law. This also includes legal language, with legal concepts as its vocabulary and the legal way of reasoning and arguing as its grammar. It may be difficult to imagine that other types of law and legal language could exist. I would contend that this is largely the case with Legal Positivism. In emphasising that they are engaged in a conceptual analysis, legal positivists imply that what they write holds not only for modern state law but for law in general. A look at non-state law - say, indigenous or religious law - may have a sobering effect. It may open our legal eyes and ears to other types of law and legal language; shake up our unwarranted self-certainties; and reveal to us things about our native law and legal language that we have not perceived before.

A Terminological Note

Law is a kaleidoscopic creature, with diverse modes of existence, multiple binary distinctions, and intrinsic perspectivism. This poses exceptional terminological problems, starting with the very term 'law'. Problems are further aggravated by legal-cultural perspectivism: in different legal cultures the same term may possess different connotations.

Because of law's elusiveness, the meaning of 'law' is impossible to pin down in an unambiguous definition. As a rule, the context indicates what I mean by 'law', whether for instance I refer only to its normative or social dimension, or both. When talking about law's plurality, I use the term 'instances of law'. If I want to stress that the instance I am discussing displays all three modes of law's existence – law as first-order sociolegal and second-order specialised practices, as well as law as a normative legal order – the term is 'legal regime'. Because of its systems-theoretical ballast, I avoid the term 'legal system';

I have recourse to it only in reference to systems-theoretical views. I also use the term 'law' of legislative speech acts; then the word can also come in the plural. Reference is not only to parliamentary statutes, but 'law' is shorthand for all legislative speech acts, including delegated legislation.

(Il)legality and a-legality refer to a particular aspect of the distinction between law and non-law. (Il)legality refers to the domain of legal ordering, a-legality to what remains outside that ordering: the unordered. In the former domain the binary distinction between legal and illegal, characteristic of modern state law, is applicable, in the latter not. Thus, the *pouvoir constituant* that lies behind a revolutionary constitution operates within a-legality but gives rise to a new (il)legality.

Depending on the legal culture, 'legal order' may connote law's normative or social dimension. German *Rechtsordnung* invokes the normative dimension, as does my 'legal order' too. If I want to emphasise that I am discussing the normative dimension, I may also use the expression 'normative legal order', defying the tautology involved. I use 'legal rule' and 'legal norm' largely as synonyms. However, when the reference is to Dworkin's and Alexy's discussion of different types of norm, I use 'rule' in the more specific sense as a contrast to 'principle'. In the social dimension of law, norms of the legal order are concretised into rights and obligations of individual subjects, as well as legal relationships among these; here the term is 'concrete order of behaviour'. In the social dimension, I distinguish between first- and second-order sociolegal practices. However, the corresponding terms are rather clumsy, so for the sake of brevity I reserve the term 'sociolegal practices' for the former and call the latter 'specialised legal practices' or just 'legal practices'. I hope the reader recalls that specialised legal practices, too, are sociolegal in nature. In specialised legal practices, such as legislation, adjudication, and legal scholarship, law (as a normative legal order) is both produced and (re)produced. My shorthand is (re)production.

I also distinguish between the subjects of first- and second-order practices or, as my terms go, sociolegal and specialised legal practices. 'Social actors' is the term for sociolegal practices and 'legal actors' for specialised legal practices. Under the conditions of modern state law, legal actors are usually legal professionals; here law-givers, which together with legislative experts make up the legislator, constitute a major exception. I may also call legal professionals 'lawyers', deviating from common Anglo-Saxon usage where 'lawyer' refers to practising lawyers or legal counsellors. If I mean practising lawyers, I spell this out. Lawyers or legal professionals constitute a legal community in the narrow sense of the term, all those subject to a legal order's jurisdiction, a legal community in the broad sense of the term.

Legal acts are acts that bring about changes in the normative legal order or a concrete order of behaviour. Legal speech acts are a distinct group of legal acts:

they constitute the legal discourse that connects diverse specialised legal practices and where the momentary contents of the legal order are determined. To further complicate my vocabulary, laws and court decisions will be called formal legal speech acts. In contrast to scholarly speech acts, the felicity conditions of formal legal speech acts, including their institutional and procedural setting, are legally determined. These speech acts are legal-institutional facts.

When discussing different types of law, 'state law' and 'national law' are used as synonyms, while 'post-national law' alludes to state law's loss of its monopoly. I am aware that the same nationalist pitfall is attached to 'national law' and 'post-national law' as to 'nation-state', which I attempt to dodge. So I hope the reader does not burden 'national law' and 'post-national law' with uni-national connotations, which would contradict the pluri-national character of perhaps the majority of states, past and present, and takes them more as technical terms. Examining law's unity and plurality requires new concepts and corresponding terms. Some of these have already been introduced, such as 'plurality', 'pluralism', 'simple diversity', and 'fundamental conflict of authority'. However, defining the concepts and terms needed for articulating the post-national condition of law presupposes more extensive discussion, in which I will only engage in Part III.

A distinct terminological issue, with potential implications regarding ontological commitments, is how to term the social sphere (the 'social Is' in Kelsen's vocabulary) which positivists want to shut outside law and which constitutes the opposite pole to legal normativity. Here my terminology vacillates. In addition to the 'social Is', I employ terms such as 'social reality', 'social facts', or 'social facticity', without trying to convey diverging meanings or ontological implications. The same goes for such terms as 'psychic (psychological) facts' and the 'psychic (psychological) Is'. Instead of 'social', I sometimes use the term 'societal'. The latter term intimates that society comprises action fields with different mechanisms of integration and coordination; social (in the narrow sense of the term) or systemic, operating behind the backs of social actors.

Some readers may be irritated by the use of German terms, such as *Vorverständnis* (preconception), *Lebenswelt* (lifeworld), *Grundnorm* (basic norm), *Stufenbau* (hierarchical structure), *Rechtswissenschaft* (legal science), *Allgemeine Lehren* (general doctrines), *Eigenbeschreibung* and *Fremdbeschreibung* ('internal description' and 'external description'), *Gemeinschaft* (community) and *Gesellschaft* (a society of formal, impersonal relations), *Kompetenz-Kompetenz*, or *Anwendungsvorrang* (primacy) and *Geltungsvorrang* (invalidation). My justification is not only, or even primarily, the terms' German origin. The terms either do not have an established English equivalent or their rhetorical force is lost in translation. In discussion of the principal ways of law's realisation, even French makes its entry.

There I find the terms *réalisation pacifique* (peaceful realisation) and *réalisation contentieuse* (contentious realisation), introduced in French legal phenomenology,[23] telling but difficult, if not impossible, to translate.

The polysemous character of not only 'law' but some other key terms, too, may cause difficulties. *Lebenswelt* (lifeworld) is one of them. It may refer to particular fields of action in society – as is the case with Habermas' distinction between *Lebenswelt* and System – a particular perspective on society – as Habermas' distinction can also be interpreted – or the world taken for granted in the experience and tacit knowledge of individuals, as it is usually employed in phenomenological philosophy. I am aware of the diversity of meanings but hope that here, too, the context will help to specify the connotation.

'Institution' is another polysemous term. It may refer to systematisation of the law, as it did with Roman jurists, as well as Savigny and his followers among nineteenth-century German *Rechtswissenschaft*. In the terminological pair of 'institution' and 'institutional fact', 'institution' also possesses a normative significance; institutional facts are considered instances or embodiments of institutions. By contrast, in sociology 'institution' has been used in more or less the same meaning as 'social practice'. In the following, I will exclude the sociological connotation, and privilege the normative and systematising one. However, in accordance with my interpretation of Savigny, I consider institutions as sets of norms arranged with a view to the social practices and relationships they address. So defined, 'institution' alludes to the interaction of law's sociality and normativity as approached from the latter side. Finally, 'institution' has an organisational connotation as well. For instance, by the institutional aspect of legal practices, I refer to the organisational sites which are the locus of these practices, such as parliament, the courts, and universities.

'Authority', like 'institution', is a difficult term to pin down. 'Authority' implies power and its recognition within a collective. Recognition can be of a legal character, which makes 'authority' a legal concept. Thus, one possible definition of 'authority' would be 'legally recognised power'. What complicates matters is that we use 'authority' also of an institution, person, or thing that possesses legally recognised power. 'Constitutional authorities' are institutions on whom the constitution confers authority and the persons who constitute these institutions. In addition, we can also speak of the authority – or claim to authority – of law. Law's claim to authority is a claim to be legally effective. Here 'authority' means approximately the same as 'jurisdiction'.

'Human' and 'fundamental' rights may also cause confusion. I use the term 'human rights' in two senses, narrow and broad. Human rights in the narrow sense are rights enshrined in international human rights instruments, while

[23] Goyard-Fabre, 1972.

fundamental rights are constitutional rights. In the broad sense, 'human rights' covers both of these, that is, rights guaranteed by both international treaties and constitutions. In turn, 'rights' can refer not only to the rights of particular individuals or collectives, but also to the surface-level norms establishing those rights and, finally, to general legal principles supporting those norms and extending their reach.

Part I
Sociality

1

Return of the Repressed

Society in Law and Law in Society

Law is not only about legal norms, about the normative legal order. It is also about first-order sociolegal practices where legal norms are realised and specialised legal practices where norms are (re)produced and their realisation is guaranteed. Characteristic of modern state law is differentiation. An important aspect of differentiation is abstraction of legal norms from sociolegal practices. In turn, differentiation of norms and practices has enabled the emergence of specialised legal practices, including legal scholarship, with their focus on law as a normative legal order. Yet differentiation does not mean isolation. The normativity of law cannot be accounted for without heeding law's sociality, nor can sociality be accounted for without heeding normativity. A relational approach is needed: normativity must be related to sociality and vice versa.

In academic division of labour and in accordance with its legal function, legal scholarship has approached law as a normative legal order. This holds not only for doctrinal research but for the greater part of legal theory too. Doctrinal legal scholarship fulfils a particular task in relation to other specialised legal practices, in particular judicial but also legislative. Its specific point as a specialised legal practice justifies its normative emphasis. Still, even doctrinal research should be aware of the importance of law's sociality; doctrinal legal scholarship, too, should assume a relational approach. In legal theory, this requirement is ever more heightened. In its reconstructions, legal theory should cover all the principal modes of existence of law, and not restrict its gaze to legal norms and the normative legal order; it should also attend to the role that sociolegal practices and specialised second-order practices play in law's functioning. Even for legal theory, it is wholly legitimate to enter law through the gateway of the normative legal order. However, in recapitulating the normativity of law, sociality keeps knocking on the door. Instead of merely taking notice of the tenacious intruder, it should be let in and the indispensable contribution of law's social aspect heeded and included in legal-theoretical reconstruction. Legal theory cannot make sense of the normative aspect of law without taking into account how the normative legal order interacts with the first- and second-order sociolegal practices that manifest law's sociality.

The relational approach I am advocating and the underlying understanding of law's sociality should be kept apart from diverse law-and-society and law-in-society calls for the renewal of legal scholarship; for shedding its dusty introvert normativism; and for breaking its self-containment. For me, the primary issue is law's inherent sociality; not law in society but, rather, society in law. I do not negate the importance of studying the (external) societal factors that lie behind legislation or the societal consequences of legislation. Nor do I want to belittle discussion of societal preconditions for a certain type of law – such as modern state law – or the pertinence of such discussion, not only for legal theorists, but for the reflexive self-understanding of other legal actors as well. Yet, by law's inherent sociality I mean something else. Law's inherent sociality is sociality without which law could not exist as a normative legal order; it provides the ontological support which anchors legal normativity in social facticity. This is the sociality to which legal normativity must therefore be constantly related and the conceptualisation of which should be an integral part of legal theory's reconstructive task.

Another feature distinguishes a legal-theoretical reconstruction of law's sociality from many, if not most, law-and/in-society movements. Legal theory, as I conceive of it, is interested in the relationships that law maintains with the external society too. At the same time, it examines even these relationships from within law, and does this in two senses. First, its particular remit is to identify the channels through which external societal influences – for example, from politics, economy, or morals – enter law, and the internal mechanisms through which those influences travel before they can leave their impact on, say, new legislation or judicial precedents. Here, specialised legal practices, such as legislation, adjudication, and legal scholarship, hold a key position. They not only perform particular internal functions in law. They also channel external societal influences, translate these into legal language, and exercise feedback impact on society. Secondly, the legal theory I am calling for shares the particular dual citizenship of legal scholarship as both a scholarly and a legal practice, and explores even the external relationships of law from an internal, participant's position. Here, too, it differs from sociology of law and law-and/in-society research.

The distinction between society in law and law in society is only possible where law retains its autonomy. If autonomy is gone, legal practices can no longer accomplish their mediating and disciplining function vis-à-vis external societal influences. Recall, though, that we are now discussing ideal-typical modern state law where autonomy, as well as respect for the principles of a democratic *Rechtsstaat*, are key assumptions. It is important to discuss deviations from the ideal type, too, but this can only be done after laying out its general features.

Breaking Points in the Pure Theory of Law

I shall try to warrant the claim of the non-repressible intrusion of law's sociality into normativist reconstructions through a critical reading of Kelsen. The purity of Kelsen's theory of law required vigilance over two separations: of Ought (*Sollen*) from Is (*Sein*) and of the legal from the non-legal - especially moral - Ought. Yet even Kelsen, often considered the extreme normativist, was not able to isolate normativity from law's social dimension. His recording of the interfaces between normativity and sociality are instructive even for a legal theorist who does not share his aspiration for normative purity but, on the contrary, seeks to articulate the interplay between the normative and the social in law. A legal-theoretical recapitulation should recognise the limits of its enterprise. Instead of trying to cover the entire motley array of topics which have been discussed under the broad title of law-and/in-society, it should concentrate on examining the interdependencies connecting law's social and normative modes of existence. Despite his avowed normative purism, Kelsen can offer guidance in localising these interdependencies.

Through a critical discussion of the way Kelsen demarcates the legal Ought from the social Is, I want to show two things. First, the philosophical foundations of this fundamental dichotomy turn out to be astonishingly wobbly. Secondly, Kelsen's structural theory of positive law cannot avoid continuously touching on the sociality of law; nor indeed does this escape Kelsen's notice. The constructions with which he attempts to ward off social pollution of the normative purity of his theory are not convincing. Emergency constructions include the *Grundnorm* as the ultimate basis of legal normativity, as well as the distinction between a condition and a reason for legal validity. A critical reading of Kelsen supports the claim that instead of struggling to keep up an appearance of normative purity, even normatively oriented legal theory should openly thematise the interrelations between the normativity and sociality of law. I also benefit from my Kelsen foray in identifying the topical areas where such thematisation should set in.

I will start developing my own account of law's social modes of existence from law's realisation in first-order sociolegal practices, hinted at by Kelsen's discussion of the efficacy of law (Chapter 3), and then move to law's (re)production in specialised legal practices - an issue related in Kelsen's Pure Theory to the mysterious metamorphosis of the legislator's subjective will into the objective will of law (Chapter 4). In examining law's sociality, my main social theoretical basis consists of the theory of social practices (Chapter 2), a theory which helps to perceive the characteristics of both first-order sociolegal practices as the setting for law's realisation and the second-order legal practices which have specialised in law's (re)production and in monitoring law's observance. Conceptualising sociality in general and law's sociality in particular through practice theory is a theorist's perspectival choice, which is not unequivocally determined by sociality 'out there'. Practice theory is a variant of cultural theories which adopt an actor-centred perspective and embed sociality in collective cognitive and symbolic structures, in 'shared knowledge'.[1] Depending on research interests, cultural theories must be complemented with approaches which emphasise the contribution of systemic, hidden-hand mechanisms in societal integration, such as Niklas Luhmann's autopoietical theory of social systems. Furthermore, an account of – or at least a reference to – the power inherent in social practices must be added to a culturally oriented theory.

In tracking law's journey from abstract norms to social reality, I also rely on recent theorising on legal institutions and legal-institutional facts, invoking Savigny and Kelsen as important precursors. In legal-institutional facts, the intertwinement of the legal Ought and the social Is is particularly conspicuous. Kelsen's remarks on legal qualification and legal norms as schemes of interpretation anticipate contemporary institutional theory of law (ITL). Yet even here Kelsen declines to concede how fatal are the consequences that this intertwinement involves for the normativist purity of his theory. Kelsen's analysis of legislative acts also contains hints at the direction of speech act theory, which will be my theoretical support in discussing legal discourse as a linkage among specialised legal practices.

The dichotomy of the (legal) Ought and the (social) Is constitutes a central pillar of Kelsen's Pure Theory, and cleansing the theory of references to social facts is an essential aspect of its purity. Legal normativity is isolated from social facticity, and legal science as a science of positive norms, relying on the principle of imputation (*Zurechnung*) or normativity, is separated from the science of Is, applying the principle of causality. Considering the constitutive role of the separation of Is and Ought, Kelsen was surprisingly unsure of its philosophical foundations. Three alternative philosophical explanations run side by side in his extensive *oeuvre*, stretching over several decades: Kantian constructivist; Humean logical; and Neo-Kantian ontological.

In a relatively early article, Kelsen seems to acknowledge that law possesses both social and normative modes of existence. He points out that positive law appears, on the one hand, as a product of an empirical human act of will, occurring in the realm of Is; and, on the other hand, as a norm – an Ought – by which actual human conduct is evaluated as lawful or unlawful. In sum, law appears simultaneously as both Ought and Is. However, he adds, logically these two categories exclude each other. This, Kelsen argues, is the problem of law's positivity.[2] After moving to the USA, Kelsen evidently felt the need to accommodate his Pure Theory to the philosophical predilections of Anglo-Saxon readers and increasingly presented the dichotomy as a basic precept of

[1] Reckwitz, 2002. [2] Kelsen, 1957, 393–394.

logic, harking back to Hume's famous guillotine: from Is-statements no Ought-statements can be logically inferred. The import of this explanation is doubtful. If the task is to vindicate the existence and separation of two distinct domains of reality, can the proof lie in the logical disconnectedness of statements about these domains? Does not the explanation transform an ontological issue into a logical one? Can we deduce qualities of reality from the logical qualities of statements about reality? And, given the existence of the two domains, can their connectedness or disconnectedness be reduced to logical relations between statements?

The formal-logical explanation never completely superseded the Kantian constructivist or Neo-Kantian ontological justifications. In the Kantian constructivist account, Is and Ought, together with the methodological principles of causality and imputation or normativity as their corollaries, are transcendental categories; that is, categories which make causal and normative sciences possible in the first place. Kantian epistemological constructivism argues that science does not find its object 'ready-made' in external reality but constructs the object through its categories. These, however, are not arbitrarily chosen but inbuilt in human rationality and discoverable through philosophical analysis. In the light of Kantian epistemological constructivism, strict separation of the legal Ought from the social Is would not be an inherent feature of reality but an ordering principle imposed on that reality by (positivist) legal science.

In particular in his pre–World War II writings, but occasionally even when already settled down in the USA, Kelsen emphasised that the human subject creates his world in and through his cognition. Accordingly, when and insofar as legal science comprehends its object as a meaningful whole, it too, just like any other field of cognition, displays a constitutive character. And just as Kant in his *Kritik der reinen Vernunft* (*Critique of Pure Reason*) set out to show that the possibility of natural science depends on transcendental categories, such as 'time' and 'space', Kelsen claimed to have shown that all cognition of positive law implies the presupposition of a transcendental and, in this sense, hypothetical *Grundnorm*.[3] Kelsen's argument suffers from two central weaknesses. First, he universalises and 'transcendentalises' the hierarchical *Stufenbau* as the structure of the normative legal order. Indeed, one can question whether even modern state law has ever corresponded to this pattern. Secondly, Kelsen drifts into intractable intricacies when assigning the *Grundnorm* not only an epistemologically but also a normatively, even ontologically, constitutive function: the *Grundnorm* is supposed to constitute the possibility not solely of legal cognition but of legal normativity as well.

In addition to the Humean logical and Kantian epistemological explanations, Kelsen invokes a third, Neo-Kantian, ontological vindication of the

[3] Kelsen, 1967, 201–202.

dichotomy of Ought and Is. On this account, the dichotomy does not actually call for further justification. Reality just happens to be composed of two independent domains, Ought and Is, and human beings are innately conscious of this fact, even without any assistance from Kantian epistemological constructivists or Humean logicians. Kelsen's early writings contain explicit references to German late nineteenth-century Neo-Kantian philosophy, especially philosophers of the Marburg school, such as Hermann Cohen. During Kelsen's US decades such express references diminish in number. Yet the second edition of *Reine Rechtslehre* (1960) still treats the separation of Is and Ought as a simple ontological fact which we cannot explain further but which we are immediately aware of.[4]

In sum, Kelsen is astonishingly ambiguous when discussing the foundation of the sharp distinction between Is and Ought. The philosophical ground does not turn any firmer when he moves to the related but more specific issue of the ontological status of legal norms. Kelsen stuck, though, consequently to the starting point that legal norms are ideal entities whose ontological domicile lies in the realm of Ought. In his writings in the 1920s, Kelsen invoked Edmund Husserl's notion of ideal entities, which Husserl had developed for logical truths. Yet legal norms differ from logical truths in one crucial respect: their existence displays a temporal dimension. By contrast, unlike spatio-temporal facts of the realm of Is, legal norms as ideal entities do not exist in space, nor are they governed by the principle of causality but by that of imputation or normativity. Beyond this premise, Kelsen struggled to keep apart four phenomena:

- legal norms as ideal entities;
- mental human acts which bring about these ideal entities;
- linguistic expressions of norms, such as texts of statutes, which constitute the object of legal interpretation; and
- legal propositions (*Rechtssätze*) produced by legal science.[5]

Dissecting Kelsen's volatile and frequently fluctuating views on the relations between legal norms, mental acts producing these norms, legal texts, and legal-scientific propositions is a tricky task, further complicated by Kelsen's (and his translators') changes of terminology. In any case, such an analysis far exceeds my present purpose to introduce the topic of law's sociality through Kelsen's aporias.

This purpose leads me to focus on Kelsen's account of how, exactly, mental human acts bring about legal norms as ideal entities. After all, these acts are inhabitants of the realm of Is, while the domicile of legal norms lies in the realm of Ought. In order to account for the leap from Is to Ought, Kelsen took recourse to a key concept of German neo-Kantianism: 'meaning' (*Sinn*).

[4] Ibid., 5. [5] See Hartney, 1991.

He argued that legal norms are to be seen as meanings of mental human acts. In Kelsen's psychology, mental acts are either cognitive or volitional, that is, acts of knowledge (thought), or acts of will. Kelsen had difficulty in making up his mind whether legal norms should be treated as meanings of cognitive or volitional acts: as statements or commands. His position shifted from a cognitivist to a volitional understanding. Initial cognitivism can be explained by two background factors.

In his early writings, Kelsen criticised his predecessors and teachers in the German late constitutional school for employing what he called concepts of will: 'legal subject' as a subject of will; 'state' as a legal subject and, consequently, a subject of will; 'state power' as state will; and 'state organs' as the mouthpieces of state will. In Kelsen's view, concepts of will tainted the positivist achievement of the late constitutional school, let factual connotations invade legal concepts, thus violating the separation of Ought from Is.[6] Kelsen's rejection of concepts of will accounts for his initial reluctance to accept command theory and his embrace of a conception of legal norms as statements: as meanings of cognitive acts. Moreover, Kelsen wanted to stress law's autonomy vis-à-vis morality, where to his mind command theory held sway. In the first edition of *Reine Rechtslehre* (1934), he argues that legal norms should not be understood as commands (imperatives) but as hypothetical statements linking together 'a conditioning material fact' and 'a conditioned consequence' through the formal category of Ought; here Kelsen alludes to the conditional 'if-then' form of legal programming. Kelsen terms legal norms which have been transcribed into such statements 'legal propositions' (*Rechtssätze*). Legal propositions, which express the basic form of positive laws (*die Grundform des Gesetzes*), are produced by legal science. However, Kelsen does not claim that legal science brings about legal norms. Rather, his point appears to be that through an effort of reformulation, legal science only lays bare the implicit structure of legal norms. Indeed, it was here that the Kelsen of the first edition of *Reine Rechtslehre* saw the essential task of legal science.[7]

The cognitivist position is afflicted by obvious problems. A risk exists of conflating legal norms produced by the legislator and legal propositions produced by legal science. Still, the main issue concerns the normativity of law. Turning legal norms into hypothetical statements and, by the same token, meanings of cognitive acts, divests them of normativity and cannot account for their obligatory effect. How can hypothetical statements obligate?

Kelsen never spelled out the reasons which led him to abandon the cognitivist view and to adopt a command or will theory of legal norms. In the second edition of *Reine Rechtslehre* (1960), legal norms are seen as meanings (*Sinngehalte*) of acts of will which command, permit, or authorise certain

[6] Kelsen, 1911. [7] Kelsen, 2008.

behaviour. Yet legal norms are not identical with the subjective meaning that legislators attach to their volitional acts; they constitute the objective meaning of those acts. An act of will, something occurring in the realm of Is, receives an objective meaning if it has been authorised by a 'higher' norm. Statutory norms constitute the objective meaning of the will of the legislator because the constitution authorises the legislator to pass such norms.[8] The notion of objective meaning is supposed to rescue Kelsen's version of command theory from the accusation of confusing Is and Ought: unlike subjective meaning, the objective meaning of legislators' act of will belongs to the realm not of Is but Ought.

Kelsen's corrected account of legal norms as the objective meaning of volitional acts raises a number of questions, not all of which Kelsen tackles. I shall bypass the often-raised objections that individual wills of individual legislators do not add up to a collective will or that many legislators do not take any position on many pieces of legislation in whose adoption they participate. These are general issues which affect all talk about the will of the legislator. Besides, Kelsen could argue that the shift from subjective to objective meaning liberates his version of command theory from such objections. What interests me now is what the 'meaning of an act of will' actually means. How can volitional acts possess a meaning and how can that meaning be ascertained?

Arguably, we can only speak of the meaning of a volitional act if that meaning is expressed – or, at least, can be expressed – in linguistic form. The same holds also for cognitive acts or acts involving thought, the other subcategory of mental acts identified by Kelsen. Complementing Kelsen's account with a linguistic element would carry it in the direction of a theory of legal speech acts: law-creating acts would be approached as a specific type of speech act and their meaning as the propositional content of those acts. What, then, about the distinction between objective and subjective meaning? In Kelsen's Pure Theory, the objectivity of the meaning of volitional legislative acts equals the validity of the legal norms they create. In the framework of speech act theory, 'objectivity' could be reconceptualised as the illocutionary force that legislative speech acts obtain if they meet their legally defined felicity conditions.

Emergence of legal norms through legislators' volitional acts is the first interface connecting law's sociality and normativity and recorded by Kelsen: the origin of legal norms lies in the social and psychic Is. One might argue that Kelsen embraced the social-sources thesis - which for Hartians is a distinctive feature of Legal Positivism, together with the separation of law and morals. Yet neither Hart nor Kelsen, nor their disciples, have been interested in probing deeper into law's social sources, or in examining the sociolegal practices

[8] Kelsen, 1967, 7–8.

specialised in law's (re)production or the legal discourse connecting these practices.

A brief discussion of legal validity will reveal further junctures where Legal Positivism is forced to register an encounter of legal normativity with the social dimension of law. As the early Kelsen explicitly noted, his dichotomous understanding of Is and Ought follows Neo-Kantian dualistic ontology which juxtaposes Nature and Spirit (*Geist*). Kelsen embraced the Neo-Kantian view of validity (*Geltung*) as the specific mode of existence of ideal entities – values, purposes, norms – populating the sphere of Spirit, where legal norms, too, find their domicile. The validity of a legal norm implies legal obligation: if we deem a legal norm valid, we also assign 'binding' force to it.[9] In Kelsen's dichotomous ontology, validity is a feature of Ought, instead of an Is quality which would exist in time and space and be subject to causality. However, the reach of the validity of legal norms must be determined in temporal and spatial terms because the contents of norms addressing human behaviour refer to spatial and temporal events.[10] Kelsen's discussion of the spheres of validity appears to question the separation of Ought from Is. All four spheres of validity that Kelsen detects – spatial, temporal, personal, and substantive – refer to properties of Is.[11] Validity is supposed to be an Ought phenomenon, but, still, it is specified through Is coordinates.

In his further discussion, Kelsen draws an equally questionable distinction between reasons and conditions for legal validity. Let us try to explicate Kelsen's argument. Because validity is a feature of Ought and because the legal Ought is separate from the moral Ought, the reason for legal validity must be sought within the legal Ought. From the two demarcations constitutive of his Pure Theory – of Ought from Is and of the legal from the moral Ought – Kelsen concludes that the reason for the validity of a legal norm can only be another legal norm; a higher norm authorising creation of that norm. Here begins the regress which all hierarchically structured theories of legal validity or political authority must tackle: where does the hierarchical continuity stop and what lies behind – and justifies – that continuity? Or, in Kelsen's version: what, if not a precedent constitution, authorises the historically first constitution or a revolutionary constitution breaking constitutional continuity? Kelsen cannot invoke, say, a mere act of power or acceptance by the citizenry; these are Is-facts and, therefore, cannot constitute a reason for legal validity as an Ought-quality. Nor can the answer lie in justification provided by moral principles; this would violate the postulate of the separateness of law and morals. Thus, the only explanation available for Kelsen is to presuppose a transcendental, hypothetical, *Grundnorm* which authorises the constitutional legislators; confers objectivity on the subjective meaning of their volitional

[9] Kelsen, 1945, 31. [10] Kelsen, 1967, 122. [11] Ibid., 12–15.

constitution-giving act; and validates not only the constitution but ultimately all subsequent enactments respecting constitutional and legal continuity and adding to the intact chain of validity.

Ever since introducing the idea of the *Grundnorm* in the 1920s, Kelsen toiled to present it in a manner consistent with other elements of his Pure Theory. Presupposing a *Grundnorm* seems to contradict the central legal positivist premise that all law is positive law. How can the edifice of positive law rest on a *Grundnorm* which has not been posited (*gesetzt*) but merely presupposed (*vor-gesetzt*)? Kelsen sought an answer in Kantian epistemology and stuck with the Kantian analogy even after adopting the will theory and abandoning the view of legal norms as meanings of cognitive acts. Kelsen characterised *Grundnorm*, too, as the meaning of a mental act, but rejected the volitional view at the very top of the hierarchical structure of legal norms. *Grundnorm* is supposed to be the objective meaning of, not of a volitional but of a cognitive act. Kelsen treated *Grundnorm* as a transcendental concept in the sense of Kantian epistemology; that is, as a concept which enables cognition of positive law and is presupposed in every act of legal cognition. Yet the Kantian analogy falters already for the reason that in the Pure Theory the *Grundnorm* does not perform a merely epistemological function. It is supposed to found the possibility not only of cognition of legal normativity but of legal normativity itself.

Kelsen assigns to the *Grundnorm* the task of founding the validity of a positive legal order. It is ultimately the *Grundnorm* that transforms the subjective meaning of the legislator's volitional acts into a legally valid, objective, meaning; or, in other words, the *Grundnorm* is supposed to account for the mysterious leap from legislative acts of will in the world of Is to legal norms in the world of Ought. Kelsen entrusts the *Grundnorm* with two functions, only one of which is compatible with Kantian constructivism. Kant's transcendental categories bring order into the manifold of natural facts, such as they appear in our perception as sense data, thus facilitating natural science as a systematising act of cognition. Correspondingly, in their epistemological role the concepts of the Pure Theory, most importantly the *Grundnorm*, bring order into the manifold of objectively valid legal norms, transforming them into a system or a legal order. Yet by the same token the *Grundnorm* is also supposed to establish legal normativity as such, 'to found the objective validity of a positive legal order';[12] that is, to provide for the existence of legal norms. The latter task finds no correspondence in Kant's epistemology of natural science: Kant's transcendental categories do not provide for the existence of the 'raw material' for scientific ordering as Kelsen claims the *Grundnorm* does. The Kantian analogy cannot but fail because the analogy between perceptions of natural facts (sense data) and legal norms fails.

[12] Ibid., 202.

Kelsen was never able to explain how a transcendental presupposition for legal cognition can found legal normativity and furnish norms created by the legislator's volitional acts with 'binding force'. His reference in the second edition of *Reine Rechtslehre* to an imaginary will present in our thinking appears as a last-ditch desperate attempt to save the very cornerstone of his theoretical construction from crumbling. Kelsen argues that because a correlation exists between the normativity – the Ought, as he puts it – of a norm and a will whose meaning it is, our thinking, which presupposes the *Grundnorm*, must also involve an imaginary will as a correlate of the *Grundnorm*.[13]

Kelsen was as vacillating about the character of the *Grundnorm* as about the philosophical foundation of the dichotomy of Is and Ought or the ontological nature of legal norms. Kelsen's axiomatic ontological demarcations barred him from deriving legal validity from the efficacy or social acceptance of constitution-giving as an act of power, or from law's harmony with fundamental moral principles and ethical values. Yet as a testimony to his nagging uncertainty, at least in one of countless expositions of the *Grundnorm*, published in 1929, Kelsen flirted with both a sociological and a Natural-Law reading. The sociological reading relates to the particular historical fact which the *Grundnorm* qualifies as the original law-making act. This is an act of power, and, accordingly, the *Grundnorm* could be understood as transformation of power into law.[14] The *Grundnorm* would sanction the power manifest by the successful issuance of a revolutionary or foundational constitution and by the maintenance of a by-and-large effective legal order based on this constitution. But this remains only flirting: in the end, Kelsen rejects the power-theoretical reading and decides to remain faithful to the strict separation of Is and Ought. Yet Kelsen's discussion of the *Grundnorm* and hinting at the possibility of a sociological or power-theoretical reading indicate a second juncture where the social dimension calls for legal-theoretical attention: the origin of, not only individual legal norms, but of the normative legal order as a whole.

Kelsen's examination of legal validity points at yet another encounter between the normativity and sociality of law: efficacy as a condition for validity. Kelsen qualifies validity as a feature of Ought, which makes it necessary to distinguish validity from efficacy. Yet he cannot ignore the connection between the two. Not all revolutionary constitutions are sanctioned by a *Grundnorm* but only those that prove to be effective; instead of establishing a novel hierarchy of legal validity, failed revolutions are conceptualised in terms of treason. Nor can Kelsen neglect the age-old doctrine and practice of *desuetudo*: loss of validity of non-efficacious law. Kelsen argues that the *Grundnorm* must meet the requirement for efficacy in the sense that norms which the law-making authority has issued in accordance with the

[13] Ibid., 9–10. [14] Kelsen, 1957, 436.

Grundnorm must, by and large, be observed, and social life must broadly conform to the legal order based on this hypothetical norm.[15] In addition to the legal order as a whole, individual norms, too, are subject to a similar requirement for efficacy: if ineffective, they lose their validity. To retain their validity, legal norms must, in general, be both obeyed by individuals subject to the legal order and applied by legal organs, particularly the courts.[16] Thus, efficacy relates both to law's primary realisation in first-order sociolegal practices and secondary realisation in judicial practices.

How can such conditioning of validity by efficacy be brought into harmony with the dichotomy of Ought and Is? Kelsen's response lies in the distinction he draws between a condition and a reason for validity. He argues that efficacy as a social fact is a condition but not a reason for validity, which, as may be recalled, can only be another, higher, norm. The implication is that the gulf separating Ought from Is can only be bridged by a condition but not by a reason for validity. The answer would probably be the same if the question were focused on the contribution that law-makers' acts of will make to legal validity: an act of will as an Is-fact is a condition but a not a reason for the emergence of a new instance of valid legal normativity.

This is not convincing. Kelsen does not explicate the difference he postulates between x being a condition and a reason for y. Neither does he explain why an Is-x being a reason for an Ought-y would contradict the separateness of the two spheres but x being a condition for y would not. Kelsen discusses logical and normative relations in the realm of Ought and causal relations within the realm of Is. But how should one characterise conditioning as a relation which connects Is to Ought but still maintains their separateness? Even when discussing validity, Kelsen sometimes treats the separation of Ought and Is as a requirement of logic. However, just as the existence of two distinct ontological spheres of Ought and Is cannot be vindicated by the logical (non-)relation between statements about these spheres, formal logic cannot solve the problem of the foundation of legal validity and obligations, either. Yet, once again, the foundering of Kelsen's reductive normativism is instructive: the connection between efficacy and validity constitutes the third juncture where law's normativity cannot be accounted for without bringing in its social modes of existence. Law as legal norms is dependent on social practices, not only in its origins, but also in its further existence.

In his discussion of efficacy as a condition for legal validity Kelsen, somewhat surprisingly, does not refer to the coercion which ultimately guarantees law's realisation and, by the same token, its efficacy. Yet, even in his very definition of law and in explaining how law differs from morals, Kelsen stresses the importance of coerciveness.[17] Thus, in his Pure Theory violence

[15] Ibid., 437. [16] Kelsen, 1967, 11. [17] See, e.g., Kelsen, 1967, 33ff.

or at least the possibility of violence hangs over legal normativity. Tellingly enough, Kelsen mentions coerciveness as a distinctive feature of legal normativity, but never articulates the complicated issue of law and violence. Once more: notice taken but no further discussion considered necessary!

The social Is disturbs the normative closure of Kelsen's Pure Theory at the origin of both individual legal norms and the legal order as a whole, as well as in conditioning legal validity through the requirement of efficacy and coercion guaranteeing efficacy. The very possibility of positive law, both its emergence and further existence, turns out to depend on conditions which in Kelsen's dualistic ontology fall to the world of Is. On the other hand, Kelsen has shown the inevitable miscarriage of extreme legal-theoretical realism; the failure of the reductionist realist effort to efface the normative element from law.

Theorists committed to ontological realism have repeatedly attempted to define legal norms through empirically observable characteristics. Some realists have even abandoned the very distinction between legal norms and practices. In American Realism, law is reduced to the decision-making of courts and defined as the actual or predicted behaviour of judges or as the rules judges in fact apply or are predicted to apply.[18] Yet realists have not succeeded in their effort to reduce the legal Ought to the social Is. Normative criteria are needed even for identifying the persons whose behaviour is supposed to be constitutive for law. Courts and judges, as well as their decision-making and decisions, are institutional facts which receive their legal significance from relevant legal norms. This is a lesson that realists could have learned from Kelsen, the arch-normativist.

Kelsen's remarks on how legal norms function as schemes of interpretation of Is-events makes him, together with, say, Savigny and Weber, a precursor to the ITL. What Kelsen calls legal qualification constitutes a further interface between legal normativity and social facticity which he notes but whose consequences for the putative separation of Ought and Is he declines to articulate or even acknowledge. Kelsen's remarks testify to the influence of Neo-Kantian and phenomenological philosophy. Legal qualification is a special case of meaning-giving (*Sinn-Stiftung*). Although Spirit and Nature, as well as ideal and empirical entities, are ontologically different, the former can invest the latter with meaning. This is exactly what, according to Kelsen, transpires in legal qualification; when, for example, killing a man is qualified, not as murder, but as execution of a death penalty.

Kelsen discusses the function of legal norms as schemes of interpretation in the opening pages of the second edition of *Reine Rechtslehre*. Legislative and judicial decision-making is made up of two elements. One is a series of events, human acts, occurring at a certain time and in a certain place, and perceivable by our senses; 'people assemble in a large room, make speeches, some raise

[18] Summers, 1982.

their hands, others not' or 'a man in a robe and speaking from a dais says some words to a man standing before him'. The other element is the meaning conferred on these events by legal norms: a law is enacted or a sentence pronounced.[19] Without legal qualification – legal meaning-giving – through legal norms, empirically observable events could never be understood or even exist as legislative or judicial decision-making. However, we could add, neither could legal norms by themselves, without the occurrence of empirically observable events, produce such decision-making. Both Is- and Ought-elements are necessary for legal qualification and, to use more recent terminology, creation of legal-institutional facts. Again, Kelsen stands on the threshold of articulating the interplay between social and normative elements. And again, true to his axiomatic ontological commitments, he declines to take the decisive step. Legal theorists not bound by the same commitments can follow the clues left by Kelsen and openly thematise this interplay.

We can now sum up the critical locations where Pure Theory cannot avoid encounters with what in Kelsen's dualistic ontology falls into the realm of Is: origins of individual legal norms and the legal order as a whole, efficacy as a condition for legal validity, coercion backing up efficacy, and legal qualification where legal norms function as schemes of interpretation of Is-facts.

[19] Kelsen, 1967, 3–4.

2

Social Practices

Why Social Practices?

In accordance with its dichotomous ontological premises, mainstream positivism of the preceding century was not interested in conceptualising the realisation of law. It considered, though, compliance of social actors with law in general and individual norms in particular necessary for law's efficacy and as such a precondition for legal validity. As a rule, its interest did not extend to exploring the process of realisation; that is, the transition from abstract norms to norm-conforming behaviour. Of course, exceptions exist. Rights, duties, and legal relationships are major steps in the transition. In the wake of Jeremy Bentham, John Austin and Wesley Newcomb Hohfeld, analytically minded positivists have continued elaborating these concepts. Yet analysis has focused on the logical relations between the concepts so that, typically, rights, duties, and legal relationships have been detached from their social context. In this respect, too, Kelsen held an extremist position. For him, 'right', 'duty' and 'legal relationship' connoted relationships between legal norms. In the realist camp, especially in Scandinavian Realism, the analytical approach has also enjoyed popularity. However, Scandinavian realists' realism was largely confined to defining the basic concepts with reference to predictable reactions from the side of authorities, thus allegedly satisfying empiricist criteria whose fulfilment the scientific character of legal scholarship was seen to require.

The search for antecedents in discussing the social contextualisation of legal relationships must be extended to the pre-positivist era. Here, Friedrich Carl von Savigny, the main proponent of the German Historical School and an international hero of nineteenth-century legal scholarship, revered even, for example, in the United States, is an important point of reference. Savigny also connects to the ITL, arguably the main legal-theoretical effort in recent decades to conceptualise law's realisation. Savigny's core concepts are 'legal relationship' and 'legal institution'. Legal relationships possess two sides, substantive and formal. The substantive element consists in 'life relationships' (*Lebensverhältnisse*), the formal side, in turn, in the legal determination of the substantive element. The formal element of legal relationships is provided by legal rules (*Rechtssätze*), arranged into legal institutions.[1]

Savigny stressed the organic character of legal relationships. 'Organicity' was a key concept for nineteenth-century German legal science, especially for the Historical School but also for subsequent *Begriffsjurisprudenz* (Conceptual Jurisprudence). Usage of the concept varied but usually it connoted two features: firstly, the interdependence of the elements of the phenomenon under examination and, secondly, its subjection to the developmental principle of living nature. The organic character of legal relationships was manifest by the interplay between their formal and substantive aspects and by their lifespan: legal relationships emerge, develop, and are extinguished. Savigny also depicted legal institutions, the building blocks of law's systematisation, as organic wholes. Legal institutions are not 'abstract' combinations of legal rules but organic, developing wholes with their elements connected by reciprocal ties. Savigny portrayed legal institutions as types (*Typus*) or models (*Urbild*) of legal relationships.[2] Legal rules can only be brought into such organic wholes because the factual life relationships they address are organically interlinked. Family law institutions derive their organicity from the interlocking life relationships on which family law confers legal determination.[3]

Savigny divided legal institutions and the corresponding legal relationships into two groups: natural and artificial. In contrast to artificial institutions, natural institutions possess a 'natural-ethical' foundation. Family law, for instance, includes natural institutions such as marriage, paternal power, and kinship, all of which rise from a natural-ethical foundation. Relationships within natural institutions can never be exhaustively governed by the law. By contrast, artificial legal relationships are subjected to law in their entirety; they are purely and merely legal relationships.[4]

Savigny's legal relationships and ITL's legal-institutional facts are proposals for conceptualising law's realisation; or, to put it differently, law's sociality. Both for Savigny and ITL, the corresponding concept on the normative side of law is 'institution'. 'Institution' provides the systematisation of law with a conceptual tool where law's normativity is still related to its sociality. 'Institution' also connects to recent theorising about social practices, where it refers to the inherent normativity of practices. Practice theory facilitates placing rights, duties, legal relationships, and legal-institutional facts in a wider social setting. At the same time, the linkage to legal normativity can be retained through the concept of institution. In addition, the theory of social practices enables discussion of both sides of law's sociality – realisation and (re)production – in the same social theoretical framework. Law is realised in first-order and (re)produced in second-order sociolegal practices.

[1] Savigny (1840) 1981, 333. [2] Ibid., 9 and 291. [3] Ibid., 342. [4] Ibid., 370.

Furthermore, practice theory stresses the importance of social actors' tacit knowledge and the routine-like nature of many practices. This corresponds to the way law is primarily realised through social actors' practical lifeworld knowledge.

Practices provide the social context for rights, duties, and legal relationships which specify abstract norms and transform them into concrete orders of behaviour. Social practices also rescue legal-institutional facts from isolation and facilitate discerning the diverse functions these facts accomplish in law's social life. Yet the question can be posed whether all law is realised in social practices so that practice theory can provide a comprehensive social theoretical framework for analyzing this aspect of law's sociality. Evidently, the answer depends on how social practices are defined.

Prominent practice theorists are inclined to consider practices a basic and omnipresent form of human sociality and human life in general. As my main guides in the prolific field of contemporary practice theory, I rely on Raimo Tuomela and Theodore Schatzki. Tuomela argues that the deepest sense in which practices are primary is that they constitute the basis for thinking and conceptual activities.[5] In turn, Schatzki claims that the intelligibility of both the world and actions taking place there depends on practices. For both Tuomela and Schatzki, social practices are central elements of Wittgensteinian 'forms of life'. Schatzki even contends that human life in general transpires within social practices. He stresses that sociality cannot be construed exclusively out of individuals and relations among them, because individuals and their interrelations exist only within practices. Furthermore, composite social formations, such as families and economies, are built out of forms of coexistence within practices. In sum, all human coexistence ultimately relates to practices, in Schatzki's view.[6]

These are bold claims. If warranted, they imply an affirmative answer to the question posed above: yes, all law is realised in social practices. If all sociality transpires within practices, law's realisation outside practices would be a conceptual non sequitur. Such a claim of omnipresence implies a broad definition of 'social practice'. If the concept is reserved only for integrative practices which display a distinct teleological structure and a corresponding differentiation of actor positions or roles – say, accounting or legislation – practice theory could hardly procure a framework for examining realisation of, say, criminal law. By contrast, adoption of a wider concept, covering even dispersed, elementary, practices, such as the discursive practices of questioning or explaining, also widens the applicability of practice theory. Inherent normativity is not as dense in dispersed as in integrative practices, but no non-normative practices exist. Law may well contribute to the inherent

[5] Tuomela, 2002, 1. [6] Schatzki, 1997.

normativity of not only more complex integrative practices but even elementary practices dispersed into diverse fields of society.

Social practices in general and sociolegal practices in particular should be examined at the level of both types and tokens. 'Family practices' can be discussed as both abstract types and concrete tokens. Types collect characteristic features, possession of which makes particular practices tokens of them. Below, I shall propose understanding legal institutions in reference to the inherent normativity of social practices as types. Legal institutions are sets of abstract norms which relate to distinct social practices understood as types; say, family law to family practices or procedural law to judicial practices. Discussion of legal institutions is always discussion of abstract types. In exploring law's realisation, we move from type to token, from abstract to concrete. Particular rights, duties, legal relationships and legal-institutional facts find their locus in social practices as tokens rather than types; in, say, particular family or judicial practices.

Dissecting Social Practices

Put in a concise definition, social practices consist of recurrent, patterned, and interlinked social actions. I shall start unravelling the concept by explaining what 'recurrent' and 'patterned' means; then go over to identifying actions and among them social actions; and finally, discuss how social actions are interlinked to form a practice.

No one-off action creates a social practice by itself, although it may well be – and most probably is – part of a practice. 'Recurrent' refers to repetition, that is, an empirical fact. The patterned nature of social actions constituting a practice means that they are rule-governed. Thus, characterising practices as patterned entails rejecting an extreme empiricist or behaviouralist position. Social practices cannot be approached as mere empirical regularities of behaviour. It is an empirical regularity, a recurrent fact, that drivers on the highways in Finland keep to the right-hand side. Yet the empirical regularity of driving in the right-hand lane does not make it part of traffic as a social practice. What is decisive is that social action is not only recurrent but also patterned, rule-governed.

What, then, are social actions and how are they are interlinked to form a practice? 'Behaviour' connotes something occurring in empirically observable reality, such as bodily movement, while 'action' is behaviour in a context which confers a sense on the behaviour and renders it intelligible. It is important to note that not only others but the actor, too, attach a meaning to action, although in most of our actions the meaning is self-evident and we do not need to deliberate it. Action may consist of both doing and saying, in some contexts even of non-doing or non-saying. Speech acts, too, are actions in the meaning of practice theory, and discursive practices are a sub-group of social practices. Specialised legal practices, for instance, are mainly discursive.

Yet, *pace* some post-structuralist theorists, not all social practices are discursive, nor is any practice exclusively discursive. Actions, including speech acts, involve bodily movement; actions are produced by body / mind, as Schatzki puts it.[7] The respective importance of doing and saying varies. In legal or scholarly practices, the emphasis is on speech acts, while in sports it lies on the bodily aspect.

Not all actions are social. Walking and biking are actions and intelligible as such, but isolated from a social context they are not social actions. By contrast, walking or biking to work on the pavement or the cycleway are. 'Social' implies an explicit or implicit reference to coexistence with other humans. According to Max Weber's classic definition, social actions consist of behaviour to which actors attach a specific meaning and which is guided by or takes account of the behaviour – the actions – of other human beings.[8] Weber has been criticised for an individualist approach and for ignoring the basic sociality in which individuals and their actions are embedded. Tuomela tries to avoid the individualist fallacy by arguing that collective social actions, constituting a social practice, imply a shared we-attitude.[9] A social practice 'in the core sense' consists of recurrent collective social actions which are performed for a shared social reason. As the primary impetus must consist of a shared social reason, individualist strategic reasoning cannot be the dominant basis for actions constituting a social practice. Tuomela emphasises that the social reason need not be conscious but may function as a presuppositional, unreflected, backdrop to action. This corresponds to the customary, routine-like, nature of many social practices.[10] What Tuomela means by shared social reasons or we-attitudes comes close to John Searle's notion of collective intentionality. Collective intentionality includes shared intentional states, such as beliefs, desires, and intentions, so that each person's individual intentionality is derived from a shared collective intentionality.[11]

It may appear that requiring a we-attitude from the social actions making up social practices would seriously limit the applicability of practice theory in examining the sociality of law. Evidently, law also addresses and is realised in strategic actions based on an individualist approach; an I-mode, as Tuomela puts it. Think of, say, the law addressing economic activities where market participants pursue, and are even expected to pursue, their strategic interests. Indeed, facilitating strategic action, often removed from local, face-to-face contexts, has been considered a major function and achievement of modern state law. In the interest theory of rights, 'subjective right' has even been defined as a legally protected interest. In the early decades of the twentieth century, Interest Jurisprudence (*Interessenjurisprudenz*) was instrumental to breaking, or at least shaking, the dominance of Conceptual Jurisprudence (*Begriffsjurisprudenz*), and in the USA, the long shadow of Interest

[7] Ibid. [8] Weber, 1978, 22. [9] Tuomela, 2002, 22–24. [10] Ibid., 84ff.
[11] Searle, 1995, 23–25.

Jurisprudence extends to Law and Economics and Critical Legal Studies as heirs to American Realism.

The importance of strategic action for law is a serious test for the relevance of a practice theory which emphasises collective intentionality, we-attitudes and shared social reasons. Strategic action cannot be ignored or downplayed. Yet, it is crucial to note that law not only facilitates and protects strategic action. Law also restricts the reach of strategic action, channels it into acceptable forms and coordinates it, for instance through contracts. As Émile Durkheim intimated with his notion of non-contractual preconditions for a contract, law also embeds strategic action in a non-strategic context, where collective intentionality, shared reasons, and we-attitudes hold sway.[12] Contracts where parties pursue strategic interests are immersed in economic practices towards which participants adopt not only an individualist strategic attitude but also a we-attitude; which they consider *our* practices. Accordingly, the restrictions that law imposes on strategic action not only give effect to moral, and maybe even ethical, considerations but, by the same token, reflect a we- perspective.

The notion of a shared social reason hints at a crucial interlinking factor in social practices, namely the point of the practice. In practices, social actors adopt a first-person plural perspective, sharing a common understanding of and commitment to the practice and its point. The point also constitutes the backdrop to the meaning that individual actors attach to their actions. It may well be that such an understanding and commitment are not conscious or only enter participants' consciousness when the ordinary course of matters is disturbed; when there is uncertainty or controversy about the point of the practice. It may also be that not all participants share a collective's understanding of and commitment to the point of the practice in which the collective is engaged: some members of the collective may be indifferent towards or critical of the dominant understanding of the practice, or even reject it. Yet when the proportion of indifferent or oppositional members reaches a critical limit, the practice comes to the end of its life cycle, at least when at issue is a practice which participants enter voluntarily. If the majority of a university club no longer sees the point in partying every Saturday night, the practice will probably be buried.

Power is the weak spot of practice theory. Some actors may be obligated to participate in the practice against their will and without accepting either its point or the role imposed on them. Talk of collective intentionality, shared social reasons and a we-attitude tends to create the impression of voluntary participation and consensual agreement on the point and the task and role structure of the practice. Such talk should be taken with caution and furnished with qualifications. From early childhood onwards, we are impelled to

[12] Durkheim, (1893) 1984, 158ff.

participate in practices where we find ourselves at the receiving end of power relations and whose declared point we do not necessarily agree upon: from day care and compulsory education through military service to working life and, finally, elderly care. Social practices also constitute the scene for the exercise of Foucauldian disciplinary power. Power is inherent in social practices, including sociolegal ones where law contributes to the internal normativity.

Many social practices are composite practices, consisting of sub-practices. In a composite practice, such as family, sub-practices are supposed to promote the point of the composite practice, and their particular points are subordinated to the overriding point. Component practices may correspond to what Schatzki calls dispersed practices.[13] Dispersed practices, such as the primary discursive practices of questioning and responding, are not confined to particular social fields but are included in more complex, integrative practices across society. A contextualised dispersed practice retains its characteristic point, but this is specified in accordance with the point of the integrative practice. In witness hearings, the point of adjudication as an integrative, composed, practice specifies the point of questioning and responding.

Participants in a social practice constitute a collective, united by a shared we- perspective, with the important caveat concerning reluctant or oppositional members. When acting within a social practice, we act as members of a collective. Membership can be examined as a subject position or a role defined through normative expectations manifesting the inherent normativity of the practice. Being a member of a football team or a symphony orchestra has normative implications: members are expected to comply with the rules governing football or orchestral music as social practices and serving the point of those practices. What Schatzki calls integrative practices are characterised by a division of tasks for achieving the point of the practice. In integrative practices, the joint membership role is complemented by differentiated subject positions, distinguished by particular 'task-right systems' as Tuomela puts it.[14] Diverging normative expectations define the subject positions of a defender and an attacker in a football team, and of a violinist and a harpist in a symphony orchestra. When a practice is structured through a differentiation of tasks and subject positions, the practice possesses an organisation. It is also possible that the differentiation covers only a part of the members. Then a division occurs into active and ordinary members. The roles of active members involve decision-making over ordinary members so that in an association, for instance, members of the board take decisions on behalf and in respect of the other members. Division into active and ordinary members also hints at a power relation, such as that prevailing between management and workforce.

[13] Schatzki, 1997, 91ff. [14] Schatzki, 1997, 100ff.; Tuomela, 2002, 160.

Social actors live their sociality through social practices, and in their daily life they are constantly participating in various practices relating to family, friendship, work, consuming, recreation, or hobbies. Participation requires that social actors possess the knowledge necessary for carrying out the actions constituting the practice and for enacting their roles. For the main part, practices rely on tacit, practical, knowledge which social actors employ without being immediately aware of doing so. In such practical knowledge, know-what and know-how, as well as factual and normative knowledge, become mixed. Even in social practices where the patterning and role-defining normativity has been codified in rule books, much of participants' normative knowledge remains tacit. It may well be that only those specialised in rule-monitoring, say, football referees, need explicit, discursive, knowledge, and even rule specialists rely most of the time on their practical knowledge.

Many of our daily social practices are routines in which we engage without deliberation so that even the shared reason motivating us remains unconscious. Expressed in Wittgenstein's vocabulary, in routine practices we do not actually act but react through spontaneous, unreflected, behaviour, without stopping to ponder its meaning or the point of the practice. Schatzki emphasises that we are immersed in social practices ever since early childhood. In these practices we learn understanding the world and acting – doing and speaking – in that world. Much of what we learn comes to stand fast for us and form part of our mostly unreflected convictions. Routine practices are customs, when the shared, mostly unconscious shared reason relates to the past: actions are performed because 'in our group we have always done so'.[15] Routine practices are facilitated by the embodiment of practical knowledge in attitudinal dispositions and bodily propensities; in what Bourdieu calls 'habitus' and Searle 'the Background'.[16]

In sum, practice theory emphasises the significance of the unconscious and unreflected; practical knowledge and habitus. This brings practice theory close to phenomenological lifeworld (*Lebenswelt*) analysis, which, in turn, has influenced Habermas, including his distinction between law as institution and medium.

For phenomenologists, the lifeworld is the world such as we take it as granted in our daily life. It forms the horizon of our everyday social action; it both provides resources for and creates obstacles to social action. In our natural or common-sense attitude to the world, we take it as granted that there exist the objective world of nature, the social world of society, and the subjective world of our personality and experiences. We take as granted the existence of mountains and rivers; roads and cars; parents, spouses, children, and neighbours; parliaments, governments, and presidents. We also take as

[15] Ibid., 118ff. [16] Bourdieu, 1977, 17ff.; Searle, 1995, 129–130.

granted that there are ways in which parents, spouses, children, and neighbours ought to act towards each other; in which parliaments, governments, and presidents ought to treat us; and in which we ought to react to the laws and decisions issued by parliaments, governments, and presidents. Most of the time I also take for granted that I am I, with my unique biography and personality. Phenomenologists emphasise the importance of the knowledge we have of our lifeworld and which enables us to cope with the world such as we confront it in our everyday activities. Every individual has at her disposal a stock of knowledge which helps her through daily routines. This knowledge contains a large number of 'recipes'; know-how guiding her in her daily activities.

Instead of articulated, discursive, knowledge, we act most of the time on the basis of the practical knowledge which we have acquired through our primary and secondary socialisation, as well as our experience from social practices. We are born and raised in a particular cultural tradition, including our language, which is transmitted to us by our parents, teachers, friends, and consociates, mostly by linguistic means. The stock of knowledge individuals possess is social, not only by its origin, but also in the sense of reciprocity. We are aware that every individual approaches the world from a distinct perspective, but we also assume that the standpoints are interchangeable at least up to a certain point. This facilitates the congruence of individual coordinates of relevance, ensures the compatibility of individual stocks of knowledge, and makes joint social action possible. Compatibility does not negate the social distribution of knowledge, which makes one an expert in a narrow field but a layman in many others. However, the lifeworld stock of knowledge also comprises knowledge of this social distribution. I know that in the fields where I am a layman I must consult an expert, say, a doctor or lawyer, whenever the ordinary course of my life is interrupted.[17]

What unites phenomenological lifeworld analysis and practice theory is emphasis on the mostly unarticulated state of the knowledge we employ in our daily activities. Social practices are possible because of participants' practical knowledge. Social practices are differentiated, as is the practical knowledge of social actors too. Members of society share a common basic stock of knowledge consisting of both know-what and know-how and enabling them to participate in general social practices with an open membership. By contrast, specialised, expert social practices with a restricted membership imply diversification. Doctors and lawyers are expected to possess expert knowledge which medical and legal laymen lack. However, it is important to note that the distinction between general social knowledge and expert knowledge does not coincide with the distinction between discursive, articulated knowledge and practical, tacitly functioning knowledge. In routine actions, experts too rely on

[17] Schutz, 1962.

practical knowledge. Indeed, what makes an expert an expert is possession of practical expert knowledge in her field of specialisation; knowledge where know-what and know-how are mixed, and which she has accumulated not only through education but also through practical experience. If our lifeworld is equal to the reach of our practical knowledge, then clearly our lifeworlds vary. My lifeworld also covers the field of my expertise – academic legal scholarship – which constitutes the setting for my daily occupational life. Yet it definitely falls outside of the lifeworld of most members of society who are laymen in law.

Habermas depicts the lifeworld as the setting of communicative action: social action where actors coordinate their action plans through a common understanding of their situation. In communicative action, only a narrow segment of the lifeworld is overtly thematised: the segment which possesses immediate relevance for planned action. The rest of the lifeworld remains an unquestioned, taken-for-granted horizon of the thematised situation. This is the realm of phenomenologists' natural or common-sense attitude. It also provides the cultural resources from which the actors can draw to reach a common interpretation of their situation. If the participants' initial interpretations differ, they can try to attain agreement through discursive means.[18]

Habermas criticises the phenomenological approach to the lifeworld for culturalist reductionism. This criticism is related to a fundamental ambivalence in Habermas' concept of the lifeworld. On the one hand he treats *Lebenswelt* and System as two perspectives on society, but, on the other hand, he ontologises them into two distinct societal fields of action. The lifeworld perspective on society is the perspective of social actors who participate in communicative action, thus contributing to the social integration of society. Habermas' portrayal of the lifeworld as a cultural and linguistic reservoir of common interpretations of situations of communicative action comes close to Alfred Schütz' depiction of individuals' socially determined stock of lifeworld knowledge. It is also akin to practice theorists' accounts of the significance of practical knowledge. By contrast, Habermas' ontologising move objectivises the lifeworld and detaches it from the actor perspective. Habermas the social theorist gives up recapitulating the first-person singular or plural standpoint and engages in constructing second-order theories which lack correspondence in social actors' experience.

In his evolutionary theory, Habermas considers the differentiation of *Lebenswelt* and System typical of modern society. Furthermore, he argues that modernisation also entails an internal differentiation of the lifeworld into the components of culture, society (or legitimate social orders) and personality.[19] Now Habermas sees in culture – Schütz' socially determined stock of knowledge – merely one of the components of the lifeworld. In Habermas' view, the

[18] Habermas, 1989a. [19] Ibid.

alleged phenomenological reductionism lies in the neglect of the society and personality constituents of the lifeworld. Habermas' criticism is unfair: phenomenologists do not embrace the sociological ontologising and objectivisation of the lifeworld proposed by Habermas. Furthermore, what Habermas in his ontologising lifeworld analysis calls 'society' and 'personality' can – and should! – be included in a reconstruction of the common-sense attitude and the practical knowledge which, according to phenomenologists, label our lifeworld. Social normativity can only be effective through a common-sense attitude and practical knowledge. These, in turn, are internalised in the processes of primary and secondary socialisation where our personality is moulded.

Communicative action and social integration, on the one hand, and strategic action and systemic integration, on the other hand, cannot be confined to specific societal action fields. The daily life of members of society involves not only communicative but also strategic action, and communicative actions, too, are coordinated through systemic mechanisms, operating behind the backs of social actors. The presence of strategic action in the lifeworld also implies the presence of power relations. Power is a weak spot, not only in practice theory, but also in the way Habermas depicts the lifeworld, creating the impression of an exclusively consensual coordination of actions. In turn, economy and administration, which for Habermas epitomise System, include not only strategic but also communicative action. Hence, it is possible to adopt a lifeworld perspective on economy and administration too. Much speaks in favour of treating the lifeworld and System as perspectives on society and refraining from ontologising them. Still, in spite of these qualifications, I would argue that 'lifeworld' and 'System' can also be used in an ontological sense; 'lifeworld' to connote the domain of our daily activities and face-face sociality – Friedrich Tönnies' *Gemeinschaft* – and 'System' the world of economy and administration where systemic mechanisms and *Gesellschaft*-type sociality hold sway. It is also possible to continue applying the distinction between law as institution and medium; a distinction which implies the ontological separation of lifeworld and System.

Grouping Social Practices

Social practices can be identified and classified on diverse grounds. 'Social practice' is a theorist's term which social actors do not use. Instead, actors have concepts for many types of social practices – say, familial, occupational, or recreational – and through these concepts they identify interlinked social actions as tokens of those types. Concepts of ordinary language also give theorists a hint of how to identify types and tokens of social practices, and how to bundle these into higher-order social formations and fields, such as family, friendship, hobbies, work, economy, or politics. There is no one correct way either for social actors or theorists to group social actions into practices, constituent practices into composite ones, or practices into higher-order social formations. Our perspective as social and legal actors or theorists affects how we conceptualise social actions and how we insert them into the nexus of social practices. Conceptualisations have consequences, not least in law. The legal qualification of an action and, consequently, its legal repercussions depend on the social practice where it is incorporated. Hitting somebody in the boxing ring and on the street are qualified differently and entail different legal consequences.

Theorists also depict types of social practice which ordinary language does not recognise. Primary and composite practices is one example, dispersed and integrative another. Dispersed practices are not confined to particular social fields but occur in diverse contexts, woven into diverse integrative practices. Schatzki's examples of dispersed practices include describing, ordering, following rules, explaining, questioning, reporting, and examining. These consist of doings and sayings which are mainly connected through common understandings: the doings and sayings which constitute X-ing are mainly linked by a shared understanding of X-ing. Integrative practices found in and constitutive of diverse social fields are more complex. They are interlinked not merely by shared understandings but also by a teleological structure of ends, tasks, and projects, and a corresponding structure of subject positions (roles), each with its particular task-right system, to use Tuomela's expression. Organisations are social practices, or bundles of practices, with a distinct teleological and role structure. In turn, institutions, in the organisational sense of the term, are a specific, formal, type of organisation.[20]

Social practices also vary with respect to their spatiality and temporality. What is crucial in the modern conception of space is the extension of space beyond the locale, the interaction between immediately experienced and merely imaginable space. Detachment of space and locale opens up the possibility to engage in social practices and to enter into social relations, not only with those in one's immediate presence, but also with those absent. The social environment of modern individuals, their spatial horizon, reaches out beyond the neighbourhood and village towards and even beyond the state.[21] Law has played an important role in facilitating social practices and relations which exceed the local, *Gemeinschaft*, contexts and, rather, epitomise *Gesellschaft*-type sociality. Yet social practices still include face-to-face, local practices too. Thus, dispersed practices are largely of a face-to-face nature.

The implicit assumption in modern state law is that the society it addresses is state society and that the social practices and relationships where it is realised are confined to state territory. Denationalisation of social practices, including sociolegal ones, has increasingly questioned this central premise of

[20] Schatzki, 1997, 116ff. [21] Schroer, 2006, 110–119.

modern state law. Recalling the enduring indispensability of face-to-face and local practices, too, social practices constitute a continuum of gradually enlarging spatiality, beginning with the local and ending up with the transnational. Practices may also possess a specific spatiality in the sense that they can only be properly acted out in certain locations; say, religious practices in churches or judicial practices in courtrooms. Furthermore, places which are reserved for certain types of practice – such as churches or courtrooms – may also display a typical internal spatiality; an architecture conveying symbolic messages or arousing desired sentiments, such as elevation of God or awe and impartiality of justice.

The temporality of social practices also displays diverse aspects and variants. With regard to their duration, primary or dispersed practices typically emerge and fade away at a rapid pace. In turn, integrated practices – say, art or law, when examined as composite practices – may be of a continuous nature, while their constituent practices – say, a theatrical performance of a play or particular judicial proceedings and legislative processes – come and go. In addition to duration, temporality can be approached as rhythms and paces of change. If theorists of spatiality and temporality hit the mark, in (post-) modernity expansion of space finds its counterpart in acceleration of time, as well as understanding of time as linear instead of cyclical and orientation towards future instead of past.[22] As is the case with spatiality, social practices show great variance even with regard to their temporality. If law enables widening the spatial scope of social practices and relationships, it also facilitates their stretching in time. Transactions need not be fulfilled immediately because the law guarantees that they will be duly carried out at a later time, and land or housing can be leased for a stretch of time exceeding the lifetime of the contracting parties.

Another central borderline of particular importance for an account of the sociality of law runs between what I call general and specialised social practices. These differ in point and membership, as well as the knowledge deployed. General practices include not only elementary, dispersed, practices but even more complex, integrated practices in, say, family, friendship, workplace, or hobbies. The point of such practices relates to social actors' everyday life. Membership is open, with no particular qualifications needed for participation, beyond such at least partly biologically determined criteria as gender and age. General social practices rely primarily on tacit, practical, knowledge but may involve explicit, discursive, knowledge too. However, this knowledge is in principle accessible to all or at least a great a majority of social actors. The social aspect of the lifeworld consists largely of nexuses of general social practices. General social practices are the typical social setting for

[22] Rosa, 2013.

communicative social action, as defined by Habermas; that is, social action where action plans are coordinated through mutual understanding among participants.

The point of specialised social practices and the focus of their specialisation are removed from ordinary social actors' everyday life. Ordinary social actors may well perceive the point and the utility, even necessity, of banking, doctoring, accounting, administrating, or lawyering. Yet such specialised practices affect and intervene in their lives only occasionally, usually when something deviating from the regular course of things transpires. Specialised practices present specific membership requirements, at least for those occupying active subject positions, such as doctors and lawyers. The role of a parent does not call for any particular qualification, but the role of an accountant does. Typically, the specialised practices of contemporary society are expert practices, within the reach of only those mastering the necessary expert knowledge, acquired through education or professional experience.

Practical knowledge is crucial also for expert practices. Administrators, bankers, doctors, accountants, administrators, and lawyers possess much explicit, discursive, knowledge which laymen lack. However, an important part of expert knowledge lies in a practical state and is only articulated when something unusual happens; when routine is interrupted by a hard case. Practical knowledge connects to and draws its contents from the expert culture of the action field at issue – banking, medical, accounting, administrative, or legal culture.

3

Sociolegal Practices

Legal Determination of Inherent Normativity

Social practices are inherently normative; no non-normative social practices exist. Yet, the extension and intensity of inherent normativity varies. The primary interlinking factor of dispersed practices is a common understanding of the criteria that acting must meet in order to be treated as a token of a particular practice; as 'X-ing'. Such thin, conceptual, normativity is not specific to social practices. All our conceptual thinking and identifying of entities and events, as well as arranging the objective, social and subjective world, involves such normativity.

Only integrative practices that possess a more complex structure display an inherent normativity in the strong sense of the term. This inherent normativity covers, first, behavioural norms addressing the way that the social actions constituting the practice ought to be carried out. At issue is no longer what criteria acting should meet in order to be in general identifiable as X-ing. X-ing can be performed rightly or wrongly, and this distinction is based on the behavioural rules included in the inherent normativity of the practice. Social actions constituting social practices are recurrent and patterned. Sociologists adhering to the phenomenological tradition examine the patterns interlinking actions as resulting from processes of reciprocal typification and habitualisation, which in this tradition is considered characteristic of social institutionalisation.[1] No matter how their origin is conceived, the patterns can be understood to reflect the inherent normativity of social practices.

The teleological and role structure of complex integrative practices also possesses a normative character. From the perspective of other participants or external observers, roles consist of bundles of normative expectations related to the tasks that role occupants are supposed to perform to promote the point of the practice. This normativity need not be codified, and it is possible that participants of a practice do not conceive of it as explicit norms. Inherent normativity may remain in an implicit, informal, state, as in the queueing practices Neil MacCormick used as a favourite example of

[1] Berger and Luckman, 1967.

spontaneous norm formation.[2] However, formalisation through codification does not spell the end of informal normativity, nor does codification necessarily entail participants' awareness of the norms. Even in practices displaying a high degree of codification, say, legislative and judicial ones, much of their inherent normativity is realised without participants being immediately conscious of it. Participants' experience and a theorist's account may diverge widely. A theorist may extract norms from a social practice and render them in a form which is totally strange to social actors. Language is a case in point. Language speakers may have a vague idea of the import of grammar, but usually they are unable to express grammar as explicit rules, not even to mention the rules formulated by speech act theorists. Another example would be indigenous law: legal sociologists, anthropologists, and theorists may discern law in indigenous practices even when the participants do not even avail themselves of a legal language.

Law does not contribute to the pattern-forming or task and role differentiation of all social practices. Elementary discursive practices are also a prime example of practices which run without intervention by law, except when inserted in legally determined integrative practices, say, judicial ones. Yet to the inherent normativity of many social practices law does contribute. When this is the case, we are dealing with sociolegal practices. Parenthood, accounting, or law-making are conspicuous examples. Usually, law merges with other types of normativity – customs or conventions (social norms in the restricted sense of the term), moral norms, technical or prudential norms expressing instrumental rationality – into what can be called general social normativity. Only theorists analyzing practices from the outside can introduce strict distinctions in general social normativity among various types of norm. As a rule, social actors do not distinguish among, say, legal, moral, conventional, and prudential norms. This usually only occurs in a situation of normative pluralism where different types of norm, say, legal and moral, pull in different directions.

Individual parents, accountants, and MPs react to role expectations and, if they are keen to continue participating in the practice, try to live up to them. Yet at the same time they must be properly equipped for the role they occupy. Some qualifications may be legally fixed: wives and husbands must be of a certain age, and government officials must meet legally defined requirements. But not all the prerequisites for successful enactment of a role can be legally determined. Role occupants must possess the knowledge needed for carrying out their tasks, but that is not all. They also need certain dispositional qualities, a particular approach to people, things, and events. Much more is required of a good centre back in football than just knowledge of the rules of the game. And to be a good judge means not only knowing the law. In Bourdieu's terms, one

[2] MacCormick, 2008, chapter 1.

must possess the habitus appropriate to the role, and such a habitus can only be acquired through legal experience; the legal experience of a legal professional. Much of what Bourdieu included in the habitus – or Searle in the Background – remains outside the reach of legal specification.

By way of analogy to 'sociolegal practices', we can speak of sociolegal roles when role expectations have been at least partly fixed by law. Sociolegal roles include employers and employees, landlords and tenants, consumers and CEOs, and presidents and ministers. To occupy a sociolegal role, specific qualifications may have to be shown or specific procedures may have to be passed: for instance, a constitution may require that a minister be a native citizen and that a government and its ministers be appointed following a constitutionally defined procedure. In addition, all sociolegal roles share a common basic presupposition. One cannot be employer or employee, landlord or tenant, consumer or CEO, president or minister without being a legal subject and possessing legal capacity. Legal subjectivity is not exactly a role in the same sense as the sociolegal roles mentioned above. It is a prerequisite for occupying distinct sociolegal roles; a meta-role, if you want. Still, in line with specific sociolegal roles, legal subjectivity displays both a legal and a social aspect. Legal subjectivity is a legal quality, but its 'deontology' and the enactment of that deontology are dependent on social conditions, as the analyses by, say, Michel Foucault and Samuli Hurri have demonstrated.[3]

Occupying a particular role entails a particular perspective on the practice, although all the particular perspectives are usually accompanied by a common understanding of participating in a shared practice; a joint we-perspective. Parents and children view their common family practice in a different way, although they also share an understanding of being members of 'our family'. Correspondingly, legislators, judges, and legal scholars hold divergent views on and of law, which they still regard as their common practice.

Law and the inherent normativity of social practices – for short: social normativity – stand in a recursive relation. In its realisation, law is submerged in and contributes to social normativity. Yet pre-existing social normativity also affects the law. Not only can law codify pre-existing social normativity; it can even expressly refer to (uncodified) social normativity and confer on it a legal quality. The *Bürgerliches Gesetzbuch* invokes *gute Sitten*, and more recent national or transnational law may grant legal recognition to 'best practice' in specialised social fields, such as banking, accounting, or data protection. Kelsen's and Hart's sketches of the transition from a primitive amalgam of rules of behaviour to a developed legal system can be read as descriptions of legal codification of social normativity. According to the narrative recited by the Masters of Legal Positivism, at the outset, all law was customary law, while

[3] Foucault, 1979; Hurri, 2014.

in a developed legal regime law posited through explicit legislative or judicial decisions has gained the upper hand.[4]

Social normativity feeds into law, but law also feeds into social normativity. Law influences the social normativity with which it enmeshes in the process of its realisation. If it did not, it would have little chance of realisation, at least without recourse to second-order, specialised legal practices. Only if legal norms manage to modify other types of norm, conventional or moral, can we speak of their internalisation and quasi-automatic realisation. During recent decades, we have witnessed impressive transformations of social normativity in Western countries which have been at least partly induced by legislative changes: gradual social acceptance of homosexuality, both in legislation and in social perception; anti-smoking legislation and incipient social ostracism of smokers; or safety-belt and motorbike helmet legislation and the social pressure supporting its observation.

Moreover, social practices exist where the inherent normativity is primarily of a legal origin. This may, for instance, be the case when the task and role structure of a practice is fixed ex ante as a legally determined formal organisation, as is usual in, say, economy and administration; that is, in Habermas' System. Here, law precedes social normativity. Still, even in such artificial sociolegal relationships – to modify an expression coined by Savigny[5] – social substance tends to overflow legal determination. Formal organisations, too, develop an informal organisational culture which impacts the social normativity where law's realisation is embedded. Once organisations are established, codified norms do not exhaust their internal normativity. In organisational practices, formal and informal normativity are mingled in the same manner as in sociolegal practices in general.

Sociolegal practices are practices where law contributes to patterning social actions, and to defining the task and role structure. Sociolegal practices include both general and specialised practices. Legal institutions provide a legal form, a legal determination, to both general and specialised social practices. Among the latter, a particular position is held by practices which are specialised in law, such as legislative, judicial, and legal-scholarly practices. These are second-order legal practices, as distinct from first-order sociolegal practices, which are the scene for law's primary realisation. They are second-order in the sense that their point and tasks relate to first-order practices. They (re)produce the law which is realised through the inherent normativity of first-order sociolegal practices, and guarantee realisation when primary realisation fails. In this essay, I also call second-order sociolegal practices 'specialised legal practices' or just, 'legal practices', for short. Distinct from scholarly practices – the third main type of second-order legal practices – legislative and judicial practices are

[4] Kelsen, 1945, 338–339; 1967, 246–251; Hart, 1961, 89. [5] Savigny (1840) 1981, 370.

legally structured and can be examined from the point of view of realisation of the law pertaining to them. Hence, they can be analyzed as first-order sociolegal practices too.

With this qualification in mind, we can argue that the point of first-order sociolegal practices lies outside the law. Their main point is neither to realise nor to (re)produce law, although they do contribute to law's realisation and sometimes, in customary law, even to its (re)production. In first-order sociolegal practices, law plays only an auxiliary part in patterning social actions and in defining task and role structures, and thus in strengthening the inherent normativity. By contrast, the very point of second-order legal practices is related to law: they exist for the sake of law. Judicial practices are there for the sake of guaranteeing law's realisation whenever primary realisation in first-order sociolegal practices has encountered difficulties; legislative practices are specialised in producing new legal norms, in legal programming, as Niklas Luhmann has put it; while legal scholarship assists other legal practices through interpretative and systematising proposals, and articulation and elaboration of legal doctrine. The focus of specialised legal practices varies, but they all participate in law's (re)production, As I will argue below, if law is treated as a comprehensive composite practice, its constituent elements consist of second- rather than first-order practices. All specialised legal practices contribute to achieving the comprehensive point of law, however this might be defined: creating social order, obtaining justice, promoting welfare, preserving ecological balance, combating climate change, fulfilling God's will, and so on.

In sum, the points of first- and second-order practices relate differently to law. This also impacts how law appears to the participants; that is, which of its three modes of existence law shows them. Participants of first-order sociolegal practices experience law mainly as 'living law'; that is, as an integral part of inherent social normativity. Social actors only become conscious of law – including its existence as a normative legal order and as secondary legal practices – in extraordinary situations: when they witness instances of illegality or a-legality; when, for instrumental, moral, or ethical reasons, complying with the law is no longer self-evident, routine-like; or when they conclude contracts or issue unilateral legal documents – say, a will – of major significance to them. By contrast, legal actors of specialised legal practices cannot but be aware of law's existence as a normative legal order to which the very point of those practices relates. As the dominance of Legal Positivism shows, what instead may recede into the background, especially in legal scholarship, is law as it exists in first-order sociolegal relationships.

Law as Institution and Medium

Crucial for law's realisation is that it forms part of the sociality taken for granted in the everyday lifeworld. Lifeworld normativity guides social actors' own behaviour and expectations of the behaviour of their consociates. What philosophers and legal theorists call legal-institutional facts and the concomitant deontology of those facts also constitutes an important element of the social lifeworld. Our lifeworld is inhabited by husbands and wives, employers and employees, professors and students, presidents and judges. How they are supposed to act is at least partly determined by law.

Corresponding to law's presence in the lifeworld, social actors' knowledge of law is mostly tacit in nature. It is practical knowledge, facilitating everyday social action and practices. It should not be understood in strictly cognitive terms, but rather as unconsciously working schemes of perception and experience, as well as behavioural dispositions: Bourdieu's habitus and Searle's Background. In the ordinary course of things, legal components do not stand out but are immersed in diffuse social know-how and dispositions. In this respect, talk of legal knowledge or legal habitus with reference to ordinary members of society is misleading. The same holds for such concepts as 'legal culture', 'legal consciousness' or 'legal *Vorverständnis*'. These are important concepts for examining specialised legal practices. By contrast, when employed in the context of first-order sociolegal practices, they may obscure the way law is realised in and through the lifeworld. They imply such distinctions in social actors' practical knowledge as do not exist in lifeworld experience. Even 'legal subject' is a problematic conceptual tool in analyzing law's realisation from a lifeworld perspective. General legal subjectivity is a central premise of modern state law. Under this premise, we are all legal subjects and, indeed, as legal subjects, are legal-institutional facts. Yet, in our everyday lifeworld experience, we do not treat ourselves or our consociates as legal subjects. No distinct legal compartment exists in our subjectivity or in our perception of the subjectivity of others.

Because of the mainly tacit and diffuse character of social actors' knowledge, sociological or phenomenological depictions of 'living' or 'real' law which imply a conscious relation to law fall short of the mark. Weber, for instance, defined law in the empirical or sociological sense as beliefs (*Vorstellungen*) that members of society have about legal norms and which, at the level of psychological motivation, causally influence their behaviour.[6] If 'beliefs' here mean consciously held beliefs, then Weber was victim of the consciousness fallacy.

Law's realisation through the inherent social normativity of everyday social practices guarantees not only the efficacy but even the legitimacy of law. Law's immersion in lifeworld normativity signals its conformity with other types of social norm, such as morals and customs, and its tacit acceptance by members of society. Continuous, largely unconscious, production of legal-institutional facts manifests the social acceptance of corresponding legal institutions, and

[6] Weber, 1978, 311.

conformity with criminal law and other rules of behaviour testifies to their implicit acknowledgement. This is an essential element of society founding law, to employ an expression coined by legal phenomenologists.

However, not all law is realised through diffuse everyday social normativity and lifeworld practical knowledge, but only what Habermas has called law as institution. Habermas bases the distinction between law as institution and medium on legitimacy considerations. What is decisive is whether legal norms need substantive legitimation or whether positivist legitimation invoking the legal procedure of their production suffices. When law is used as medium, closely intertwined with the media of money and administrative power, substantive legitimation from a lifeworld perspective is neither needed nor possible. In contrast, so Habermas argues, law as institution cannot be legitimated merely by reference to the legally defined legislative procedure. If legitimacy is contested, substantive legitimation is required, because law as institution forms part of the lifeworld and, together with informal norms of action, constitutes the social horizon of communicative action.

The distinction between law as institution and medium implies ontologising of lifeworld and System. As I have argued above, such ontologising is not unproblematic. On the one hand, strategic action occurs even in social fields which Habermas includes in the lifeworld. On the other hand, economy and administration possess even a lifeworld aspect which is relevant for law too. We live much of our sociality as, say, employees and consumers, with labour law and consumer law structuring our working and consuming practices. Between law as institution and medium no strict boundary can be drawn supposedly corresponding to the boundary separating lifeworld from System. Nevertheless, Habermas reminds us of the important fact that not all law enters the everyday lifeworld perspective of social actors. Increasing instrumentalisation of law, its growing employment in social engineering, has expanded the branches of law which have severed immediate ties to lifeworld normativity and ordinary social actors' practical knowledge; for example, interventionist and regulatory economic and administrative law. Legal-institutional facts play an important role in the realisation of regulatory law too. Still, corporate taxes do not constitute such an integral element of our lifeworld as do families and partnerships.

Even those fields of law which match Habermas' depiction of law as medium call for realisation in social practices and relationships. Realisation involves strategic administrative or economic action, which in turn often presupposes deliberation and explicit, discursive, knowledge. Above, I have argued that the strategic action which law addresses and facilitates is embedded in wider social practices, based on shared social reasons and we-attitudes. Accordingly, regulations of economic and administrative law are surrounded by a legal framework which, arguably, connects to or even manifests law as institution, as well as moral and ethical considerations. Marxist criticism cannot – and, indeed, does not – negate contract law's connection to liberty and equality, and general administrative law pays respect to fundamental rights and rule-of-law principles. Framework law is implicated in the realisation of interventionist law. Here the tacit practical knowledge of economic and administrative actors makes a contribution, and here law as institution moderates the strategic orientation of law as medium. By the same token, law as medium can benefit from the substantive legitimation with which the lifeworld connection of law as institution feeds into the law in general.

So the conceptual framework of social practices and practical knowledge is relevant for examining the realisation of instrumentalist, policy-oriented law too. Law as medium is often, perhaps even primarily, realised in specialised expert practices: administration, banking, accounting, and the like. The contribution of law to structuring these practices endows them with a sociolegal character. These practices offer examples of where law plays a constitutive role, preceding social normativity and giving rise to what Savigny termed artificial legal relationships; let me only refer to economic and administrative organisations established in the form indicated by law. Yet an approach which stresses the significance of the knowledge that actors must possess also applies to such practices. Experts even need legal knowledge to cope with their tasks: knowledge about the often extensive, detailed, and complicated norm work addressing specialised practices. Explicit, discursive, knowledge plays a more prominent role in specialised expert practices than in general lifeworld practices. Still, in line with the practical knowledge of ordinary social actors, the expert culture of specialised sociolegal practices involves a legal component which mostly remains in a tacit shape. Bankers are not constantly aware of the banking law nor accountants of the accounting law which pattern their actions and structure their expert practices. They only gain consciousness in extraordinary situations or when they are uncertain of what the law regulating their practice really says.

Legal Institutions

Social practices can be discussed as both types and tokens. When discussing types, common, typical, features are abstracted from tokens. These features include the inherent normativity patterning social actions and defining the task and role structure and expectations of the practice at issue. Football or adjudication can be approached both as types of social practice and as particular football matches or judicial proceedings. In practice theory, the concept of institution has been related to the normative aspect of social practices. This connects to the age-old jurisprudential notion of legal institution, as well as recent theorising about institutional facts. Legal institutions can be understood as anticipations of law's realisation in sociolegal practices. The calling of law as a normative legal order is to be realised. Accordingly, legal norms are only intelligible in the light of their foreseen realisation. We need relational concepts which link legal norms to the social practices they address and where they are expected to be realised. 'Sociolegal practice' heeds the link from the social and 'legal institution' from the normative side of law.

'Institution' has a long pedigree in legal scholarship, harking back to Roman times, when it was used in such well-known contexts as *Institutiones Gaii* or *Institutiones Justiniani*. The primary reference was to systematisations of law for educational purposes. In the nineteenth century, at the dawn of modern *Rechtswissenschaft*, 'institution' was reintroduced by German Romanists, such as Savigny, the main proponent of the Historical School. Savigny retained the concept's focus on systematising legal norms (*Rechtssätze*), but related systematisation to the social relationships, *Lebensverhältnisse*, which legal norms were destined to structure. 'Institution' has preserved a place in the systematisation of law, particularly in German-influenced legal scholarship. However, starting from the Historical School's transformation into *Begriffsjurisprudenz*, the explicit linkage to law's realisation in legal relationships which was a hallmark of Savigny's theorising has mostly been lost. Reconnecting to Savigny, I would propose understanding legal institutions – such as marriage, contract, fundamental rights, and the like – as sets of legal norms addressing distinct social practices. Thus, the criteria for grouping and ordering legal norms would be drawn from the social practices which the norms are called on to pattern and structure.

Theorists of institutional fact have brought new life to the concept of institution and reconnected it to law's realisation. I shall return to their conceptual proposals below, when discussing the contribution that institutional facts make to law's realisation. Kelsen produced sharp-eyed observations on legal qualification and legal norms as schemes for interpreting spatio-temporal events, foreshadowing the theory of institutional facts. Yet he had no use for the notion of legal institution. He renounced any substantive systematisation of law. The legislator had full discretion over the substance of law, which could not, so Kelsen argued, display anything permanent or stable. Furthermore, attempts at substantive systematisation threatened to dissolve one or other of the two constitutive demarcations in Kelsen's Pure Theory: law's separation from either morals or the social (and psychic) Is. Kelsen blamed Savigny's *Volksgeist* doctrine for confusing legal with non-legal normativity.[7] In turn, Savigny's concept of institution appears to establish a connection of Ought to Is that contradicts Kelsen's normativist premises. Yet it is this very connection which makes Savigny's theorising pertinent to my purposes of relating law's normativity to its sociality. Savigny also offers a clue to a question which theorists of institutional facts do not really tackle: on what grounds should legal norms be grouped into institutions and how should individual legal-institutional facts be contextualised? Savigny's response lies

[7] Kelsen, 1957, 299.

in the organically interlinked social relationships (*Lebensverhältnisse*) which legal institutions transform into legal relationships. Only a step separates Savigny from embedding legal relationships in sociolegal practices which, according to my proposal, constitute the main scene for law's realisation.

In the dialectic between legal institutions and legal relationships as their realisations, Savigny's focus was on legal institutions. By contrast, contemporary theorists have more to say about institutional facts than institutions. Searle points out that, as a general rule, institutional facts presuppose existing institutions. Yet he also allows for the possibility of institutional facts emerging without the support of pre-existing institutions; for example, when a tribe starts to treat one of their members as a leader or a line of stones as a border. MacCormick, too, stresses that legal institutions must precede institutional facts, which he treats as instances of institutions.[8] However, MacCormick has also provided a description of queue formation before a ticket booth which proceeds without the support of pre-existing norms.[9] Norms only arise in tandem with queue formation; that is, norm formation and realisation coincide in the way typical of customary law. Both Searle and MacCormick have an idea, not only of how legal institutions are realised through institutional facts and, thus, impact society, but also of how legal institutions arise from society; that is, of the deeper social sources of law.

Yet theorists of institutional facts tend to depict institutions in general and legal institutions in particular in a more formalistic way than Savigny. Indeed, the relational view of law which Savigny inaugurated threatens to be buried under norm-theoretical considerations. Searle defines institutions as systems of constitutive rules. Such rules follow the formula 'X counts as Y' or, to make it more comprehensive, 'X counts as Y in context C'. In turn, regulative rules can be presented as imperatives: 'do X' or 'do X in C'. These rules regulate activities which exist or can exist independently of rules. By contrast, constitutive rules define activities whose existence is logically dependent on these rules and thus they facilitate new forms of behaviour. The rules of a game create the possibility of playing the game and, we could add, rules on the legislature, its powers, and the procedure it is supposed to follow create the very possibility of legislating.

However, the formulas for constitutive and regulative rules are not meant to facilitate an unequivocal distinction between two fundamentally different types of rule. Searle points out that regulative rules can be twisted into the form of constitutive rules. Criminal law consists of regulative rules, but when somebody violates a rule of criminal law, a crime is committed. The crime is an institutional fact, and in qualifying the act as a crime, the rule performs a constitutive function. On the other hand, the rules of a game not only

[8] MacCormick, 1986, 55. [9] MacCormick, 2008, chapter 1.

accomplish a constitutive function in establishing the possibility of playing the game. They also regulate the correct way of doing so. Probably not all constitutive rules can be converted into the paradigmatic form of regulative rules or all regulative rules into that of constitutive rules, but many of them can. Thus, the distinction between constitutive and regulative relates to two distinct normative functions rather than two mutually exclusive categories of rules.[10]

I have proposed relating legal institutions to the legal aspect of the inherent normativity of social practices. Let me introduce yet another norm-theoretical distinction, linked to the above analysis of social practices. Legal institutions, codifying the inherent normativity of sociolegal practices, can include, first, rules of behaviour, which convert doings and sayings into recurrent and patterned social actions, and perform a predominantly regulative function, and, secondly, organisational rules, which define the task and role structure of a practice, and perform a predominantly constitutive function. This is not a watertight division, either: organisational rules, too, may include rules of behaviour. Rather, at issue are diverse functions of the inherent normativity of sociolegal practices and of legal rules codifying that normativity.

Let us try to recapitulate. On the side of law's normativity, 'legal institution' is a conceptual counterpart to 'sociolegal practice' on the side of sociality. Both concepts adopt a relational view on law where normativity and sociality are seen as interlinked. Legal institutions gather together legal norms addressing sociolegal practices as types. Institutions are realised in distinct sociolegal practices, that is, sociolegal practices as tokens, and contribute to the inherent normativity of those practices. In this account, institutions and institutional facts are, in a way, disconnected. On the one hand, institutions cover a wider set of norms than just the rules constitutive of institutional facts. On the other hand, realisation of legal institutions is no longer explored merely through institutional facts but in the wider context of sociolegal practices.

Alternative ways exist of grouping social actions into social practices. One and the same action can be seen to enact diverse practices. Correspondingly, there is no one correct way of arranging legal norms into institutions or institutions into fields of law. Contracting can be examined as a particular type of social practice 'on its own' or as a moment in a wider practice, say, banking, and the norms addressing banking contracts as elements of contract or banking (financial) law.

Concrete Orders of Behaviour

When institutions are related to the inherent normativity of social practices and legal institutions to the legal aspect of that normativity, practices are seen

[10] Searle, 1995, 27ff.

not as tokens but as abstract types. Yet, at the end of the day, law is realised in particular sociolegal practices; in practices treated not as types but as tokens. Legal relationships among individual social actors emerge, develop, and expire within particular sociolegal practices, where legal-institutional facts, too, receive their legal meaning and unfurl their legal consequences. In sociolegal practices and through the contribution of legal-institutional facts, abstract norms of legal institutions are concretised into rights and duties of individual social actors; individual legal subjects. The normative legal order, comprising abstract norms, is transformed into a myriad of concrete orders of behaviour, which manifest the legal aspect of the inherent normativity of particular sociolegal practices.

The legal aspect of legal relationships consists of reciprocal rights and duties of the parties. For examining legal relationships, Analytical Jurisprudence has produced more detailed schemes where rights and duties have been dissolved into more specified legal positions, such as the one elaborated by Wesley Newcomb Hohfeld.[11] Such schemes were still unknown in Savigny's time. This does not diminish the value of Savigny's account, which lies in his effort to link together the factual social relationship (*Lebensverhältnis*) as the substance and its legal determination as the form of a legal relationship. To the contrary, Savigny's approach is an important complement to analytical schemes, where rights and duties are detached from their social substance, leaving them, as it were, hovering in an intermediate state between abstract norms and their realisation. In his extreme normativism, Kelsen, who confessed an affinity with Anglo-Saxon Analytical Jurisprudence,[12] was even more categorical in severing the ties which Savigny knit between social relationships and their legal determination. Kelsen reduced legal relationships to relations between legal norms and severely criticised understanding them as a combination of factual substance and legal form. For Kelsen, matrimony as a legal institution is not a complex of sexual and economic relations shaped into a specific form by law, but a complex of legal duties and rights or – which for Kelsen amounts to the same – a complex of legal norms. Kelsen generalises: for legal science, no legal relationships exist other than those among legal norms. Yet Kelsen concedes the possibility of something like Savigny's artificial legal relationships. He adds that law can contribute to creation of actual relations between individuals. However, such relations do not enter the view of legal science, but can only be examined 'from the point of view of a cognition directed toward actual reality'.[13]

The substance of a legal relationship – Savigny's *Lebensverhältnis* – can be a power relation, say, between family members, management and workforce, or administrative authorities and their clients. In such cases, legal determination reinforces and legitimates a factual power relation. Evidently, this is an

[11] Hohfeld, 1919. [12] Kelsen, 1945, xv. [13] Kelsen, 1957, 168.

instance of power *by* law. Yet, when we approach first-order sociolegal practices as a particular mode of existence of law, we can also examine their inherent power relations as examples of power *in* law. Indeed, the power aspect in concrete orders of behaviour is conspicuous in, for instance, the will concept of subjective right or the conceptual pairs of Hohfeld's analytical theory of 'jural' relations; think especially of the correlatives of right and duty, and power and liability.

Legal relationships, and the rights and duties they involve, constitute an important but still only intermediary phase in the realisation of law. In legal relationships, abstract legal norms, grouped together into legal institutions, are converted into rights and duties of particular social actors, involved in particular social practices, and establishing particular social relationships among themselves. In and through legal relationships, the practical possibilities created by abstract norms are actualised, and the norms are concretised in substantive, personal, spatial, and temporal respects. The substantive dimension is specified as particular rights and duties; the personal dimension as the individual subjects of these rights and duties; the spatial dimension as the spatial setting of the legal relationship and the sociolegal practice in which it is lodged; and the temporal dimension as the lifespan of the legal relationship. Legal institutions are transformed into concrete orders of behaviour, participating in the intrinsic legal normativity of a particular sociolegal practice.

Law's realisation does not end with the permutation of abstract norms into concrete orders of behaviour. It only ends with the norm-conform behaviour through which duties are fulfilled and rights satisfied and, as a consequence, legal relationships expire. Still, fixation on individual legal relationships conveys a misleading image of 'living law'; law in its process of realisation. In integrated, complex, social practices, stretching out in time, concrete orders of behaviour are in constant flux; when legal relationships are extinguished, they are replaced by new sets of rights and duties. Thus, 'concrete order of behaviour' is a pointilliste and momentary concept, referring to a particular moment in the flow of 'living law' within a distinct sociolegal practice.

Legal scholars treat the normative legal order, consisting of abstract norms, as a unified, ordered, whole. Legal positivists see the source of ordering in the hierarchical chain of authorising and validity, terminating with the Master Rule, such as the *Grundnorm* or the rule of recognition. In contrast, pre-Kelsenian German *Rechtswissenschaft* relied on substantive ordering, where systematisation through legal institutions also played a role. I shall discuss the ordering principles of the normative legal order in Part II. What is important to note here is that the pointilliste and momentary concrete orders of behaviours do not add up to a unified counterpart to the normative legal order. Particular social practices can be bundled into larger social formations, analysable as composite practices – family practices into family and economic practices into economy – and law's realisation in these composite practices can be discussed in terms of composite concrete orders of behaviour. But it would be far-fetched to examine society as a whole as a parallel to the state legal order as a maxi sociolegal practice with its composite but unified momentary concrete order of behaviour. If in general it is justified to treat law as a composite social practice, its constituent parts cannot consist of first-order sociolegal practices. Reference should be to specialised, second-order, legal practices.

Legal-Institutional Facts

What, then is the role of legal-institutional facts in law's realisation? By itself, the concept of institutional fact is an insufficient conceptual tool in a legal-theoretical recapitulation of law's realisation. Legal institutions are realised through the inherent normativity of concrete sociolegal practices; concrete orders of behaviour consisting of particular rights, duties, and legal relationships. Legal-institutional facts make an important contribution, but they must be analyzed in a wider conceptual framework, such as the one I have tried to elaborate. In addition, not all legal-institutional facts play exactly the same role, and classifications are needed in order to account for their distinct significance.

I use John Searle as my guide to the theory of institutional facts. For Searle, institutional facts are objective facts, but both their emergence and further existence presuppose human agreement. Objective facts come in two groups. Brute facts exist independently of human intentionality; they are both ontologically and epistemically objective. But there are also facts whose existence depends on human intentionality; these facts are ontologically subjective but epistemically objective, as Searle puts it. They result from human imposition of functions on facts which have existed independently of human intentionality. Our tools, such as Searle's screwdriver or Heidegger's hammer, are examples of intentionality-relative facts whose existence is due to human imposition of function. The imposition of function follows the formula 'X counts as Y' or 'X counts as Y in context C'. In Searle's account of intentionality-relative facts, human values and purposes are imposed on the world reminiscently of the way the German *geisteswissenschaftliche* tradition articulated cultural meaning-giving (*Sinn-Stiftung*). Kelsen, as also might be recalled, was raised in this tradition, the impact of which can be discerned in his account of legal qualification. Yet Kelsen discussed legal qualification as cognitive interpretation of spatio-temporal, empirically observable reality where legal norms served as schemes of interpretation. By contrast, for Searle and other theorists of institutional facts, what Kelsen calls legal qualification amounts to a production of new facts adding to social reality.

On Searle's account, social facts are a sub-class of intentionality-relative facts; what makes them social is the involvement of collective intentionality. Institutional facts are distinguished from other social facts by the specific nature of the function imposed; that is, the specific characteristic of Y in the formula 'X counts as Y'. Institutional facts result from the collective imposition of status functions. Status functions are positive and negative deontological powers, such as rights and duties. 'All institutional facts carry a deontology', as Searle puts it. The deontology of institutional facts also implies that the collective imposition of status functions displays a normative basis. Institutional facts presuppose the existence of institutions; sets of constitutive rules, which follow the familiar formula 'X counts as Y in context C'.[14]

Searle discusses institutional facts at a general level, without restricting his focus to law. Still many, if not the majority, of his examples are taken from law: Mr Smith marrying Miss Jones, Mr Green being convicted of larceny or Congress passing the Appropriation Bill. In turn, institutions which in these examples account for the transformation of brute facts into institutional facts are legal institutions, consisting of rules of marriage; criminal law rules on larceny, and procedural rules on the establishment and procedure of courts; and constitutional rules on Congress, its powers, and the procedure it is supposed to follow when exercising those powers. All in all, what Searle says about institutional facts in general also holds for legal-institutional facts.

In spite of Kelsen's exclusively cognitivist focus, his depiction of legal qualification can be used to complement Searle's account. Legal-institutional facts result from legal qualification where legal norms confer a distinct legal meaning, that is, the Y-term in Searle's formula, on constituent facts, or the X-term. However, legal qualification is not an achievement of merely a particular class of legal norms - 'constitutive rules' in Searle's terminology. Every time a piece of objective, social, or subjective world is interpreted through a legal norm, legal qualification occurs: the legal meaning expressed by the Y-term is conferred on the X-term and a legal-institutional fact has emerged.

To elucidate their role in law's realisation, legal-institutional facts should be divided into sub-classes. Classification can connect either to the constituent fact, the X-term, or to the legal meaning conferred on it, the Y-term. A wide array of potential X-terms exists. Almost any imaginable entity or event in the objective, social, or subjective world can be attributed a legal meaning. Accounts of institutional facts have relied on the dichotomy of brute and institutional facts. Brute facts are empirically observable spatio-temporal facts, which a normative interpretative scheme transforms into institutional facts. Yet, chaining also occurs so that the X-term, that is, the constituent fact, can be not only a brute fact but another institutional fact too. Labour law qualifies particular kinds of contract, that is, institutional facts, as labour contracts.

The X-term can also be a speech act. Laws and judicial decisions are legal-institutional facts whose constituent facts consist of speech acts of the legislator and judges. They are also examples of chaining. Speech acts in general can

[14] Searle, 1995, 8ff.

be examined as institutional facts; indeed, Searle introduced his view of institutional facts as an elaboration of J. L. Austin's speech act theory.[15] In contrast to primary speech acts, say, asserting or commanding, in formal legal speech acts the constitutive function is performed by legal norms. The particular character of formal legal speech acts is determined by the Y-term, as defined by the constitutive legal norms. At issue can be a 'private' legal speech act performed within a first-order sociolegal practice; say, a contract or a will. Or at issue can be a legal speech act issued within a specialised, second-order legal practice; such as a law or a court decision concluding a distinct token of legislative or judicial practices.

Searle defines the Y-term - the legal meaning conferred on the constituent fact, the X-term - as a status function and the status function as a particular deontology consisting of a bundle of rights, duties, and powers.[16] Searle is not very precise in explicating what he means by 'status function'. But this is not a problem. 'Status function' can be taken as just another term for the legal meaning or qualification – the Y-term – which the constitutive rule confers on the constituent fact – the X-term. Some legal qualifications do involve a deontology of rights, duties, and powers. A sociolegal role occupied by a particular person – say, the Presidency of Finland – is an institutional fact of which the specific legal meaning can be examined as the kind of deontology that Searle identifies the status function with. Yet the legal significance of legal-institutional facts does not always consist of such a deontology; not all legal-institutional facts carry a deontology. Some legal-institutional facts do; they activate rights, duties, and legal relationships, and convert abstract legal rules into a concrete order of behaviour. Signing a promissory note creates rights and duties for creditor and debtor, and a legal relationship between the two. Yet other legal-institutional facts de-activate or extinguish rights, duties, and legal relationships. Paying back the debt extinguishes the legal relationship created by signing the promissory note. MacCormick's classification of rules making up an institution into institutive, consequential, and terminative points to the lifespan of legal relationships. Institutive rules relate to institutional facts which establish the legal relationship and terminative rules to those which extinguish it, while consequential rules define the rights and duties of the parties, activated by the former and extinguished by the latter institutional facts. Rules of matrimonial law on weddings are institutive, rules on the rights and duties of the spouses consequential, and rules on divorce terminative.[17]

Legal-institutional facts are not solitary phenomena but come in groups. They come in groups because they are inserted in sociolegal practices where they perform different tasks in converting abstract norms into particular rights, duties, and legal relationships, and in creating and extinguishing

[15] Searle, 1988. [16] Searle, 1995, 41; 2010, 8. [17] MacCormick, 1986, 49–54.

concrete orders of behaviour. And just as alternative ways exist to bundle social actions into social practices, so legal-institutional facts can be grouped together in diverse ways and analyzed in the context of diverse sociolegal practices. Searle has also emphasised that institutional facts do not exist by themselves but only in systematic relations to each other. Yet he has not stopped to examine these relations, although he has offered impressive descriptions of the role of institutional facts in everyday life; for instance, of the thicket of institutional facts through which he makes his way in the morning to his office at the university. Here Searle's depiction of institutional facts and underlying constitutive rules calls for complementing. Social practices establish systematic relations among institutional facts and provide a criterion for grouping legal norms into legal institutions.

4

Specialised Legal Practices

Detachment of Second-Order Legal Practices

Among legal theorists, as well as sociologists and historians of law, broad agreement prevails that differentiation of practices specialised in particular legal functions has been decisive for the emergence of modern law, if not law in general. Particular significance has been accorded to detachment of the judicial function: complementing primary realisation of law in first-order sociolegal practices and private forms of enforcement, such as blood feud, with secondary realisation through judicial practices and accompanying coercive execution. Kelsen and Hart, the Masters of Legal Positivism, tended to treat positive law exclusively as a normative legal order and largely ignored analyzing first- or second-order sociolegal practices. However, in their brief sketches of the transition from a primitive regime of rules to state law (Kelsen) or a developed legal system (Hart), differentiation of specialised legal practices holds centre stage.

Kelsen argues that, in primitive law, both creation and application of general norms is decentralised. General norms are established through custom and applied by the subjects themselves whose normatively protected interests have been violated. Self-help and blood feud are typical techniques of decentralised primitive law application. Centralisation sets off from law-application, while centralisation of the legislative function is a later development. What turns primitive law into state law – and the primitive community into a state – is centralisation of the judicial and administrative rather than the law-making function.[1]

Hart's concise sketch of the passage from a set of primary rules of behaviour to a developed legal system also implies differentiation of specialised, second-order legal practices, although Hart confines his discussion to the normative dimension. He elevates secondary rules - and, implicitly, second-order sociolegal practices - to the distinctive feature of a developed legal system. According to his well-known account, social ordering consisting merely of primary rules of behaviour runs into three problems: uncertainty about the

[1] Kelsen, 1945, 338–339; 1967, 246–251.

rules and their contents; the static character of rules; and the inefficacy of social pressure for upholding and enforcing them. These problems are remedied through secondary rules: substantive uncertainty through a rule of recognition; inertia through rules of change; and inefficacy through rules of adjudication.[2] It is easy to note that Hart assigns a key position to judicial practices, which both the rule of recognition and rules of adjudication address. The rule of recognition is Hart's Master Rule, replacing Kelsen's *Grundnorm* at the top of a hierarchically arranged legal order. The rule of recognition is a rule in two meanings. On the one hand, it refers to an empirical regularity, expressing the criteria that judges in fact adhere to when identifying applicable rules. On the other hand, for judges the rule of recognition is a pivotal element of the inherent normativity of judicial practices. Both meanings of the rule of recognition accord judges a central role in law.

In their forays into legal evolution, both Kelsen and Hart ignore the input of legal scholarship. This reflects their view of the specialised legal practices of modern state law and of the status of legal scholarship. Neither of them treats legal scholarship as a legal practice which would participate in the (re)production of the normative legal order and in the legal discourse determining the momentary contents of this order. They both treat legal scholarship as a merely cognitive enterprise, qualitatively different from legislative and judicial practices. By contrast, the contribution of legal scholarship to both legal development and the functioning of modern state law has been acknowledged by German historically oriented *Rechtswissenschaft* and, in its wake, by German sociologists of law, such as Max Weber and Niklas Luhmann.

For Savigny, the doyen of the German Historical School, law had developed from folk law (*Volksrecht*) to scientific law or jurists' law (*Juristenrecht*). Law followed a general trend of social and cultural differentiation, which involved the emergence of professional 'estates' (*Stände*) specialising in particular activities. In law, too, the further development and application of law fell to such a professional estate: learned lawyers.[3]Related to his *Spezialistendogma*, Savigny granted legal science the status of a source of law. This view was anathema to Kelsen, who severely criticised Savigny's and his disciples' position for assigning volitional, normative, functions to legal science. In Kelsen's view, legal science was purely cognitive by nature.[4]

Pace Kelsen, Savigny's *Spezialistendogma* has exercised great influence among subsequent historians and sociologists of law, including Weber and Luhmann. For Weber, the distinctive feature of modern law lies in its formal rationality, which secures the legal security and predictability required by a capitalist market economy and bureaucratic public administration. In Weber's ideal-typical presentation of modern law, creation of law is based on systematic enactment, while application is entrusted to professional lawyers

[2] Hart, 1961, 89ff. [3] Savigny, (1814) 2002, 67. [4] See, e.g., Kelsen, 1957, 440–441.

employing a specific juridical method, which Weber called 'logical interpretation of meaning'. On Weber's account, university-based legal science has - especially in Continental Europe - been crucial in securing the formal rationality of law. Employing the method of logical interpretation of meaning, legal science has guaranteed the systematic nature and autonomy of the normative legal order.[5]

Finally, Luhmann examines modern law as a functionally differentiated social sub-system whose specific function is to stabilise normative expectations in society.[6] Modern law constitutes an autopoietical system which produces and reproduces its elements through its own operations. The basic elements – and, simultaneously, basic operations – consist of legal communications. What makes a communication legal, and maintains the boundary between law and its environment, is employment of the binary code of legal/illegal. Luhmann argues that the differentiation of law into an autopoietically operating social sub-system is only possible because law includes second-order observation of first-order application of the legal code. Indeed, it is second-order observation that maintains legal autopoiesis, that is, the specific mode of reproduction of law as a social sub-system. The differentiation of law as a functionally specialised social sub-system is accompanied by internal differentiation of networks of second-order observation. Luhmann agrees with the Masters of Legal Positivism that internal differentiation sets off from the judicial function, with the formation of particular procedures and organisations deciding on application of the binary code of legal/illegal. Only at a much later stage does differentiation continue with the procedural and organisational separation of the legislative function as well. In an autopoietically operating legal system, courts, and legislature constitute an organised decision-making sub-system which alone is allowed to decide on legal validity; that is, to transfer validity as a symbol of law's (diachronic) unity, as Luhmann puts it in his typically rather convoluted terminology. Because courts are not allowed to decline taking decisions, they keep legal autopoiesis going and occupy the centre of the system of law.

What, then, about legal scholarship? On Luhmann's account, doctrinal research has played a vital role in legal evolution and law's differentiation into a distinct social sub-system. Legal evolution proceeds through the stages of variation, selection, and stabilisation. New cases entering the courts provide variation, while judicial decisions, later complemented by legislative ones, accomplish the function of selection. Doctrinal legal scholarship ('legal dogmatics') specialises in the stabilising function. Legal scholarship is pertinent not only to legal evolution but also to ongoing legal autopoiesis. Scholarship condenses into and confirms as doctrine selections effectuated through legal decisions. Doctrine, then, provides the basis for subsequent legal

[5] Weber, 1978, 657–658. [6] Luhmann, 2004.

decision-making. In their reasoning courts invoke doctrine, which guarantees the self-reference – the connection (*Anknüpfung*) of legal communications to previous ones – necessary for legal autopoiesis. Legal scholarship operates outside the decision-making sub-system of law and does not participate in transferral of the validity symbol. Yet the arguments, concepts, and theories that it elaborates are related to legal decision-making, and its outputs are legal communications which employ the code of legal/illegal. Legal scholarship forms part and parcel of the communicative network of law, more exactly of the second-order observation which keeps legal autopoiesis going.

In sum, all the above accounts of legal evolution and functioning of modern state law emphasise the significance of the differentiation of second-order, specialised, legal practices. They also agree on the centrality of the judicial function. Where views diverge is on the status of legal scholarship. Kelsen and Hart exclude legal scholarship from legal practices, while Savigny, Weber, and Luhmann assign it an important role in both the emergence and functioning of modern state law. Below, I will join the latter camp. I will defend a position which I dub the dual citizenship of legal scholarship. Legal scholarship is a legal practice and participates in the (re)production of law and in ongoing legal discourse. At the same time, it is also a scholarly practice and subject to academic commitments and requirements. This dual citizenship explains much of the specificity of legal scholarship both as a legal and as a scholarly practice.

The history of the emergence of modern state law testifies to the crucial contributions of legal scholarship, especially on the European Continent. Legal scholarship created a European transnational legal-cultural basis, which universities transmitted to the transnational corps of learned jurists. In some regions, such as Northern Italy and – from the sixteenth century onwards – Germany, legal scholars were even granted a formally recognised role in legal proceedings. In the German procedure of *Aktenversendung*, the record of a case was dispatched to a faculty of law for its collective opinion.[7] The procedure bore a conspicuous resemblance to the Roman practice of turning to learned jurists for their opinion (*responsa*). The prominence of legal scholarship in Germany in the decades preceding adoption of the *Bürgerliches Gesetzbuch* could build on centuries-old antecedents. Still, it was only the Historical School of Savigny and Puchta that clearly formulated legal scholarship's self-understanding of its dual citizenship: of its peculiar character as both a legal and scientific practice.

The Point of Specialised Legal Practices

At present, evolutionary theories of society and law are often met with suspicion. They are seen to imply a whiggish view of social and legal development which inevitably, in a law-like manner, is leading to a preordained goal:

[7] Dawson, 1968, 200ff.

contemporary Western society and law. A linear view of cumulative progress shakes hands – so the criticism goes – with a Western cultural bias. Anti-evolutionary sensitivity incites to caution towards simplified summaries of legal development and the prehistory of modern state law. Yet we cannot make sense of law's three modes of existence and their interdependence without sketching a narrative of their differentiation as a background.

Law plays but an auxiliary, supportive, role in first-order sociolegal practices, the point of which lies elsewhere than in law. By contrast, the point of second-order, specialised practices is related to law itself. Parallel to the differentiation of specialised second-order legal practices from first-order sociolegal practices, another process of differentiation transpires: legal norms are abstracted from the internal normativity of social practices. The point of secondary legal practices is connected to the (re)production of abstract(ed) legal norms and securing the realisation of those norms. Along the way towards modern state law, the need arises for particular legal functions which first-order sociolegal practices and their inherent normativity cannot cope with: judicial, legislative, and doctrinal. Specialised legal practices emerge to accomplish these functions.

The detachment of particular legal functions and second-order legal practices is a process parallel to the abstraction of legal norms from the inherent normativity of social practices. Through these processes, the sociality of law adopts a two-pronged character: realisation and (re)production of law decouple. Law is primarily realised in first-order sociolegal practices, while its (re)production moves to second-order, specialised, legal practices. When all law was customary law, law was realised and (re)produced in the same social practices. Not even in modern state law has customary law lost all its significance, but has even experienced a renaissance in the 'best practices' of specialised action fields of contemporary society. Yet a long distance separates these practices from the customary law of premodern *Gemeinschaft*-type society.

The judicial function also blurs the boundary between realisation and (re)production. It responds to the problem of inefficacy; that is, the need to secure the realisation of law. Second-order judicial practices are expected to step in when realisation in first-order sociolegal practices runs into difficulties; when rights or duties of concrete orders of behaviour are breached, or when uncertainty and disagreement arise about their contents. The problem of inefficacy is one of the three problems which, on Hart's account, ordering that relies merely on primary rules of behaviour confronts and which secondary rules set out to resolve. Rules of adjudication address the problem of inefficacy, while the problem of inertia is met with the rule of change and the problem of uncertainty with the rule of recognition. Expressed in the language of practice theory, these problems emerge when the inherent, spontaneous, normativity of social practices does not suffice to produce social order. Inefficacy becomes a problem when custom-like social normativity loses its self-evident character; inertia when social change accelerates and the static tranquillity of a

Gemeinschaft-type society is disturbed; and uncertainty with expansion of the body of legal rules and its increasing detachment from generally acknowledged customs. The response to these problems can also be formulated in terms of legal functions and practices. Guaranteeing efficacy falls to the judicial function and practices; overcoming inertia to the legislative function and practices; and reducing uncertainty to the doctrinal function and practices.

In modern state law, diverse practices are specialised in judicial, legislative, and scholarly functions, respectively. If we are to lend credence to the accounts of the emergence of modern state law such as those summarised above, differentiation started from the judicial function. Emergent judicial practices also performed legislative and doctrinal functions, whatever the need in general was to facilitate normative change and condense applicable norms into doctrine. Only subsequently were these functions transferred to distinct legislative and doctrinal practices. We can surmise that the necessity to separate the legislative from the judicial function only arose parallel to instrumental use of law. In turn, the legal pluralism of late medieval society enhanced the importance of the doctrinal function, while adoption of this function by legal scholarship was facilitated by the birth of universities, intimately linked to the reception and modification of Roman law.

Yet not even in our ideal-typical 'mature' modern state law does the division of labour between legal practices match a strict 'separation of powers'. In a democratic *Rechtsstaat*, the autonomy of the judicial function, reserved exclusively to judicial practices, is buttressed against interventions by the legislator too. Neither is Continental legal scholarship any longer directly involved in the exercise of the judicial function; the era of *Aktenversendung* is long past. In contrast, judicial practices have retained their multi-functional character. Depending on the legal culture, judicial practices accomplish a more or less prominent legislative function, too, most conspicuously through the precedents of appellate courts. The main burden of law-making, though, falls on legislative practices, particularly in the civil-law countries of Continental Europe, but increasingly even in the common-law area. This holds especially for instrumental legislation where law is used as medium and where courts lack both democratic legitimation and organisational competence. Here the potential legislative role of courts is confined to introducing rule-of-law restrictions and safeguards; that is, disciplining policy-oriented legislation through principles, to put it in Dworkinian terms, or law as medium through law as institution, to employ Habermas' vocabulary.

Judicial practices exercise doctrinal functions, too, most importantly in common-law countries but even on the Continent, though with more substantive support from legal scholarship. In judicial practices, legislative and doctrinal functions are intertwined, and it may be difficult – even unnecessary – to tell whether a precedent should be treated as contributing to judicial law-making or doctrine. Doctrine, too, displays normative effects. Legal doctrine is about concepts, principles, theories, and methodologies, and new concepts, principles, theories, and methodologies impact the way law will be interpreted and applied. As I shall argue at more length in Part II, legal doctrine, sedimented into legal culture, itself forms part of law. Finally, the multi-functionality of judicial practices is also manifest by their participation in both of the two principal tasks which specialised legal practices accomplish with regard to law's other modes of existence: (re)producing the normative legal order and guaranteeing law's realisation when primary realisation in first-order sociolegal practices founders. Multi-functionality entails that judicial speech acts address widening circles of addressees. Court decisions are directed not only to the parties in the case and the executive authorities, but, particularly if they possess precedent value, the community of legal professionals, too, and at times even society at large.

Specific legal functions and practices respond to the three problems Hart discerned in a primitive system of primary rules of behaviour: inefficacy, inertia, and uncertainty. In the normative dimension, judicial function and judicial practices correspond to secondary rules of adjudication, and legislative function and practices to rules of change. But what about overcoming uncertainty? How do doctrinal function and scholarly practices relate to Hart's rule of recognition? Or is there any relation?

Uncertainty about applicable law is reduced by condensing and systematising the contents of preceding legal speech acts into legal doctrine, which can then be resorted to in future legal practices. Established legal doctrine exercises much of its impact unconsciously, through the *Vorverständnis* of legal professionals. I would propose dismounting the rule of recognition from the pedestal to which it has been lifted by Hart and his disciples and treating it simply as an element of doctrine; more precisely, as a summary of the prevailing doctrine of legal sources. The doctrine of legal sources is an indispensable part of the methodical dimension of legal doctrine. It combats uncertainty about applicable law and promotes legal certainty, not only within judicial practices but in society at large too. Yet in highlighting the importance of the rule of recognition, understood as the prevailing doctrine of legal sources, we should not ignore other elements of legal doctrine, such as legal concepts, principles, theories, and patterns of reasoning. These, too, promote legal certainty and stability.

Whatever other, more focused, functions they perform, all three main specialised legal practices of modern state law – judicial, legislative, and scholarly – contribute to law's (re)production. What, exactly, do I want to convey via my shorthand '(re)production'?

The input of legal practices to the production of legal norms varies. Even in common-law countries, the emphasis in legal programming has shifted to legislative practices while the relative importance of judicial law-making has decreased. On the other hand, in civil-law countries where the legislator's hold on the throne of law's empire has long been uncontested, courts also participate in developing the normative legal order. They not only specify and confirm implications of abstract norms as particular rights and duties of particular legal subjects. Kelsen is not alone in characterising this as issuing individual legal norms. I deviate from this parlance; for me all norms are general. Yet through interpretation, courts also contribute to clarifying the sense of general legal norms; no strict boundary between interpretation and norm-creation can or need be drawn. Especially in hard cases, courts elaborate legal doctrine and from legal principles derive more focused norms applicable to the pending case. And although the days are long past when legal scholarship was in some jurisdictions a serious pretender to the throne of law's empire, its interpretative and doctrinal interventions still carry weight in determining the contents of the legal order, especially in civil-law countries.

Legal practices contribute not only to production but, by the same token, also to reproduction of the normative legal order. When a court applies a legal norm to the case at hand, it also confirms the norm, thus reproducing it. However, such pointwise confirmation does not exhaust the sense of reproduction. Usually second-order legal practices focus on and, by the same token, confirm only a limited set of surface-order legal norms. Yet these norms are in multiple ways networked with other norms to which they refer or which they implicitly presuppose and confirm. Applying the criminal law rule of larceny to Mr Green's act involves assessing the act in the light of other prima facie relevant criminal law rules on, say, shop-lifting or robbery. It also involves rules of general criminal law on, say, premeditation or mitigating circumstances; rules on criminal procedure; and, ultimately, constitutional rules on legislative power and procedure. No legal norm is either intelligible or applicable in isolation but only in a broader normative setting. Correspondingly, the reproductive implications transcend the norms that legal speech acts expressly invoke. Furthermore, legal practices share an inherent call for coherence – a call that extends beyond their immediate normative reach. In judicial practices, this call connects to the principle of equality; legal expertise injected into law-drafting and parliamentary deliberations serves to ward off the threat to law's coherence which new legislation always entails; and promoting coherence is an integral element of the stabilising and certainty-creating doctrinal function of scholarly practices.

It is also important to perceive that the reproductive effects are not confined to expressly formulated surface-level norms. Specialised legal practices would be impossible without the legal-cultural reservoir of sub-surface law. Without the normative, conceptual, and methodological resources provided by the prevailing expert legal culture, laws could not be drafted; court decisions arrived at, justified and formulated; or scholarly treatises and articles composed. In their facilitating, constitutive, task, sub-surface layers largely function through practical knowledge, the *Vorverständnis* of legal actors. This holds particularly for routine tasks. It would be an error to suppose that in routine tasks legal-cultural support is not needed. It is precisely internalisation of professional legal culture and its functioning through practical knowledge that makes routine tasks routine for legal actors. In hard cases, too, only segments of professional legal culture are openly articulated, while the rest remains the uncontested, self-evident horizon where expressly thematised legal normativity is immersed. Even so, when drawing - consciously or unconsciously - on law's cultural layers, legal practices simultaneously confirm and reproduce them.

Specificities of Legal Practices

In line with first-order sociolegal practices, specialised legal practices possess their inherent normativity. Law participates in the inherent normativity of especially legislative and judicial practices. Accordingly, these practices can be examined not only as specialised legal practices but also as (first-order) sociolegal practices where constitutional norms, parliamentary rules of procedure, and procedural law are realised. Indeed, compared to sociolegal practices in general, judicial and parliamentary procedures are determined extensively and minutely. Two explanations can be suggested. First, final judicial and legislative speech acts are legally binding and backed up by the possibility of coercion, which is a vital *differentia specifica* of legal normativity. Therefore it is important to define the formal 'felicity conditions' of these speech acts as unambiguously as possible. Secondly, law is needed to secure the substantive requirements which judicial and legislative practices are expected to meet in a democratic *Rechtsstaat*: in adjudication, neutrality, legal security, and attention to all relevant interests; and in law-making, respect for democratic principles, free and equal deliberation in parliament, and engagement of civil society and the public sphere. Yet in legislative practices the degree of legal determination is significantly lower than in judicial ones. In law-making only the final phase is legally determined, while in judicial proceedings even the stages preceding decision-making are ordered in great detail. Furthermore, in adjudication the law is supposed to determine not only the procedure but even the content of the decision. By contrast, in law-making the free political discretion of the legislator prevails, within the outer limits staked out by the constitution, and international and, possibly, transnational law. In its inherent normativity, legal scholarship differs fundamentally from legislative and judicial practices. In line with other social practices, legal scholarship is norm-governed, but now the norms are not legal in nature. At issue are largely non-codified requirements of scholarly research, reasoning, and argumentation. Thus, the intensity of legal determination decreases when moving from judicial through legislative to scholarly practices.

Often enough, sociolegal practices comprise power relations which legal determination reinforces and legitimates. This also holds for specialised legal practices. Approaching legal practices through Habermasian discourse theory as examples of practical discourse easily obscures the power aspect – power *in* law – which is most obvious in judicial practices. Laymen, too, are allowed – and, except for plaintiffs in civil and administrative cases, even obligated – to participate, but merely in subordinate roles. Legal proceedings, too, may be examined through the lens of discourse theory, as Klaus Günther in particular has done.[8] Yet in the putative discourses of application the word is not accorded to laymen, nor can the discursive features efface the taint of power, even violence, which is most conspicuous in criminal cases.[9] Even as plaintiffs, laymen lack the legal-cultural resources that boost the power position of legal professionals, including their own counsellors. Neither are legislative or scholarly practices governed merely by the force of better argument, as discourse theory would like to have it, but are also traversed by power relations. When examining power *in* law, these should not be ignored, either. Yet, differing from adjudication, power relations in legislative and scholarly practices are not legally determined. To the contrary, constitutional provisions on legislative procedure and political fundamental rights support the discourse-theoretical reading, as do academic norms on scholarly debates.

In a sense, judicial practices constitute legal practices *par excellence*. The step from other forms of social normativity to law arguably requires at least embryonic forms of judicial practice, differentiated from first-order social practices. Furthermore, of the three main legal practices of modern state law, only judicial ones are 'purely' legal, while legislative and scholarly practices possess a characteristic dual citizenship. Legislative practices are both legal and political, while scholarly practices are both legal and scholarly.

Judicial practices pursue an exclusively legal point, which is not supposed to be subordinated to extra-legal aims. In modern state law, such subordination would be considered a pathological symptom, a breach of the principles of a democratic *Rechtsstaat*. If the judiciary and judicial practices are seen as politicised, this is taken as criticism. By contrast, even talk of politicisation of legislative practices would sound absurd. Legislative practices also serve a political point, and assessing them by political aims and criteria is considered entirely natural and appropriate. If in general applying goal-rational terms to judicial practices is justified, the only legitimate goal is to realise the law. In legal interpretation, goal-rational arguments, alluding to the expected factual, social, or individual consequences of alternative interpretative options, may play a role. Still, even here goal-rational viewpoints are subordinated to the principal objective of judicial practices, that is, realising the law. Moreover, teleological interpretation is exercised only if allowed by the methodological tenets of the prevailing legal culture.

[8] Günther, 1993. [9] Cover, 1986.

The 'purely' legal character of judicial practices is manifest by the heightened requirement for autonomy, the edge of which is directed not only at the legislative, executive, and administrative branches of government but also at the surrounding society. Yet autonomy does not amount to autarchy. Thus, autonomy from the legislator means only autonomy in deciding particular cases, including legal interpretation. And in a crucial respect judicial practices remain dependent on their social environment. Society feeds judicial practices with cases, which have emerged as concrete social problems. Moreover, courts are not free to choose the social problems which appear as legal issues on their agenda. These are channelled to the courts through particular mediating practices, such as policing, prosecuting, and practical lawyering. Courts function under a decision-making imperative. They are legally obligated to receive cases – whether penal, civil, or administrative – and to produce a decision which puts a legal end to the controversy. Yet autonomy starts functioning the moment social issues enter judicial practices.

When reaching the courts, social problems are translated into legal language and endowed with a formulation which may make them unrecognisable to the parties who have encountered them in their social practices. The prevailing legal culture of modern state law conceives of judicial decision-making as application of pre-existing law to the facts of the case. Decisions are formulated as, or at least should be convertible into, judicial syllogisms where the major premise consists of a general norm – a decision norm, as it might be called – the minor premise of (a description of) the facts of the case and the conclusion of the ruling. The syllogistic description of court decisions is telling. It tells not only of the dominance of legislation (civil-law jurisdictions) or the significance of precedents and *stare decisis* (common-law countries). It also tells about the prevalent conception of justice in modern Western state law. The syllogistic formula is not supposed to describe how a judge arrives at a decision but how she justifies it; the syllogistic logic is logic, not of discovery but of justification. It is supposed to guarantee the generalisability of the ruling; justice in a formal or abstract sense, reduced to treating like cases alike. What matters for such a conception of justice are the common and abstract features of cases rather than their concrete uniqueness. Welfare-state legislation may be animated by a different conception of justice, such as social justice related to substantive rather than formal equality, and requiring redistribution and counterbalancing of the non-egalitarian social effects of the market economy. Yet when welfare-state legislation is applied in courts, the formal and abstract justice of judicial syllogism tends to gain the upper hand over social justice, whose relevance is relegated to interpreting legal texts.

While judicial practices confront social problems in concrete guise, in legislative practices these are treated in a generalised form, and general solutions are called for instead of decisions in particular cases. Law-making is not only a legal but also a political practice. Ultimately, the political aspect dominates and determines the contents of new laws, although in the procedural forms and within the substantive limits defined, in the first place, by the constitution. Legislative practices are the main vehicle of law's *voluntas*. As I have stressed, *voluntas* should not be identified with irrationality or even a-rationality. As the Godfathers of Anglo-Saxon Legal Positivism, Hobbes and Bentham, made clear, *voluntas* is associated with instrumental rationality. In the twentieth century, the increase of instrumental legal regulation for the purposes of the welfare state and mitigation of the dysfunctionalities of the capitalist market economy led to a preponderance of legislative practices in legal programming and in the legal discourse determining the contents of the momentary legal order. Typically, law as medium is legislator's law, the product of legislative practices with the clear dominance of political over legal aspects. However, in a democratic *Rechtsstaat*, politics is supposed to exercise its dominance under the control of law, and moral and ethical reason, say, in the guise of fundamental rights, are supposed to impose limits on the free rein of instrumental reason. The endpoint is a formal legal speech act, a law, destined to have legal effects. Yet laws, too, can be examined, not only in the legal framework, but also as results of political practices, registering political power and bargaining, as well as social-scientific expertise. As a political practice, legislation views beyond law towards society: generalised social problems and generalised regulatory responses to them. To put it in Luhmann's terms, laws and legislative practices manifest a structural coupling between law and politics.

Bracketing the procedural forms of the final stages intended to secure the formal validity of laws, the legal aspect of legislative practices comes to the fore mainly in two contexts. Instrumental legislation aims to implement political programmes, based on political goals and social-scientific knowledge on the societal preconditions for achieving these. In law-drafting, legal expertise is needed to translate programmes and goals into legal language, and to keep an eye on the coherence of the legal order. Secondly, legal expertise is also needed to ensure that new legislation respects restrictions on the legislator's discretion deriving from the constitution and international or transnational law. Most important is the restrictive effect of fundamental and human rights, which defend the cause of moral and ethical reason against over-indulgent instrumentalism. Alternative organisational arrangements have been designed for the specific legal tasks in legislative practices. Connected to the importance of the legislative initiative of the executive, administrative law-drafting units usually hold a key position. Fundamental and human rights control may be entrusted to an administrative unit such the Swedish *Lagrådet*; a parliamentary committee included in parliamentary deliberations such as the Constitutional Law Committee of the Finnish Parliament; or a constitutional court, which can be invoked after the termination of parliamentary procedure but before the entry into force of the law, as in Germany, for instance.

Legal scholarship, too, is a legal practice which participates in legal discourse and contributes to law's (re)production. All second-order legal practices fulfil distinct legal functions. Legislative practices have taken over the main burden of legal programming – production of new legal norms – especially for the purposes of law as medium, and judicial practices react to disturbances in the primary realisation of law. Both the legislative and judicial functions can be related to external society: they respond to either generalised or concrete social problems, although only after translating these into legal language. By contrast, the doctrinal function connects to other legal practices; in particular judicial but also legislative ones. Doctrinal condensation and confirmation promote the stability and coherence of the law as applied in adjudication and, thus, further legal certainty. Legal concepts, elaborated by doctrine, provide the vocabulary for transforming social problems into legal issues, and in hard cases courts can turn to legal doctrine in their search for prima facie pertinent principles. Legal doctrine also articulates the legal methodology which legal actors employ in their professional activities: a doctrine of legal sources; interpretative canons with which the meaning of legal texts is specified; and patterns of reasoning and argumentation relied on in legal decision-making and justification.

Legislation can only exercise its legal function because of its dual nature as not merely a legal but also a political practice. Correspondingly, legal scholarship can only accomplish its doctrinal function because of its dual nature as not merely a legal but also a scholarly practice. As a legal practice, it is related to other legal practices and accomplishes important functions within law. Yet, in interpretation and systematisation, legal scholarship employs scholarly methods and shares with other scholarly practices certain fundamental commitments, such as openness of argumentation, transparency and identification of sources, and justification of standpoints. Speech acts where the results of legal scholarship are presented are not only legal but also scholarly, and their validity claims are assessed not only in legal but also in scholarly discourse. In universities, legal scholarship possesses a joint institutional site with other branches of scholarship.

Legal scholarship's citizenship among scholarly practices facilitates fulfilling its tasks as a legal practice. Interpretation and systematisation are intellectual activities which call for scholarly qualifications, methods, and commitments. The scholarly side of legal scholarship's dual citizenship accounts for its distinctive features among legal practices. Unlike laws or court decisions, scholarly standpoints do not acquire formal validity, they are not legally binding, nor are they backed up by external coercion. The results of legal scholarship can only receive binding force mediately, through other speech acts, judicial or legislative. Yet, depending on the prevailing doctrine of sources of law, legal scholarship participates in legal discourse on the contents of the legal order, and in this discourse its interventions carry weight, also indicated by the doctrine of sources of law.

Ever since the late eleventh century, the history of legal scholarship has been inseparably linked to universities. Still, although universities have provided – and still provide – the main institutional loci for legal scholarship, they do not enjoy a similar legally protected monopoly as do legislative bodies over law-making or courts over adjudication. And although legal scholarship constitutes a norm-governed practice, its internal normativity derives from its scholarly rather than its legal character.

In sum, the distinctive features of legal scholarship as a legal practice are largely due to the scholarly aspect of its dual identity. The same holds conversely: the particular features of legal scholarship as a scholarly practice largely derive from its being a legal practice too. Its character as a legal practice accounts for its peculiar dual normativity. Legal scholarship not only studies norms, but its results have normative effects and contribute to development of the law, its very object. Through their normative consequences, legal scholarship's outcomes affect what counts as law. This holds in particular for doctrinal research, which is one of the three main participants in legal discourse alongside legislation and adjudication. Here we have the backdrop to the often weak scholarly self-identity of legal scholarship and its perpetual qualms about its scientific nature.

Different legal practices accomplish different tasks in law: legislative practices focus on creation of general legal norms, responding to generalised social problems and channelling the influences of politics into law; judicial practices aim at securing the realisation of law when first-order sociolegal practices misfire; and doctrinal legal scholarship provides other legal practices with interpretative standpoints and systematisation proposals, and inserts the outcomes of legislative and judicial practices into the overall framework of the normative legal order. Still, despite their different functions, second-order legal practices are interconnected. They all contribute to law's continuous (re)-production and to achieving its overall point, however this might be defined. And they all produce legal speech acts which are interlinked to form a common legal discourse. Such interconnections facilitate analyzing law as a composite social practice, with specialised legal practices as its constituents. The contested nature of the overall point is no obstacle to such an analysis. In the wake of Dworkin, law, along with, say, art, can be treated as an interpretative practice of which an integral part consists of an ongoing discussion of its very point.[10]

Legal Professionals

Legal professionals play a dominant role in specialised legal practices, particularly in adjudication and legal scholarship. Even in legislation the contribution

[10] Dworkin, 1986, 45ff.

of legislative experts is indispensable; they translate social issues, goals, and programmes into the language of law, monitor the coherence of the normative legal order and point to the substantive limitations which the constitution and transnational or international law impose on new legislation. Laymen appear in judicial practices but merely as visitors, as parties and witnesses, and even as parties they mostly remain silent while counsellors plead their case. In legislation, the final decision on the substance falls to legal laymen, politicians, but in the framework and linguistic form defined by legal professionals.

Legal professionals are distinguished from laymen by their legal knowledge, acquired through education and professional experience. They possess knowledge not only of surface-level law but also of sub-surface legal-cultural layers: legal concepts, principles, theories, and methodologies. They master the language of law, where legal concepts constitute the vocabulary and the specific legal way of reasoning and arguing the grammar. The expert language of law can be as incomprehensible to laymen, in whom it suscitates a similar mixed feeling of awe, apprehension, and impotence as medical Latin.

Specialised legal practices focus on law; consequently, legal professionals must have explicit, discursive, knowledge of the segment of law with and on which they are working. Contrary to law's realisation in first-order sociolegal practices, specialised legal practices are inconceivable without the involvement of explicit knowledge of law. Yet practical knowledge plays a vital role even in expert practices, including specialised legal practices. Legal professionals approach their judicial, legislative, and scholarly tasks through their legal *Vorverständnis*; the expert legal culture they have internalised during their legal education and professional career. They are in possession of a legal-cultural stock which provides them with the basic normative, conceptual, and methodological means needed for successful performance of professional tasks. Even in specialised legal practices, most of the knowledge that legal actors employ lies in a practical state, without the actors being immediately conscious of its input. Legal *Vorverständnis* as the reservoir of internalised expert legal culture is at work in all legal activities; in both routine and hard cases. Hard cases require that a segment of legal culture – say, a controversial legal principle, an unclear legal concept or the source value of a putative legal text – must be openly thematised and legal knowledge transformed from a practical, tacit, state into a discursive, explicit, one. Yet, in hard cases, too, a major part of expert legal knowledge retains its character as a taken-for-granted cultural horizon.

Much of the lifeworld knowledge needed in general everyday practices is acquired already in primary socialisation. By contrast, expert legal knowledge can only be accumulated and a distinct legal *Vorverständnis* developed in secondary socialisation. The expert knowledge required by and internalised in diverse legal roles – as a judge, a legislative expert, or a legal scholar – varies, as does, accordingly, the *Vorverständnis* of diverse groups of legal professionals. This is a backdrop to what I have called perspectivism of legal roles.

However, legal *Vorverständnis* also includes common features, such as the legal language which facilitates discourse among legal professionals involved in diverse legal practices: judges, legislative experts, and scholars. Furthermore, the basics of this language have a cross-border character and are shared by professionals raised in different legal cultures and occupied in different legal regimes. Expansion of transnational law or contemporary interlegality connecting legal regimes would have been unthinkable without such a border-transcending 'deep-cultural' foundation.

In the – to some ears evolutionary-smacking – narrative of the emergence of modern state law, formation of an expert legal culture is one of the key processes of differentiation. A distinct legal *Vorverständnis*, informed by expert legal culture, distinguishes professional legal actors from the social actors of first-order sociolegal practices, with their diffuse lifeworld practical knowledge. Legal professionals constitute the legal community in *sensu stretto*, engaged in specialised legal practices and in a common legal discourse. If law is treated as a comprehensive, composite practice, the legal community in the narrow sense can even be treated as a collective agent of this practice. Legal professionals share an understanding that they are promoting a common point of law by their different tasks in different legal practices, although they may disagree as to what, exactly, that point is. And in spite of their different perspectives on law they share a common legal view. On my terminological proposal, ordinary legal subjects of a distinct legal regime form the legal community in *sensu largo*. Their practical lifeworld knowledge may, in all its variation, include common traits, too, and even talk of a general legal culture – as distinct from the expert culture of legal professionals – can be justified. Yet, as I have argued above, the concrete orders of behaviour of particular practices or the points these practices pursue do not add up to a comprehensive whole. The term 'legal community in the broad sense' does not imply any idea of a collective agent of such a higher-order practice.

How, then, should we characterise the legal point of view which legal professionals are supposed to share? How does it differ from the point of view of the social actors of first-order sociolegal practices? In legal theory, various distinctions have been proposed to catch the specificity of the legal point of view; such as those between practical and theoretical, internal and external, cognitive and volitional.

Legal phenomenologists apply the distinction between practical and theoretical approaches. Let me try to express the phenomenological view with the terminology adopted in this essay. Social actors of first-order sociolegal practices treat law in a practical manner: law operates in their practical activities inconspicuously so that they are not even immediately aware of its presence. By contrast, legal actors of specialised legal practices detach law from its practical involvement, approaching it theoretically and primarily as a normative legal order. Ordinary social actors also shift the gear from practical to theoretical in the exceptional circumstances when the threshold of consciousness is transcended. Then ordinary social actors, too, gain awareness of law as an order of abstract, objectified norms and as specialised legal practices; that is, those modes of law's existence which social actors usually ignore when engaged in their sociolegal practices. In sum, phenomenologists would characterise the legal point of view of legal professionals as a theoretical approach, distinct from the practical view of ordinary social actors.[11] My main criticism of this account would be that it may lead to downplaying the indispensable role that practical knowledge plays even in the expert tasks of specialised legal practices.

Discussion of the Hartian school is dominated by the distinction the Master made between the internal and external points of view. In *The Concept of Law*, Hart appears to argue that legal officials necessarily adopt an internal, participant's point of view and that this also implies an acceptance of the normative legal order, although not necessarily on moral grounds. Hart does not expressly discuss the approach of legal scholars. Yet he agreed with Kelsen on restricting legal scholarship to a cognitive function and excluding it from the legal practices (re)producing the law. Hart would probably have concurred with MacCormick in ascribing to legal scholars a hermeneutic point of view which includes awareness of – but does not share – the internal point of view of legal officials.[12]

Kelsen drew the decisive distinction between cognitive and volitional approaches. Kelsen's privileged perspective, from which he embarked on his theoretical reconstruction of positive law, was that of legal science, a perspective that involved – so he argued – a purely cognitive approach. Thus, Kelsen emphasised that, in legal interpretation, legal science must content itself with presenting interpretative alternatives and refrain from choosing among these. A normative choice would add a forbidden volitional aspect to scientific practice and trespass on the field reserved for legislation and adjudication.[13] These Kelsen considered legal practices *par excellence*, while legal science, to his mind, is merely a scientific and not a legal practice. Still, Kelsen saw an overlap between the legal practices of legislation and adjudication and the scientific practice of legal science. Legislation and adjudication include a cognitive phase which precedes normative position-taking and the final act of will. Legislators and judges must gain knowledge of the existing legal order in order to canvass the normative possibilities of and restrictions on their volitional acts.

It is not entirely clear how the legal point of view should be defined in the framework of Kelsen's Pure Theory. On the one hand, legal practices specialised in the (re)production of the normative legal order are distinguished by a volitional aspect and normative position-taking. On the other hand, it appears

[11] See, e.g., Lindahl, 2013, 121–122. [12] MacCormick, 1981, 37. [13] Kelsen, 1967, 355–356.

to be impossible to recapitulate Kelsen's conception of the legal point of view without taking into account the necessary assumption of the *Grundnorm*, an assumption that is related to the cognitive and not the volitional aspect. Everyone engaged in legal cognition must presume the existence of the hypothetical and transcendental *Grundnorm* of the legal order; without that presumption, knowledge of valid law would be impossible. The implications of Kelsen's *Grundnorm* thesis are not restricted to legal science but extend to the cognitive phase of legislation and adjudication too. Indeed, on Kelsen's view even legal laymen must presuppose the *Grundnorm* when they try to gain knowledge of valid law and, as legal phenomenologists would say, give up the usual practical approach to law and assume a theoretical one.

Joseph Raz has based his interpretation of the Kelsenian legal point of view on a problematic reading of Kelsen's conception of legal normativity and the perspectival elements in the Pure Theory.[14] Raz squeezes the discussion of normativity within the dichotomy of social and justified normativity, where, as I shall argue in Part II, Kelsen's conception does not really fit. As concerns the perspectival elements in the Pure Theory, Raz implies that at issue are individual choices and that legal normativity is, in a sense, a consequence of such choices. It is true that by invoking the characters of an anarchist and a communist, Kelsen pointed out that individuals can adopt or reject the legal *Grundnorm* and, as a consequence, the legal order as a frame for assessing social reality.[15] Yet this is not Kelsen's only - nor even the most important - perspectivist point. The communist and anarchist Kelsen refers to stand outside the law. Kelsen never says that individual judges, legislators, or legal scholars would have a similar option. He argues that an anarchist professor of law could describe positive law as a system of valid norms without having to approve that law.[16] This the anarchist professor could do because assuming the purely epistemological *Grundnorm* does not imply any moral or political commitment. However, it is important to add, although Kelsen here leaves it unsaid, that the anarchist professor not only could but also would have to presuppose the *Grundnorm*. The *Grundnorm* is presupposed by everybody engaged in legal cognition and treating the legal order as objectively valid norms. This certainly includes legal scholars – even anarchists or communists, if they ever managed to secure an appointment – but it also includes legal professionals involved in other legal practices, such as judges and legislative experts. Before the concluding act of will, both legislation and adjudication involve a cognitive phase necessitating assumption of the epistemological *Grundnorm*. For those standing outside the law, presupposing the *Grundnorm* and employing the objectively valid legal order as a frame of interpretation is a possibility but not a necessity. By contrast, for legal

[14] Raz, 1979, 134ff. [15] Kelsen, 1957, 44 and 226. [16] Kelsen, 1967, 218n8.

professionals engaged in specialised legal practices, it is a sine qua non, legal cognition being an indispensable element of their activities.

Thus, Raz is only partly right in his claim that Kelsen discusses perspectivism in terms of individual choices. Kelsen does, but only in relation to persons not belonging to the legal community in *sensu stretto*. In fact, Raz comes closer to Kelsen's understanding when describing the uncommitted adoption of the perspective of the legal order by 'legal man'. Raz argues that Kelsen distinguishes between a personal and a scientific point of view. Legal science adopts 'the point of view of the hypothetical legal man, i.e. of a person accepting from a personal viewpoint all and only the legal norms, without assuming that such a person actually exists'. Yet 'acceptance' does not imply any moral or political assessment but must be understood in a professional and uncommitted sense.[17] The same holds for other legal actors who engage in legal cognition as a moment of their professional activities. Here Raz is groping for Kelsen's notion of the *Grundnorm* as a necessary epistemological presupposition for all those involved in legal cognition, but shuns defining the point of view of the hypothetical legal man in Kelsen's Neo-Kantian terms. Moreover, Kelsen would probably not subscribe to characterising the subject of legal cognition as a *hypothetical* legal man. In Kelsen's framework, the role of legal man is by necessity played by legal professionals engaged in specialised legal practices and by choice by those members of the legal community in *sensu largo* who decide to adopt the objectively valid legal order as a cognitive frame of reference.

Raz reproaches Kelsen for creating confusion by not distinguishing between legal scholarship and the activities of lawyers and judges, and discussing both under the title of juristic cognition. Still, Kelsen's point is very clear: all those involved in legal cognition, whatever their particular legal role, inevitably presuppose the *Grundnorm*. What, however, may sometimes cause misunderstanding is Kelsen's use of the term 'legal science' in both a broad and narrow sense; both as a synonym for legal cognition in general and to connote legal scholarship in particular.

Both Kelsen and Hart define the legal point of view through the distinction between cognition and volition. Kelsen emphasises the role of volition in judicial and legislative practices but understands the specific legal point of view in purely cognitive terms. Adopting a legal point of view means adopting a positive legal order as one's cognitive frame of reference, which – so Kelsen argues – inevitably entails presupposing the *Grundnorm* of the legal order. Commitment to the *Grundnorm* is purely epistemological, with no normative implications whatsoever, so that even anarchists and communists can undertake it. To call such an epistemological stance acceptance, even 'uncommitted, professional, acceptance' (Raz), confuses epistemological and normative

[17] Raz, 1979, 141.

commitments. Another issue is that Kelsen's effort to keep epistemological and normative commitments strictly apart ultimately fails. The reason lies in the ineradicable ambivalence of the *Grundnorm*: as we have already learned, it is supposed to found not only legal cognition but even legal normativity itself. This makes assuming the legal *Grundnorm* more complicated for an anarchist or a communist than Kelsen perceives. Kelsen is sensitive to the mostly unconscious nature of epistemological presuppositions. By contrast, he treats the volitional aspect of legal practices exclusively in terms of explicit normative choices. He does not recognise that normative commitments, just like epistemological ones, can be of a tacit nature or that epistemological commitments can imply normative ones. If the *Grundnorm* plays a foundational role in both epistemological and normative respects, as Kelsen implies, it is difficult to see how an epistemological commitment – explicit or, most often, implicit – would not entail a normative commitment too.

In Hart's portrayal of the critical-reflective attitude towards rules, typical of the internal point of view, epistemological (cognitive) and normative (volitional) aspects are explicitly interwoven. For legal officials, the rule of recognition is not only a cognitive criterion but also an obligatory rule. Applying the rule of recognition implies acceptance of the law in a non-epistemological sense, although not necessarily a moral one. I would also emphasise the intertwinement of cognitive and normative presuppositions and the implicit normative commitments that participation in legal practices (re)producing the law entails. However, Hart shares with Kelsen some fundamental defects in his depiction of law and legal knowledge. These defects also affect specification of the legal point of view from a participant's position. First, the Masters of Legal Positivism tend to reduce the normative contents of the legal order to its surface level and ignore the sub-surface, legal-cultural (principle) layers. Secondly, they tend to reduce knowledge of the contents of law to explicit, discursive, knowledge and ignore the role of tacit, practical, knowledge. These two flaws are interrelated: in legal practices, legal-cultural layers primarily exercise their influence through the practical knowledge of legal professionals; in other words, their *Vorverständnis*.

Legal *Vorverständnis* defies distinctions such as internal and external or cognitive and volitional, and internalisation of the prevailing legal culture in the formation of legal professionals proceeds simultaneously and inseparably in cognitive and normative dimensions. Legal *Vorverständnis* as internalised and accumulated practical knowledge of the law is at work in all professional activities, hard and routine cases alike. When professional routines are interrupted by hard cases, a section of practical knowledge is converted into a conscious, discursive, form, but only insofar as the case requires reflecting on the exact significance and repercussions of legal concepts, principles, theories, or methodologies. The reproductive effects of specialised legal practices are not confined to immediately relevant surface-level norms but cover the normative legal order as a whole. Legal actors also confirm and reproduce the legal concepts, principles, theories, and methodologies they rely on, mostly in an unconscious way. At the same time, by promoting reproduction of the legal order as a whole, legal actors also undertake an (at least) implicit normative commitment to it. Were they to deny this commitment, they would be guilty of a performative contradiction: their claim would stand in contradiction to the contribution they make to the reproduction of the law. Here we can discern the fundamental normative commitment implicit in the legal point of view and shared by professional legal actors of second-order practices, even by legal scholars.

5

Legal Discourse

Demarcating Legal Discourse

Despite their different functions in law and society, specialised legal practices are interlinked. They produce legal texts: laws and *travaux préparatoires*, court decisions, and scholarly papers and treatises. These are legal speech acts which are recursively linked with each other to constitute a common legal discourse. It is this discourse which, at the surface level of law, determines the momentary contents of the normative legal order, that is, the law in force. In modern state law, legislators bear the main responsibility for establishing new legal norms. During the legislative process, *travaux préparatoires* are published by law-drafting and deliberative bodies, such as legislative bills submitted to parliament, and reports by governmental and parliamentary committees. These may be considered as legal speech acts on their own. The main task of judicial practices is to apply the law in force to concrete cases and thus to secure its realisation. Yet, especially through precedents issued in hard cases, courts also exercise legislative and doctrinal functions and modify what counts as the law in force. Finally, through its interpretative and systematising, doctrine-developing interventions, legal scholarship, too, impacts the contents of the momentary legal order.

Legal speech acts are speech acts which participate in the continuous legal discourse on the contents of the law in force. Which speech acts are considered legal and allowed entry into legal discourse is defined legally. The prevailing doctrine of legal sources determines the participants of legal discourse, as well as the prima facie weight of their speech acts in specification of the momentary normative legal order. The throne of law's empire has been claimed by three main pretenders – the legislator, the judge, and the legal scholar – whose respective positions have displayed great historical and legal-cultural variation. The prevailing doctrine of legal sources indicates what sources - namely what preceding legal speech acts - say, a judge should consult and what respective importance is attributable to them when identifying what the law is in the case pending before the court. By the same token, the ruling exercises an impact on the law in force. What, exactly, the impact of the ruling will be also depends on the prevailing doctrine of legal sources.

The prevailing doctrine of legal sources is a legal doctrine and part of the law. Yet it is but deficiently specified at the surface level of the law, in explicit constitutional provisions. The constitution usually enshrines the internal hierarchy of legislative and judicial bodies, and, accordingly, of the speech acts these bodies issue. In contrast, the constitution is silent on the respective significance of legislative and judicial speech acts, nor does it tell us anything of the weight of legal scholarship or *travaux préparatoires*. The doctrine of legal sources is not primarily a matter of surface-level law but of legal culture. In judicial practices, it is articulated merely in hard cases, and even then only fragmentarily; to the extent its exact bearing appears controversial. Whatever codification exists is due to legal scholarship. In line with legal culture in general, the doctrine of legal sources functions primarily through the practical knowledge, the *Vorverständnis*, of legal professionals.

Legal practices are specialised in not only producing but also reproducing the normative legal order. They face not only the future - subsequent legal speech acts - through which they are interpreted, applied, and systematised. They also face the past - precedent legal speech acts which they consult in ascertaining what the law in force is, and which they interpret, apply, and systematise. Legal speech acts always refer, explicitly or implicitly, to other legal speech acts, past and future. Reference to past legal speech acts implies affirmation: acknowledgement of their validity and illocutionary force. When a court applies a law in its decision and follows the interpretation advocated by a legal scholar, it also recognises the validity and illocutionary force of the legislator's and the scholar's speech acts. In turn, laws include references to other laws, and in *travaux préparatoires* proposals for new legislation may be supported by judicial precedents or standpoints professed by legal scholars. Again, reference implies recognition of validity and illocutionary force. The same goes for the laws and precedents which legal scholars subject to interpretation and systematisation, as well as the opinions of their colleagues which they invoke. Legal speech acts raise a claim to validity and illocutionary force. Simultaneously, they assess - implicitly or sometimes explicitly - claims raised by previous legal speech acts.

As a rule, the validity and illocutionary force of past legal speech acts are accepted tacitly, simply by invoking them and treating them as contributions to legal discourse. Yet it also happens that validity claims, in particular substantive ones, are explicitly discussed. If this occurs in judicial practices, we are dealing with a hard case. In routine cases, the validity of the speech acts referred to is taken for granted. By contrast, in scholarly practices, routine cases are ignored. Scholarly routine involves discussing controversial validity claims raised by earlier legal speech acts; laws, *travaux préparatoires*, court decisions, and the standpoints of other legal scholars. Yet, even in scholarly debates, merely a small segment of the normative legal order and corresponding legal speech acts is thematised; the rest is taken as given. When validity claims are overtly appraised, the focus is usually on the substantive dimension, while formal validity or illocutionary force is not questioned. On the contrary, discussing the substantive validity of a law or a judicial decision or the merits of a scholarly standpoint implies recognising the illocutionary force of the legal speech act, acknowledging it as a contribution to legal discourse.

When examining legal discourse as consisting of legal speech acts which amend and modify the contents of the law in force and assess validity claims of preceding speech acts, the spotlight is on the final phases of legal practices. Yet there is much more to legislation, adjudication, and legal scholarship than issuance of legal texts. Neither are the discursive elements in law restricted to the end results of specialised legal practices and their interrelations. Legislative, judicial, and scholarly practices involve internal discourses, which may also be linked to discourses outside the institutional sites of those practices. This is especially true of legislation, which is not only a legal but also a political practice. In a democratic *Rechtsstaat*, in order to guarantee the substantive validity of laws, legislation is expected to maintain discursive contacts with civil society and the public sphere, particularly with regard to the ethical and moral implications of legislative projects.

Legislative, judicial, and scholarly speech acts create constant turbulence on the surface level of law. Focusing the analysis of law on legal speech acts runs the risk of confining our attention to what happens on the surface and neglecting the more sedate transformation that is characteristic of the sub-surface, legal-cultural, layers. It is important to keep in mind that legal practices, inclusive of the concluding speech acts, also draw from and (re)produce the legal-cultural reservoir. This holds not only for legal-theoretical treatises or the reasoning of appellate courts in hard cases but also for specialised legal practices in general. Issuing legal speech acts would be impossible without relying on and, at the same time, confirming and modifying, the conceptual, normative, and methodological resources of professional legal culture.

Legal Speech Acts

Approaching the outcomes of specialised legal practices as speech acts is not a novelty. In legal phenomenology, Adolf Reinach's *Zur Phänomenologie des Rechts. Die apriorischen Grundlagen des bürgerlichen Rechts* (1913)[1] is an early example of theorising which bears a resemblance to subsequent speech act theory. Kelsen, too, came close to an understanding of legislative and judicial acts as speech acts. Recall that he defined general and individual legal norms as the objective meaning of the volitional acts of legislators and judges. Kelsen did not elaborate on the implications of attributing a meaning to volitional acts. Yet, evidently, such a meaning attribution presupposes that the act be

[1] Reinach, (1913) 2013.

given linguistic expression. In turn, a linguistically articulated volitional act comes close to what speech act theorists have termed performatives. Indeed, legislative and judicial acts are favourite examples of speech act theory. In J. L. Austin's classification, judicial speech acts fall under 'verdictives' and legislative speech acts under 'exercitives',[2] while John Searle treats them as Declarations. In Searle's vocabulary, laws and constitutions are standing Declarations.[3] For Habermas, laws and judicial decisions are prime examples of regulative speech acts which raise claims to normative correctness. When contested, so Habermas argues, such claims are discussed in practical discourses, as distinct from theoretical discourses which are about controversial claims of truth.[4]

In line with other speech acts, legal speech acts can be dissected into locutionary, illocutionary, and perlocutionary elements. A locution is the act *of* saying or writing. Locutionary speech acts possess a sense (meaning); performing 'a locutionary act … is roughly equivalent to uttering a certain sentence with a certain sense and reference, which again is roughly equivalent to "meaning" in the traditional sense'.[5] In Austin's distinction, illocution is what one does *by* and *in* saying or writing something; that is, through locution. Illocutionary acts include arguing, contesting, promising, and baptising. Illocutions attach an illocutionary force to the meaning of a locution. Finally, the perlocutionary element refers to the consequences of speech acts; to what is achieved *through* saying or writing something. While locutions convey a meaning and illocutions possess illocutionary force, successful perlocutionary acts produce an effect; for instance, the addressee of a command to shut the window shuts the window.[6]

Austin argues that, in order to obtain illocutionary force, speech acts must meet particular felicity conditions. These may be legally enshrined, as is the case with, say, concluding a marriage or issuing a law. Yet the felicity conditions of many speech acts rely merely on social conventions. A speech act is a promise if it fulfils the culturally determined felicity conditions of this type of speech act. Felicity conditions include following a certain procedure, as well as the appropriateness of the persons invoking the procedure and of the circumstances where this happens.[7] Searle has further elaborated speech acts' felicity conditions and formulated them as rules to be followed in performing speech acts. Searle treats these rules as constitutive rules and successful speech acts as institutional facts.[8]

The propositional sense of legislative speech acts refers to general and abstract norms (laws), as well as to justifications for and specifications of such norms (*travaux préparatoires*); the propositional sense of judicial speech acts to rulings, namely application of general norms to individual cases; and the propositional sense of scholarly speech acts to interpretative

[2] Austin, 1984, 153–157. [3] Searle, 2010, 12–13 [4] Habermas, 1984, 18–22.
[5] Austin, 1984, 109. [6] Ibid., 109–121. [7] Ibid., 12ff. [8] Searle, 1988.

and systematising doctrinal standpoints. Legislative speech acts claim illocutionary force as generally obliging and applicable laws and as *travaux préparatoires* guiding interpretation of those laws; judicial speech acts as executable legal decisions; and scholarly speech acts as scholarly standpoints possessing argumentative weight in other specialised legal practices. Legislative speech acts aim overtly at perlocutionary effect. Corresponding to legislation's dual character as not only a legal but also a political practice, laws are intended to produce an impact in and on surrounding society. Court decisions may also pursue such effects through, say, teleological interpretation or the presumed preventive repercussions of sentences meted out in criminal cases. Yet external, extra-legal, societal objectives are secondary to the primary point of securing the realisation of law. Finally, any perlocutionary effects that scholarly speech acts may have are usually mediated through judicial or legislative practices. A critical observer may, though, detect in both judicial and scholarly speech acts covert perlocutionary objectives related to institutional, professional, or personal interests. These, of course, are crucial in examining the strategic, power-related, aspects of legal discourse and the distance which separates 'real-world' legal discourse from Habermas' ideal practical discourse.

In an analysis of legal discourse, the claim to illocutionary force merits particular attention. If the participants of legal discourse do not recognise the illocutionary force of a putative legal speech act as a law, *travail préparatoire*, court decision, or scholarly standpoint, it does not enter legal discourse in the first place. Laws and court decisions are prime examples of speech acts which find their major felicity conditions enshrined in explicit legal norms. I shall call them formal legal speech acts. The competence and composition of legislative and judicial bodies are defined by the constitution, rules of procedure of parliament, and other organic or ordinary laws. Legislative and judicial procedures, including issuance of the final speech act, are also legally determined. Legal determination turns legislators and judges, as well as legislative and judicial procedures, into legal-institutional facts. It may be recalled that Kelsen used legislative and judicial procedures as examples of the legal qualification of empirically observable events transpiring in time and space.

The felicity conditions of *travaux préparatoires* are also partly legally defined but not as comprehensively as those of laws and court decisions. Legal determination is confined to speech acts which constitute regular or even obligatory phases in the law-making procedure, such as bills and motions, as well as reports by parliamentary committees. By contrast, particularly in the early law-drafting stages, memoranda and reports are produced which may also possess legal source value, although their felicity conditions have not been legally specified. Finally, in contrast to formal legal speech acts, the felicity conditions of scholarly speech acts have not been legally codified. Legal scholarship's participation in legal discourse is based on the prevailing doctrine of legal sources, which, as I have emphasised, is part of the law. Yet this doctrine is silent on the criteria that putative pieces of scholarship must meet in order to be acknowledged as contributions to legal discourse. To a large extent, they are conventions relating to the academic credentials of the authors of the texts, as well as the manner of argumentation and presentation.

As so much in law, the illocutionary force of legal speech acts is a perspectival phenomenon. There is no illocutionary force as such but only within a particular audience. What complicates the issue is that legal speech acts may be directed to several addressees. Legal positivists, among them Kelsen, have had difficulties in making up their mind about who the primary addressees of general legal norms are: the social actors who are expected to comply with the norms, or the judges and other law enforcers who are expected to apply them. Laws are addressed to both the legal community in *sensu largo* - social actors at large - and the legal community in *sensu stretto* - legal professionals engaged in the ongoing legal discourse. Accordingly, laws claim illocutionary force in both audiences; in the legal community in both *sensu largo* and *sensu stretto*. In turn, court decisions, in particular those by appellate courts, fulfil not only a judicial but also a legislative and doctrinal function. Correspondingly, they are directed not only at the parties and the executive authorities, but also the legal community in both the narrow and broad sense. Judicial speech acts claim illocutionary force among all these addressees, and the exact character of the claim varies according to the audience. In respect of the parties and executive authorities, judicial speech acts claim illocutionary force as definitive and authoritative solutions to a particular case. In the legal community, both narrowly and broadly defined, the focus is on their character as precedents. This is an important distinction: a judicial speech act may lose its illocutionary force as a precedent – think of *Lochner*! – while still retaining its status as a definitive solution to the case where it was once issued.

According to my definition, in legal discourse validity claims of legal speech acts are reciprocally assessed. How, then, is the illocutionary force of legal speech acts related to legal validity? Are 'illocutionary force' and 'validity' synonyms; or, if not synonyms, do they at least partly overlap? I will discuss validity more thoroughly in the context of the normativity of law, and confine myself here to some preliminary remarks.

In the framework of speech act theory, the focus shifts from validity to claims to validity that legal speech acts raise. By the same token, validity becomes conditional: validity is not acquired once and for all but can be lost. I shall connect to legal theorists who distinguish between formal, empirical, and substantive dimensions in legal validity.[9] What is crucial for the

[9] Wróblewski, 1979; Aarnio, 1987, 33–46.

illocutionary force of legislative and judicial speech acts is formal validity. These speech acts obtain illocutionary force and, simultaneously, formal validity when they meet the legally defined felicity conditions concerning the composition and competence of legislative respectively judicial bodies and the procedure these are supposed to follow. Usually, formally valid legal speech acts both attain and retain illocutionary force, unless they are duly repealed or overturned by other, formally valid, legal speech acts. Yet the empirical and substantive dimensions make the validity of legislative speech acts conditional. In the empirical dimension, *consuetudo*, formation of law through custom, has its opposite pole in *desuetudo*, loss of validity because of non-use. Empirical validity is identical with what Kelsen and Hart called efficacy and attempted to keep separate from validity. This is a particularity of the validity of legislative speech acts, with no correspondence in judicial or scholarly speech acts. While the felicity conditions of scholarly speech acts are not legally determined, their illocutionary force cannot be equated with formal validity or in general examined within the framework of legal validity. The only relevant validity dimension for scholarly speech acts is the substantive one. In sum, the validity claims of legislative speech acts possess formal, empirical, and substantive dimensions; those of judicial speech acts formal and substantive; while for scholarly speech acts only the substantive dimension matters. As a rule, the illocutionary force of legislative and judicial speech acts coincides with their formal validity.

The validity claims of all the main types of legal speech acts display a substantive dimension. Indeed, to the extent that the validity claims of preceding legislative, judicial, or scholarly speech acts are in general questioned in legal discourse, it is usually substantive validity that is at stake. In a democratic *Rechtsstaat*, a strict distinction between the formal and substantive validity of laws and court decisions is, in an important sense, misleading. Constitutional and other procedural rules which lay down felicity conditions and criteria for formal validity are not ends in themselves. Ultimately, they aim to secure the substantive validity of legislative and judicial speech acts. Of course, adherence to procedural rules cannot provide an absolute guarantee of substantive validity. However, formal validity establishes an assumption of substantive validity too. Enactment of a law in a democratic law-making procedure, as set out in the constitution and parliamentary rules of procedure, creates the presumption that the law meets the substantive criteria of validity as well. Correspondingly, formally valid court decisions can be assumed to possess substantive validity too.

Yet the presumption is fallible, and the substantive validity of formally valid laws or court decisions can be raised at any moment in subsequent legal discourse. Austin pointed out that although a speech act meets its felicity conditions and obtains illocutionary force, this does not preclude criticism employing other yardsticks. These vary according to the type of speech act, such as the truth/non-truth of assertions or the right/wrong of performatives.[10] Only subsequent to recognition of a speech act as an assertion can the truth or non-truth of its propositional content be judged. Correspondingly, recognition of legal or judicial speech acts as formally valid laws or rulings that entail the intended legal effects does not prevent subsequent examination of substantive validity.

So even when a law or court decision has attained illocutionary force, its substantive validity is always open to fresh assessment. To take a conspicuous example, the merits of pivotal US Supreme Court rulings – say, *Dred Scott*, *Lochner* or *Brown v Board of Education* or (why not?) *Roe v Wade* – are constantly re-examined in US legal discourse. Often enough, substantive reassessment of past legal speech acts of a landmark character is due to a change in yardsticks. Under the dominance of positive law, criteria for substantive validity are drawn from the sub-surface layers of law. And, contrary to the prescriptions of universal and eternal natural law, these criteria are subject to alteration, originating in surface-level legal discourse but also reflecting a more general mutation of moral principles and ethical values. In line with empirical – but differing from formal – validity, substantive validity is a quality which, though once possessed, may subsequently be lost.

Although the reasons supposedly supporting the substantive validity of legislative or judicial speech acts can be challenged, this does not usually affect the illocutionary (legal) force that these acts possess or the legal consequences they have already brought about. In this respect, substantive validity differs from the formal and empirical: as a rule, lack of formal or empirical validity of a putative law entails non-achievement or loss of illocutionary force. However, sometimes a formally valid law stands in such contradiction with substantive criteria – say, fundamental human rights principles – that courts reject its illocutionary force and leave it unapplied. Rights-based constitutional review, as it were, formalises substantive validity control and assigns it an immediate legal bearing. Furthermore, a court decision which is no longer considered substantively valid – say, *Dred Scott* or *Lochner* – may lose its illocutionary force as a precedent but not as a definite and authoritative solution to the particular case where it was issued.

Within the framework of Habermas' discourse theory, legal speech acts fall under regulative speech acts, which, as distinct from the truth claims of propositions, raise a claim to normative correctness. This claim is specified differently in different kinds of legal speech act. In legislative and judicial speech acts it displays both a formal and a substantive aspect. In turn, the exact content of the claim to substantive correctness varies in accordance with the divergent functions that legislative, judicial, and scholarly practices fulfil in law and society. On Habermas' account, when contested, claims to truth are

[10] Austin, 1984, 146–147.

discussed in theoretical discourses and claims to normative correctness in practical ones. In this division, legal discourse constitutes a particular variety of practical discourse where participants of diverse specialised legal practices discuss the contents of the law in force and engage in an implicit or explicit appraisal of the validity claims of past legal speech acts. It is not the only kind of practical discourse relevant to law. Habermas has analyzed different forms of practical discourse – pragmatic, ethical, moral, and juridical – which law-making in a democratic *Rechtsstaat* should include in order to secure the substantive correctness of laws.[11] In turn, Klaus Günther has elaborated on a theory of an application discourse which would promote the substantive correctness of court decisions; that is, their appropriateness.[12] These are discourses supposedly preceding issuance of the legal speech act that concludes the legislative or judicial procedure. Yet discussion of the normative correctness of laws and court decisions can continue after the procedure has ended, not only in the legal discourse interlinking specialised legal practices but also in discourses in civil society and the public sphere.

[11] Habermas, 1996, 157–168. [12] Günther, 1993.

Part II
Normativity

6

Specificities of Legal Normativity

Textuality

Legal normativity cannot – *pace* Kelsen – be examined without reference to sociality, that is, the social practices where law is realised and (re)produced. Conversely, exploring law's sociality requires attention to normativity. An analysis of sociolegal practices must heed the contribution of legal normativity to the internal normativity of those practices: to the patterning of the social actions making up the practice and to defining its task and role structure. Neither can legal relationships, legal-institutional facts or concrete orders of behaviour - all playing a vital role in law's realisation - be grasped without alluding to the legal norms that provide legal relationships with legal form; which accomplish the function of constitutive rules in creating legal-institutional facts; or which are specified into rights and duties of particular individuals in concrete orders of behaviour. Furthermore, second-order legal practices would not be possible without the constitutive and facilitating contribution of legal culture, operating primarily through the *Vorverständnis* of legal professionals. Law also provides the framework for legal discourse among legal professionals occupying diverse roles within diverse legal practices. Law, comprising even sub-surface, legal-cultural, layers, defines the participants of the discourse, as well as the relative weight of their interventions.

Although legal normativity cannot sever its ties to sociality, it can obtain an autonomy that facilitates taking a legal point of view typical of legal professionals of specialised legal practices and focusing on law as a normative legal order. Legal phenomenologists call this the theoretical approach, to distinguish it from the practical approach of the social actors of first-order sociolegal practices. Recall that our discussion still proceeds under the assumption of ideal-typical modern state law. On an equally ideal-typical evolutionary account, modern state law is a product of intertwined processes of differentiation. One of these is the abstraction of (legal) norms from the inherent normativity of social practices. The process, closely connected to the differentiation of the judicial function, originated under the dominance of customary law. A qualitatively new step was taken with subsequent separation of the legislative function, too, especially when the legislative authority was seen to include establishing new norms, not only codifying existing customary normativity.

How is such an abstraction possible? This is one of the crucial issues with which Kelsen struggled but to which he never managed to proffer a convincing solution: how could the legislators' act of will, a spatially and temporally anchored and empirically observable fact of Is, give rise to a legal norm, an entity of Ought, lying outside spatial and temporal coordinates and the reach of empirical observation? Or, to put it in other words, how can the subjective meaning of an act of will of the legislator be transformed into the objective meaning of law? Above, I proposed searching for the answer by recourse to speech act theory. Laws and court decisions are formal legal speech acts and as such institutional facts.

Norms can be seen as the propositional contents of formal legal speech acts, which obtain their typical illocutionary force, that is, a legally obligatory character, when they fulfil particular felicity conditions. But how can the propositional contents of successful speech acts detach themselves from their initial spatio-temporal context and embark on a life of their own as ideal entities – as standing Declarations, to use Searle's term? Credit is due to the same human invention which has facilitated preservation, accumulation, and tradition of even other cultural achievements which owe their origins to singular speech acts: writing. Legislative and judicial procedures include oral elements, but from the very dawn of Western legal tradition much of the propositional contents of legal speech acts has been enshrined in writing. Anthropological and historical evidence intimates a parallel and mutually enforcing development of law and writing. Law has needed writing in order to be recorded and memorised, and legal writing has contributed to the development of writing in general. Recognition of the pivotal role of writing shears much of the unnecessary mysticism of the notion of law as consisting of ideal or abstract entities.

Historically, the first written legal speech acts – say, Hammurabi's law, the Law of Twelve Tables, or European medieval compilations, such as the *Sachsenspiegel* – were not understood as producing new law but as extracting, codifying, and preserving the law as it existed in the sociolegal practices of the community, for the purposes of both the authorities and the community at large. Written records of compilations of customary law and decisions of magistrates were the two main forms of legal text through which the abstraction and objectivisation of law proceeded. Only towards the end of the Middle Ages were legislative speech acts seen as capable not only of authenticating but also creating law.

Not even in modern state law do all legal norms emerge from formal legal speech acts, performed with the intention of producing law and adhering to legally determined procedures. In customary law, realisation and (re)production coincide. Yet, in order to acquire formal validity, customary law must be recognised by legislative or judicial speech acts. By the same token, customary law, too, receives written form. In modern state law, 'spontaneous' or 'wild' customary law of general social practices has lost perhaps most of the relevance it had in premodern societies. Instead, specialised practices typical of a technology-driven, highly differentiated, and globalised world society have acknowledged law-producing power, often through explicit legislative authorisation or recognition. National and transnational law abound with references to best practices within specialised action fields of contemporary society: banking, accounting, data protection, and so on. Often enough best practices have been codified by national, international, or transnational organisations. Customary law, whether in its traditional or contemporary guise, does not really constitute an exception to the textuality of law.

Norms and norm texts are not identical. Norm texts give information about norms but are not themselves norms. This points to an important truism which legal theorists often – I would say surprisingly often – ignore, for instance when treating validity assessment and interpretation as two separate intellectual enterprises. Because of the conveyance function of writing, legal norms are only accessible through interpretation. Above, in the framework of speech act theory, I have examined norms as the meaning or propositional content of legal, primarily legislative, speech acts. These are issued in written form, and their meaning can only be deciphered by way of interpretation. Legal norms are always interpreted norms, identified and specified through interpreting legal texts; this holds not only for the 'penumbra' but also for the 'core'. With interpretation enters legal-cultural perspectivism: interpreters always carry with them a particular legal *Vorverständnis* through which they read legal texts. Legal interpretation is usually discussed in the context of surface-level law, as a phase in judicial reasoning preceding construction of the decision norm which is applied to the facts of the case and which constitutes the major premise of the judicial syllogism. Yet legal culture, too, is preserved in and (re)produced through legal texts, and interpretation is as necessary for explicating its contents as it is for ascertaining surface-level law. Legal-cultural principles, concepts, theories, and methodologies owe their origins to distinct legal speech acts; no shortcut leads to law's sub-surface layers but the contents of legal culture must be reconstructed from the traces it has left on law's surface. This is only possible through interpretation of legal texts; an inevitably perspectival exercise.

To recap, legal norms have become abstracted from the inherent normativity of – and attained a certain autonomy vis-à-vis – social practices. Legal texts provide us with information about, but are not identical with, legal norms. In order to account for the existence of legal norms, we must subscribe to an ontological dimension of ideal or thought entities, distinct from entities identifiable by spatio-temporal coordinates and observable by the senses. Yet legal norms and the normative legal order taken as a whole are safely rooted in the social practices without which they would never have emerged or continued their existence. Furthermore, the textuality of law adds to the ontological support that law enjoys in the spatio-temporal world.

Textuality is the first specific feature of legal normativity to which I want to draw attention. It is a foundational feature in the sense that it explains how legal norms can have become abstracted from the internal normativity of social practices, and obtained and maintained a relatively autonomous existence as a normative legal order. How should we in general approach and detect the *differentia specifica* of legal normativity? Many contemporary legal theorists, especially those adhering to the Legal Positivism of either the Hartian or the Kelsenian strand, adopt an essentialist standpoint. Here they follow the footsteps of the Masters, at the price, though, of downplaying Hart's overtures to 'descriptive sociology'. The essence of law is what defines law as law and not something else. The *differentia specifica* are supposed to detach law from the contingencies of particular territorial or historical contexts. Moreover, contemporary legal positivists are prone to emphasise the conceptual character of their enterprise. Historical, anthropological, or sociological research is argued to focus on what is contingent and accidental, by contrast with conceptual analysis, with its focus on the necessary and universal: the essence of law.[1]

Neither essentialism nor conceptualism are self-evident starting points for legal theory; to the contrary, they can be seriously flawed premises. What if what is called law consists and has consisted of such a variety of phenomena that it would be futile to search for features common to all of them; that this variety should rather be approached through the interrelated ideas of family resemblances, networks, and cluster concepts; that instead of essentials we should focus on, say, typicalities? The cognitive powers of conceptual analysis and its superiority over, say, history, anthropology, and sociology, also appear to be but poorly justified, if indeed at all. Where does conceptual analysis derive these powers from? Are the *differentia specifica* of law supposed to be analytical truths and, if they are, how do they withstand the Quinean criticism of the very distinction between synthetic and analytic judgements? Unanswered questions keep heaping up.

In the following, I shall discuss legal normativity in the setting of ideal-typical modern state law. Instead of essentials, my focus will be on typicalities, which do not necessarily add up to a general concept of law. My main legal-theoretical interlocutors will again be the Masters of modern Legal Positivism, Kelsen and Hart.

Positivity

Sociologists have proposed grouping norms into formal and informal, and the latter into social and moral. Formal norms involve mechanisms of legislation and adjudication, which informal norms lack. Formal norms also imply the

[1] See, e.g., Shapiro, 2011, chapter 1.

threat of coercive enforcement through tangible sanctions, while informal norms mainly rely on the force of disapproval. Furthermore, formal norms apply only to external actions, while informal norms may address attitudes and modes of deliberation as well. Finally, formal norms always apply to a limited group of persons and, sociologically, they can only exist if they are somehow accepted by that group.[2]

Moral and social norms constitute the primary types of informal norms. In this distinction, moral norms are practice-independent and social norms practice-dependent: social norms emerge out of corresponding practice, while the source of moral norms may lie elsewhere. Legal normativity clearly falls under formal norms, at least in modern state law. It is furnished with mechanisms of legislation and adjudication, and buttressed by tangible sanctions - coercion. Within the normative legal order, the sociological characteristics of formal norms imply the existence of Hartian secondary rules; a normative meta-level complementing primary rules of behaviour. The sociological depiction of formal norms corresponds to what legal theorists call the positivity of law.

It is hardly surprising that for Legal Positivism all law is positive law. However, often enough another distinctive feature is elevated to the principal characteristic, such as the alleged separation of law and morals. Evidently, however, this putative feature derives from the more fundamental premise of positivity, although, as I shall argue, the inference is unjustified. Kelsen, who vehemently defended the positivity of all law, vindicated with positivity the randomness of law's contents and the pure contingence of any substantive overlaps between legal and moral norms. With Kelsen, extreme normativism, manifest by the exclusion of law's social dimension from the scope of legal theory, shook hands with extreme voluntarism. With reference to positivity, Kelsen drew a boundary towards Natural Law, which in all its variegated versions committed the mortal sin of blurring the distinction between law and morals. For Kelsen, the positivity of law relates to its creation and annulment through human acts. We can agree with Kelsen's definition of positivity but still disagree with his inference that law is thus independent of morality and other non-legal normativity. The inference can only be warranted if the normative contents of the legal order are reduced to its surface level and the legal-cultural layers are bypassed. The conclusion also presupposes that Legal Positivism and Natural Law are the only available alternatives; that no third way exists for legal theory. The dichotomy, also cherished by Hartian positivists, is false.

Positivity anchors law in time and space, although it does not convert legal norms from ideal into empirical entities. Kelsen's definition of positivity connects the emergence of law to explicit legislative decisions – occurring in

[2] Brennan et al., 2013.

time and space. This is not the only temporal and spatial anchoring of positive law. In order to achieve their perlocutionary effects, legal speech acts must gain illocutionary force, which in turn requires that relevant addressees accept their validity claims, in particular the formal one. Positive – posited – law does not call for universal validity and bindingness: validity and bindingness for all times, places, and persons. The claim is limited territorially, temporally, subjectively, and substantively, with regard to particular behaviours. Accordingly, Kelsen distinguishes among four spheres of validity: spatial, territorial, personal, and substantive.[3] Together, these demarcate the claim to authority of posited law.

Positivity has been connected to law's temporality in a still more fundamental sense. The reputation of the early nineteenth-century German Historical School is often tarnished by caricatures of its *Volksgeist* notion, where some not too meticulous historians of ideas have even discerned roots of the Nazi *Volksgemeinschaft* ideology. Yet the Historical School was in many respects a path-breaker which articulated many of the tensions of law that have ever since puzzled legal scholarship.[4] For the Historical School, positive law was not yet identical with legislation or explicitly posited law in general. The epithet 'positive' derived from German idealist philosophy and alluded to historical determination in general; this was the sense in which Hegel, for instance, understood positivity. The Historical School renounced conceiving of the law's *ratio* as the time-and-place-independent reason of *Vernunftrecht*. Yet this did not prevent Kelsen, for whom positivism and Natural Law were the only available options, from affiliating the Historical School to the latter.

During the nineteenth century, understanding of law's positivity changed, especially after Germany's unification and subsequent adoption of the Constitution of the *Reich* in 1871 and the *Bürgerliches Gesetzbuch* as the 'basic law' of private law at the end of the century. Legal-scientific positivism was transformed into statutory positivism (*Gesetzespositivismus*). Kelsen stands at the end of the development where positivity is seen to entail the unhindered malleability of law and the free substantive discretion of the legislative will. With regard to the mixture of *ratio* and *voluntas* in law, Legal Positivism emphasises the latter at the expense of the former. Kelsen's voluntarism epitomises the fundamental change in law's temporality which definitely broke through towards the end of the nineteenth century and which was reconfirmed by the emergence of the regulative welfare state in the course of the twentieth century. The future became the dominant temporal dimension in law, especially for the legislator as the emblematic legal actor of modern state law; the new prince now occupying the throne of law's empire. By the same token, in legal theory positivity has lost its connection to the past, to law's historicity, and now connotes openness to the future, the law's unbounded pliability. For

[3] Kelsen, 1967, 10-14. [4] Tuori, 2011, chapter 3.

Savigny and Puchta, positivity had nothing to do with voluntarism and instrumentalism, which subsequently became hallmarks of Legal Positivism, perhaps most conspicuously in its Kelsenian version.

Kelsen connects positivity in a self-evident way to the state, not only treating judicial and legislative bodies as state organs, but even claiming that a state is reducible to a positive legal order, and concluding that every state is a *Rechtsstaat*. For Kelsen, the spatiality of positive law coincides with the spatiality of the state: the spatial sphere of validity of a positive legal order equals the territory of the state concerned.[5] Kelsen's Legal Positivism attached to the state two features which in legal history have gone together with law but not always with the state. The *voluntas* of law was now conceptualised as the will of the state, and the sword of Iustitia, that is, the coercion guaranteeing realisation of law, was put firmly in state hands. Kelsen not only presupposed but even enhanced the voluntarist element which he had criticised in the theorising of his teachers of the German Late Constitutional School and took for granted that the coercion accompanying positive law was wielded by the state.

In Hart's version of Legal Positivism, the voluntarist element, ensuing from the positedness of law, is pronounced too. The difference between Continental, German-oriented, and common-law legal cultures comes to the fore in the locus of the *voluntas*. Hartian Legal Positivism has been elaborated in a common-law context, and judge-made law occupies a more pivotal position than in Kelsen's Continental theorising. Voluntarism is conspicuous for example in the ardour with which Hart and his disciples have defended their view of judicial discretion. The 'state' has never had such currency in the common-law world as on the Continent. Still, a Continental legal theorist who reads Hart and the disciples through her legal-cultural *Vorverständnis* can easily discern the state behind the voluntarism and coerciveness of Hartian Legal Positivism. The very term 'state' hardly appears in *The Concept of Law*. Yet too much emphasis should not be put on terms. We should recall the crucial role that English political philosophy – in particular Hobbes – played in introducing the modern idea of the state; in performing the 'double abstraction of state'.[6] And we should also recall that Hobbes is a key player in the history not only of the idea of the state but also of modern Legal Positivism. In Hobbes' figure of the Sovereign, the voluntarist and coercive traits of law come together: the *voluntas* of the law consists of the instrumentally oriented will of the Sovereign, backed up by the sword also held by the Sovereign. Instead of reason, the authority that makes the law is will which, if needed, can make its way through coercion. From Hobbes runs a line to Jeremy Bentham and John Austin and, through them, all the way to Hart. Hart did dislodge 'sovereignty' from the position to which his positivist

[5] Kelsen, 1967, 286ff. [6] Skinner, 1989.

predecessors, most importantly Austin, had elevated it. In his criticism of Austin, Hart also pointed to the non-coercive, facilitating elements, of law. Still I would claim that Hart, under the influence of earlier English Legal Positivism, shared much of the state-centrism of the Kelsenian strand.

Kelsen's and Hart's voluntarist understanding of the positivity of law gives rise to several intricate problems. The first of these concerns the validity and obligatory force of law.

Positive law – in the sense of expressly posited law – had a role both in Natural Law and in the traditionalist conception where law was primarily identified with the age-old customs of the community. Yet legislation was not expected to create new law but to clarify existing law; to specify the requirements of natural law or to codify and preserve customary law. As Savigny's famous debate with Thibault demonstrates, in the nineteenth century and even within the Historical School, which in many other respects already heralded the dawn of modern law, this view of legislation still survived.[7] The validity of positive law was not a problem for natural lawyers or traditionalists, for whom legislation was not an independent source of law but only gave expression to law which flowed from other sources: the objective reason of the universe or the subjective reason of human beings (Natural Law), or the ingrained customs of the community. For Natural Law, positive law which broke against the maxims of natural law was not law at all. To use concepts anachronistically, the validity of positive law derived from the foundational law it expressed: natural or customary law.

Validity only became a problem after law's positivisation and the breakthrough of the voluntarist view which allowed for new law to be created through legislation. Only Legal Positivism raised 'validity' into a central – if not *the* central – concept and problem of legal theory. If law could no longer draw its validity and consequent obligatory force from the foundational law it expresses, where to draw it from? Only an extreme decisionist would contend that the mere fact of law having been posited suffices to prove its validity or explain and justify its obligatory nature; such a view would vindicate unbounded arbitrariness and naked power. Legal positivists' solution is authorisation. Yet this solution engenders a new problem. The chain of authorisation cannot continue *ad infinitum*. What authorises – forms the basis of – authorisation? Kelsen responds with the *Grundnorm*, Hart with the rule of recognition. If Legal Positivism has been very conscious of the issue of validity, it has largely ignored two other, closely related, problems which also ensue from a voluntarist understanding of positivity: justification and limitation. How to prevent unjustified coercion through law: that is, legally disguised totalitarianism?

[7] Hattenhauer, 2002.

Positivity is a fundamental feature of modern state law. Here I agree with the positivism of Kelsen and Hart. Where I disagree is the voluntarist view of positivity which ignores the disciplining effect that legal culture exercises on *voluntas*. A new understanding is needed which brings the sub-surface layers into harmony with surface-level positivity. Only such an understanding can show a way out of the cul-de-sac where Legal Positivism has enclosed itself and facilitate a satisfactory solution to the problems of validity and justification/limitation. As I shall argue below, a new reading of positivity is also needed to bring order and coherence to the voluntarist disorder created by policy-driven legislation.

Coerciveness

In defining law as distinct from morals, Kelsen concurred with Kant. Law addresses external behaviour and is backed up by external coercion; unlike morals, law is a coercive order. Law also differs from morals in its positivity, in resulting from human acts of will. Indeed, Kelsen connects the necessity of coercion to positivity. In contrast to natural law, the rules of positive law cannot be immediately self-evident. Positive law is an arbitrary human order which needs support from an agency of coercion and shows an inherent tendency to evolve into a coercive organisation. This coercive organisation, Kelsen adds, is identical with the state.[8]

The positivist understanding of legal validity leads to another, more fundamental issue of coercion and violence. The regress of validity and authorisation leads positivists to the postulate of the Master Rule. Yet contemporary critical legal theorists, familiar with their Schmitt, Benjamin, and Derrida, discern under the veil of the Master Rule non-authorised and a-legal exercise of *pouvoir constituant*, accompanied by foundational violence. This aspect of coercion has largely escaped the attention of legal positivists. Kelsen, though, hinted at it when toying with a power-theoretical interpretation of the *Grundnorm*. Can law ever erase the taint of original a-legality, naked power, and even foundational violence or prevent their outburst anew and a break of constitutional continuity?

Order

Legal norms never come alone but refer, implicitly or explicitly, to other norms, weaving normative networks. Law has a calling for order. Not only is it tasked with creating order and stability of normative expectations in society: it also craves internal order. The general personal scope and abstractly defined substance of law contribute to social order and stability. Yet the generality and

[8] Kelsen, 1957, 392–393.

abstractness of individual norms do not exhaust the requirement for the order of the legal order.

In modern state law, a call for a more comprehensive order is warranted by such fundamental principles as the rule of law and formal justice. The principle of the rule of law presupposes that law offers clear and equivocal guidance to those whom it addresses. Internally contradictory law is not able to do this. In turn, formal justice requires that like cases are treated alike and unlike cases unalike. To enable this, legal norms must display not only logical consistence but also substantive coherence. In addition, the requirement for coherence is relevant even for individual court decisions. Contradictions among the implications of prima facie applicable norms must be resolved so that none of these loses its validity. Thus, formation and justification of the decision norm finally applied to the case presuppose mutually coherent interpretation of all relevant norms. Through their justification, these norms (norm interpretations) are connected to other norms that are not directly relevant to the case at hand. Hence, as Klaus Günther has argued, the demand for coherence extends more widely than just the norms of immediate pertinence.[9]

The doctrinal function belongs – alongside the judicial and legislative ones – to the specific legal functions which have emerged in the historical course of Western legal tradition. The doctrinal function responds to law's internal need for certainty and stability. Ever since Roman antiquity, satisfying this need has been one of the major tasks that legal scholarship has set out to accomplish. At the dawn of modern law, the German Historical School considered law not only a historical but also a systemic phenomenon, which called for not only a historical but also a doctrinal, systematising, approach. A systematising approach was necessary even for meeting the very criterion for science: if *Rechtswissenschaft* aspired to be a *Wissenschaft*, it must understand its object as a systematic whole, in line with other branches of science.

Legal Positivism's voluntarist understanding of the positivity of law poses a serious threat to the order of law. Positivity becomes a menace to order when 'positivity' starts to denote, instead of historicity, the changeability of law through explicit legislative decisions. The legislator does not prioritise systematic considerations but produces ever-new normative material which endangers the consistence and coherence of law. Legal Positivism does not seem to be left with any other possibility to conceive of the order of law than to shift the emphasis from substantive to formal criteria. Yet formal criteria cannot respond to law's call for internal order; it is a call for substantive coherence rather than logical consistence.

In the following, I start elaborating an alternative view of positivity by showing that law cannot be reduced solely to its visible surface of legal speech

[9] Günther, 1993.

acts; that 'sub-surface' legal-cultural layers must be considered an integral part of law as a normative legal order (Chapter 7). Insight into the multi-layered character of law resolves the dilemma of the order of positive law: legal-cultural layers bring coherence to the disorder of surface-level law (Chapter 8). The same insight also facilitates articulating a substantive dimension in legal validity; dissolving the aporias of the legal positivist understanding of the foundations of validity; and reassessing the relations between law and morality in a way that shows how coercion in the name of law can be justified and circumscribed (Chapter 9). I wrap up my discussion of legal normativity by discussing the role of the constitution in a multi-layered normative legal order (Chapter 10).

7

Layers of Law

Legal Culture as Law

Few legal scholars would deny the influence of legal culture on legal interpretation and argumentation, although agreement on what legal culture consists of could be difficult to attain. One of the central tenets of this essay is that legal culture not only impacts legal interpretation and reasoning but forms an integral part of law. The normative legal order is not made up merely of surface-level norms produced by formal legal speech acts; it also includes sub-surface, legal-cultural layers. This claim is likely to raise severe opposition, in particular in the legal positivist camp. How do I warrant my claim?

One of the specificities of legal normativity is textuality. Legal norms are only accessible through legal texts. To be exact, what we encounter on the surface of law is not legal norms but legal texts providing information about norms. The road from text to norm goes through interpretation. The need of interpretation does not distinguish easy from hard cases, or core from penumbra. Interpretation is necessary even in easy cases; 'literal' interpretation is interpretation too. In order to be accepted by relevant addressees in legal discourse, interpretation must rely on the tenets prevailing in legal culture. These may be codified in scholarly treatises but only very rarely, if ever, in formal legal speech acts. Still they are legally effective: if not complied with, the interpretation, expressed implicitly or explicitly in another legal speech act, does not obtain illocutionary force. Primacy of 'literal' interpretation may appear as a self-evident canon in legal regimes where it is adhered to. Yet it, too, is an interpretative precept and its almost axiomatic nature is due to its being so deeply ingrained in legal culture.

Even apart from the necessity of interpretation, individual legal speech acts always imply not only explicitly identified surface-level norms but legal-cultural layers too. In every legal case they decide, whether easy or hard, judges apply not only the decision norm which constitutes the major premise of the judicial syllogism but even legal-cultural principles. In every criminal law ruling, *nulla poena sine lege* or the broader principle of legality is resorted to, explicitly or, most often, implicitly. The difference between hard and easy cases lies not in the necessity to take recourse to principles but in the need to articulate sub-surface principles which usually, in easy cases, are operative through the practical knowledge of legal professionals. The fact that the primacy of literal interpretation is experienced so 'naturally', especially in criminal law, is due to the criminal law principle of legality and the internalisation of this principle in legal *Vorverständnis*. Correspondingly, in every contract-law case the *pacta sunt servanda* principle is applied, although most often implicitly and explicitly merely in hard cases where its exact significance and implications appear uncertain or controversial.

Not only interpretative canons and sub-surface legal principles but even other elements of legal culture are involved in individual legal speech acts. This holds for the doctrine of legal sources, which indicates the surface-level normative material – previous legal speech acts – whence judges and other legal actors draw information on applicable norms. It is this very doctrine that makes legal professionals turn to books of statutes or precedents for guidance. Furthermore, legal speech acts use a particular legal language, with legal concepts as the vocabulary and patterns of legal reasoning and argumentation as the grammar. Mastering this language is a prerequisite for participation in legal discourse; interventions in another language neither obtain illocutionary force nor are accepted as contributions to that discourse. Legal speech acts represent legal *parole*, while legal concepts and methods constitute the *langue* that facilitates and is employed in *parole*.

The meaning of legal texts can only be deciphered by recourse to interpretative precepts, which constitute an integral part of legal culture. Moreover, legal speech acts, including laws and court decisions, would not even be possible without the contribution of legal-cultural layers, nor would the specialised legal practices where speech acts are produced or the ongoing legal discourse where these practices are interrelated. Legal-cultural layers accomplish a constitutive function with regard to legal speech acts and practices. Without the resources provided by legal culture, judges could not issue rulings, legislative experts draft - and consequently legislators adopt - laws, or legal scholars compose doctrinal writings. Yet in relations between surface-level law and sub-surface, legal-cultural, layers, constitution comes with limitation. Legal-cultural layers not only constitute the possibility for legislating, judging, interpreting, and systematising; they also restrict, again mostly unconsciously and through legal *Vorverständnis*, what kinds of law, ruling, and doctrinal standpoint are possible. As I shall argue below, of particular importance is the internal normative censorship exercised by general legal principles.

In sum, surface-level law is inseparably intertwined with legal-cultural layers, which must also be acknowledged as an integral part of law. But note that at issue here is the elite or expert culture of legal professionals. Detachment of an expert culture from the general culture of the legal community in *sensu largo* is one of the characteristic differentiations of modern state law. Legal texts are written in legal language, using legal concepts and methods, and, in order to perceive their meaning, they must be interpreted by employing interpretative tenets and against the background of general legal principles. Legal professionals and laymen approach the law through different cultural filters, and consequently the law for laymen cannot be exactly the same as for professionals. This may be the fundamental legal-cultural perspectivism of modern state law; more fundamental even than the perspectivism of legal roles or legal regimes. In spite of all the differences, the legal culture of diverse legal roles in diverse state legal regimes shares much in common. It is this common basis that facilitates legal discourse interconnecting diverse legal practices within a distinct legal regime, as well as dialogue among legal professionals from diverse regimes.

I distinguish between three types of element of expert legal culture: conceptual, normative, and methodological. In this triad, the normative element refers to general legal principles. The distinction is analytical in the sense that the elements are interwoven and that not only principles but also concepts and methods possess normative implications. In legal doctrine, the same normative phenomena have sometimes been discussed as concepts, sometimes as principles. In both Germany and the USA, the late nineteenth century was an age of concepts. Concepts were seen as clusters of norms, and derivation of norms from concepts was considered a wholly legitimate legal-scientific operation. After analytical and realist critique – even derision – of conceptualism, an era of principles seems to have dawned. Principle-based reasoning has conquered ground, not only in common-law countries, but also on the European Continent, including Germany. Still, even if mainly analytical, the distinction among legal-cultural elements is important because legal concepts, principles, and methodologies accomplish different functions in law. The distinction is also important because it clarifies my criticism of one of the fundamental reductions of Legal Positivism. My claim that Legal Positivism adopts a uni-level conception of law and ignores the legal-cultural layers focuses on what I identify as the normative element – that is, general legal principles – as distinct from the methodological and conceptual dimensions.

Legal theories are a mixture of diverse legal-cultural elements; conceptual, normative, and methodological. Legal theories aim to make sense of legal institutions. Thus we have theories of property, contract, fundamental rights, and separation of powers. As may be recalled, legal institutions are related to distinct social practices. Accordingly, legal theories also reflect a particular view of these practices: an implicit economic or social theory of property or contract, or an implicit political theory of judicial independence or separation of powers. Controversies among rival legal theories may have their backdrop in differences in such implicit economic, social, or political theories.

Positivity of Legal Culture

Legal Positivism ties law to time and space in two respects. Firstly, although they give rise to ideal entities, law-making acts are spatio-temporal events.

Secondly, even though positive legal norms are ideal entities, their validity is spatially and temporally circumscribed.

While anchoring law in spatio-temporal legislative acts, Legal Positivism adopts a voluntarist view of those acts and loses sight of the limitations that legal culture, law's historically determined *ratio*, imposes on legislative *voluntas*. Even modern state law is not only a manifestation of legislative *voluntas*; even under the dominance of posited law, the dialectic of *voluntas* and *ratio* continues. The task is to reconstruct law's *ratio* in a way that brings it into harmony with the positivity of modern state law; retaining Legal Positivism's understanding of positivity as positedness, yet, by the same token, reconnecting to the Historical School's view of positivity as historicity.

Through legal culture, law maintains the link to its history. Furthermore, legal culture disciplines the discretion of legislative *voluntas* reigning on the surface of law. But what about positivity? How can my account of law's legal-cultural layers be reconciled with its posited nature? Legal concepts, principles, theories, and methodologies have not fallen from heaven, nor can they, in the era of positive law, be conceived of as universally valid natural law. They, too, share the positivity of modern state law. They have originated from individual legal speech acts on the surface of law: from court decisions, laws and *travaux préparatoires*, and scholarly writings. Through a process of sedimentation lasting decades, maybe even centuries, doctrinal insights and proposals have been converted into elements of the legal culture which in legal education is transmitted to new generations of lawyers and which, through legal *Vorverständnis*, exert their constitutive and restricting impact. Genealogies of both private- and public-law doctrine could be written, starting, from, say, the reception of Roman law in the late Middle Ages (private law), and the political and legal philosophy of the early modern age and the constitutional speech acts influenced by this philosophy (constitutional law). Legal-cultural layers are not connected to the surface level merely through relations of constitution and limitation; they are also connected through a relation of sedimentation. This relation enables us to trace distinct elements of legal culture back to individual legal speech acts and, hence, to conceive of legal culture, too, as positive law.

Talk of sedimentation and definition of legal culture as law's sedimented *ratio* easily arouse an image of a harmonious process of advancing rationality. This is not how I see things. In diverse legal cultures, the process of sedimentation has included controversies and contradictory readings of law's *ratio* and the concepts, principles, theories, and methodologies that legal practices should adhere to. Instead of linearity the road has been much more twisted. And most probably, only rarely have the debates through which sedimentation has proceeded approximated the ideal conditions of Habermasian discourse theory but have, rather, in various ways, manifested power *in* law. The history of law's *ratio* is a history of the winners, a history whose temporary denouement can be read in the prevailing legal culture – the contents of which can also be highly contested and susceptible to contradictory readings.

Not only surface-level law but even the legal-cultural layers are spatially and temporally circumscribed. Yet legal-cultural layers obey a different temporality and spatiality from the surface level. Validity is a quality of surface-level law, and speaking of the 'validity spheres' of legal culture does not make sense. Instead of 'validity', 'relevance' might be a suitable term. As distinct from natural law, the relevance of legal culture is temporally and spatially limited, though the limits cannot be expressed with exact parameters. The ideas of French annalists of the multi-temporality of history are applicable to legal history as well. The pace of change is much more laggard in the legal-cultural layers than on the turbulent surface, and the relevance of legal culture is measured in longer temporal units than the validity of surface-level law. The foundational layers of legal culture, constituting 'legal deep culture', obey the *longue durée* of law, reaching back to Roman law, if not even further. The spatial validity of modern state law follows the contours of state territory. In the territorial respect, too, the relevance of legal culture adheres to criteria other than the validity of surface-level law. National legal cultures display idiosyncrasies – but they may also share much in common. Legal-cultural boundaries but rarely coincide with state borders, which by and large the spatial validity of surface-level law follows. This facilitates the talk of a deep culture, shared by diverse legal regimes.

Because of their porosity, as well as temporal and spatial ambiguity, the legal-cultural layers of law cannot be unequivocally identified or demarcated by a Master Rule: a rule of recognition or *Grundnorm*. Escaping the reach of the Master Rule, legal culture also relativises the autonomy of law, in respect of both other legal orders and non-legal normativity, in particular morals. Western legal culture – tracing its origins back to the writings of late medieval glossators and commentators of Roman law, and early modern philosophical writings and constitutional documents – has always possessed a transnational foundation, ignoring state borders or the validity spheres of surface-level law. Even if a legal-positivist Master Rule could guarantee the autonomy of surface-level law, it would be impotent in front of the interlegality between the legal-cultural layers of state legal orders. The same holds for the relationship between law and morals. As I will argue below, Legal Positivism has only been able to uphold the separability thesis by confining its gaze to surface-level law.

All in all, the emergence of a distinct legal expert culture has an ambivalent impact on the autonomy of law. The very phenomenon of an expert culture testifies to cultural autonomy, connected to the professional autonomy of law. The primary roles in legal practices – the roles of judges, legislative experts, and legal scholars – are reserved for legal professionals who have received a legal education, internalised a legal *Vorverständnis*, and master legal language. Legal methodology employed in legal practices and discourse creates a methodological autonomy for law and distinguishes legal from, say, moral and political reasoning and argumentation. Insofar as the Master Rule succeeds in circumscribing formally valid law, it guarantees a certain autonomy for surface-level law. In the sub-surface layers, substantive autonomy is mellowed by the porosity of legal culture and the intertwinement of general legal principles with non-legal normativity. This relativises the substantive autonomy of even surface-level law, due to the fact that legal texts can only be read through a legal-cultural filter.

Evoking law's alleged standing between politics and morals, politics with its hectic temporality and territorially circumscribed spatiality could be argued to unfurl is impact at the surface-level of law, while morals and its more languid temporality and open spatiality would be effective in the sub-surface layers. Yet this is a simplification. The surface level is not only about law as medium but also law as institution, and legal speech acts may refer to and even incorporate moral norms. Neither is the sedimentation process or the legal discourse through which legal culture is distilled from individual legal speech acts free from political influences and stakes, as is most conspicuously proved by eras when intense doctrinal and legal-theoretical debates coincide and interlock with political and ideological fault lines; think of the Weimar Republic. And, to repeat, no strict separation exists between surface-level law and the sub-surface legal-cultural layers. In legal practices, they work together and through legal *Vorverständnis*, legal culture influences the contents of surface-level law too. In legal practices and speech acts, the layers of law, with their different temporalities and spatialities, join forces.

Master Rules in Multi-Layered Law

In its voluntarism, Legal Positivism rejects the idea of substantive sub-surface principles which would curb the discretion of the legislator. Still, it would be incorrect to maintain that Kelsen and Hart were blind to the legal-cultural presuppositions of legal practices. The *Grundnorm* and the rule of recognition are susceptible to a legal-cultural interpretation. Furthermore, both Kelsen and Hart attended to basic legal concepts and appreciated the analytical strand in Legal Positivism. Hence, the claim that Legal Positivism holds a uni-level view of law is not entirely true. It is true but only as regards the substantive contents of law.

Let us pursue the legal-theoretical reading of Kelsen's and Hart's Master Rules. Kelsen privileged the perspective of legal science, Hart that of judicial practices. However, insofar as law-making and adjudication also – according to Kelsen – involve a cognitive phase, what he writes about legal science is meant to be relevant for those legal practices too. With his *Grundnorm*, Kelsen claims to reconstruct, in a Kantian epistemological vein, the necessary implicit presupposition for all legal cognition. In turn, Hart's rule of recognition is intended to explicate the criteria that judges in fact employ when identifying the law in force. Kelsen is deeply conscious of the reconstructive thrust of his enterprise. The *Grundnorm* is supposed to be 'merely the formulation of the assumption necessary for any positivistic grasp of legal materials', which 'merely raises to the level of consciousness what all jurists are, even unconsciously, doing when, in the comprehension of their subject, they reject natural law . . . and yet consider the data of their cognition not as mere facts of power, but as laws, as norms'.[1] Thus, 'by offering this theory of the basic norm, the Pure Theory of Law does not inaugurate a new method of legal cognition' but 'merely makes conscious what most legal scientists do, at least unconsciously, when they . . . consider as law exclusively positive law'. In sum, 'the theory of the basic norm is merely the result of an analysis of the procedure which a positivistic science of law has always applied'.[2] Kelsen is also explicit about the Kantian analogy.

Thus, in discussing epistemological presuppositions of legal practices, Kelsen draws attention to the significance for legal practices of legal actors' *Vorverständnis*. The problem is that he tries to reconstruct this *Vorverständnis* in a-historical terms. He contends that assumption of a *Grundnorm* and the concomitant hierarchical understanding of the normative legal order amount to transcendental presuppositions necessarily involved in all legal cognition and practices. However, legal *Vorverständnis* is not transcendentally fixed for all times and places. Legal actors draw their *Vorverständnis* from the temporally and spatially variable legal-cultural reservoir available to them. In addition, faithful to his voluntarist positivism, Kelsen conveys an epistemologically truncated view of the *Vorverständnis* that constitutes the possibility of legal practices. Legal culture, informing legal *Vorverständnis*, includes not only methodological and conceptual but, in the guise of substantive legal principles, even normative elements.

The exact nature of Hart's rule of recognition is a seemingly inexhaustible topic within the Hartian school. Questions abound: In what, if any, sense is the rule of recognition a rule? If it is a rule, is it part of or a presupposition for law? Is it a duty-imposing or a power-conferring or perhaps a constitutive rule? If it is a social rule, what is meant by a 'social rule'? Can a social rule also be a legal rule? Let me comment briefly on John Gardner and Matthew Kramer's analyses, which belong to the most insightful recent interventions. Both Gardner and Kramer lend support to my proposal to treat the rule of recognition as a concise articulation of the prevailing doctrine of the sources of law and as such part of sub-surface law.

Gardner treats the rule of recognition as a norm of customary law *in foro*. According to him, customary law differs from legislative law in not being made by acts of communicating it; 'not by what people say is to be done, but by what they actually do'. Customary law *in pays* is made by what people at

[1] Kelsen, 1957, 396. [2] Kelsen, 1967, 204–205.

large do, customary law *in foro* by what judges do. Customary law *in foro* – judicial customary law – is not to be confused with judicial case-law, which, for Gardner, constitutes a sub-type of legislative law and is made by acts communicating it. *Stare decisis* is judicial customary law, which addresses reception and use of case-law. Analogously, the rule of recognition has emerged from judicial custom; from what judges do, not from what they say is to be done. In that sense, the rule of recognition is a social rule as distinct from a posited rule. Yet it is a normative, even a legal, rule - not a mere empirical regularity. Perhaps Gardner would have allowed us to express his point as follows: the rule of recognition is an extract of the internal normativity of judicial practices.[3]

Gardner's account can be read as an attempt to explicate the process of sedimentation which the rule of recognition undergoes and through which it participates in the positivity of modern law. It also shows that social and legal rules are not mutually exclusive descriptions of the rule of recognition, although Gardner has difficulty in making up his mind whether, at the end of the day, the rule of recognition is a legal rule or not. This may be due to legal positivists' unease with the insight that law is not exhausted by its surface level. Gardner does hint at this possibility by distinguishing between explicit formulations of the rule of recognition and its primarily tacit way of functioning. Thus, he stresses that no canonical formulations of the rule of recognition exist.

I am not sure whether the distinction Gardner draws between judicial customary law, arising from what judges do, and judicial case-law, emerging from what judges say is to be done, holds. What judges do consists mainly of judicial speech acts. The (re)productive implications of judicial speech acts are not confined to surface-level law but extend to sub-surface, legal-cultural layers. Implicitly, these speech acts always also apply a doctrine of legal sources; a rule of recognition, as Hartian legal scholars would put it. The difference is not between saying and doing but between what is said and done explicitly and implicitly.

Kramer's reading of the rule of recognition also displays an affinity to my interpretation of the rule of recognition as a legal-cultural doctrine of legal sources. Kramer argues that law rests on an array of normative presuppositions that underlie the efforts of officials, especially in law-ascertaining, and that the rule of recognition belongs to such presuppositions. He distinguishes between an epiphenomenal and a foundational level, implying that explicit formulations can never fully capture the tacitly operative rule of recognition. Kramer seems to intimate that the rule of recognition does not form part of but is merely a presupposition for law; again we are confronted with the positivist reluctance to include sub-surface legal culture in law. Somewhat

[3] Gardner, 2012, 65, 82–83, and 288–290.

confusingly, Kramer, in line with Gardner, discusses whether at issue is a duty-imposing or power-conferring rule. His conclusion is that the rule of recognition consists of a bundle of precepts, both duty-imposing and power-conferring.[4] The discussion is confusing because it appears to mix up two differently functioning levels: surface-level law and legal culture. The rule of recognition is synonymous with the prevailing doctrine of legal sources, and it makes no sense to confer qualities of surface-level law on legal-cultural doctrine; even to call the rule of recognition a 'rule' can be misleading. Closer to the point is the constitutive function, which Kramer also attributes to the rule of recognition. Another issue is that it may be justified to derive justiciable surface-level norms from legal-cultural doctrines. Thus, a judge who deliberately sets aside a statutory norm - whose applicability to the case pending before the court is obvious - may be guilty of punishable malfeasance.

In sum, the Master Rules of Legal Positivism can be seen as proposals for reconstructing vital legal-cultural presuppositions of the surface-level legal order. In my analytical tripartite classification of elements of legal culture, the doctrine of legal sources falls in the methodological compartment, together with patterns of legal reasoning and argumentation – such as analogy, *argumentum a minore ad maius*, *e contrario* or, to take a more recent example, proportionality – and interpretative canons, such as literal and teleological interpretation. The methodological elements of legal culture are intermixed; the division employed here is an analytical one as well. The doctrine of legal sources not only indicates the sources of the law in force. It also defines what kinds of argument are legally relevant and admissible in legal reasoning and discourse.

In addition to epistemological presuppositions, Legal Positivism's other primary field of interest is the conceptual structure of law. Kelsen's Pure Theory has a wider reach than just explicating the hypothetical *Grundnorm* as a transcendental precondition for legal science. Pure Theory is a general theory of positive law, which 'furnishes the fundamental concepts by which the positive law of a definite legal community can be described'.[5] The central concept is 'legal rule' (*Rechtssatz*), while other fundamental concepts include 'sanction', 'delict', 'legal duty', 'legal right', 'legal person', and 'legal order'.[6] Kelsen also calls his theory structural. The Pure Theory aims to purify legal concepts of substantive content and to (re)define them as structural concepts connoting formal relationships among legal norms. This is an impoverished and a-historical view of legal concepts. It ignores concepts whose reference consists of legal-institutional facts or legal institutions, such as 'marriage' or 'contract', and which reflect the intertwinement of law's normative and social aspects. Arguably, these constitute the basic type of legal concepts.

[4] Kramer 2008, 110ff. [5] Kelsen, 1945, xiii. [6] Ibid., 50.

In *The Concept of Law*, Hart does not explicitly deal with legal concepts. However, as editor and commentator of Bentham's writings he showed a keen interest in the conceptual analyses of his legal positivist predecessors in English legal theory; representatives of the Anglo-Saxon tradition of Analytical Jurisprudence which Hohfeld continued in the twentieth century and with which Kelsen professed kinship.[7] The analytical trend in Legal Positivism has engaged in articulating and elaborating the fundamental conceptual structure of modern state law; especially the concepts that relate to the abstract legal order's transformation into a concrete order of behaviour; rights and duties of particular persons. The analysis has its undoubted merits. Yet it is afflicted by the twin problems of normativism and a-historicism. Rights and duties are detached from the social relationships they structure, and fundamental legal concepts are presented as universally relevant. Yet these concepts, too, have undergone a similar of process of sedimentation as elements of legal culture in general.

[7] Ibid., 17.

8

Orders of Law

Plurality of Orders

Law never works in isolation but always in conjunction with other law. This holds for all legal practices, and for all legal speech acts. Laws and court decisions include explicit or implicit references to other laws and decisions, and to other legal norms than only those explicitly applied to the case at hand. Furthermore, surface-level law is not even intelligible without the filter provided by sub-surface layers. The normative legal order possesses an order which makes it into a unity and which provides it with its identity. The question can only be how order, unity, and identity should be conceived of. Here my focus is on order and unity, while below, in discussing the plurality of law in Part III, it is on unity and identity. Yet the link between order, unity, and identity should be kept constantly in mind.

As so much in law, even its order is perspectival. Diverse criteria of order exist, and order is not the same once and for all. There is no right order of the law. All legal practices aspire to order and unity, but the backdrop to this aspiration or the point of the order is not identical. A judge wants primarily to bring order into prima facie applicable norms, while the legislator (or at least the legislative expert) wants to secure that new laws cohere with existing ones and that their realisation is not affected by contradictions. For legal scholarship, in turn, systematising the law has ever been a vital task. Scholarly systematisation connects to legal education; in universities, legal scholarship and legal education have shared a common institutional site. Yet systematisation also relates to the legal side of the dual citizenship of legal scholarship. Through its proposals for systematisation, legal scholarship creates prima facie coherence which can then be capitalised on in adjudication and legislation. Yet within legal scholarship, too, diverse options for systematising criteria are available, and the specialisation of the scholar and the specific purpose of the systematising exercise impact the choice among them. Doctrinal scholars are usually committed to a particular field of law, while legal theorists at least aspire to a position above disciplinary divisions.

It is sometimes asked whether order is inherent in the law or whether it is created by legal scholarship. My answer would be: both. Legal scholarship is a legal practice and a participant in legal discourse and, as such, part of law in its social mode of existence. When systematisation proposals by legal scholars gain adherence in subsequent legal speech acts, a process of sedimentation is launched through which, if the process succeeds, the proposals are included in the prevailing legal culture. Thus they also find their way into legal *Vorverständnis*, and become part of the filter through which legal professionals read and interpret legal texts and conceive of the law's order.

Diachronic or Synchronic?

Alternative positions taken on the order of law can be arranged around three pairs: diachronic or synchronic; substantive or formal; and local or comprehensive. Those privileging diachronic coherence emphasise historical contextuality and continuity, while those embracing synchronic coherence tend to depict the order of the law in an a-historical, universalist manner. Classic common-law thinking, as elaborated in debates with the early representatives of English positivism, such as Hobbes and Bentham, is a clear example of a diachronic view. Diachronic coherence links the present and future of the law with its past, the past being the principal time horizon. Diachronic coherence is substantive by nature, created by age-old, tradition-bound, and localised principles, further elaborated by intricate common-law methodology.

The synchronic conception detaches law from its history, preserved in its traditions. If Natural Law and Legal Positivism have something in common, it is the synchronic and, by the same token, a-historical way of apprehending order and unity. Early modern common-law writers had to wage a two-front war. The idea of comprehensive, synchronic, and substantive, and, at the same time, a-historical coherence, embraced by Thomist Natural Law, was rejected as contradictory to common law's localised traditionalism. Yet common law found its main opponent in early Legal Positivism, with its equally universalist but formal rather than substantive understanding of the order of the law. For Hobbes, the law's unity was guaranteed by its origin in the Sovereign's will. The Natural Law elements in Hobbes' thinking vindicated the necessity of Sovereign and positive legislation but, differing from the Thomist view, did not determine the content of law: law as the Sovereign's command was obligatory irrespective of its content. In turn, Bentham aspired to a formal systemic order, produced by analytical concepts and classificatory premises corresponding to a Linnaean notion of science. Bentham advocated a code or set of codes which would be organised by a new conceptual apparatus, indicating a precise location for different types of norm and legal relation. Bentham belonged to the international codification movement of the turn of the eighteenth and nineteenth centuries. Yet the codification he espoused did not amount to such a recording of customary law as in, say, Prussia's *Allgemeines Landrecht* or Austria's *Allgemeines Bürgerliches Gesetzbuch*. His codification purported to serve the cause of instrumental reason, to enhance the stability and transparency of a *Gesellschaft* society. Bentham also inaugurated a particular strand in the systematisation of law: systematisation through analytical concepts, considered universal in their application. Here, too, Austin was destined to be his most important follower, transmitting Bentham's influence to twentieth-century jurisprudence, including Hart. Hart is often recalled only as a critic of Austin, but this is a one-sided perception of Hart's relationship to his nineteenth-century colleague. Hart is heir to both the voluntarist and the a-historical analytical approach of his positivist predecessors.

In accordance with its two-pronged historical and systematising approach, the German nineteenth-century Historical School sought to reconcile diachronic and synchronic order. Diachronic – and, by the same token, substantive – order was supposed to be produced by the embedding of law in society and culture, the latter link forged through the historically evolving *Volksgeist*. In line with the common-law movement, the Historical School fought against not only the dominance of legislative *voluntas* but also the a-historical Natural-Law view of substantive coherence, primarily in the guise of Christian Wolff's axiomatic system.

Michel Foucault argued that, in the aftermath of the French Revolution, a new epistemological mindset, a modern episteme, broke through. The new episteme was championed by disciplines such as biology, which studied the organic nature of living creatures, and historically oriented linguistics, which treated languages as organism-like entities.[1] The Historical School's conception of the order of the law manifests the same epistemic rupture. The system of the law is supposed to derive from its organic character – the interdependence of its elements and its subjection to historical change. Law was a product of the *Volksgeist*, just as language, which, according to the linguistics of the day, also demonstrated internal interdependence and historical evolution. Through the *Volksgeist* as its main source of origin, law was bestowed an organicity, much the same as language. For Savigny, the law constitutes a system, an organic whole, of interdependent institutions. Taken separately, institutions, too, are organic unities, composed of interdependent parts and subject to historical change. As might be recalled, legal institutions, on Savigny's view, are grounded in factual life relationships (*Lebensverhältnisse*) through the intermediary of legal relationships. The systematic order of the law grows from the systematic order of society, from its organic character.

In the latter half of the nineteenth century, systems-thinking in German legal science was transmitted to the new discipline of state law by Carl Friedrich von Gerber and Paul Laband, both of them with a private-law background. At the same time, the view of the systematic traits of law and legal science altered. The system of law lost much of its organic character and cut its link to organic system(s) of social life. In the conceptual constructions

[1] Foucault, 1974.

of *Begriffsjurisprudenz*, as well as in contemporary US conceptualism, the order of law shed its diachronic features and acquired a prominently synchronic character. *Begriffsjurisprudenz* considered the truncated historicity of *Gesetzespositivism* not as a source of the order of the law but as a threat to it. The legislator did not always heed systematic concerns, and yet positive law restricted the freedom of doctrinal system-formation.

Kelsen is a successor to nineteenth-century German *Rechtswissenschaft*, especially the state-law strand of Legal Positivism initiated by Gerber and Laband and strongly influenced by private-law *Begriffsjurisprudenz*. One of the legacies that Kelsen inherited from his predecessors is a preoccupation with the order and unity of law. With Kelsen, awareness of law's historicity and the diachronic dimension of unity has wholly faded away: the 'historicity' in Kelsen's reconstruction of the law's unity is the regress in the validity chain leading to the historically first constitution and the *Grundnorm* as the transcendental, hypothetical reason for the validity of that constitution and the basis of legal normativity in general. Kelsen calls his system of law dynamic in contrast to the static system of Natural Law. In a static system, all norms can be deduced from the *Grundnorm* by a mere intellectual operation. By contrast, in a dynamic system the *Grundnorm* merely authorises a human will to create norms. For Kelsen, his Pure Theory with its dynamic (and formal) order and unity was the only alternative to the static (and substantive) view of Natural Law.[2] However, ironically, in respect of the diachronic and synchronic features, Kelsen's Pure Theory and Natural Law are not really alternatives but both fall to the latter, synchronic, side of the divide. In Kelsen's dynamic system, dynamism is confined to the turbulent movement on the surface of law. The Pure Theory ignores the historicity of sub-surface layers – law's sedimented tradition and reason – which alone can replace universal natural law as the fount of substantive coherence and lend that coherence a diachronic twist.

Even within his Pure Theory, Kelsen distinguished between dynamic and static parts. The object of the static part is law as a system of valid norms - law, as it were, in a state of rest - while the dynamic part addresses law in motion - the process in which law is created and applied. To dispel any misunderstandings, Kelsen clarified that legal cognition considers acts of law creation and application only insofar as these are determined by legal norms and, thus, form the content of legal norms. Hence, the dynamic part of the Pure Theory, too, deals exclusively with norms. In turn, the static part of Pure Theory has nothing to do with examining the contents of law, which would take it dangerously close to the static principle of validity embraced by Natural Law. Kelsen's objective was to develop content-independent structural concepts and purify them of any factual or moral connotations; concepts such as

[2] Kelsen, 1967, 195–197 and 217–219.

'legal right' and 'duty'. The static part of Pure Theory is not an effort to construe substantive, content-based order and unity. To the contrary, Kelsen viewed all such efforts with suspicion, as steps on the path to Natural Law. Under his critical gaze, both the *Volksgeist* doctrine of the Historical School and systematisations through the divisions of law were merely camouflaged versions of Natural Law.

In twentieth-century Legal Positivism, order and unity are conceived of in synchronic terms, reflecting a uni-level and a-historical view of law and rejection of the lingering importance of legal tradition. Both Kelsenian and Hartian Legal Positivism acknowledge the indispensable contribution of methodological and conceptual presuppositions – though not sub-surface legal principles – but discuss them in a-historical terms and hesitate to include them in the law proper. The diachronic dimension is reduced to the continuity of formal identity under a Master Rule. Legal positivists take pride in bringing in dynamism and order after the stagnation of Natural Law and the antiquated chaos of common law. Kelsen called his view of law dynamic, while Hart praised the secondary rules of a developed legal system for providing a solution, not only to uncertainty and inefficacy, but also to inertia. Yet the dynamism of Legal Positivism curtails law's temporality into a mere formal principle of changeability, opens law to the future but cuts its ties to the past and succumbs to unrestrained voluntarism. The traditions of law fall victim to positivist purification; paradoxically, even diachronic unity loses its historicity and is pruned into formal continuity.

Formal or Substantive?

On Joseph Raz' account, the material (substantive) unity of a legal system depends on the content of its laws and on the manner in which these are applied: 'the all-pervasive principles and the traditional institutional structure and practices that permeate the system and lend to it its distinctive character'. By contrast, formal unity, which also constitutes the identity of the system, lies 'in the criterion or set of criteria that determines which laws are part of the system and which are not'. Evidently - because Raz is now discussing formal as distinct from substantive unity - these criteria cannot be substantive, either. Accordingly, the examples Raz provides are all content-independent and fall to the formal side: enactment by the Sovereign (Austin); authorisation by the basic norm (Kelsen); and recognisability by the rule of recognition (Hart). As Raz puts it, none of these three philosophers was concerned with substantive unity, nor did they ground unity on the content or spirit of its laws, or on legal traditions and practices. Unlike Kelsen, Raz does not outright condemn the search for substantive unity as suspicious and entailing the risk of succumbing to Natural Law. Still, he clearly does not consider articulating or elaborating substantive unity a task worthy of an analytically oriented positivist legal theorist. Moreover, he accords formal unity a logical or epistemological priority over substantive unity. He argues that an investigation into material unity presupposes a concept of the identity of a legal system, that is, its formal unity.[3]

After excluding law's sociality and sub-surface normative layers, Legal Positivism cannot bring much in the way of order or system to the law. A rather thin conception of formal unity seems to be the only remaining alternative. Kelsen explicitly assigns to the *Grundnorm* the task of creating the order and unity of the legal order. For him, an order is a set of norms the unity of which is constituted by having the same reason for their validity, and that reason is the *Grundnorm*. Raz follows Kelsen in defining (formal) unity by the criterion or criteria determining membership in the legal order or system, as Raz calls it. In Hartian Legal Positivism, the criterion is the rule of recognition.

But does merely bringing a multitude of legal norms together under a common *Grundnorm* or rule of recognition produce such a structure and organisation as the notion of a legal order or legal system implies? Are not further organising principles needed? Here Kelsen could invoke the idea of a legal *Stufenbau*, that is, the hierarchical structure which ensues from the 'dynamic' notion of validity and the principle of authorisation: the norms of a legal order are interconnected through chains of validity and authorisation. Yet that is not all. An additional criterion for unity lies in non-contradictoriness. In some writings, Kelsen includes the requirement for non-contradictoriness in the *Grundnorm*, arguing that the *Grundnorm* must facilitate comprehending a legal order as a meaningful - that is, non-contradictory - whole. The pure principle of authorisation is not able to guarantee this because 'it bestows validity upon any content' and 'justifies any norm, regardless of its content, on condition that it has been created by a certain procedure, even a norm with a self-contradictory content or two norms whose contents are logically incompatible'.[4]

It may appear that, with non-contradictoriness, Kelsen introduces a substantive aspect into his conception of order and unity. Yet Kelsen was careful to discuss non-contradictoriness in terms of logical consistence, instead of substantive coherence. In line with many others interested in deontic logic, Kelsen struggled with the question whether one can speak of logical contradictions between legal norms or merely propositions describing those norms. Even if norms themselves cannot stand in logical contradiction, propositions describing them can, so that the non-contradictoriness of the legal order can be reformulated as the non-contradictoriness of norm propositions. Over his long career, Kelsen kept returning to the subsequent problem of how contradictions could be eliminated from the legal order, expounded as a meaningful whole.[5] In some contexts, he put his trust in interpretation. Still, the possibility

[3] Raz, 1979, chapter 5. [4] See, e.g., Kelsen, 1957, 403. [5] Hartney, 1991.

remained that contradictions cannot be effaced through interpretation. Then - Kelsen argued - a contradiction that involves norms of the same hierarchical level should be resolved by means of the precept *lex posterior derogat legi priori*, which in his view is implicit in the principle of authorisation. In the case of a contradiction between norms of different levels, the Kelsenian solution is evident: the higher norm prevails over the lower. Higher norms not only validate but also invalidate.

Kelsen's analysis has three weaknesses. First, it is doubtful whether all relevant contradictions in law can be compressed into logical inconsistences. Laws, enacted at different times and under different political majorities, may pursue contrary policy objectives and, if effectuated, annul each other's social (perlocutionary) effects, even in the absence of any logical contradiction between individual norms. Secondly, it is also doubtful whether the age-old canons of legal methodology aiming at eliminating logical contradictions can be applied without recourse to substantive arguments. In addition to *lex superior* and *lex posteriori* a third precept belongs to the established methodological toolkit: *lex specialis derogat legi generali*. When *lex superior* does not apply, both *lex posterior* and *lex specialis* may be prima facie applicable. Which precept should be given precedence cannot obviously be decided without recourse to substantive reasoning. Thirdly, even when discussing non-contradictoriness, Kelsen assumes that all norms of a legal order are of legislative origin and can be arranged in a hierarchical *Stufenbau*. Yet this is not the case.

Even if the supplementary criterion of non-contradictoriness could be successfully employed, the order which the *Grundnorm* can supply is rather weak and confined to hierarchical structuring. It produces a monistic unity which ignores the substantive divisions – starting from public and private law – which for precedent German *Rechtswissenschaft* had been an essential phase in the systematisation of the legal order. The only division Kelsen discusses at length is that between international and national law. However, this is not a division internal to a legal order but distinguishes between two legal orders, although, as we shall see in Part III, Kelsen throws a monistic veil over this division too. For Kelsen, law's division into distinct branches was the first step on the road to the static, substantive, systematisation typical of Natural Law. Neither do his conceptual reformulations of, say, 'sanction', 'delict', 'obligation', 'right', 'legal capacity', 'competence' or 'legal subject' serve systematising purposes. Faithful to his purifying mission, he tries to demonstrate that these concepts express particular non-substantive legal normativity, cleansed of any references to morals or social facts. They are meant to be formal concepts, devoid of substantive normative contents and lacking such interconnections as would make them a unifying conceptual skeleton.

The characteristic reductions of Legal Positivism lead to a dominance of formal criteria and an impoverished account of order and unity; an account where law has lost its social and cultural embedding and cut ties to its history.

Both synchronic and diachronic unity are emptied of normative content, while historicity is drained into a combination of unconstrained voluntarism and hollow continuity. In the Kelsenian framework, a legal order as the multitude of legal norms gathered together under a common *Grundnorm* remains a loose whole, lacking internal organisation beyond the hierarchical structure of the legal *Stufenbau*. And, as we shall see in Part III, even such thin formal unity is threatened by the effects of post-national plurality.

Leaving these effects aside for the moment, we can lend some credence to Raz' argument that the formal unity provided by a Master Rule can help in identifying national legal orders at the surface level of law and guarantee their autonomy vis-à-vis other legal orders and non-legal normativity. However, even here some scepticism is necessary. In Continental Europe, too, courts and scholars have always used legal sources which simply cannot be organised in a hierarchical *Stufenbau*. Not only do the Master Rules neglect and prove unable to grasp the sub-surface, legal-cultural, substance of law. They also tend to exclude important, non-legislative sources of surface-level law. The idea of a Master Rule, especially the Kelsenian one, reflects a public lawyer's view of law: hierarchically arranged legal norms are explicitly posited by state organs which also constitute a hierarchically structured, unified organisation: the state in organisational or institutional guise. It can be doubted whether formal order can really fulfil law's internal need of certainty and stability. Neither does it respond to the call for order which arises from the requirements of the rule of law and formal justice, as well as the justifiability of individual legal decisions. This a call for substantive coherence, not merely for formal unity under a Master Rule, complemented by logical consistence. Finally: no sensible legal education can be grounded in and organised in accordance with the formal order provided by a Master Rule.

Local or Comprehensive?

For pre-Kelsenian German *Rechtswissenschaft*, the divisions of law played an important systematising role. The basic division into public and private law dated from Roman law, as did the compartments of private law. By contrast, fields of public law, such as constitutional and administrative law, were of more recent date. The divisions delineated not only fields of law but also corresponding disciplines of *Rechtswissenschaft*. Fields of law received their substantive unity and identity through their general doctrines (*Allgemeine Lehren)*, consisting of legal concepts, principles, theories, and methodologies articulated by the respective discipline of *Rechtswissenschaft*. Taken together, divisions of law and the substantive unity of each field of law were supposed to guarantee the overall order of the law; a coherence transcending mere logical non-contradictoriness. In Anglo-Saxon legal cultures, divisions of law have probably never been of such a constitutive significance as in Continental Europe. They have, though, especially in the USA, played a certain role, as is proved by, say, the ingrained distinction between property, contract, and tort, as well as the sporadically reviving classification debates.

Pace Kelsen's criticism, traditional systematisation through divisions of law has proved long-lived. On the Continent it has dominated not only textbooks and books of statutes, but organisation of law faculties and law teaching as well. Yet it had already run into difficulties in the first decades of the twentieth century, due to increasing regulation and social engineering through law, reaching out to domains previously preserved for private law, as well as subsequent welfare-state policies; that is, developments which manifested the growing instrumentalisation of state law, its use as medium. Systematisers have responded by rather artificial additions. In German debates, new compartments have included special private law and special administrative law, the former comprising, for instance, labour law, economic law, competition law, and environment law, and the latter, say, tax law or financial law. As our discussion in Part III will show, growth of non-state law and its intertwinement with state law have dealt an even more serious blow to traditional systematisation.

Yet post-national plurality has not quelled interest in the classification of law: dividing surface-level law into distinct fields and elaborating field-specific general doctrines is discussed as eagerly as ever. Indeed, we are witnessing a revival of classification debates. However, their focus has shifted, so that nineteenth-century discussants – or even those of, say, the first post–World War II decades – would have a hard time in orienting themselves in present debates on putative legal departments such as social law, medical and bio-law, sports law, information law, or communication law. Recent interventions are no longer concerned with comprehensive systematisation of the national legal order. Some decades ago, when labour law waged its battle for independence, it was, at least in Continental Europe, still considered important to ponder its location in respect of the basic distinction between private and public law. Contemporary discussants do not seem keen to insert the new fields and disciplines they are advocating in a comprehensive system. The aim is more modest: to create local coherence in a limited body of law. The local coherence sought in contemporary debates may even contradict the aspiration for comprehensive coherence. The putative new branches of law typically gather together norms which, within traditional divisions, would fall into several compartments; they even transcend the basic boundary between public and private law. This was already the case with labour law and environmental law, which were among the first new fields to shake up the traditional system and to bring their battles for independence to a successful conclusion. Distinct branches of law are no longer expected to add up to a single and unified, self-contained legal order. Divisions of law are not static but in constant movement. They are not exclusive but overlap, so that a set of norms can be examined as belonging to more than one branch of law: for instance, provisions on patient insurance fall under both tort and medical law. The divisions are openly perspectival: they admit that other classifications are both conceivable and justifiable, for other purposes and adopting another perspective.

Kelsen was right in his observation that efforts to create order and unity through systematisation by means of law's divisions involve substantive criteria. The divisions question Legal Positivism's foundational delineations: the separation of legal normativity from social facticity and non-legal normativity. Diverse fields of law are demarcated primarily through the social practices and relations they address; in this respect they problematise the strict demarcation of the legal Ought from the social Is. They obtain their unity and identity through general doctrines, largely elaborated and articulated – at least on the European Continent – by legal scholars. An integral part of these doctrines consists of field-specific principles with obvious links to morals – *nulla poena sine lege* in criminal law, *pacta sunt servanda* in contract law, proportionality in constitutional law, or *détournement de pouvoir* principles in administrative law. In turn, legal concepts and theories of legal institutions imply a particular view of the social practices and relations addressed by the field of law: a hidden social theory, as it were. All this invokes substantive criteria, as Kelsen noted. Where he erred was to claim that establishing order and unity on substantive criteria would necessarily entail embracing Natural-Law premises.

Systematisation through divisions of law is still a pertinent objective, not only for pedagogical purposes, but also for doctrinal construction and rationalising of legal argument. Yet, the unity and coherence that contemporary systematisation can bring about is local rather than comprehensive and openly perspectival rather than valid for all purposes. Whatever unity, transcending the thin formal unity of Legal Positivism, there can be in the normative dimension of law can only be of a substantive character, deriving from unifying principles as well as common concepts, theories, and methodologies, which also possess normative implications. The supports of order and unity lie in the cultural, sub-surface, layers of law which positivist theorists in their voluntarist normativism tend to overlook. The surface level of law is the domain mainly of policies, and policies are shifting, a source of contradictions rather than coherence.

Both/And

I have discussed the order and unity of the normative legal order through three binary options: diachronic or synchronic; formal or substantive; and local or comprehensive. As is so often the case with binary distinctions of law, these options should not be conceived of mutually exclusively but, rather, complementarily; adopting a logic of both/and rather than either/or. Thus, both synchronic and diachronic coherence are needed. The coherence which legal practices try to achieve and maintain is primarily of a synchronic nature; coherence of the momentary legal order. Yet synchronic coherence is only possible due to the principles sedimented into the sub-surface layers of law, and manifesting continuity, tradition, and diachronic coherence. Such synchronic coherence is substantive rather than formal, created as it is by subsurface legal culture, which brings order to the disorder of policy-dominated surface-level law. However, formal order, emphasised by legal positivists, should not be neglected, either. The hierarchical model possesses its own field of application in law produced by legislative speech acts, and the importance of eliminating logical contradictions from the law should not be ignored. Yet it is also important to note that logical inconsistence does not exhaust possible contradictions; that the age-old canons supposed to eradicate logical contradictions do not function in isolation from substantive legal argumentation; that not all applicable law can be arranged in a hierarchical *Stufenbau*; and, finally, that the thin formal order that a Master Rule can offer does not respond to law's internal call for coherence.

The coherence which can be produced by the divisions of law and field-specific doctrinal construction is local rather than comprehensive, confined to the field at issue and not even aiming to cover the whole (national) legal order. Yet the existence of a legal deep culture testifies to the lingering relevance of an even more comprehensive coherence, crossing the boundaries of fields of law and even those of legal orders. Such greater comprehensive coherence can be created by principles related to fundamental and human rights, as well as the legal concepts and methods which constitute the vocabulary and grammar of legal language.

9

Morality of Law

Separability Thesis

Legal Positivism discusses the autonomy of law in three directions: in respect of social and psychological facts; non-legal normativity, particularly morals; and other normative legal orders. In Kelsen's Pure Theory, all three aspects are explicitly present. In the Hartian camp, the main emphasis is on the relationship between law and morals; especially on what has come to be called the separability thesis, which has sometimes been elevated to the core idea of Legal Positivism. Hartians have never been equally strict about the distinction between law and society; the Kelsenian dichotomy of Is and Ought has even been explicitly disclaimed. In the preface to *The Concept of Law*, Hart famously characterised his project as an exercise in descriptive sociology and, in the same vein, some contemporary Hartian positivists even declare the social-facts or social-sources thesis, instead of separability, the central tenet of Legal Positivism. The same theorists are wont to see an important difference from Dworkin in the social-facts thesis. Yet what the social-facts thesis actually boils down to is the claim of the rule of recognition as a social rule or a convention: legal validity ultimately depends on and is defined by a social rule; hence, the edifice of law rests on social facts. The way Hartians specify the rule of recognition and, for instance, demarcate legal validity from efficacy is remarkably similar to Kelsen's treatment of the *Grundnorm*. In line with the *Grundnorm*, the rule of recognition, although itself breaking the separation of Is and Ought, produces autonomy in all three dimensions: in respect not only of morals and other legal orders but also of society and social facts. And because legal positivists derive the separability thesis from the rule of recognition as a social rule, the difference between the separability and social-facts theses as characterisations of the core of Legal Positivism vanishes.

For Kelsen, the separation of law and morals was an evident consequence of the main premise of his Pure Theory – the *Grundnorm* – and did not require much further discussion. The separation of law and morals followed from each of these norm orders being subordinated to its *Grundnorm*; law to a dynamic and morals to a static one. Law and morals provided two diverse perspectives on the world of Is; two alternative and mutually exclusive frameworks for normative assessment. For Hart and the Hartians, the matter has not been equally straightforward but has spawned an apparently never-ending internal debate and school-formation. At the end of the day, the Hartian discussion of the separation of law and morals, just like the Kelsenian one, returns to the role and character of the Master Rule.

Kelsen's *Grundnorm* is substantively empty: it only involves the order to behave in accordance with the historically first constitution, whatever the contents of that constitution might be or whatever authorised its issuance. If the dichotomy of duty-imposing and power-conferring rules is in general applicable to the Master Rule, the *Grundnorm* is both duty-imposing and power-conferring. It is supposed to establish both legal normativity and validity. At least in one context, Kelsen played with an interpretation of the *Grundnorm* in terms of the requirement for justice but in the end concluded that the seeming similarities between the *Grundnorm* and justice were purely formal. In turn, substantive overlaps between legal and moral norms are in Kelsen's view purely accidental and have no impact whatsoever on the validity of the former – or, for that matter, of the latter, either.[1]

Yet, in spite of Kelsen's explicit pronouncements on the strict separation of law and morals, attempts have not been lacking to prove that Kelsen was in fact a crypto-natural lawyer; a natural lawyer against his own knowledge. Some of these attempts can be traced back to the rival positivist - Hartian - school. Perhaps the crudest argument derives from the connection between the separability and the social-facts theses: because the former derives from the latter, which Kelsen does not accept, and because the only alternative to Legal Positivism is Natural Law, Kelsen must be a natural lawyer![2] More sophisticated, although ultimately rather similar, is the argument put forth by Raz.

Raz examines Kelsen's position in the framework of the alternatives of justified and social normativity. Those embracing the former alternative require of legal normativity that norms be justified, either by objective and universally valid reasons, or through personal commitment or intuitive perception of their bindingness. For those espousing the social view, law is normative because of certain social facts and not because it is just. Raz contends that, for Kelsen, law's normativity is justified normativity, and as the *Grundnorm* is supposed to be the reason for legal normativity, it must be a justified norm. Kelsen was a moral relativist and therefore the *Grundnorm* cannot be just in an absolute or objective sense but only for subjective reasons. Raz invokes the passages where Kelsen stresses that assuming the *Grundnorm* is a matter of choice, which an anarchist or a communist may refuse to make. Raz jumps to the conclusion that, in Kelsen's view, only those who consider the *Grundnorm* just presuppose and accept it, and regard the law as normative.[3] Yet this is not Kelsen's view, nor does the non-necessity of presupposing

[1] Kelsen, 1957, 438. [2] Gardner, 2012, 7ff. [3] Raz, 1979, 134–145.

the basic norm imply it. For Kelsen, the choice of the legal order as a scheme of interpretation was not a moral but a cognitive choice, and the *Grundnorm* was not a moral but an epistemological presupposition.

If Raz' reading of the *Grundnorm* and the normativity it establishes were correct, Kelsen's strict separation between law and morals would collapse at the very heart of the Pure Theory. Raz' discussion takes a wrong direction even in the setting of the scene. Raz treats social and justified normativity as the only available alternatives and defines the latter in moral terms, as related to justice. Yet Kelsen's constitutive demarcations of Ought from Is and the legal from the moral Ought led him to reject both of these alternatives, and opt for 'pure' or formal legal normativity, beyond and independent from not only social facts but even moral norms, whether objective or subjective. It was this kind of purity, the need to keep legal normativity distinct from both social facts and morals, which made the *Grundnorm* a necessary presupposition not only for legal cognition but for legal normativity in general. Another issue is whether Kelsen's argument is convincing; whether he succeeds in showing the possibility of a legal normativity untainted by social facts or moral norms or commitments.

The Hartian separability thesis has taken many guises, but its primary focus has remained the same: the validity criteria of law. Thus specified, it includes two sub-theses: first, the validity of law does not necessarily require conformity with morals and, secondly, a moral principle does not possess legal validity simply *qua* moral principle.

For Hart, the rule of recognition is a social rule, born out of the congruent practice of legal officials, mainly judges. The social-facts thesis holds for the rule of recognition but not necessarily for the criteria by which the rule of recognition defines the scope of valid legal rules. The criteria can imply not only such social facts as legislative and judicial speech acts but moral yardsticks as well.[4] Because these are not necessarily but only contingently involved in the validity criteria of legal rules, the separability thesis is not shaken. While Hart leaves the door ajar for moral criteria of validity, his is not a 'pure' pedigree doctrine as Dworkin termed the social-sources view.

The concession that Hart made to Dworkin lies at the origin of the division of Hartians in soft and hard or inclusive and exclusive positivists. While the labels of the opposing camps vary, the contents of their views remain by and large the same. In line with Hart's final standpoint, the soft, inclusive, positivists argue that the rule of recognition can, but need not, involve moral precepts. By contrast, hard, exclusive, positivists claim that the rule of recognition would forsake its point if moral criteria were included. Alongside the division into soft or inclusive and hard or exclusive positivists runs another one: into incorporationists and non-incorporationists. The

[4] Hart, 2012, 269.

former would allow for applying moral principles as law-application, the latter not. Though much has been made of the differences in internal debates, the opposing camps agree on certain fundamental but controversial issues. There is a common understanding that the separability thesis concerns legal validity and boils down to the two claims of the non-necessity of moral yardsticks of validity and lack of legal validity of moral principles *qua* moral principles. These claims draw the boundary to Natural Law; no third way is open between positivism and Natural Law. Although some Hartian positivists would have expelled Kelsen to the Natural-Law camp, he would have subscribed to the claims in their hard, exclusive, and non-incorporationist version: reasons or criteria for legal validity can only be of a legal but never of a moral nature, and the principles of law can only be legal but not moral principles. An agreement among the fractions of Hartian positivism also exists on the rule of recognition as the arbiter of the correctness of the separability thesis. A lively, although sometimes rather tribal, debate has been waged on the exact nature and implications of this Master Rule, but the criterial premise and the authority of the rule of recognition has remained sacrosanct. Agreement also covers depiction of the rule of recognition as a social rule.

Thus, for both Kelsenian and Hartian positivism, it is ultimately the Master Rule that supports the separation of law and morals. Before elaborating my view of legal validity and legal principles, the time has come for a comprehensive assessment of this core legal positivist tenet. Let us start with the tasks the Master Rule is supposed to accomplish.

The basic functions are epistemological and validating, while the other tasks, such as creating unity, order, identity, and autonomy, are in a way by-products. The two basic functions are closely intertwined. In their argument, both Kelsen and Hart start with the epistemological function and only as a second step introduce the validating one. As we have already learned, Kelsen treats the assumption of the *Grundnorm* as a transcendental-logical presupposition for all legal cognition, analogous to Kantian categories as presuppositions for natural science. In all legal cognition, the *Grundnorm* is tacitly assumed, just as, according to Kant, in all natural science the transcendental categories, such as those of time and space, are assumed. It does make sense to argue that legal cognition and legal practices in general rest on certain presuppositions which – and this is my addition – function through legal *Vorverständnis*. Kelsen's problem consists in reducing these presuppositions to a doctrine of legal sources and in presenting the doctrine in universal, a-historical, terms, which include the hierarchical view of the normative legal order. Even more important for my present discussion is that the reach of the Kantian analogy comes to an end when Kelsen attaches a validating function to the epistemological one. As the ultimate source of legal validity, the *Grundnorm* is entrusted with the heavy burden of founding legal normativity.

The epistemological function can rely on the Kantian analogy but the validating function cannot. The *Grundnorm* is supposed to accomplish a foundational task in both the epistemological and normative sense: to create the possibility not only of legal cognition but also of legal normativity as such. When historicised, Kant-inspired epistemology can warrant tacit presuppositions of legal cognition too. What Kant-inspired epistemology cannot vindicate is the thesis that the whole edifice of legal normativity rests on the transcendental presupposition of a substantively empty *Grundnorm*.

Hart, too, introduces the rule of recognition as a solution to an epistemological problem but, in line with Kelsen, glides almost unnoticeably into attributing even a validating function to his Master Rule. The epistemological problem is uncertainty about the rules of behaviour that members of a community are expected to respect. The rule of recognition specifies some feature or features by which the rules supported by the social pressure of the community are identified. Hart is more conscious than Kelsen of the variety of legal sources, although tends to reduce these to legislation, custom, and judicial precedents. When discussing a developed legal system, Hart sometimes speaks of rules of recognition in the plural – wavering between the singular and the plural labels Hart's discussion in general – and points to their complexity. He seems to imply that in contemporary England separate rules of recognition exist for legislative, customary, and judicial law, in addition to which 'provision may be made for their possible conflict by their arrangement in an order of superiority, as by the common subordination of custom or precedent to statute, the latter being a "superior source" of law'. Hart argues that not only officials but even private persons and their counsellors use the rule of recognition for purposes of identification. In this point we confront a recurring problem in portrayals of the rule of recognition; a problem which is further aggravated by the acquiescent standpoint of soft positivism vis-à-vis moral principles. The more complex the rule of recognition is made, the less credible becomes the epistemological or identifying function, responding to the problem of uncertainty. Legal laymen may be aware of the supreme position of legislation but not of the complicated relations among different sources of law, keeping track of which can be hard even for legal professionals. It is only consequent that the clear emphasis in Hart and his disciples' subsequent treatment of the rule of recognition lies in the social practice of the officials of law.

How does the validating function enter the discussion? Hart presents validity as an issue of linguistic analysis. He argues that what is meant by saying that a rule is valid is that the rule has passed all the tests included in the rule of recognition. Usually at issue are internal statements, made from the internal point of view and applying an unstated but accepted rule of recognition. Hart calls the ultimate rule of recognition the rule which provides the supreme criteria of validity of other rules of the system. Hart explains the need to arrive at an ultimate rule of recognition in a rather similar way to Kelsen, by following a hierarchical chain of validity, conceived of as authorisation. The starting point is a by-law of Oxfordshire County council and the endpoint the rule of recognition, which states that what the Queen in Parliament enacts is law.[5]

On its face, Hart's is a very Kelsenian argument, the only difference being that, on the top of the hierarchical edifice of legal norms, Hart refuses to take the leap to the transcendental – and, by the same token – hypothetical *Grundnorm*. Unlike Kelsen, Hart is not committed to Kantian epistemology, by which Kelsen warrants his *Grundnorm*, or to the strict (neo)Kantian separation of Is and Ought, which makes it impossible for Kelsen to stop the validity regress with a social rule, as does Hart. Still, exactly like Kelsen, Hart slides from the epistemological – in Hart's case identifying – function to the validating one. In introducing the hierarchical staircase of legal validity, Hart not only refers to criteria by which valid norms can be identified but also, again exactly like Kelsen, treats these criteria as reasons or grounds for validity. And if with Hart's rule of recognition validity is taken to imply bindingness and obligation, exactly as with Kelsen's *Grundnorm*, we are dealing with the foundation of legal normativity. In the context of the *Grundnorm*, the question arises how a mere epistemological presupposition can have such fateful consequences as establishing legal normativity. In the context of the rule of recognition, the question is how legal normativity can be founded on a social rule which has emerged from social practice among officials of law to facilitate identifying legal norms and thus to respond to the issue of uncertainty. Hartians may retort that at issue is not only a social rule but a social rule accepted by officials from an internal viewpoint. If they do, they hasten to add that acceptance may rest on diverse reasons but not necessarily moral ones. Thus, legitimacy in the sense of moral approval is not necessarily involved; the separability thesis applies here too.

Let us assume that acceptance by judges, even if not necessarily on moral grounds, of a social rule born out of their social practice could explain vis-à-vis judges themselves the normativity of this rule, and, indirectly, the binding and obligatory nature of the whole edifice of law drawing its validity from this rule. Yet, at the end of the day, legal norms, other than secondary ones, address the behaviour of ordinary citizens. It is hardly credible that legal normativity vis-à-vis ordinary citizens could rest on such a narrow and precarious basis as morally non-committed acceptance by judges of a social rule of recognition.

Somewhat surprisingly, Hart restricts his discussion of legal validity to legislative law which can be arranged in a hierarchical *Stufenbau*. Hart or his disciples do not discuss the validating aspect of the rules of recognition which they assume to exist for non-legislative sources of law, such as customs

[5] Hart, 1961, 100–109.

(customary law), precedents (judicial law) or – as is allowed for by soft positivists – principles. Yet we can assume that rules of recognition are supposed to accomplish the same dual epistemological and validating function for non-legislative as legislative law. If so, the above questions repeat themselves: how can a morally neutral commitment to a social rule extracted from a practice among judges legally validate rules deriving from the sources this rule indicates, vis-à-vis either officials or ordinary citizens?

In previous sections of this essay, I have focused on the epistemological or identifying function and proposed treating the Master Rules as doctrines of legal sources, internalised in the *Vorverständnis* of legal professionals. I have in particular criticised Kelsen's version of this doctrine for its a-historicity and the unfounded premise that the normative legal order always adheres to the hierarchical template. I have also argued that, in their epistemological function, the Master Rules have difficulty in including non-legislative law and in heeding relations among legal sources of diverse kinds. Finally, I have pointed out that whatever success the Master Rules may have in identifying and demarcating modern state law, that success is constrained to surface-level law. When confronted with the sub-surface, legal-cultural layers, the Master Rules inevitably fail even in their identifying task. Now we are able to add a new item to the list of failures of the Master Rules: the unjustified transition from the epistemological to the validating function, as if successful accomplishment of the former could explain and vindicate the latter.

The problems the Master Rules confront in their epistemological and validating tasks also affect the order, unity, identity, and autonomy they can produce. Here failure can facilitate a new start: acknowledging the multi-layered nature of law and bringing in the sub-surface, legal-cultural layers can point to new ways of understanding and establishing order, unity, and identity. For the alleged autonomy of law the problems are more critical. If the Master Rule is capable neither of circumscribing reliably the scope of law nor of accounting for the foundation of legal validity and normativity, the justification which it was claimed to offer for the separability thesis collapses.

Validity

When discussing the sociality of law in Part I, I proposed examining validity in the framework of speech act theory. This proposal has several important consequences. I want to make seven points.

Firstly, the discussion extends from formal legal speech acts, such as laws and judicial decisions, to all speech acts contributing to legal discourse and recognised by the prevailing doctrine of legal sources; such as *travaux préparatoires*, and interpretation standpoints and systematisation proposals by legal scholars. Yet laws and judicial decisions hold a special position. This is due to their binding force, buttressed by coercive sanctions, and their capacity to engender, together with legal-institutional facts, rights and duties, characteristic of the interplay of legal normativity and sociality.

Secondly, speech act theory shifts the emphasis from validity as a quality of legal norms to validity claims raised by legal speech acts. 'Validity' denotes the precarious situation where the validity claims of a legal speech act are accepted by the relevant audience. This audience consists of participants in the legal discourse where the claims are assessed and which determines the contents of the momentary legal order.

Thirdly, the shift of emphasis implies that validity is a quality that can be lost; it is not obtained once and for all but only for the time being. Validity and validity claims display three dimensions: formal, empirical, and substantive. The formal dimension is relevant only for formal, that is, legislative or judicial, legal speech acts and the empirical one, equivalent to efficacy, merely for laws. Formal validity is measured by the compliance of formal legal speech acts with constitutional and procedural norms determining legislative and judicial competences and procedures. Reflecting the pertinence of the empirical dimension, laws can be deprived of validity through *desuetudo*; that is, non-compliance by social actors or non-application by judges. The validity of scholarly standpoints and *travaux préparatoires* is appraised merely in the substantive dimension. What is important for a discussion of the morality of law is that the substantive aspect remains relevant for formal legal speech acts too; including those that meet the other criteria for validity.

Fourthly, speech act theory highlights the relational and perspectival character of validity. When discussing validity, a specification is needed: validity in respect of which addressees? Validity claims are always directed to a particular audience, and legal speech acts obtain validity when the audience accepts the claims. Legal validity claims are primarily addressed to legal professionals, so that validity depends on their acceptance. Among legal professionals – the legal community in *sensu stretto* – sub-audiences can be discerned, such as judges, scholars, and legislative experts, and acceptance by one of the sub-audiences can be more consequential than acceptance by the others. Evidently, the crucial sub-audience consists of judges. In what I call the typical validity situation, a judge weighs the validity of a legislative speech act. Acceptance of validity claims need not be – and usually is not – explicit but can be manifest simply by references to the speech act in future legal discourse – in subsequent legislation and *travaux préparatoires*, court decisions, and scholarly interventions. Yet sometimes validity claims, in particular substantive ones, are put into debate.

Confining the discussion on validity claims to legal discourse among legal professionals as the main actors of legal practices does not imply that legal speech acts would not be addressed to other audiences too. Of course they are. Laws are intended to make a difference in society at large and not merely, or even primarily, in specialised legal practices and legal discourse among law professionals. The primary audience of legislative speech acts remains the legal community in *sensu largo*. In turn, the primary addressees of court decisions are the parties, as well as the executive authorities. Sometimes, though - especially when fundamental principles are involved - judicial speech acts turn to the legal community, and not only in *sensu stretto* but in *sensu largo* as well. Laws and judicial rulings intervening in general debates in the public sphere claim correctness before the public at large too. Yet I propose discussing these claims in terms of legitimacy rather than validity.

Fifthly, adoption of the framework of speech act theory intimates that validity is an issue of surface-level law; that is, of distinct legal speech acts and norms as their meanings. In this framework, it makes sense to speak of the validity of principles only insofar as they are explicitly enshrined in legal texts and manifest as surface-level norms. General legal principles, sedimented from surface-level speech acts into sub-surface legal culture, form part of the law, along with the conceptual and methodological elements of legal culture. Yet their belonging to the law should not be discussed under the concept of validity but, rather, that of relevance. In my conceptual scheme, law raises claims to normative correctness. These comprise, first, claims to validity by individual legal speech before the legal community in *sensu stretto*; secondly, claims to relevance by general legal principles and other elements of legal culture; and, finally, claims to legitimacy directed to the legal community in *sensu largo*.

Sixthly, validity is a quality of individual legal speech acts and norms enshrined in them. My conceptual framework does not enable speaking of the validity of the legal order as a whole. We may ask questions of the foundation of legal validity and normativity, as did the Masters of Legal Positivism. I concur with the Masters, who both argued that legal validity and normativity rest on a non-legal foundation. Where I do not agree is the claim that this foundation would consist of a transcendental epistemological presupposition or a social rule emerging from social practice among judges.

Seventhly, acceptance of validity claims has consequences. Instead of validity, Austin and Searle speak of successful speech acts which obtain their intended illocutionary force. Like validity, illocutionary force is perspectival; illocutionary force is not universal but confined to the relevant addressees. Moreover, when speech acts have multiple audiences, the implications of the illocutionary force of one and the same speech act may vary. I have suggested equating the illocutionary force of formal legal speech acts – that is, laws and court decisions – with their formal validity. Typically, judges feel obligated to apply formally valid laws and the reasoning of formally valid precedents. Only exceptionally can loss of empirical or substantive validity lead to loss of the illocutionary force of formally valid laws. Laws claim normative correctness and aspire to illocutionary force among the legal community in *sensu largo* too. In a democratic *Rechtsstaat*, compliance with legislative competences and procedures usually suffices to secure laws' illocutionary force among the wider audience too. Yet this is not always the case, at least not for all members of the legal community. Concerns about legitimacy may arise and interrupt the quasi-automatic adherence typical of law's realisation in first-order sociolegal practices.

For discussion of the separability thesis, substantive validity is the crucial dimension. This is also the dimension shared by all types of legal speech act – laws, court decisions, *travaux préparatoires*, and scholarly contributions. Yet the substantive validity claims of diverse legal speech acts are not identical but vary in accordance with the point of the legal practice at issue. Again, with regard to the separability thesis, legislative speech acts are the most important.

Let me analyse the claim to substantive validity in the light of the Kantian triad of practical reasoning: pragmatic (instrumental), moral, and ethical. Pragmatic reasoning is about goals and means: goals of public policy and the means – the programmes – conducive to their realisation. Concisely put, pragmatic reasoning focuses on policies. Ethical reasoning pursues reflexive clarification of the strong values at the core of personal and collective identities. Ethical questions are questions about the determinants of a good life, and strong values are answers to those questions. Except for value proclamations typical of the preambles to and opening chapters of constitutions, modern state law mainly promotes instrumental or moral reason. Law formulates and implements policies or provides solutions to intersubjective conflicts of action, which constitute the province of morality. Only rarely does subconstitutional law directly address issues of a primarily ethical nature, that is, confer legal force on strong values. Consequently, substantive validity claims are primarily of either a pragmatic (instrumental) or a moral nature. In the ever-widening use of law as medium, the pragmatic dimension prevails. The success of legislation is measured in terms of social engineering, its ability to contribute to solving social problems and achieving social goals.

However, in spite of the dominance of pragmatic reasoning, ethical and moral aspects are also implicitly involved in the claims to correctness of policy-oriented legislation. The goals pursued by legislation are ultimately based on particular values, although these are not always spelled out even in *travaux préparatoires*. In turn, involvement of the moral aspect can be warranted by Robert Alexy's argument. Alexy's point is that if the legislator or a judge attached an explicit claim to unjustness to their speech acts, they would be guilty of a performative contradiction; if, for instance, in the preamble to a statute, the Finnish Parliament stated that 'we hereby issue the following unjust statute' or the district court of Helsinki declared in a decision that 'the Court hereby unjustly sentences Mr. Virtanen to prison for two years'. In a performative contradiction the propositional content of a speech act contradicts its claim to correctness. Alexy argues that we instinctively realise that something is wrong with speech acts such as the above examples; that this 'wrong' can be categorised as a performative contradiction; and that this shows that formal legal speech acts raise a claim to justice.[6]

I buy Alexy's argument but only half way. On the face of it, most contemporary laws are morally – and ethically – more or less indifferent, and their substantive claims to correctness are primarily of a pragmatic nature. I agree with Alexy on the argument from performative contradiction but would formulate the conclusion differently: legal speech acts do not always claim to be just but they always do claim not to be unjust. I would also formulate the negative claim more broadly: policy-oriented legislation claims not to contradict legally relevant moral principles or ethical values. Thus, not only principle- but also policy-oriented legislation can be submitted to principle- and value-oriented assessment.

In the judicial practices of a democratic *Rechtsstaat*, the validity of prima facie applicable norms is but exceptionally made into an issue. The assumption is, first, that the norms meet the criteria of formal validity and, secondly, that they also pass the negative test of substantive validity. What is important to note is that formal validity entails a presumption of substantive validity too. Constitutional provisions on legislative competences and procedures together with political fundamental rights reflect democratic principles which are supposed to guarantee that, in legislation, not only pragmatic but even moral and ethical aspects are duly attended to.

Yet it may occur that addressees of legislative speech acts question the presumption of substantive correctness. The pragmatic dimension need not occupy us here; in the typical validity situation where a judge thematises the validity of a prima facie applicable legislative norm, relevance is granted merely to the moral and ethical dimensions. The norm may stand in such a contradiction with moral or ethical validity criteria – say, human rights principles – that it loses its illocutionary force before the judge. Rights-based constitutional review, as it were, institutionalises substantive validity control and assigns it an immediate legal bearing, which may include declaring the law null and void.

The threat that constitutional rights and constitutional review pose to the separability thesis has not escaped legal positivists. Kelsen was critical of judicial fundamental-rights review of legislation. He was concerned about the intrusion of natural into positive law and the elevation of a constitutional court to a third legislative chamber.[7] Hartian inclusive positivists are more tolerant. They allow for including morally related criteria in the rule of recognition through explicit constitutional provisions, such as the US Bill of Rights or the Canadian Charter. Still, they insist that these examples do not testify to a necessary or conceptual connection between law and morality; the link is contingent, based on a discretionary choice of the constitutional

[6] Alexy, 2002. [7] Kelsen, 1929.

legislator. Because of the near ubiquity of national, transnational, and international rights-based review, the borderline between what is contingent and what Hartian theorists call necessary or conceptual is increasingly blurred. Furthermore, it is possible that even in the absence of a formalised procedure of judicial constitutional review, a court finds a legislative act falling so short of substantive validity that it denies the act illocutionary force. The post–World War II examples that illustrate the 'Radbruch formula' cannot just be explained away as mistakes committed by the German courts. Even in England, 'general principles of common law' provide ample opportunities for camouflaging employment of substantive criteria of validity in the absence of a constitutional Bill of Rights. Finally, validity assessment and interpretation may come close to each other. It may be a matter of preference whether a judge formulates the conclusion as a denial of the illocutionary force of a legislative norm because of its contradiction with a constitutional right or as an interpretation of the norm text in conformity with such right.

In sum, substantive criteria are not usually explicitly employed in judicial validity assessment, and legislative speech acts obtain illocutionary force due to their meeting the criteria for formal validity. To this extent, legal positivists with their source-based, pedigree, criteria of validity are right. Yet cases occur where substantive criteria stand in the foreground, most conspicuously in rights-based constitutional review in a constitutional court or a corresponding body of constitutional jurisdiction. However, such cases may crop up even in jurisdictions with no specialised practice of ex post constitutional review or even no constitutional Bill of Rights. Then, the yardsticks of substantial validity are drawn from sub-surface legal principles, relying on other kinds of surface-level support than explicit constitutional provisions.

Not only legislative but other legal speech acts, too, come with particular substantive validity claims. Neither the formal nor the substantive validity criteria of judicial speech acts are identical to those of legislation. In line with legislative speech acts, formal criteria, enshrined in constitutional and procedural law, aim to facilitate substantive validity, for example through giving the word to all relevant interests and securing attention to all relevant facts. Specification of the substantive criteria would require a separate discussion. Let me just point to requirements such as attending to all interests involved; heeding all prima facie applicable norms; employing the methodological precepts of prevailing legal culture; and accomplishing a balanced weighing of relevant principles. Diverging from legislative speech acts, the pragmatic dimension does not play a predominant role. Judicial speech acts are supposed to apply the law and secure its realisation when primary realisation in first-order sociolegal practices has failed; their point is not related to determining or implementing policies. Instrumentalist reasoning may only enter judicial practices through interpretation of legal texts, and even then only if prevailing interpretative canons permit this. When teleological reasoning is allowed, the ethical aspect is also implicated by the value basis of the goals pursued. By contrast, the moral dimension is relevant for all judicial decisions. Alexy's argument from performative contradiction, warranting a claim not to be unjust, holds for judicial speech acts as well. Yet such a negative claim does not exhaust the significance of justice for judicial speech acts. As Hart noted, these always claim to be just, at least in the minimum sense of respecting the requirement for formal equality to treat like cases alike and unalike cases unalike.[8]

As is the case with legislative speech acts, the substantive validity of court decisions, too, can at any time be (re)made an issue in subsequent legal discourse, without this in any way affecting the illocutionary force that the decisions have attained through their formal validity. Meeting the substantive criteria remains always susceptible to new assessment, and debate can reignite after decades or even centuries. As I have argued above, British and US legal history abounds with illustrious examples of cases the merits of which are subjected to ever-new appraisals: the trials of the wives of Henry VIII, the impeachment of Charles II, *Dred Scott*, *Riggs v Palmer*, or *Lochner*. Reappraisals cannot affect the illocutionary force of court decisions as final settlement of a concrete case after they have acquired *res judicata*. Rulings by appeal courts also aspire to illocutionary force as precedents. That illocutionary force a ruling may well lose as a consequence of questioning of its substantive validity in subsequent legal discourse.

Legitimacy

Validity is an issue for the legal community in *sensu stretto*, to be discussed in the legal discourse among legal professionals. Yet legislative speech acts are also, and even primarily, addressed to ordinary social actors – the legal community in *sensu largo* – and claim normative correctness before them too. In civil society and its public sphere, debates may be waged not only about the expediency of legislation but also about its moral or ethical correctness – in short, its legitimacy. Social actors take a position on legitimacy in situations when the threshold of consciousness is transcended and actors gain awareness of the significance of the law; when complying with the law loses its self-evident, quasi-automatic character; and when compliance or non-compliance becomes an issue of individual or collective deliberation. Civil disobedience implies rejection of the legitimacy of a piece of legislation on moral, and conscientious objection on ethical grounds. Validity and invalidity are qualities of individual legal norms and speech acts. By contrast, the issue of legitimacy, that is, moral and ethical acceptability among the legal community

[8] Hart, 1961, 159.

in *sensu largo*, can be extended to cover the law as a whole. Anarchists reject the legitimacy of law as individuals, revolutionaries as members of a collective.

According to legal positivists, the Master Rule accounts not only for the validity of individual norms but also for the foundation of legal validity and normativity as such. Here Hart's rule of recognition is more convincing than Kelsen's *Grundnorm* as a mere transcendental epistemological presupposition, but still not convincing enough. Hart's point seems to be that ultimately, legal validity and normativity rest on acceptance of the law by officials of the legal regime, yet not necessarily on moral grounds. This calls for two critical remarks. First, it is doubtful whether the legal regime would survive if the majority of officials did not accept it at least partly for reasons of legitimacy; that is, moral and ethical justifiability. Secondly, it is also doubtful whether legal normativity vis-à-vis ordinary social actors – the legal community in *sensu largo* – can ensue from and repose on acceptance by the officials of the regime. In the long run, a legal regime whose legitimacy is not recognised by the citizenry at large is doomed.

The requirement for acceptance connects the present discussion to Searle's depiction of institutions and institutional facts. Searle is aware of the regress issue which has concerned legal positivists from Hobbes to Kelsen and Hart. Searle considers laws as speech acts: standing Declarations. As speech acts, laws are institutional facts, with their constitutive rules enshrined in the constitution, which again is a standing Declaration. But does a standing Declaration itself, such as a constitution, always require a further Declaration to exist? Searle answers bluntly that it does not; if it did, there would be an infinite regress.[9] This is exactly the problem; the very problem which led Kelsen to postulate his *Grundnorm*, and Hart to introduce his rule of recognition.

Naming the problem does not yet amount to resolving it. However, Searle's discussion of institutions and institutional facts as their instances does indicate a solution. Searle argues that institutional facts and institutions comprising the constitutive rules of those facts only exist due to human agreement. Both the emergence and continuing existence of institutional facts, including standing Declarations such as laws and constitutions, depend on recognition and acceptance of those facts and the corresponding institutions by members of the community. Acceptance is not necessarily expressed through explicit speech acts but can be manifest simply by employment of the institution in the creation of new institutional facts: if people continue getting married, they also display their acceptance of the legal institution of marriage. Searle's comparison is illustrative: contrary to shirts and shoes, use of institutions does not wear them out but, on the contrary, strengthens them.[10] Furthermore, acceptance of an institution can be interpreted as entailing acceptance of the

[9] Searle, 2010, 14. [10] Searle, 1995, 57.

institutional facts created under it. If members of a polity accept its constitution, they can be presumed also to accept the presidents elected and the particular laws enacted under the constitutive rules of the constitution.

Acceptance is a social fact and, to be more precise, a brute and not an institutional fact. Though acceptance may be manifest by creation of institutional facts, it does not continue the chain of institutional facts. Neither does it continue the chain or hierarchy of validity which Kelsen and Hart interrupted with their Master Rules. At least in the long run, acceptance presupposes legitimacy. In turn, acceptance produces and is manifest by efficacy; observance of the law in first-order sociolegal practices and its application in judicial practices. Efficacy is equivalent to empirical validity, which laws can lose through *desuetudo*. If that happens, they also lose their illocutionary force. The contention of the link leading from legitimacy to acceptance and from acceptance to efficacy is empirical. If the contention is warranted, we are also justified to conclude that legal validity – and legal normativity in general – rests on acceptance and, through acceptance, on legitimacy. Such a conclusion ignores both the separation of the legal Ought from the social Is and the legal from the moral Ought.

When tracing the grounds for legal validity and normativity, the regress of the hierarchical validity chain stops at the constitution in force. In modern state law, legislation is by far the most important source of law, and social acceptance of the constitution implies – though does not necessarily guarantee – acceptance of not only legislation enacted in accordance with the constitution but the normative legal order as a whole. There may be laws, falling under law as institution, whose acceptance by the legal community at large requires more than just compliance with the constitutional provisions on legislative competences and procedures: substantive harmony with the non-legal normativity imbuing social actors' lifeworld. Acceptance of the law as a whole and acceptance of individual laws are two distinct things. Acceptance of the constitution arguably transfers its legitimating effect on some – in a democratic *Rechtsstaat* probably even the majority – of the laws enacted under the constitution, but not all of them. Diverging from Kelsen's *Grundnorm*, social acceptance is not a postulate but an empirically verifiable claim. So are the grounds for acceptance. I would suppose that moral and ethical reasons are involved but argue here, too, for a negative test: the law presents itself as not being morally or ethically unjustifiable. This is the very title which is rejected by anarchists as individuals and revolutionaries as members of a collective.

Legal Principles

Arguably, we live in an age of principles. After the focus on concepts by conceptualists and their analytical critics, principles dominate scholarly debates. Principles are a central issue in discussing the morality of law too;

here I agree with the Hartian school. In his extreme voluntarism, Kelsen was rather brusque with principles, which could contaminate the purity of his theory and violate the separation of law and morals. Kelsen stresses that legal principles can never be a presupposition for or a source of a legal order; on the contrary, they can only be created by that order. Kelsen admits that the legislator can be guided by principles, yet these are not legal but moral or political.[11] In general, in Kelsen's brief and scattered remarks on the contents of positive law, the clear emphasis is on interests and thus on policies rather than principles. His unmasking critique of the use of principle-related arguments is astonishingly similar to contemporary CLS scholars' endeavours to reduce principles to policies.[12]

If Kelsen did not consider principles worth much attention, for Hartian legal positivists they have become a central preoccupation, particularly after Dworkin's criticism of Hart and Hart's response in his celebrated *Postscript*.[13] At least three issues, which Hart, too, touched on in the *Postscript*, have occupied Hartians in their by-and-large one-sided debate with their chosen nemesis: (1) whether the rule of recognition can recognise principles too; (2) whether the legal validity of norms can depend on their congruence with moral principles; and (3) whether moral principles can possess legal relevance simply *qua* moral principles so that judges, for instance are obligated to apply them in hard cases. The first issue is an easy one for Hartians. The distinction between rules and principles introduced by Dworkin cannot be read backwards into the language of *The Concept of Law*, and when Hart discussed identifying and validating rules he did not mean to exclude Dworkinian principles. Many principles are enshrined in formal legal texts – laws or precedents – and a pedigree-based rule of recognition can cope with them as easily as with rules in their Dworkinian sense.[14]

The two other issues relate to the two sub-theses of the separability argument. The position taken on morals-related principles as criteria for validity distinguishes soft from hard and inclusive from exclusive positivists. The former – among them Hart himself – argue that whether judges in their social practice resort to morals-related principles in assessing legal validity is a contingent social fact. Sometimes reference is made to the US Constitution and the Canadian Charter, which expressly enshrine such principles. The argument is not very successful: in Hartian theory the written constitution cannot function as the ultimate rule of recognition, which necessarily lies beyond or above the written constitution and accounts for its validity. In contrast to soft or inclusive positivists, hard or exclusive positivists argue that the rule of recognition could not accomplish its epistemological or identifying function if it included moral criteria.

[11] Kelsen, 1945, 249. [12] Kelsen, 1957, 438–439. [13] Hart, 2012, 238–275.
[14] Ibid., 263–266.

On the third issue Hartian positivists again agree: moral principles are not legal principles nor are they applicable in hard cases simply *qua* moral principles. Yet incorporationists and non-incorporationists specify the common position differently. In the incorporationist view, law can - depending on the rule of recognition - incorporate moral principles whose application, then, is law-application. In the non-incorporationist view, judges may have an obligation to take recourse to moral principles in hard cases, but if they do, they do not apply but make law. Non-legal principles which judges are obligated to heed are comparable to foreign law or rules of associations, which judges may also be obligated to take into consideration but which are not part of the legal order under which judges act.

The debate on legal principles seems to be riddled with mysteries. An author may treat legal principles as norms applicable to cases before the courts; as a type of norms alongside rules. Yet the same author may also characterise principles as sources of law. If legal principles are legal norms, which must find support in legal sources, how can they themselves constitute such sources? The mystery evaporates if we perceive that legal principles as applicable legal norms are not exactly the same as legal principles as sources of law. In their discussion of rules and principles – a discussion which Hartian legal positivists have largely ignored – Dworkin and Alexy examined legal principles primarily as directly applicable legal norms, distinct from legal rules.[15] This is only one of the senses of 'legal principle'. The following list indicates the plethora of meanings:

- legal principles as norms applicable in judicial decision-making (decision principles)
- legal principles as summarising the normative contents of a branch of law or the normative legal order as a whole (general legal principles)
- legal principles as arguments employed in interpreting formal legal texts, such as laws (interpretative principles)
- legal principles as legal sources supporting legal norms (source principles)

For my present discussion, general legal principles are the most important token. Together with legal concepts, theories, and methodologies, general legal principles constitute a major element in the doctrinal infrastructure of distinct branches of law. Identity-building general legal principles include *pacta sunt servanda* in contract law; *nulla poena sine lege* in penal law; *détournement du pouvoir* principles or the reasonability principle in administrative law; and democracy, separation of powers, and proportionality in constitutional law. When emergent fields of law – say, communication law, information law, or medical law – try to assert their distinctness, they point to putative general

[15] Dworkin, 1978; Alexy, 2002.

legal principles which are supposed to create coherence in surface-level law. In addition to field-specific principles, legal principles exist whose relevance covers the entire normative legal order; say, fundamental rights.

The insight into law's multi-layered character facilitates grasping the role of different types of principle, as well as their interplay. Decision principles and general legal principle have different domiciles: decision principles are surface-level norms, while general legal principles are inhabitants of sub-surface, legal-cultural, layers. However, general legal principles, too, receive expression in surface-level legal texts, such as constitutional and other statutory provisions, *travaux préparatoires*, judicial precedents, and scholarly writings. General legal principles must be reconstructed starting from such explicit manifestations. These are also a sine qua non for their legal relevance. In line with other elements of legal culture, legal principles have emerged through a successful process of sedimentation, which brings them into harmony with the positivity of modern state law. General principles are not valid or invalid; they are legally relevant or irrelevant, and they obtain their relevance from explicit or implicit references in surface-level legal texts. Surface-level manifestations of legal principles accomplish both an identifying and relevance-affirming function. Moral principles are not legal simply *qua* moral principles; they must find what Dworkin called institutional support that renders them legally relevant. Yet it is important not to reduce general legal principles to their surface-level expressions. Fundamental rights may be enshrined in explicit constitutional provisions and function as 'pedigree-based' decision principles. In a modern state legal regime approximately matching the template of a democratic *Rechtsstaat*, fundamental rights also function as general legal principles, with their domicile in sub-surface layers and with their relevance covering the law as a whole.

Legal scholarship alone cannot provide the institutional support which the relevance of legal principles presupposes. Still, in its doctrinal function vis-à-vis other legal practices, legal scholarship plays an important role in articulating and systematising general legal principles, thus also contributing to the sedimentation process which establishes the relevance of those principles.

The notion of general legal principles has been subjected to severe criticism by analytically oriented scholars, among them the Finnish legal theorists Kaarle Makkonen and Aulis Aarnio.[16] Their critique is a critique of legal inductivism and premised on the assumption that general legal principles are inferred through induction from individual surface-level norms enshrined in legal texts. However, reconstructing legal principles from the traces they have left in legal texts is something other than an exercise in inductive logic. At issue is perception of the normative point of the field of law in question; the point which brings coherence to fragmented surface-level law. Rather than

[16] Makkonen, 1965; Aarnio, 1979.

inductive logic, the intellectual operation at play in recognising general legal principles is akin to the *Anschauung* which, according to the German Historical School, is needed for comprehending organic normative entities.[17]

Decision principles, on which Dworkin's and Alexy's debate on rules and principles focused, form part of the normative basis from which judges derive the decision norm for the case before them – the major premise of the judicial syllogism. In their source and interpretative role, principles accomplish important tasks even in preceding stages of judicial decision-making. Source and interpretative principles are general legal principles as approached from the perspective of their two specific functions. General legal principles, sedimented into the law's sub-surface layers and fulfilling the criteria for relevance, may provide source support for valid surface-level norms, which, in turn, may be either rules or principles. Furthermore, general legal principles are used as arguments in interpreting other sources of law. As interpretative principles they provide guidance in specifying the meaning of formal legal texts and extracting applicable norms from these. A principle may in some cases function as a decision principle and in others as an interpretative principle. This dual character is typical of fundamental-rights principles. Fundamental rights can serve as decision principles, especially in the absence of other, complementary legislation. In general, though, courts do no resort to fundamental rights as decision principles but as interpretative principles. In some legal regimes, courts are legally bound to a fundamental rights-affirmative interpretation. The New Zealand Bill of Rights Act of 1990 and the UK Human Rights Act 1998 include explicit provisions on such an interpretative duty.

In addition to rules and principles, Dworkin introduces another distinction, which is of equal, if not even greater, importance for his argument. Principles in the broad sense are of two kinds: principles in the strict sense, and policies. Policies are goals and programmes focusing on economic, political, or social development. In the Kantian triad of practical reason, they fall under pragmatic, instrumental, reasoning. By contrast, principles in the strict sense express moral requirements, such as the demand for justice. In Germany, Alexy has been criticised for downplaying the distinction between principles and policies.[18] I am inclined to concur with Alexy's critics on the importance of this distinction for constitutional interpretation. If policies aiming at collective goods are equated with and given equal argumentative weight as principles justifying individual rights, then the power-restricting edge of the constitution would be blunted. The constitution of a democratic *Rechtsstaat* would be in danger of losing one of its two main legs. The distinction is needed to provide a democratic *Rechtsstaat* with doctrinal means to ward off excessive instrumentalisation of law; for the purposes of self-defence of a democratic

[17] Tuori, 2011, 85–86. [18] See, e.g., Maus, 1989.

Rechtsstaat. This, of course, presupposes that principles can in general be distinguished from policies.

Not all agree that they can. Radical critics of Dworkin have challenged the very foundations of the distinction. In this criticism, CLS scholars have shaken hands with Richard Posner, the leading figure of Law and Economics, who has written off principles as rhetorically embellished policies. Both CLS scholars and Posner argue that principles can be reduced to policies and that even the very distinction between principles and policies is policy-based. They both attack Dworkin for 'rhetoric of rights', and detect policy considerations underlying this rhetoric too. I concede that drawing the distinction is not always easy and that, as Kelsen already noted, language of principle can be abused to camouflage particular interests. Still, I consider it evident that the leading principles from different fields of law which I have used as examples – such as *nulla poena sine lege*, *pacta sunt servanda*, or fundamental rights – connect to morals and in that respect differ from policies oriented towards political, economic, and social goals. Moreover, the distinction between policies and principles is supported by the Kantian analysis of the triad of practical reasoning – pragmatic, moral, and ethical.

In a democratic *Rechtsstaat*, general legal principles of distinct fields of law or the normative legal order as a whole are closer to morals-related principles than to policies. The legislator of modern state law primarily resorts to law as medium and is mainly driven by goal-rational, instrumentalist, considerations. Legislation is policy-oriented, and policies are even explicitly invoked in *travaux préparatoires*, or in preambles to or introductory sections of laws. In judicial practices, policies may gain legal relevance in teleological interpretation but hardly as independent norms. Neither is it probable that policies could attain a similar status as elements of legal culture as morals-related principles. Political power-constellations vary over time, as do policy considerations underlying individual laws; they may even – and most likely to some extent do – contradict each other. Policies do not undergo a similar process of sedimentation or acquire similar stability as morals-related principles. The temporality of policies is closer to that of law's surface than the sub-surface layers where the domicile of general legal principles lies.

The debate between Dworkin and Hartian legal positivists has hinged on the role that principles play in hard cases. Dworkin claims that in hard cases, too, judges apply law and that the principles they resort to are legal principles. In contrast, Hartians, with the qualified exception of incorporationists, maintain that in hard cases the law runs out. In relying on principles which are not explicitly enshrined in legal texts and as such enjoy legal validity, judges make law instead of applying it. Even if judges were obligated to decide hard cases in accordance with principles, this would not make the principles legal. Judges may be legally obligated to apply even norms that do not belong to the legal order under which they work; say, foreign law where private international law (conflict of laws) so determines.

Hartians make much of the distinction between core and penumbra, introduced in *The Concept of Law*. Law in general and distinct norms in particular are supposed to possess a core of settled meaning, which is surrounded by a penumbra of uncertainty. In the core area of settled meaning, law-application approximates a quasi-mechanical, deductive, template, whereas in the penumbra other types of reasoning are needed. Hartians have conceded that principles may be identifiable by the rule of recognition. This is a consequential concession: principles are prone to inject law with uncertainty typical of the penumbra and jeopardise the settledness of the core. The more room principles take from rules, the more space the penumbra conquers from the core. And the more and vaguer principles the rule of recognition identifies, the less effectively it accomplishes its task of reducing uncertainty about the contents of the law.

The penumbra may also expand because of the ambiguity of legal texts; the more room for interpretation legal texts leave, the larger the area the penumbra occupies. The postulate of a settled core implies that at least a relevant part of the legal texts recognised by the rule of recognition are unambiguous and lend themselves to literal interpretation or some other generally accepted interpretative canon which is expected to produce uncontroversial results. Exact speed limits are an often-invoked case in point. Penumbra engendered by principles and penumbra engendered by need of interpretation may come together. Constitutional provisions on fundamental rights, for instance, often employ vague terms – say, 'fair trial' – which need specification by interpretation and whose significance in a particular case cannot be determined by deductive reasoning.

Hartian theorists acknowledge that within the penumbra judges take recourse to principles which may also involve moral considerations. In hard cases, legal norms, identified by the rule of recognition, do not indicate an unambiguous solution. Consequently, judges must heed other, non-legal grounds; say, moral principles or policy arguments. Here judges leave the terrain of law-application and enter that of law-making: yet another strict distinction, cherished by Hartian legal positivists. Judicial decision-making in hard cases is supposed to proceed in two stages: first, by resorting to non-legal considerations, the judge establishes a new legal norm for the purposes of the case at hand; and, then, secondly, applies the newly established norm to the facts of the case. Depending on the status of the court and the position which the rule of recognition accords to precedents, the new norm is relevant only for the particular case or possesses wider pertinence.

When countering criticism for strong judicial discretion, Hartians are prone to emphasise the constraints of judicial law-making, which distinguishes it from legislation where discretion is much wider. Reasoning in judicial law-making, too, is supposed to be legal by nature – reasoning not about the law but according to the law. Still, it remains unclear where reasoning about the law aiming to ascertain the law in force ends and reasoning according to the law aiming to establish new law for the purpose of deciding a hard case begins; what the distinctive features of reasoning according to law are; what legal constraints it is subject to; and how, exactly, it differs from the reasoning involved in legislative law-making.

To recap, Hartian legal positivists argue that we must and can separate the settled core of law from the penumbra of uncertainty; non-interpretation from interpretation; easy cases implying deductive, mechanical law-application from hard cases calling for another kind of legal reasoning; and reasoning about the law which aims to determine the law in force from reasoning according to the law which judicial law-making necessitates. Why are Hartians so anxious to stick to such rigid binary distinctions, which probably appear rather counter-intuitive to judges' phenomenological self-understanding, and, even if corresponding to everyday judicial experience, would fail to withstand critical theoretical examination? Most likely, in hard cases, demarcating judicial law-making and 'reasoning according to the law' from establishing the law and 'reasoning about the law' would seem a strange idea to a majority of judges, not only in the USA and the United Kingdom but in other jurisdictions as well. Identifying routine or easy cases which neither cause interpretative difficulties nor involve competing principles is more likely to strike a chord with judges. For a legal theorist trying to penetrate the foundations of judicial experience, the idea of law which could be arrived at without interpretation is harder to accept. Law is expressed in legal texts, and no legal texts exist which would not need interpretation. The need to articulate an interpretative problem depends on the canons of interpretation rooted in the prevailing legal culture. These are an integral part of the legal *Vorverständnis*, which functions mainly at an unconscious level, as practical knowledge. Quasi-mechanical application of speed limits does not tell of non-interpretation of legal texts but of deeply ingrained interpretative tenets. Because the law is preserved in legal texts produced by previous legal speech acts, interpretation is an inescapable companion of judicial decision-making and legal practices in general. The boundary separating the settled core of meaning - where established interpretative precepts point to an unambiguous and uncontroversial interpretation - and the penumbra of uncertainty - where competing interpretations and interpretative precepts clash - proves to be blurred. The same holds for the borderline between easy and hard cases, be the hardship due to problems of interpretation, difficulties in identifying the implications of principles, or conflicting ramifications of rival prima facie applicable principles.

The above distinctions are variations of the basic theme of post-Hartian Legal Positivism: the separability thesis and the related differentiation of law from non-law. The fervour with which the distinctions are shielded probably derives from the threat that Dworkin's writings were experienced as posing for the separability of law and morals, and for the sharp demarcation of law from non-law. Dworkin evoked moments in judicial practice which at least on their face defy a watertight sequestration of law and legal argumentation: legal texts which used morally flavoured terms like 'fairness' and required specifying interpretation to extract the norm relevant for the case at hand; principles which in particular cases only provided direction but could not as such be employed as a decision norm, that is, the major premise of the judicial syllogism; as well as competing or even conflicting principles which called for weighing and balancing.

The Hartian position reflects a uni-level view of the contents of law. My contention of the legal relevance of general legal principles, with their domicile in the sub-surface, legal-cultural, layers, and the functioning of those principles as source and interpretative principles contradicts the premises of the Hartian view. Yet this is not the only point I want to make. I shall argue that hard cases have been devoted excessive attention, not only by legal positivists but also by their critics. In depicting how legal principles exert their effects, easy cases are as important as hard, if not even more important.

As I have repeatedly argued, modern state law is preserved in legal texts, such as laws, *travaux préparatoires*, precedents, and scholarly writings. Legal texts only disclose their sense and the content of legal norms through interpretation. Most often, in routine activities, interpretation proceeds in an automatic, unconscious, way. Legal actors rely on the practical knowledge they possess of the legal culture. They understand legal terms in their established meanings and employ established interpretative tenets. Even identification of legal texts and assessment of their source value mostly transpires through practical knowledge. In judicial decision-making, and in legal practices in general, morally laden legal principles are operative not only in hard but in easy cases too. Every contract-law case, whether easy or hard, implies applying *pacta sunt servanda* or at least weighing it against a counter-principle, such as protection of the weaker party. The easiness of easy cases is not due to the redundancy of legal principles or legal culture in general; legal culture is as indispensable for easy as for hard cases. This holds equally for legal concepts, principles, theories, and methodologies. Easy cases are not easy because of the irrelevance of legal culture but because its implications are so evident that there is no need to articulate them. Easy cases are easy for legal professionals who have internalised the prevailing legal culture in their legal *Vorverständnis*, but not for laymen, who may stumble at the first legal term in a legal text. Easiness is a subjective, phenomenological, experience rather than an objective, measurable, quality. The experience may vary among professionals, too, reflecting the perspectivism of legal orders, roles, and disciplines. Instead of sharply distinguishable easy and hard cases, legal actors encounter easier and harder cases situated along a continuing line. What indicates the difficulty of a case is the necessity to articulate elements of legal culture; that is, to ponder whether a text is legally relevant or not; what the text means and what legal norm(s) it expresses; how a particular legal concept should be understood; what the implications of a general legal principle are in the case at hand; and how the principle weighs against other, competing principles. It is also important to note that practical knowledge continues its indispensable work in hard cases. Not all elements of the prevailing legal culture are thematised but only those that are relevant for the pending case and that necessitate clarification. The rest remain in the tacit domain of legal *Vorverständnis* as the unquestioned horizon of decision-making.

What is crucial is that legal-cultural layers are at play in all legal practices, whether these are dealing with routine or more complicated legal issues, and that this concerns all the main elements of legal culture, including general legal principles. Morally laden principles are not called on merely to help to resolve hard cases. Nor in hard cases can two steps be separated: first, establishing the law in force and reasoning about the law; and, secondly, judicial law-making beyond the law in force and reasoning according to the law, where extra-legal morally laden principles would also have their legitimate place.

It may be difficult to determine what principles, concepts, theories, and methodologies enjoy such institutional support and possess such legal relevance that they are to be included in the legal culture that constitutes an integral part of the law. Reconstruction and interpretation are necessary, starting from references in and implications by legal texts. In the absence of clear-cut criteria – another Master Rule – which would decide on inclusion in legal culture, it is to be expected that reconstructions differ; for instance, that legal actors disagree on the identification and substance of general legal principles, as well as their prima facie order of preference. Such disagreements are a major impetus to and topic of the ongoing legal discourse among legal professionals. In addition, scholarly disagreements may connect to wider ideological and political controversies; think, say, of *pacta sunt servanda* and equity in contract law or democracy and fundamental rights in constitutional law.

Still, the range and depth of disagreements should not be exaggerated. Recapitulation of general legal principles is not arbitrary guesswork but proceeds under obvious constraints. First, rather evident candidates for general legal principles exist. In ideal-typical modern state law, it would be audacious to challenge the candidacy of my two main examples, *nulla poena sine lege* in criminal and *pacta sunt servanda* in contract law, or the status of fundamental-rights principles with repercussions across diverse compartments of law. Secondly, the porosity of the borderline between law and non-law in the legal-cultural layers does not entail that moral principles would be legally relevant just because of their moral justification. The legal relevance of putative general legal principles presupposes institutional support in legal texts, such as laws, *travaux préparatoires*, or precedents. Dispersed references are not sufficient for reconstructing the nexus of legal principles sustaining a field of law or the normative legal order as a whole. General legal principles never come in isolation but in clusters or networks, and referring to and prima facie sustaining but also contradicting each other; principles and counter-principles are as much part of legal culture as are mutually supportive principles. As may be recalled, finding examples of principles and counter-principles – such as, individualism and altruism, say – used to be a favourite exercise of Critical Legal Studies, and alleged proof of the indeterminacy and fundamentally political nature of law. Articulation of the relevant principles, whether by a theorist, a judge, or a legislative expert, should aim – this is my third point – at a coherent arrangement where prima facie preferences are proposed and principles pulling in contrary directions find their places. Even if coherence were acknowledged as a regulative idea, the coherence which can be reached is inevitably fragile and open to attack from the side of counter-principles and alternative orderings; in brief, agonistic coherence.

In a reconstructive effort, one should also keep in mind the functions ascribed to general legal principles in law and in the legal practice one is engaged in, say, dealing as a judge with a hard case or articulating and elaborating legal doctrine as a scholar. What are the functions that general legal principles are expected to fulfil? First, as source and interpretative principles, they accomplish vital tasks in judicial decision-making, especially in hard cases. Secondly, they summarise the normative premises of a distinct field of law, thus contributing to law's coherence; some principles – again fundamental-rights principles spring into mind – may promote coherence even across the divisions of law. Thirdly, in line with the conceptual and methodological elements of legal culture, legal principles exert a constitutive function. By providing the necessary cultural resources, they create the very possibility of legal practices, legal discourse, and legal speech acts which engender the constant movement on the surface of law but which extend their (re)productive effects to the sub-surface layers. Fourthly, the constitutive function has its reverse side: legal culture – internalised by legal actors and established in their *Vorverständnis* – not only facilitates but restricts too. It imposes restrictions on the laws that legislative experts can draft and, consequently, legislators enact; the rulings that judges can issue; and the doctrinal standpoints that legal scholars can put forth. Kelsen was wrong: modern state law cannot have any content whatsoever.

In their limiting function, morally laden principles sedimented to the sub-surface layers of law control policy-based legislation and teleological interpretation, and exercise a kind of normative censorship. For the major part, this censorship is realised through the *Vorverständnis* of legal professionals, who occupy the key positions in specialised legal practices. The normative censorship that guarantees the law's self-limitation is operative every time when, for example, a judge employs morally laden principles to interpret laws which the legislator has issued from its mainly instrumentalist perspective, or when a legislative expert quasi-instinctively avoids legislative proposals whose contradiction with fundamental rights would be obvious. Conceived of in this way, the self-limitation of law is a mundane, daily occurrence, proceeding through routine legal practices.

In modern state law, legal practices specialised in constitutional review have been developed to complement tacit control by practical knowledge. Yet the cases where the substantive validity and even illocutionary force of formal legal speech acts is openly challenged and tested in constitutional review form but the tip of the iceberg; the conspicuous culmination of a normative censorship unravelling most of its effects inconspicuously, through the practical knowledge of legal actors. Insight into these effects demonstrates the disproportionate attention that legal positivists have dedicated to discussing whether or not the rule of recognition can include moral criteria. When discussing the morality of law, the emphasis should be elsewhere than on the criteria of legal validity allegedly codifiable in a Master Rule. Sub-surface legal principles also provide the answer to the vital question that Legal Positivism is incapable of tackling: how to ward off the danger of totalitarianism in legal disguise, a danger engendered by the positivity of modern state law?

Closely related to limitation is the fifth function I wish to pinpoint, namely that of criticism. Appraisal of the substantive validity claims of legal speech acts poses the ineradicable problem of criteria. Sub-surface principles proffer intersubjective, non-arbitrary yardsticks for criticising past legal speech acts and for assessing their substantive validity claims, even in situations where the illocutionary force of the speech acts is not at stake. Such yardsticks respect the positivity of modern state law and demonstrate the existence of a third road between Natural Law and Legal Positivism; a third road whose possibility legal positivists of diverse hues have always obstinately denied.

Sixthly, justification is the reverse side of limitation and criticism. Justification of coercion cannot be said to be the point of law; the point lies elsewhere and coercion is its servant. Yet the Kantian problem of justifying external coercion should be taken seriously, even by those who reject Kant's treatment of the problem. But Legal Positivism, whether in its Kelsenian or Hartian version, has not been interested. Indeed, the reductive normativism of Legal Positivism offers as little by way of means to indicate a solution to justifying coercion as to warding off legal totalitarianism. In a democratic *Rechtsstaat*, the solution to Kant's problem lies in the sub-surface layers of law. Yet it is important to keep in mind the restricted scope of justification. Law can only provide justification for coercion securing its realisation; constituted violence, as we could put it. What law cannot justify is constitutive violence related to constitution-giving.

General legal principles relativise the normative autonomy of law, although they do not negate it. They interact with - but are not identical to - moral principles. The relationship of sedimentation, which connects principles to the surface of law, and the institutional support which their legal relevance presupposes prevents us from confusing legal with moral principles. Moral principles are not legally relevant simply *qua* moral principles. Because of their border-crossing, transnational, character, general legal principles also relativise the autonomy of law vis-à-vis other normative orders.

Necessary, Conceptual Links?

So, are there necessary, conceptual, links between law and morals? By analyzing the claim to normative correctness and the role of general legal principles, I have charted the main links between law and morals in modern state law. By the same token, I have criticised the legal positivist position, manifest by Kelsen's postulate of the different *Grundnorms* of different normative orders and the Hartian separability thesis. Yet I do not claim that, with my observations, I have demonstrated the existence of necessary, conceptual, links between law and morals. Serious doubts can be raised about the possibility and viability of an unequivocal, universally applicable general concept of law. I have consciously confined my discussion to ideal-typical modern state law, more or less matching the criteria of a democratic *Rechtsstaat*. In fact, many of my observations are based on empirical hypotheses which I have not tested. It is possible - although improbable, at least, in the long run - that legal regimes exist where laws or court decisions openly profess to be unjust and where the law rests, not on acceptance, but on fear. It is also an empirical question to what extent general legal principles have managed to pass a process of sedimentation; to what extent legal actors have internalised the principles in their *Vorverständnis*; and to what extent principles perform the diverse functions I have ascribed to them. Ideal types do not answer empirical questions but help to pose them. In addition, they can be used as crutches in normative argumentation.

As legal theorists, we should be wary of over-sweeping empirical generalisations; of turning empirical into conceptual questions; and of confusing empirical claims and normative argumentation.

10

Constitution

Aspects of Constitution

'Constitution' in its present sense belongs to the history of modern law and polity, with the American and French revolutionary constitutions from the end of the eighteenth century as the decisive watersheds. The sedimentation of the new meaning of 'constitution' took time. After Russia had gained possession of Finland from Sweden, Alexander I received the estates in Borgå in 1809 and solemnly pledged to preserve the 'constitution' of the land. The Russian and Finnish sides could never come to an agreement on what Alexander meant by 'constitution'.

Written or formal constitutions are legal speech acts – standing Declarations – whose meaning, deciphered through interpretation, consists of constitutional norms, including both rules and principles. The concept of material constitution evokes the typical contents or functions of constitutional norms and is thus specified in accordance with what these are held to be. For Kelsen, the main function of a constitution is to regulate production of new legal norms; this view, then, shaped his conception of 'material constitution'.[1] The norms making up the constitution in the material sense may, but need not, be codified in a single constitutional speech act (a constitution in the formal sense). As every undergraduate student in comparative constitutional law well knows, the United Kingdom has a constitution in the material but not in the formal sense.

'Constitution' involves the idea of a higher law which assigns the constitution a privileged position with respect to other law. This idea can be given either a formal or a substantive reading. The formal reading is evident in Kelsen's depiction of the hierarchical structure of the normative legal order where the constitution occupies the highest level next to the *Grundnorm*. A constitution authorises adoption of lower-level norms and, in cases of conflict, prevails. The requirement for a qualified procedure to amend the constitution or to issue a new constitution is related to the formal reading as well. Because the constitution stands higher than – and provides the legal

[1] Kelsen, 1967, 222.

foundation for – other law, it should enjoy exceptional stability and legitimacy; hence such requirements for constitutional amendments as qualified majority, approval by more than one parliamentary composition, or ratification by referendum. Some constitutions – the German Basic Law, for instance – have declared certain constitutional provisions unamendable, thus introducing an internal formal hierarchy within constitutional law.

The substantive sense of a higher law connects to the normative contents of constitutional law. In this sense 'higher' equals 'basic' or 'fundamental': a constitution is supposed to give expression to the basic normative premises of the polity and its law, even society in general. Here the modern constitution has taken over the legacy of premodern *lois fondamentales*. What the basics are that a constitution should affirm is, of course, open to contestation. Equally controversial is the extent to which the political legislator, armed with a democratic mandate, is and should be formally bound by constitutional provisions. In many states, including Germany, debates have focused on the role of fundamental rights as general legal principles unfolding their effects throughout the legal order and imposing restrictions even on the legislator. The formal and substantive status of a constitution as higher law implies or at least makes intelligible the need of particular specialised practices – constitutional review – which are expected to guarantee observance of the constitution.

Constitutional law and particular constitutional institutions share the general relational character of law and legal institutions. What complicates constitutional analysis is the fact that a constitution relates to both legal and political regimes. Not only can a constitution be analyzed in both legal and political contexts so that a formal constitution can be understood as not only a legal but also a political speech act; even as a legal speech act a constitution attends to both law and politics. Thus, not only does 'constitution' possess a legal and political sense; in a legal sense, too, constitution displays two legs, juridical and political. One could even speak of two legal constitutions: a juridical one, addressing the legal regime, and a political one, addressing the political regime. If constitutional theory sometimes seems confusing, the reason may be that the theorist does not make clear what constitution is under discussion: legal or political and, if legal, the juridical or political dimension.

The juridical constitution is a token of the reflexivity of modern law and culture: through the constitution, law addresses itself. The constitution is the law of laws. Positivity of law would be unthinkable without cultural reflexivity: production of new law through explicit law-making decisions presupposes existing law's openness to criticism. The reflexivity of positive law did not escape Kelsen's sharp theoretical gaze. Kelsen pointed to the peculiarity of (positive) law that it regulates its own production, and attached the material concept of the constitution to this reflexive function.[2]

[2] Ibid.

The conceptual framework elaborated above for analyzing the sociality and normativity of law is applicable to the constitution as well. The legal constitution does not consist merely of its surface-level expressions; surface-level constitutional law is underpinned by constitutional culture. In addition, the legal constitution possesses its social dimension in constitutional practices. Even in discussing constitutional culture and practices, the two-pronged nature of a constitution should be heeded. Thus, constitutional culture should be examined not only in legal but also in political terms. Political actors – members of parliament, government ministers, opposition politicians – are animated by a political culture – a *Vorverständnis*! – through which they tackle their practical political tasks. The political culture includes constitutional ingredients, that is, elements of constitutional culture. The legal culture of constitutional lawyers and the political culture of political actors interact, sharing common themes and emphases. Still, they may display significant divergences too. The borders may be fluid but they exist; a politician does not usually approach constitutional issues in the same way as a justice of a constitutional court or a professor of constitutional law. What appears as an end in itself for a constitutional lawyer – say, protection of fundamental rights – may be judged by politicians in instrumental terms; as a means of, or an impediment to, attaining policy goals and executing political programmes. We should be wary of empirical over-generalisations. Still, it seems warranted to assume that a constitutional lawyer is inclined to adopt the standpoint of legal *ratio* and a politician the standpoint of political *voluntas*.

In accordance with law in general, a constitution possesses a social aspect too: it is both (re)produced and realised in sociolegal practices. In the field of constitutional law, we find counterparts to the main second-order practices specialised in (re)production of the normative legal order: constitution-making, constitutional adjudication, and constitutional scholarship. Constitutional law evolves and changes through constitutional speech acts, while the prevailing constitutional culture defines the participants in constitutional discourse and the relative weight of their interventions. The constitutional discourse where the contents of constitutional law are specified is an elite discourse. It is a legal discourse and embedded in legal practices, where legal actors hold a key position. However, especially constitution-making but even constitutional adjudication and scholarship are intimately interlinked with political practices and discourse, which extend beyond constitutional bodies to the public sphere, civil society, and the citizenry at large.

Constitutional law is not only (re)produced but is even realised in constitutional practices. A polity as the object of the political dimension of the legal constitution can be examined in a tripartite relation among the organisational, communal, and individual poles. Constitutional law qualifies institutions as state authorities and what they do as legislative, executive, administrative, and judicial practices. By the same token, constitutional law is realised in those institutions and practices. The community is constitutionally qualified as the citizenry – or *demos*, the collective subject of democracy – jointly exercising citizenship rights; such as electoral rights and political fundamental rights. Citizenship rights are exerted in citizenship practices. These hold a peculiar intermediary position: they channel the influence of the everyday lifeworld into second-order legal practices, and engender the communicative power which in a democratic *Rechtsstaat* is supposed to guide and control the administrative power wielded by state machinery.

At the individual pole, constitutional law qualifies individuals as citizens. Through fundamental rights, constitutional law promises to guarantee them both public and private autonomy. Fundamental rights related to, say, human dignity, bodily and personal integrity, privacy, family life, and confidentiality of correspondence are realised through everyday lifeworld practices. As part of law as institution, fundamental rights are enmeshed in the general social normativity which impregnates the practical knowledge of social actors.

To add further to the intricacy of constitutional analysis, not only constitutional practices but even constitutional culture should be examined from a perspective transcending the standpoint of legal and political elites. In particular, when exploring the political functions of the constitution, heeding only the elite culture does not suffice. One function clearly depends on the existence or at least subsequent formation of a supportive constitutional culture among the public at large: legitimation. If a receptive general constitutional culture does not exist, the constitution cannot contribute to the legitimacy of the polity and its political regime. In the general constitutional culture, the borderline between the two dimensions of constitutional culture is effaced: no clear distinction can be drawn between legal and political aspects. Constitutional culture emerges and evolves through constitutional practices, political and legal. Constitutional practices – or, as they may also be termed, citizenship practices – are crucial for the formation of general constitutional culture as well. In these practices – such as elections, political debates, and associational activities – citizens contribute to democratic law-making and thus to the substantive validity and legitimacy of legislative speech acts.

The functions that a constitution is expected to accomplish should also be discussed in respect of both law and polity; this holds for the legal constitution, too, with its two-pronged juridical and political nature. Furthermore, not all constitutions are alike and their functions may vary. Here. the particular *occasio constitutionis* of constitution-making plays an important role. State constitutions can be roughly divided into four groups. Firstly, revolutionary constitutions signal the beginning of a new political regime, and perhaps even a new social order. The classic examples are the American and French constitutions of the late eighteenth century. Secondly, constitutions may amount to Declarations of Independence. Drafting a constitution is the first thing a newly independent state engages in; adopting a constitution reinforces its claim to autonomous existence. Let me take two Nordic examples: the Norwegian

Constitution of 1814, the oldest constitution still in force in Europe, and the Constitution of Finland of 1919, adopted after Finland had seceded from the Russian Empire. Let us call these secessionist constitutions. Yet not all constitutions herald the beginning of a new political or social era, or reaffirm newly won independence. In addition to revolutionary and secessionist constitutions, a third type of reformist constitution exists as well. Reformist constitutions are adopted in the procedure laid down in the previous constitution so that constitutional continuity is not breached. They introduce changes to the political or legal regime, but these are of a reformist – not a revolutionary – nature. Finally, codifying constitutions, the fourth type, limit themselves to codifying and sanctifying de facto legal, political, and social developments. Again, the Nordic countries offer two examples: the 1974 Swedish Constitution, which replaced the Constitution dating back to 1809, and the Finnish Constitution of 2000, which replaced the secessionist constitution of 1919. In our two examples, the codifying constitution respected constitutional continuity: it was adopted in the procedure laid down in the previous constitution. Yet it is possible that the historically first constitution – the starting point of constitutional continuity and in this sense a founding constitution – is not a revolutionary or a secessionist but a codifying one, which merely confers constitutional sanctity on existing political and legal regimes. Evidently, this was the case for many of the constitutions octroyed by monarchs of German states in the nineteenth century. The boundary between reformist and codifying constitutions is not sharp, and a constitution can involve elements of both. Thus, in addition to codification, the 2000 Constitution of Finland involved some minor reforms of both the political and legal regimes.

Heeding the variation that diverse types of constitution entails, four main functions which the legal constitution is supposed to perform with regard to the legal and political regimes can be pinpointed:

- constitutive
- positioning
- restrictive
- legitimating

What and how does a constitution constitute, position, restrict, and legitimate?

Constitutional Functions

A legal constitution possesses constitutive effects both in respect of the polity and the political regime, and in respect of law and the legal regime. In the political dimension, a constitution defines, and revolutionary and secessionist constitutions even constitute, the basic institutional structure of political power: the main authorities, and their competences and mutual relationships. In this sense, constituting comprises organising and authorising. By the same token, revolutionary and secessionist constitutions turn the constitutive power – *pouvoir constituant* – lying behind and expressed in the act of constitution-giving into constituted power – *pouvoir constitué*. Furthermore, the constitution of a democratic *Rechtsstaat* constitutes individual subjects as citizens. In a nascent polity, the constitutive function should be examined in even broader, foundational terms. The political constitution is expected to contribute to the emergence of the polity itself. Constitutional bodies and individual citizens do not suffice. Individual citizens should be interlinked as a citizenry; a *demos* capable of engendering the communicative power without which democracy would remain an empty promise of the formal constitution. Again, the reverse side of constitution is restriction, mainly accomplished by the constitutional system of checks and balances and, with regard to citizens, fundamental rights. The constitutive function is accompanied by positioning: defining the relations of the polity to other polities. The basic positioning relates to the claim to autonomy – political and legal sovereignty – that a constitution typically involves.

In a democratic *Rechtsstaat*, constitutive and restrictive functions are inseparable from the legitimising one. For individuals, the political constitution of a democratic *Rechtsstaat* promises autonomy, citizenship, and democracy. These promises are intimately linked to the claim to legitimacy which a democratic *Rechtsstaat* raises through its constitution. Yet a constitution can legitimate only if it is considered legitimate in itself.

From where does a constitution draw its legitimacy? In general terms, two principal explanations can be suggested: origin- and content-based. Origin-based legitimacy derives from the circumstances in which the constitution has been adopted: the constitutional moment which gave birth to the constitution. The constitutional moment of a revolutionary constitution is marked by wide political mobilisation and intensive discourses within civil society and among the citizenry as the *demos* – the ultimate subject of the constituent power – perhaps culminating in a referendum. The constitutional moment of secessionist constitutions symbolises a turning point in the history of the polity; here we could speak of symbolic legitimacy. For instance, the Norwegian Constitution of 1814 evokes the memory of Norway's detachment from Denmark and entry as an autonomous entity into a personal union with Sweden.

Content-based legitimacy flows from the substance of the constitution; from its accordance with the basic moral principles and ethical values of society. Origin-based and content-based legitimacy can be, and often are, mutually supportive and complementary. The US or Norwegian constitutions can only have retained their origin-based legitimacy because reinforced by content-based legitimacy. However, the two types of legitimacy may also be detached from each other. So it seems that the legitimacy which the German Basic Law has gained over the years is mainly content-based: the circumstances in which the Basic Law was adopted were not very conducive to its legitimacy. On the other hand, it may happen that origin-based legitimacy loses its edge because of an increasing discrepancy between constitutional provisions – for example, an outdated Bill of Rights – and the moral principles and ethical values of society.

The juridical constitution constitutes, facilitates, the law both as a normative legal order, especially as it appears at its surface level, and the legislative and judicial practices which (re)produce that order through formal legal speech acts. In the legal dimension, too, constituting entails organising: determining and authorising the institutional sites of legislative and judicial practices. The juridical constitution also defines the territorial jurisdiction of surface-level law and the legal practices (re)producing it. State borders delineate the territorial sphere of validity of the legal order, as well as the territorial reach of the authority of legislative and judicial institutions. In the temporal dimension, a constitution establishes the peculiar dialectic of change and stability, which derives from a combination of the malleability of positive law with the relative stability of the constitution. In the social dimension of law, a constitution exerts a constitutive effect in respect of not only legislation and adjudication, but even first-order sociolegal practices. Through fundamental rights, a constitution not only converts subjects into citizens but also guarantees the autonomy where lifeworld practices and relationships become possible.

The constitutive function of a constitution is important but its importance should not be overestimated. The constitution is an innovation of modern state law; there is legal history predating the constitution and there may be legal history succeeding it. Even in modern state law, a constitution's constitutive function covers merely surface-level positive law. Emergence and stabilisation, that is, constitution, of the sub-surface, legal-cultural layers follows a different logic: the logic of sedimentation. In this logic, constitution-giving is only one leg in a process of longer duration.

In the juridical dimension, too, the constitutive function is closely linked to positioning. And in this dimension, too, the crux of positioning consists of the claim to autonomy. Through the constitution, a polity and its political regime claims political sovereignty and a legal regime legal sovereignty. The latter claim is two-pronged, covering both normative and institutional autonomy. The legal regime asserts exclusive authority to identify the norms it comprises, and to determine their legal effects and relations to other normative orders. Such normative autonomy cannot be defended without judicial and concomitant interpretative autonomy. Yet note: the assertion of normative and interpretative autonomy only concerns surface-level law.

Beyond the Constitution

A constitution accomplishes a constitutive function with regard to all three modes of existence of law: it facilitates the surface-level legal order as a hierarchical normative structure; it contains the constitutional norms that qualify particular spatio-temporal events as legislative and judicial practices and their outcomes as formal legal speech acts contributing to (re)production of the legal order; and through fundamental rights, it constitutes a sphere of private and public autonomy where social actors can engage in their lifeworld activities.

The constitutive function has often been discussed in still more fundamental terms and related to the emergence of legal normativity and centralised political power as such; this could be called the foundational function. At this level, discussions on political and juridical constitutions intertwine. The question of the foundational constitutive function can be posed with regard not only to the law but also the state or sovereign power. In theorists' search for ultimate foundations, crossing from the juridical to the political or vice versa also occurs; the key to unlocking a cul-de-sac in the juridical dimension might be sought in the political dimension and vice versa.

In the background of the discussion lies the Kantian issue of the justifiability of coercive power. According to Max Weber's well-known definition, what characterises the modern state is a monopoly over legitimate violence, and sovereignty, too, is usually connected to supreme authority over internal and external use of coercive power. In turn, from Kant to Kelsen and beyond, law has been distinguished from morals by the coercion guaranteeing its realisation. Thus, even when the focus is on the foundations of legal normativity, also at stake is the justifiability of coercion or, to put it more bluntly, violence. The problem is not only, and perhaps not even primarily, historical, but accompanies the law here and now: what justifies *hic et nunc* coercive power and the obligation to obey and apply the law? Even if the explanation invokes historical origins of political power and law, the claim is that these carry over their justifying effects to the present day.

Explanations of the foundational function fall into two main groups: normativist and power-theoretical or political. The distinction is far from clear-cut: power-theoretical accounts may involve normative elements and normativist ones may turn out to be apologies for naked power. A major point in normativist criticism of power-theoretical explanations is a claim of hidden normativism. In turn, power theorists tend to denigrate normativism as a mere ideological veil over factual power. Common to most accounts – both normativist and power-theoretical – is a hierarchical reading where higher levels of norms or power authorise lower ones. Yet, as we have seen in discussing legal positivists' Master Rule, at some point one arrives at a supreme norm or instance of power which cannot be authorised by a still higher level. The unauthorised supreme echelon clearly calls for an extra-systemic explanation; an explanation that locates the foundational function and provides for the legitimacy of coercive power.

Hobbes was an early power theorist. He did not yet employ the modern constitutional idiom, but relied on the vocabulary of sovereignty and social contract. Hobbes' problem was to justify subjects' obligation to obey the

Sovereign and show the illimitability and indivisibility of sovereignty. Laws are commands of the Sovereign, and subordinate powers ought to be obeyed because they are authorised by the Sovereign. The chain of authorisation stops at the Sovereign, whose authority to issue commands – positive laws – which subjects are obligated to obey derives from the social contract and natural law. The typical normativist critique points to the role of natural law in facilitating the conclusion and binding nature of the social contract. Hobbes, the archetypical power theorist, is argued to rely ultimately on a normative point.[3]

The power-theoretical account came to have a long-lasting influence on English political and legal theory, although in an impoverished form. After the social contract and natural law had lost their credibility as justifications of sovereignty and positive law, all that was left was sovereignty as a social fact. Thus, John Austin defined sovereignty in purely factual terms, by reference to the habit of obedience on the part of the subjects. By the same token, the aspect of legitimacy was lost: if legal normativity springs from sovereignty as a social fact, how can coercive power and the obligation to obey and apply the law be justified? The constitution was not an answer. For Austin, constitutional law was not really law at all but a species of political morality.

The peculiarities of English constitutionalism go a long way to explaining why the constitution has played such a minor role in accounts of the foundations of legal normativity. Even Hart, who demolished Bentham's and Austin's power-theoretical accounts of legal normativity, hardly mentions constitution, although his notion of secondary rules – at least as concerns rules of change and adjudication – can be given a constitutional reading. With Hart, English legal theory took a step from a power-theoretical to a normativist direction, but largely bypassing the constitution. In contrast, on the Continent both normativists and power theorists have discussed the foundational function in constitutional terms. Both camps agree that the constitution cannot be the final answer but the solution must be sought beyond it. If Hobbes is the archetypical power theorist, Kelsen is the archetypical normativist. For him, the problem of the foundational function concerns the reason for the validity of the historically first constitution, and the solution is supposed to lie in the transcendental, hypothetical, *Grundnorm*. Kelsen clearly recognises that the historically first constitution cannot accomplish the foundational function because it does not possess the capacity to auto-authorise. Yet in some contexts Kelsen characterises the *Grundnorm* as a constitution in the logical sense of the term. The *Grundnorm* as a constitution in the logical sense of the term authorises adoption of the historically first constitution and, by the same token, accounts for the validity of all norms subsequently created in accordance with that constitution.[4]

[3] Lagerspetz, 1995, 105ff. [4] Kelsen, 1967, 199.

The *Grundnorm* as a solution to the problem of the foundational function is riddled with paradoxes. Kelsen depicts the realm of the legal Ought as a product of volition: legislative acts of will. Yet the *Grundnorm* is not a product of volition but a presupposition for cognition. The hypothetical, presupposed, *Grundnorm* contradicts positivity as the basic tenet of Legal Positivism. Law clearly needs a non-legal basis, but for an extreme positivist such as Kelsen this should be a problem: How can the edifice of posited norms arise on a non-positive foundation? German expressions convey the idea of the *Grundnorm* being somehow pre-posited; if legal norms are posited, *gesetzt,* the *Grundnorm* has been *vor-gesetzt,* that is, not only 'presupposed' but even 'pre-posited'. If this was Kelsen's point – which I doubt – it would not come to more than a semantic trick: to call the *Grundnorm vor-gesetzt* – pre-posited - would hardly account for how it can found the validity – and, by the same token, normativity – of positive law. It is a sign of how puzzled Kelsen was of the exact nature of his *Grundnorm* that he even flirted with a power-theoretical account. In a relatively early article, he argued that, in a certain sense, the *Grundnorm* signals the transformation of power into law.[5] And in the second edition of *Reine Rechtslehre,* he remarked that the historically first constitution has become valid in a revolutionary way, 'either by a breach of a former constitution or for a territory that formerly was not the sphere of validity of a constitution and a national legal order based on it'.[6] The *Grundnorm* appears to be but an apology for a successful revolution or secession. This also means that the *Grundnorm* can only be identified ex post; it can never have any ex ante guiding impact. If Hobbes was a crypto-normativist, Kelsen appears to have been a crypto-power theorist.

Kelsen declines to clothe the power-theoretical implications of the *Grundnorm* in any legitimacy garb. This distinguishes him from overt power theorists, who employ the notion of constituent power (*pouvoir constituant*). The people as the sovereign power behind the constitution are supposed to confer legitimacy on the powers constituted in accordance with the constitution (*pouvoirs constitués*). The normativist criticism of the notion of constituent power boils down to the claim that constituent power can be neither identified nor exercised without a normative framework. Norms are needed to define who belongs to the *demos* entitled to wield constituent power, and norms are needed to determine the procedures and forms in which the subjects of constituent power take their decisions on the constitution. If no such norms exist, constituent power and its effectuation are matters of assertion, and constitutional developments are left at the mercy of factual power relations. But can such norms exist? If it is the constituent power that accomplishes the foundational function, how could the norms qualifying the

[5] Kelsen, 1957, 437. [6] Kelsen, 1967, 200.

constituent power be constituted? If Kelsen ultimately turns out to be an apologist of naked power, theorists of constituent power do not fare any better.

The oeuvre of Carl Schmitt, Kelsen's nemesis in twentieth-century legal and constitutional theory, epitomises the perils of the power-theoretical position relying on the notion of constituent power. Schmitt makes a pivotal distinction between a constitution – or constitution in the positive sense – and a constitutional act (*Verfassungsgesetz*). As distinct from a constitutional act, the constitution is not a norm but a decision (*Entscheidung*) on the nature and form of political unity, taken by the constituent power (*verfassungsgebende Gewalt*); in a democracy by the people as a pre-existing political entity. Schmitt replaces Kelsen's *Grundnorm* as the foundation of the constitution as a normative entity – *Verfassungsgesetz* for Schmitt – with a non-normative, existential, decision of the constituent power. A positive constitution and a constitutional act specifying its normative implications are valid because they emanate from the constituent power. Schmitt brushes aside Kelsen's *Grundnorm* and contends that Kelsen's view of validity leads to natural law.[7]

What made Schmitt's influential theorising especially dangerous in the Weimar Republic was the latent presence of the constituent power, allied with what Schmitt called sovereign dictatorship, as a continuous menace, not only to the constitutional act but even the underlying existential decision on the constitution in its positive sense. As distinct from the constitutionally defined emergency powers of a commissionary dictator, sovereign dictatorship does not aim to restore the conditions for implementing the constitution in force but to create the conditions for a new constitution; a new decision by the constituent power on the specific nature and form of political unity. Schmitt's notions of the positive constitution, constituent power, and sovereign dictatorship display almost limitless flexibility. Only ex post can one recognise that sovereign dictatorship has paved the way for a new existential decision by the constituent power. Schmitt simply dismisses the normativist criticism related to identification of the *demos* and the procedure and form of its decisions. These are trivialities which should not derail attention at crucial moments in the nation's history.[8] With his theorising, Schmitt made a major contribution to the constitutional and political instability, and, ultimately, the demise of the Weimar Republic.

What conclusions should we draw from the preceding discussion? First, whether we focus on the political or legal aspect, in a hierarchical framing of the issue the search for the location of the foundational function cannot escape the problem of regress. To solve the problem an extra-legal explanation is

[7] Schmitt, (1928) 2008, 75–79. [8] Schmitt, (1921) 2014.

needed. Even Kelsen's *Grundnorm* as a 'constitution in a logical sense of the word' is not a valid norm but as a transcendental presupposition lies outside the sphere of validity and invalidity. Secondly, the division into normativist and power-theoretical accounts of the foundational function is not as unambiguous as may seem at first glance. If natural law is excluded, normativists appear to have difficulties in avoiding taking recourse to factual power, which can only be authorised ex post but not ex ante. This was even Kelsen's predicament, which he could not hide behind the epistemological veil he threw over the *Grundnorm*. In turn, power-theoretical accounts owe us an explanation for the authority of the supreme power, the Sovereign, and this may involve them in a normative discussion. Here Hobbes' recourse to natural law is instructive. In our contemporary era, natural-law justification can no longer accomplish its task. More promising is the alternative of invoking the democratic idea of self-legislation, advocated by, say, Rousseau and Kant, and inherent in the notion of a democratic *Rechtsstaat*. This alternative is also adopted by those employing the constitutional idiom, including the concepts of *pouvoir constituant* and *pouvoirs constitués*. But, as I have already observed, these theorists owe an answer to questions concerning the definition of those entitled to wield constituent power – the *demos* – and the procedures and forms in which this is supposed to occur. Schmitt's Weimar writings and their influence should work as a cautionary illustration of the potential consequences of ignoring these normatively oriented questions.

We seem to be moving in a circle: normative accounts take us to naked power as a social fact, and power-theoretical interpretations call for normative justification and specification. This has been acutely noted by theorists who argue that law is founded on a fundamental paradox. For Luhmann, the fundamental paradox of the legal system is that the distinction between legal and illegal, which separates legal communications constituting the legal system from non-legal communications in its environment, cannot be applied reflexively to this distinction itself. Distinguishing between legal and illegal is neither legal nor illegal. In that sense, the legal system as a whole lies beyond the distinction between legal and illegal ((il)legality in short). The fundamental distinction which a system uses in its observations is a blind spot which remains unobservable to the system and can only be observed from the outside, applying another distinction. Hans Lindahl calls this the Kelsenian paradox and attributes to the *Grundnorm* the function of dissolving it. Lindahl argues that the paradoxical foundation of law shows the primacy of a-legality over (il)legality and entails the constant presence of a-legality as a spectre overshadowing present (il)legality. Lindahl's argument seems to be that if law is ultimately founded on a-legality, the way it now allocates (il)legality and draws the limit between legally relevant and irrelevant is ultimately arbitrary, and cannot be insulated against questioning by subsequent acts of a-legality; subversive acts which defy the binary categorisation of legal/illegal. The original sin of a-legality cannot be atoned for.[9]

I am not sure that the argument holds. Lindahl himself evokes the counterargument from acceptance.[10] Acceptance by the legal collective, which can simply take the form of actualising the practical possibilities opened up by the law, might expiate the original sin and redeem the a-legal origin of (il)legality. This is also Searle's answer to the question how production of institutional facts can get going in the first place in the absence of constitutive rules which those facts would actualise; that is, Searle's proposal for managing the foundational paradox, which has occupied Western thinkers at least since Hobbes.[11] Lindahl takes note of the counterargument from acceptance, but at the end of the day brushes it off as insufficient and sticks to the intractability of the fundamental paradox, the inerasable taint of foundational a-legality.

Let us recall to mind what the issue is to which proposals for identifying the foundational function have been proffered as a solution. It is the foundation for and legitimacy of legal normativity and the accompanying centralised coercion. This is not an innocent theoretical issue but the stakes can be high, especially in times when theoretical contributions also intervene in general political and ideological discourse. This was the case in Hobbes' mid-seventeenth-century England and Schmitt's (and Kelsen's) Weimar Republic.

The cul-de-sac of normative regress, from which Kelsen sought exit with his *Grundnorm* and Hart with his rule of recognition, is inevitable only on three premises. Firstly, law is examined merely as a normative legal order. Secondly, law is understood as a uni-level, self-contained normative order, separate from non-legal normativity, such as morals. And thirdly, the self-contained, uni-level normative legal order is hierarchically structured with the constitution occupying the top echelon. If these premises are acknowledged, we inescapably stand before the legal positivist dilemma. The dilemma cannot be resolved within the closed, hierarchically structured normative legal order but takes theorists to look for support outside positive law; be it Kelsen's *Grundnorm*, located beyond legal validity; Hart's rule of recognition, a social but also an obligatory rule; the *pouvoir constituant* of revolutionary constitutionalists; a Schmittian existential *Entscheidung* by the *Volk*; or Hobbes' social contract, backed up by natural law. Yet, instead of resolving the dilemma, the proposals seem only to engender new aporias and paradoxes.

The aporia starts to dissolve the moment we question the premises and perceive that a normative legal order does not consist merely of surface-level norms, which could be organised in a hierarchical *Stufenbau* topped by a constitution, but includes legal-cultural layers not only enabling but also justifying and limiting what can appear on law's surface; and that in addition to the normative aspects, law also consists of sociolegal practices where legal

[9] Lindahl, 2013, 147–148. [10] Ibid., 150. [11] Searle, 1995, 41.

norms are realised and (re)produced. It turns out that exactly those aspects which Kelsen and other legal normativists tend to exclude from law are vital for understanding the foundations of legal normativity and explaining its legitimacy. Sub-surface, legal-cultural, layers keep the law receptive to moral and ethical influences, and prevent it from drifting too far from lifeworld normativity and losing its overall legitimacy. Even in a democratic *Rechtsstaat*, some laws may contradict prevailing moral or ethical premises, as instances of civil disobedience or conscientious objection show. Yet such discrepancies are ultimately manageable by democratic law-making procedures and specialised practices of constitutional review.

At the end of the day, legal normativity rests on the correspondence of legal deep culture to the general moral and ethical groundwork of society. Without such a broad correspondence law could not be realised as part of the general normativity structuring everyday first-order social practices. Here we are dealing with law as institution, deeply enmeshed in the normative structures of the everyday lifeworld of social actors. Quantitatively speaking, law as institution may be in retreat in front of increasing legal instrumentalisation and expansion of law as a medium of social engineering. Yet, for the overall legitimacy of law and the foundation of legal normativity, the role of law as institution is as indispensable as before. With regard to substantive legitimacy, law as medium is parasitic on law as institution.

Establishing legal normativity is not a one-time achievement as is implied by all theories which locate the foundational function in a foundational norm, such as the *Grundnorm*, or a foundational act, such as a social contract or an exercise of *pouvoir constituant*. Legal normativity must be constantly re-established. Legal normativity, which involves coercive power and an obligation to obey and apply the law, cannot survive without renewal of acceptance and consent by those it addresses; the legal community in its broad and narrow sense. Origin-based legitimacy of a constitution wears out without reconfirmation of the commitment of the legal community, which in turn presupposes a minimum of content-based legitimacy; correspondence to moral principles and ethical values. Re-ratification of the commitment of the legal community to the constitution and the law in general can occur – and arguably does primarily occur – through realisation of the practical possibilities that the law and the constitution offer; creation of instances of legal institutions.

It is to the credit of Hart that he does not define his foundational rule as a one-time achievement; that he links it to judicial practice and thus draws in the social aspect of law; and that by presupposing the adoption of an internal point of view by judges, he also introduces an element of acceptance which must be constantly reaffirmed. Still, Hart, too, tends to reduce the normative contents of law into its surface-level manifestations; to ignore the legal-cultural layers with their moral and ethical linkages; and to bypass law's presence in the everyday lifeworld and the importance of acceptance not only by the legal community in *sensu stretto* but also the legal community at large.

Lindahl is right that the Kelsenian paradox proves that behind the order of (il)legality lies a-legality. The historically first constitution was not issued on a legal authorisation; the regress of the chain of formal validity necessitates an extra-systemic break-up; and the foundational function must find its location outside the constitution. Another matter is what conclusions one can draw from the a-legal origins of (il)legality. To claim that due to original a-legality an ineradicable stigma of illegitimacy or a threat of subsequent (legitimate) a-legality accompanies the law certainly overstates the case. Such a claim ignores the healing and redeeming remedy of acceptance and content-based legitimacy. Yet absence of acceptance and legitimacy may of course signal the moment of a-legality that questions the present order of (il)legality and its constitutional premises. For theorists adopting a power-theoretical conceptual framework, this is the moment when the dormant constituent power is reactivated and when it tends to break out from the constitutional cage where constitutional procedures of constitutional amendment attempt to imprison it.

We should not overestimate the importance or reach of the debate on the foundational function; on the a-legality of the issuance of revolutionary and secessionist constitutions; on the constitutional moment as a moment of exception and sovereign dictatorship as paving the way for a new start to constitutional continuity; or on the violence underlying law. Neither in politics nor in law do constitutions, not even revolutionary or secessionist ones, signify a completely new beginning; revolutionary constitutions do not revolutionise everything nor do secessionist constitutions start from scratch. Revolutions usually strive for political rather than legal upheaval, and what the revolutionary constitution revolutionises is primarily the political and not the legal regime. In Kelsen's terms, a successful revolution leads to a new *Grundnorm* which, formulated as a duty-imposing rule, involves the order to behave in accordance with the new constitution and the legal order established under its authorisation. Yet, in spite of changing the basis of authorisation, revolutions may leave much of the lower-level legislation intact. And where a successful revolution does not have any direct impact is non-legislative law and subsurface legal culture. It is possible that a revolutionary constitution launches a new process of sedimentation which, as time passes, leads to legal-cultural renewal. Yet such an impact is not immediate; legal culture follows the reformist logic of small steps rather than the revolutionary logic of complete breaks.

Perhaps paradoxically, the discussion on constituent power and the foundational violence on which law allegedly rests shares the regress argument and the fallacies of the legal positivist thesis of the Master Rule. It is the public-law fallacy of law consisting of a hierarchical *Stufenbau* that leads to searching the foundations of legal normativity beyond the constitution, in legally unauthorised, a-legal exercise of *pouvoir constituant* or sovereign dictatorship, manifesting, if not necessarily illegitimate, at least non-authorised violence. The first constitution of independent Finland – a typical secessionist constitution – was adopted in 1919 by a rump parliament, with only one socialist member attending. Constitutional continuity with eighteenth-century Swedish constitutional acts was largely a camouflage. Constitution-giving in 1919 was an a-legal act of the *pouvoir constituant* or sovereign dictatorship of the victorious white side – a counter-revolutionary rather than revolutionary constitution – and the preceding civil war in 1918 was a textbook epitome of foundational violence. So all the elements were there: a-legality, *pouvoir constituant*, sovereign dictatorship, foundational violence. Still, not much changed in the legal regime, either in the normative dimension of the legal order or the social dimension of legal practices. Arguably, though, the constitution launched a renewal of constitutional culture, continuing well into the post–World War II decades. Yet to claim that the law in Finland is ultimately grounded in the foundational violence of the civil war in 1918 would not be very convincing.

The Great Mediator

The constitution belongs to both the political and legal domains of society, and performs important functions in both of these. Equally important is that the constitution mediates between politics and law, establishing a structural coupling between the two, as Luhmann put it in his terminology of autopoietic systems theory. The constitution facilitates and even justifies the influence of politics on law and law on politics. A formal constitution is simultaneously a political and a legal speech act, as are the laws produced in the politico-legal legislative practices determined by the constitution. As the constitution enshrines the positivity of modern state law, it also gives legal permission to the political determination of the contents of law. Yet the constitution not only empowers – authorises – politics; through its restrictive function, primarily performed by fundamental rights and the system of checks and balances disciplining constitutional authorities, it also imposes limitations. Finally, revolutions and secessions, leading to revolutionary and secessionist constitutions, are both political and legal events; interruptions of both political and legal continuity, although, as I have argued, in the legal respect their repercussions may not be as dramatic as is often imagined.

The constitution plays a mediating role, not only between law and politics but within law as well. A formal constitution is a legal speech act – a standing Declaration – on the surface of law, and even in states with no single integrated written constitution, constitutional law is inferred from formal legal speech acts. Although an element of surface-level law, the constitution maintains intimate links with sub-surface, even deep-cultural principles, defining the basic features of a democratic *Rechtsstaat*; principles related to fundamental rights, democracy, and the rule of law. The constitution mediates between surface-level law and deep-cultural principles. Fundamental rights, for instance, appear both as surface-level, applicable constitutional norms – with properties of both rules and principles – and as general legal principles with relevance as, say, interpretative principles across diverse fields law. As general principles, fundamental rights result from a similar, often twisted and conflictual, process of sedimentation as elements of legal culture in general. Moreover, again in line with other sub-surface law, fundamental-rights principles must be reconstructed starting from their surface-level manifestations. Once sedimented in legal culture, fundamental-rights principles affect the turbulent developments on the surface of law, mostly through the *Vorverständnis* of legal professionals. This is recursiveness, typical of modern state law. On the one hand, the constitution occupies the uppermost echelon in the Kelsenian *Stufenbau* of legislative law. On the other hand, it manifests deep-cultural legal principles. The constitution is higher law both in a formal and a substantive sense. In the constitution, two ways of conceiving law's internal relations of determination and subordination meet.

In the dialectic of *voluntas* and *ratio*, deep-cultural principles, specific to a democratic *Rechtsstaat*, exemplify the moral and ethical dimensions of practical reason. The constitution provides this *ratio* with a surface-level expression. In reaffirming the positivity of law, the constitution facilitates the decisive influence of legislative *voluntas* on the law's contents. Yet fundamental rights and constitutional review monitoring their observance restrict the free rein of this *voluntas*. Thus, the constitution also mediates between the *voluntas* and *ratio* of law.

Finally, as we have seen, some constitutions, but not all, manifest a-legal *pouvoir constituant* and establish legal *pouvoirs constitués*; are grounded in foundational violence and legitimate state monopoly of violence; and result from the exercise of sovereign dictatorship and facilitate constitutional (commissionary) dictatorship. The great mediator also mediates between *pouvoir constituant* and *pouvoir constitué*; foundational and constitutionally legitimised violence; and sovereign and constitutional dictatorship.

Part III
Plurality

11

The Black-Box View

Unity and Plurality

This essay employs the perspective of modern state law. In this Part, I discuss developments which problematise the taken-for-granted state-centrist features of my framework. I have already questioned two of the foundational reductions of Legal Positivism: law's reduction to normativity and legal normativity's reduction to its surface level. The time has come to attack even the third one: the reduction of law to state law. The rise of non-state law has profoundly altered the setting for examining the plurality of law. Yet in the following the dominant perspective from which non-state law will be examined will still be that of state law. The conceptual language will be the legal language of modern state law, and the distinctions that govern my approach to non-state law derive from this particular type of law.

Unity and plurality of law stand in a dialectical relationship. Unity is conceived against the background of plurality, and plurality consists of unities. How unity is understood affects the view of plurality and vice versa. Here the black-box view of Legal Positivism is instructive. Although Kelsen's and Hart's Legal Positivism did not ignore plurality – this holds in particular for Kelsen – the clear focus was on the unity of a distinct state legal regime. Yet implicit in Legal Positivism's construction of unity was the coexistence of the particular state legal order with other instances of state law.

Unity relates to identity. Unity confers on an instance of law an identity, and how unity is depicted determines how identity is conceived. If unity is understood as formal unity, created by formal ordering criteria, identity is understood as formal identity. For Legal Positivism, unity is formal unity of surface-level law: in synchronic respect, unity under a common Master Rule, complemented by logical consistency; in diachronic respect, continuity of the Master Rule. Such unity can only produce formal identity: identity as sameness. Legal Positivism ignores substantive unity, created by sub-surface, legal-cultural layers. Consequently, it also ignores substantive identity, or identity as selfhood.

The connection between unity and identity highlights the implicit presence of plurality. Identity implies non-identity; existence of the non-identical, the other.

Portrayal of the unity and identity of a particular instance of law also demarcates this instance from its other; the non-identical. Legal Positivism relates unity and identity to autonomy. The Master Rule is supposed to guarantee not only the unity and identity but also the autonomy of a state legal order, and in two directions: in respect not only of non-legal normativity but also of other instances of state law. Only as such autonomous legal orders are instances of state law seen to participate in plurality. Legal Positivism approaches law from the perspective of a particular state legal order. The default assumption is that law is state law, and that state law is positive law, posited by legislative and judicial bodies. Plurality is plurality of instances of state law, including international law as interstate law.

In its black-box model, Legal Positivism treats national legal orders as mutually closed normative entities, isolated in their respective compartments. They are supposed to exist in plurality, but plurality is understood as simple diversity; as the mere coexistence of self-contained and self-sufficient national legal orders, without any hint at their interconnections, be they of conflictual or cooperative and dialogical character. Plurality is subordinated to unity. What matters for positivist legal theory is to reconstruct and explain the self-contained unity of a positive national legal order. This is legal plurality as solipsism or legal plurality in accordance with the black-box model. Each state legal regime is engaged only with its own national legal order and does not interfere with the territorially delineated exclusive and universal jurisdiction of other instances of state law.

The solipsist black-box view is built on the foundational reductions of Legal Positivism. First, all law is supposed to be state law; non-state law is treated, explicitly by Kelsen, as a *contradictio in adjecto*. Neither indigenous and religious nor transnational non-state law is recognised on a par with state law. International law has its place in the black-box model, but it is state law as well; interstate law, to be more exact. Secondly, law is examined merely under its normative aspect, as a normative legal order: unity means unity of the state legal order, and plurality means plurality of such unities. Construction of both unity and plurality hints at the indispensability of legislative and judicial practices for maintaining unity, identity, and autonomy. National legal orders can only preserve their self-contained character if normative autonomy is complemented by the legislative and judicial sovereignty of the respective state. Although Legal Positivism hardly thematises the issue, the tacit premise is that the legislator of the self-contained legal regime is the national legislator and that the courts are national courts, as defined by the national constitution. Thirdly, both unity as formal unity and the solipsist view of plurality as simple diversity, instead of interlegality and pluralism of overlapping claims to authority, build on the premise that the normative legal order only exists as surface-level law. Indeed, it would be hard to maintain the black-box model even with regard to state law if the multi-layered nature of law and the porosity of state legal orders at the legal-cultural levels were acknowledged.

Kelsen's Dialectic of Unity and Plurality

Kelsen elaborated his Pure Theory before the rise of transnational law. For him, plurality had two main manifestations: the plurality of national legal orders, and the plurality of national and international law. One might expect that neither of these manifestations of plurality would cause major problems and that Kelsen would conceive of them in accordance with the black-box model. Diverse national legal orders, on the one hand, and national and international law, on the other hand, would appear as self-contained entities, which receive not only formal unity but also identity and autonomy from their submission to a particular *Grundnorm*. Conflicts may occur but merely on the borders of the validity spheres of legal orders.

Indeed, in Kelsen's Pure Theory, relations among national legal orders, all with distinct territorial spheres of validity, correspond to the black-box model. Within its territory, each national legal order, submitted to its *Grundnorm*, enjoys exclusive sovereignty with regard to other national legal orders, and no interdependence worthy of inclusion in the formal, structural, account of the Pure Theory, breaches the isolation of the black boxes. The relations between national and international law are different, and here the black-box model falls short of conveying an accurate image of Kelsen's views.

Kelsen's starting point is the same as in examining the plurality of national legal orders: national and international law are subordinated to their respective *Grundnorm*. Formulation of the *Grundnorm* of international law must heed the fact that much of international law is customary law. Kelsen's proposal is the following: 'the states ought to behave as they have customarily behaved'. The formulation is perhaps not very convincing, bearing in mind that the *Grundnorm* is also supposed to establish legal normativity as such, now in international relationships. What is important for our present discussion is that, despite their diverse *Grundnorms*, in their mutual relations national and international law are not self-contained but interdependent. International law presupposes national legal orders and national legal orders presuppose international law.

Kelsen stresses that all law regulates the behaviour of individuals, and that legal obligations and rights cannot have for their contents but the behaviour of individuals. The immediate object of international law is the mutual behaviour of states. International law treats states as juristic persons, which means it addresses the behaviour of individuals only indirectly, through national legal orders. International law is incomplete in the sense that it leaves national legal orders to determine the individuals whose behaviour constitutes the contents of international duties and rights. International law usually determines only the material or substantive element, and to identify the personal element must be complemented by national law.

Even more important is the dependence of national legal orders on international law. The scope of national legal orders is defined by the four spheres of validity: territorial, personal, temporal, and material. The spheres of validity also define the state, which for Kelsen is identical with the national legal order. Kelsen argued that the identity of the state and the national legal order can be demonstrated by examining the three elements by which the preceding German state law theory – Georg Jellinek, for instance – had defined the state: state territory, state people, and state power. Kelsen's point is that none of these elements can be defined independently of the legal order. Because of the ultimate identity of state and law, Kelsen can demonstrate national law's dependence on international law from the viewpoint of both the state and the national legal order. The territory of a state can only be a part of space, and its people only a part of mankind. States are sovereign with regard to each other, and no state is allowed to interfere with the sovereignty of another state within its territorial and personal sphere. The territorial and personal spheres cannot be delineated by any state legal order because its validity is limited to the territory and the people of the respective state. Delineation is only possible through a normative order whose territorial and personal spheres of validity cover those of all the national legal orders; that is, international law. International law accomplishes this essential function through the principle of effectiveness. It acknowledges a permanently efficacious, coercive order of human behaviour as valid law within a distinct territory and population: in short, a state. Through the principle of effectiveness, international law also determines the temporal sphere of validity of the national legal order and, by the same token, the 'lifespan' of the state. A coercive order is valid and the community it constitutes a state only as long as it is efficacious. Finally, international law may also bear on the material sphere of validity of the national legal order. International law can address any substantive issue, including those that can also be regulated by national law, thus restricting the material sphere of validity of the latter.

Of the two aspects of plurality Kelsen discusses, the plurality of international and national law turns out to be constitutive. The other aspect - coexistence of national legal orders - would not be possible without the contribution of international law, which defines the territorial, personal, and temporal spheres of validity of national legal orders, and, by the same token, enables the coexistence of those orders, as well as the coexistence of a plurality of states. Thus, not only are national and international law interdependent; in addition, the plurality of national legal orders is dependent on international law.

Kelsen's Pure Theory focuses on the unity, identity, and autonomy of an individual national legal order and stops at its *Grundnorm*. Yet when Kelsen moves from unity to plurality and brings in international law, the analysis cannot halt at the plurality of national *Grundnorms*. On Kelsen's account, international law not only determines the territorial, personal, and temporal spheres of validity of national legal orders. International law also provides the reason for the validity of national law. The hypothetical *Grundnorm* which qualifies the 'Fathers of the Constitution' as a law-creating authority is the ultimate reason for validity only when the national legal order is examined in isolation from other national legal orders and international law. When the isolation is breached, it turns out – so Kelsen argues – that the national *Grundnorm* derives from a positive norm of the international legal order, namely the principle of effectiveness. From the perspective of international law, a coercive order based on the historically first constitution is valid because of its efficacy, and only because of this efficacy can the national *Grundnorm* authorise 'the Fathers of the Constitution'. In the discussion restricted to an individual national legal order, Kelsen treats efficacy as an extra-legal, factual condition for validity, distinguishing it sharply from normative reasons. When discussing the dialectic of national and international law, he transforms efficacy into a legal principle and a normative reason for validity. Efficacy proves to possess two aspects: factual and normative. This may seem somewhat surprising in a theoretical (re)construction premised on an axiomatic separation of Is and Ought.

Kelsen's account of the interdependence of national and international law does not affect the plurality of national legal orders. Although from the perspective of international law all national legal orders derive their *Grundnorms* from the international legal principle of efficacy and thus share the same basis for their validity, they remain united merely on the top; beyond the national *Grundnorm*. Below the national *Grundnorm*, they are self-contained and self-sufficient in accordance with the solipsist black-box model. Neither does the dialectic between international and national law have any consequences for the three reductive moves on which the black-box model is premised: the reduction of law to state law, of law to its normative aspect, and of legal normativity to its surface level. Yet Kelsen's depiction of international law as incomplete and dependent on national law could also facilitate understanding transnational law and its interaction with national law: typically, transnational law, too, is incomplete and parasitic on state law.

Still another lesson remains to be learned from Kelsen's treatment of the interrelations between national and international law: perspectivism. This comes clearly to the fore in his discussion of the final unity of the plurality of international law and national legal orders.

For Kelsen, two fundamentally different legal-theoretical readings exist of the relations between national and international law: pluralist and monist. He mounts a devastating critique of the pluralist interpretation. Pluralists do not accept the reasoning which derives the *Grundnorm* of each national legal order from the international-law principle of efficiency. In the black-box model that pluralists embrace, not only national legal orders in their mutual relations, but even national legal orders and international law are independent of each other, all possessing their particular validity bases. The pluralist position assumes the simultaneous validity of national and international law. For Kelsen this is logically impossible. In legal cognition – for instance, in a legal-theoretical reconstruction of law – one must make a choice between the perspectives of the national and international legal order. The situation is analogous to the necessity of choosing between legal and moral orders (or legal and moral cognition). A jurist must ignore morality and a moralist law, and correspondingly, an international jurist must ignore national law and a national jurist international law. In Kelsen's view, pluralists are inconsistent as they treat national and international law as simultaneously valid legal orders. And, Kelsen adds, such inconsistence is unavoidable because, as he believes he has shown, international law is meaningless without the national legal order, and the legal existence of a state cannot be understood without taking into account international law. Furthermore, even in recapitulating plurality, one must choose the perspective of a referential legal order. If the choice falls on national law, one must – provided, of course, that one is consistent – deny the validity not only of international law but also of all national legal orders except the referential one. Thus, paradoxically enough, pluralist premises lead to renouncing both types of legal plurality: both the plurality of national and international law, and the plurality of national legal orders.[1]

I am not sure that Kelsen's argument – that the pluralists implicitly deny the plurality of national legal orders – is valid even on his premises. On the face of it, the argument appears analogous to Kelsen's claim of the impossibility of the simultaneous and independent validity of law and morals, and national and international law. Yet there is a difference. Kelsen claims that two national legal orders can only be held to be simultaneously valid if they can be conceived to form one single system and that only international law can achieve this. However, if one disconnects national and international law, as pluralists do, one also disconnects diverse national legal orders. None of the reasons Kelsen presents to support the impossibility of the simultaneous and independent validity of law and morals or national and international law are applicable to relations among national legal orders. Seen through the Kelsenian framework, national legal orders are not rival normative orders which would possess overlapping spheres of validity, as are law and morals, nor are they connected by structural interdependencies, as are national and international law. Even if we were persuaded by Kelsen's thesis that only one valid normative system can exist within a particular spatio-temporal sphere of validity, what would prevent us from presupposing the parallel coexistence of several normative orders, each confined to a distinct sphere of validity?

Kelsen's contention that two national legal orders can be conceived of as simultaneously valid only if they are treated as one single system is at bottom epistemological; it relates to his epistemological search for the unity of law culminating in universal law bringing all the wayward pluralist sheep safely into an ultimate monist pen. The theorists that Kelsen labels pluralists reject

[1] Kelsen, 1967, 363–365.

this epistemological claim. Pluralists may well concede that the plurality of national legal orders presupposes the existence of international law which delineates the bordering spheres of validity. Still, by no means does this concession entail that simultaneously valid national legal orders must be thought of as forming one single system.

Kelsen deserves merit for introducing perspectivism to the discussion on the interrelations of unity and plurality. Yet Kelsen's is a typical example of what I call extreme perspectivism; a perspectivism which does not allow for any overlaps or dialogue among perspectives but sees these as enclosed as are the compartments in the black-box model. Kelsen's legal-theoretical dexterity is amazing, but for understanding contemporary post-national pluralism his extreme perspectivism is not an option, if it ever was. Kelsen's perspectivism connects to his contention that two simultaneously valid normative orders cannot share the same spatio-temporal sphere of validity. We have seen that he puts forth his claim in two contexts: when discussing the relations between law and morals, and, again, those between national and international law. The case for the necessity of choosing between the perspectives of law and morals is supposed to be equivalent to the necessity to opt for the perspective of either national or international law. The simultaneous validity of law and morals – or of positive and natural law – is logically excluded, and any attempt in this direction leads either classifying positive as natural or natural as positive law.[2]

Kelsen seems to have two arguments. When invoking formal logics, reference is to inevitable contradictions between legal and moral norms, and the requirement for non-contradictoriness. Yet there is another explanation too. Normative orders can be used as a frame of interpretation in assessing spatio-temporal facts, but only one at a time. Thus, one can judge a spatio-temporal event in the light of both legal and moral norms, but not simultaneously. Neither of the two explanations is convincing. Kelsen does not explicate where, exactly, the inevitable logical inconsistence of an overlapping validity of two diverse normative orders lies or why it would be impossible to rely simultaneously on two different normative frameworks. These are crucial defects. They seriously impair the applicability of his theoretical framework to post-national plurality, where overlapping claims of authority, as well as mingling of and dialogue among perspectives, play an essential role.

Farewell to the Black-Box Model

Positivist reductions of law to its normative aspect and the contents of legal normativity to their surface-level expressions have always prejudiced Kelsen's and Hart's formal, hierarchically structured unity of state legal orders and the related black-box model of legal plurality. Attention to the sociality of law and

[2] Kelsen, 1967, 329.

inclusion of legal-cultural layers would have opened state legal orders to each other and turned their borders fuzzy and porous. Yet the rise of non-state law, which had no place in either Kelsen's or Hart's legal worldview – except as a highly stylised starting point of legal evolution or an anthropological or historical curiosity – has drastically undermined the credibility of their view of formal unity even as an account of surface-level law. Not only has the rise of non-state law enriched legal plurality with new instances. It has also produced new evidence of the inadequacy of the black-boxist assumption of self-contained legal orders. Post-national plurality cannot be conceived of in terms of simple diversity, as mere coexistence of distinct legal orders. Diversity has increasingly taken the guise of legal pluralism where different legal regimes raise overlapping and rival claims of authority. And due to the reciprocal opening of state legal regimes, black-boxism and simple diversity convey an increasingly distorted image of the plurality of state law as well. Instead of black-boxist closure, the relations of instances of law adhere to the principle of interlegality.

Unity and plurality form a unity. The way we conceive of the unity of law affects the way we conceive of its plurality, and vice versa. If unity is depicted, as it is in Legal Positivism, as hierarchically structured formal unity, plurality is seen primarily as simple diversity. If pluralist constellations of rival claims to authority are in general conceded, they are portrayed as legally irresolvable confrontations of self-contained, solipsist, legal orders, in accordance with Kelsenian extreme perspectivism. Conversely, when plurality is presented in terms of simple diversity and extreme perspectivism, it leaves the formal unity of state legal orders intact. Yet, as I have already argued, we should be sensitive to the legal-cultural overlaps and interchanges which have been part of law under the dominance of the Westphalian model too. Moreover, we should incorporate the legal-cultural layers in our account of the unity of national law; unity should not be reduced merely to surface-level formal unity. Such a modified view of unity makes it clear that solipsism misrepresents even the diversification of modern state law.

In the era of post-national law, the defects of the solipsist view are more conspicuous than ever. The self-containment of legal orders has been punctured even at the surface level. Interlegality should substitute for state-sovereigntist solipsism as the main organising principle of legal plurality, and plurality, seen primarily as interlegality, should assume the dominant position in its dialectic with unity. What I am proposing here is a reversal of the positivist subordination of plurality to unity. Unity as identity has always been (re)constructed against the backdrop of plurality; the implicit coexistence of other national legal orders. The implicit should be made explicit, and the unity of an instance of law should from the very start be thought of as participating in plurality. It is easy to see that such a turnabout entails revising Legal Positivism's notions of both unity and plurality. The emphasis in plurality shifts from simple diversity to interlegality and pluralism of overlapping jurisdictions, while formal unity gives way to unity created by substantive principles and discursive processes. I do not dispute the significance for legal theory of either unity or plurality, nor, for that matter, their interdependence. Post-national plurality does not negate the unity, identity, or autonomy of the instances of law partaking in the plurality, but it profoundly impacts how these qualities should be conceived of. Sharp-cut distinctions, exclusive dichotomies, and insurmountable borderlines do not help us to make our way in the post-national legal world. And extending the discussion beyond normativity and attending to the social dimension of law, too, facilitates new insights into unity and plurality, as well as their dialectic.

In sum, in a legal theory of and for the post-national era, the unity of a particular instance of law must be recapitulated against the background of the plurality in which it partakes. Post-national plurality, marked by pluralism and interlegality instead of exclusive solipsism, constitutes the context where the internal unity of instances of law should be examined. This holds even for state legal orders, which Legal Positivism has – together with international law – recognised as the only instances of law. This would be a legal theory of the future. This essay, though aspiring to pave the way for the reversal necessitated by the post-national lawscape, has still proceeded in the traditional way, opting for the perspective of a single state legal regime and articulating plurality only at a subsequent stage. Moreover, conscious of the inevitable perspectivism of legal-theoretical enterprises, it has chosen to examine non-state law and its interrelations with state law from the point of view of the latter, using the legal language of that particular type of law and employing its characteristic distinctions.

In the following, I start discussing post-national plurality by examining in Chapter 12 what non-state law is and how it differs from state law. As main categories of non-state law I explore transnational law, indigenous and religious law, as well as human rights law. I am especially interested in seeing how well the conceptual framework I have elaborated in Parts I-II functions in the context of non-state law. Studying non-state law can teach us things about our modern Western state law that otherwise would remain hidden under the veil of the self-certainties of our legal *Vorverständnis*, and remind us that the language we have learned to speak is not the only legal idiom in the world. When characterising its enterprise as conceptual and as focusing on what is essential in law, Legal Positivism has fallen into the universalist trap. Acquainting ourselves with non-state law may save us from a similar fate. My coverage of non-state law in Chapter 12 is far from complete. The field is immense, and I have had to content myself with, I hope, representative examples. Thus, as regards religious law, I only discuss the so-called religions of the book: Judaism, Christianity, and Islam.

After analyzing types of non-state law, I focus on how relations among instances of law have changed under post-national plurality: how interlegality and pluralism of rival claims to authority have supplanted the simple diversity of the black-box template; and how controversies between instances of law have altered so that fundamental conflicts of authority have become an ever-present possibility, threatening 'peaceful' interlegality (Chapter 13). I wrap up by discussing in Chapter 14 how plurality has impacted unity; both as internal unity of particular instances of law and as unity of diverse instances. I bid farewell to Kelsen by arguing that instead of the unity of universal law we must content ourselves with a plurality of unities.

Especially when discussing indigenous and religious law, I move in unfamiliar terrain. Mine is the perspective of legal theory. The ambition is not to contribute to debates on legal history or anthropology, or religious studies, but, rather, to sieve legal-theoretical implications from the findings and insights of the craft. These, of course, may be controversial, and I may on some issues fall into the very trap of unwarranted generalisation against which I have cautioned. In this essay, my interest in transnational law, including human rights, is legal-theoretical by nature as well. However, thanks to previous expeditions, here the ground under my feet feels somewhat more solid.

12

Non-State Law

Epistemological Difficulties

Merely sixty years have elapsed since Kelsen published the second edition of *Reine Rechtslehre* and Hart *The Concept of Law*. For the Masters of Legal Positivism, the self-evident premise was that all law is state law, either intra- or interstate. Non-state law entered their field of vision primarily as an imaginary primitive normative regime which constituted both a contrast to a developed legal system and a starting point for legal evolution, ending up with fully fledged state law. Whether they considered the primitive regime as law or not remains unclear. During the decades separating us from publication of the *chefs d'oeuvre* of Legal Positivism, the monopoly of state law has been threatened by the rise of what has come to be called non-state law. Usually, a distinction is drawn between non-state law above and below the state. In this distinction, transnational law represents non-state law above, with indigenous and religious law below the state. Yet the distinction may be misleading: transnational law displays a local and the law of world religions a transnational dimension. In most cases, transnational legal regimes are genuinely new formations, whose background consists in the social mega-trend dubbed globalisation or, to use a less pretentious expression, denationalisation. By contrast, indigenous or religious normative regimes are no recent newcomers but predate modern state law. What is new is recognition, though haltingly, of their legal relevance by state law.

I have defended the epistemological primacy of modern state law by the differentiations which this type of law has undergone; such as the detachment of legal norms from sociolegal practices; the separation of specialised legal practices from first-order sociolegal practices; and a corresponding detachment of secondary rules from primary rules of behaviour or of constitution from other law. These differentiations facilitate construing an heuristic conceptual framework with which other types of law, too, can be approached. However, the crucial difference between modern state law and other instances populating the contemporary legal universe may lie – and most probably does lie – in the very fact that the latter do not display all these differentiations. And even if they did and a distinction could for instance be drawn between norms and practices, neither the normative nor the social would necessarily possess the same features as in modern state law. Legal normativity would not necessarily be distinguished from non-legal normativity by the characteristics of textuality, positivity, coerciveness, and order, nor would there necessarily be similar second-order legal practices specialised in judicial, legislative, and doctrinal functions. We stand in front of a dilemma. On the one hand, the legal language of modern state law or the conceptual frameworks elaborated in its self-observation – to resort to a Luhmannian term – do not appear to travel very well, in particular to indigenous and religious law. On the other hand, as children of this particular type of law we are not able to abandon our mother tongue or to develop a meta-language liberated from the influences of the mother tongue. No alternative exists to admitting the non-negatable and trying to make the best of it. We must concede the inescapable perspectivism in the treatment of non-state law and attempt to exploit the analytical potential of the conceptual framework worked out to capture the differentiations typical of modern state law. If this is Eurocentrism or legal-cultural imperialism, it is Eurocentrism and legal-cultural imperialism that can hardly be avoided.

Classifying instances of non-state law is also a perspectival exercise which is denied the privilege of a bird's-eye view. Even talk of state and non-state law implies the use of state law, not only as the template of 'complete' or 'fully fledged' law, but also as the premise for analyzing post-national plurality. Other instances of law are not only defined but also arranged in relation to state law, as becomes clear by the subsequent division into non-state law below and above the state. My proposal is to retain the state-law perspective and, as a corollary, the basic distinction between state and non-state law, although at the same time emphasising that the boundary is far from clear-cut; that the autonomy of both state and non-state law is increasingly compromised; and that transnational law is not only transnational but often also state law. By contrast, I suggest abandoning the division into non-state law above and below the state. Transnational law is not only law above the state but often enough also part of state law and effective at a local level within the state. The law of the religions of the book possesses both a transnational and an intra-state aspect and may even constitute state law. It is state law where the constitution expressly accords it that status, as does the constitution of Saudi Arabia to sharia; it is non-state law below the state as the law of religious minorities; and its written sources claim transnational authority. Indigenous law could be argued to be an uncontroversial case of non-state law below the state. Still, the protection offered and the restrictions imposed by human rights law add to it a transnational ingredient, as does the transnational networking of indigenous peoples; sometimes called globalisation from below.

I would suggest that non-state law, typical of post-national plurality and fatal to the black-box model, be examined as the following sub-types:

- transnational law
- indigenous law
- religious law
- human rights law

Transnational Law

Transnational law includes a heterogeneous array of normative formations beyond the distinction between national and international law. How should its boundaries in these two directions be drawn? As is the case with distinguishing law from non-law, sharp divisions within the legal universe are to a large extent quasi-issues – relics from the era of the dominance of the black-box model. These divisions, too, are perspectival, and no right way of drawing the boundaries exists. Furthermore, wherever they are drawn, they are bound to be blurred and porous. Transnational law is produced above the level of states, by public or private international or transnational organisations. Its normative authority traverses state borders. Unlike international law, it is not interstate law, focusing on relations among states, but addresses intra-state and cross-border practices. Unlike national law, it does not circumscribe its claim to authority in territorial but in substantive, issue-specific, terms. Its focus may, like national law's, be intra-state but typically – and as distinct from national law – it also attends to social practices and relationships that transcend state borders. Transnational law is transnational in both its sociality and normativity; in both its (re)production and realisation and the claim to authority of its norms.

Transnational legal regimes may have their background in international agreements, as do, say, EU and WTO law, as well as human rights law. International organisations under international law also play an important role in transnational norm-production. The United Nations Commission on International Trade (UNCITRAL) and the International Institute for the Unification of Private Law (UNIDROIT) are two prominent examples. Even when established under international law, transnational regimes have detached themselves from their international legal background. However, the divorce is never complete, as is shown, for example, by the dual constitutional and international legal nature of the Founding Treaties of the EU. In turn, soft-law norms produced by international organisations for harmonising national legislations are inserted in transnational legal normativity and transnational legal regimes, and do not significantly differ from norms created by private actors such as the Lando group. Yet transnational and international law remain intertwined, and what scholars of transnational law dub transnational legal regimes, their international legal colleagues may examine as regimes of international law. Furthermore, transnational law remains intertwined not only with international but also with national law, co-opting segments of national legal orders and practices.

Common to instances of transnational law is the primarily substantive character of the scope of their normative authority. As distinct from multipurposive state law, transnational law is issue-specific, each instance focusing on particular cross-border concerns. The backdrop to the expansion of transnational law lies in the denationalisation of social practices and relationships; in the impotence of state legal regimes to respond to the problems that denationalisation raises, including those of an ecological character; and the often detrimental effects of the simple diversity of national legal regimes. Fragmentation of national responses to transnational problems is a major cause of the growth of transnational law. Yet, in reacting to black-box fragmentation, transnational law engenders a new, issue-specific type of fragmentation.

Whatever substantive coherence a state legal order displays, coherence is mainly principle- and not policy-based. In transnational law, the contrary holds: whatever substantive coherence instances of transnational law display, coherence is mainly policy- and not principle-based. If state legal regimes can in general be said to possess a common normative point, the closest we can come to it is what has come to be called constitutional identity, manifest by the fundamental principles and values enshrined in the constitution. Constitutional identity may be highly controversial: a matter of ongoing debate. In transnational legal regimes, the point is easier to identify: it relates to the transnational policy issue that the regime has been established to address. In the division between law as medium and institution, transnational law typically falls to the former side, with the notable exception of human rights law.

A natural premise for an internal classification of transnational law consists in the social practices and corresponding policy fields on which instances of transnational law focus. Thus, there are transnational legal regimes concentrating on cross-border trade, such as the WTO and regional regimes of which the EU, though, has transcended its original purpose; cross-border commerce, such as the debated *lex mercatoria*; cross-border financial markets and practices, such as prudential regulation and supervision of financial institutions, or cross-border bankruptcy regulation; and industrial standardisation for the purposes of cross-border trade, consumer protection, or occupational safety. It is no surprise that economy dominates my examples; that is where the emphasis of denationalisation and globalisation have lain. Yet examples from other societal fields, too, can be brought in, such as *lex sportiva* or *lex digitalis*. Together with *lex mercatoria*, they are the favourite tokens of transnational law produced by autonomous global social sub-systems; at least, this is what systems-theoretically oriented legal theorists, disciples of Luhmann, maintain.[1]

There is no one correct internal classification of transnational law; this exercise, too, is perspectival and, to a certain extent, conventional. Policy issues and fields can be defined broadly or narrowly, and putative instances of transnational law range from norms and practices focusing on a precisely delineated transnational concern, such as access to medicines (ATM), to such a pluri-functional and fragmented regime as the EU. Instances of transnational law do not exclude each other but overlap in both normative and social respects. When norms and practices relevant to ATM are examined as a

[1] See esp. Teubner 2004a, 2004b, 2012; Teubner and Fischer-Lescano 2004.

distinct instance of transnational law, elements of intellectual property, WTO, and human rights law will be included and inserted in a new context. Correspondingly, EU norms and practices may function as elements of not only EU law but also other instances of transnational law, with a more specific substantive but wider territorial scope: transnational trade or financial law, or law of industrial standardisation.

In important respects, transnational law lies closer to modern state law than indigenous or religious law. It shares the textuality and language of modern state law, and problems of translation are not equally consequential as in indigenous or religious law. Differentiation has also proceeded further in transnational law. Moreover, within the social dimension, first-order practices where transnational normativity is realised are distinct from the second-order practices of norm-production, and of monitoring compliance and sanctioning non-compliance. Yet a confusion of norms and practices, as well as of first- and second-order sociolegal practices, seems to exist where 'best practices' are assigned normative relevance by either transnational or national norms. However, blurring is more apparent than real. The domicile of 'best practices' lies in the specialised practices of contemporary society, and as a rule their normativity has been codified in guidelines and codes of conduct adopted by relevant organisations, such as Good Accounting Practice, Good Auditing Practice, or Good Banking Practice. All in all, the conceptual apparatus elaborated above in Parts I–II appears to travel rather well.

Difficulties in analyzing and even identifying instances of transnational law ensue from its incomplete and parasitic nature. Much of transnational normativity, produced by public or private 'norm entrepreneurs', consists of norms of soft-law character. If law is reduced to its normative aspect, if coerciveness is considered a necessary feature of legal normativity and if transnational law is examined in isolation from state law, much of transnational normativity would be shut outside law. Thus, transnational law – much ado about nothing. But law cannot be reduced to normativity; coercive sanctions can be replaced by other ways of ensuring compliance; and under post-national plurality, instances of neither national nor transnational law can be explored in isolation. What legal qualities transnational normativity lacks it can obtain by attaching itself to state law. The cure to transnational law's incompleteness lies in its parasitic character. Most instances of transnational legal regimes are not purely transnational but assimilate segments of national or international law, and exploit their practices and institutions. In that sense, construing a pure theory of transnational law would be ill-advised from the very beginning.

I will concentrate on two specific features that affect discussing putative instances of transnational law in the conceptual framework elaborated above. The first is the dominance of soft law, which complicates pinpointing the legal element in transnational normativity and in the practices (re)producing and realising that normativity. The basic distinction between law and non-law is far from clear; indeed, one of the main tasks confronting transnational legal theory is to analyse the way from non-law to law. Secondly, typical of transnational law is a convoluted and instance-specific interplay among three levels: transnational, national, and local.

Transnational normativity is an Eldorado of soft law. 'Soft law' is a difficult concept, for some discussants even an oxymoron. For them, law is either hard or not law at all.[2] Yet, in non-state law, binary and exclusive distinctions function but rarely, which also goes for the binary code legal/illegal or the distinction law/non-law. 'Hard law' might be defined as consisting of norms backed up by coercive legal sanctions. Transnational hard law includes, say, EU law and WTO law. Soft law is also intended to guide the behaviour of addressees but it lacks the coerciveness of hard law. Transnational soft law shares with transnational hard law, as well as modern state law, the characteristic of textuality. Soft-law texts include codes of conduct, guidelines, recommendations, and standards adopted by private and public organisations; model laws and contracts drafted by international organisations such as UNIDROIT and UNICITRAL; and private codifications of contract and commercial law, such as the Lando Principles of European Contract Law or the Draft Common Frame of Reference composed by the von Bar group. Some soft-law norms, for instance standards and model laws, can and are even expected to be converted into hard law; they are norms on their way from soft law to hard law. Yet soft law also includes norms compliance with which is secured by other means than coercive sanctions; say, peer review or threat of loss of reputation and, consequently, professional or business opportunities. Even when non-compliance entails no identifiable negative consequences, respect for the expertise of the transnational norm authority may induce wide acceptance at national and local level of norms dubbed recommendations or guidelines. Moreover, transnational soft-law normativity may provide national or transnational courts with interpretative support even where it is not accorded the status of binding, hard, law. Thus, referring to opinions and studies of the Venice Commission has become routine in the jurisprudence of the European Court of Human Rights (ECtHR). In sum, soft law involves various grades and types of normativity, approaching or related to but not quite equivalent to hard law. Denying it legal relevance reflects obstinate clinging to binary distinctions which are beginning to be obsolete even in state law.

Various mechanisms exist for converting transnational soft law into hard law. The most straightforward way is incorporation in national hard law. This is what happens when a national legislator adopts a law based on a model law produced by, say, UNICITRAL or UNIDROIT. Formally, states maintain legislative sovereignty and are not under legal obligation to incorporate a

[2] See, e.g., Klabbers, 1996.

model law. In practice, however, pressure from the side of economically and politically powerful states may suffice to induce dependent states into incorporating transnational soft law advocated by the former. Another way of conversion is reference in or delegation by national or transnational hard law. This appears to be the favourite method in assigning a hard-law quality to transnational technical standards.

In both the WTO and the EU, divergent technical standards – a token of simple diversity! – are treated as non-tariff barriers to cross-border trade. The WTO Agreement on Technical Barriers to Trade refers to transnational standards and establishes the presumption that national regulations relying on these are consistent with WTO obligations. The Agreement does not explicitly identify the relevant standards or the organisations producing them. In practice, it confers on the leading standard producers - the International Standardization Organization (ISO) and the International Electrotechnical Commission (IEC) - a role which approaches delegated regulatory authority. Unlike UNICITRAL and UNIDROIT, these are private organisations, not subject to international law.[3] The EU's New Approach to regulatory standardisation also includes widespread delegation of regulatory functions to private standardisation bodies. Harmonising EU directives lay down essential requirements for health, safety, and environmental and consumer protection but leave the technical specifications to three major private European standardisation organisations: the European Committee for Standardization (CEN), the European Committee for Electrotechnical Standardization (CENELEC) and the European Telecommunications Standards Institute. Products that meet standards issued by these organisations at the request of the European Commission are presumed to conform with EU essential requirements.[4] Yet in both the WTO and the EU regime harmonised standards remain in a grey zone between hard and soft law. Compliance with them remains voluntary in the sense that states in the WTO regime and producers or service providers in the EU regime are free to choose not to follow a harmonised standard. However, if they so do they run the risk that WTO obligations or EU essential requirements are not met

Transnational soft law may also gain legal recognition through contracts, enforceable in a national, international, or transnational legal regime. Transnational law may be incorporated in contracts as contract terms. The parties may agree that, say, the Model Clauses for Use by Parties of the UNIDROIT Principles form part of their contract. Furthermore, the parties may also agree to use transnational soft law, say, the Lando Principles of European Contract Law or the UNIDROIT Principles, as meta-norms applicable to their disagreements. By the same token, when arbitration awards are enforceable in national courts, soft law is transformed into hard law. Contracts

[3] Mataija 2020. [4] Schepel, 2005, 2013; Cantero Gamiton, 2020.

that make transnational soft law legally binding can also be concluded under international law. Thus, transnational standards on cross-border trade and finance can be made legally effective through bilateral or multilateral treaties.

Yet, often enough, transnational soft law does not need the support of national or transnational hard law to secure compliance. In cross-border trade, economically powerful states can put pressure on dependent ones to implement standards they wish to promote, and in cross-border commerce loss of reputation or business opportunities may be as effective a deterrent as coercive sanctions. Last but not least, especially in standardisation transnational expert culture and networks are crucial for ensuring implementation. The major part of transnational normativity addresses specialised practices and is interwoven with the technical expert culture of those practices. Technical experts play a dominant part in drafting both transnational soft law and national legislation, as well as in the specialised practices where these are executed. Transnational expert networks are also the locus for formal and informal peer review as a second-order monitoring practice.[5]

Transnational legal regimes which have developed spontaneously, without any support from international law, possess particularly potent sanction mechanisms of their own. Violation of *lex mercatoria* can lead to boycotting and exclusion from business relations; violation of *lex digitalis* to blocking of a domain name or denial of internet-based services; and violation of *lex sportiva* to suspension or disqualification of an athlete. Systems theorists tend to exaggerate the independence of these regimes. They have been able to produce their norms without the involvement of states, and they avail of distinct dispute-settlement or sanctioning practices. Still, they have not been able to cut all ties to state law. They, too, share the incomplete and parasitic nature of transnational law. In particular, when coercive execution is needed, recourse to state practices is indispensable. Furthermore, when parties are not content with the second-order monitoring practices of *lex mercatoria, lex sportiva*, or *lex digitalis*, they are free to seek justice in the judicial practices of state legal regimes.

Thus, the dominant role of soft-law-type normativity in transnational law makes it impossible to draw a sharp and unequivocal boundary between law and non-law. Let us now turn to the other difficulty in demarcating instances of transnational law: the characteristic dispersal of norms and practices, and the complicated interplay between different levels. With the partial but significant exception of the above-mentioned spontaneous regimes of global social systems, transnational law usually works at three levels: transnational, state, and local.[6] Both the normative and social dimensions display such a three-level structure. To put it concisely, the transnational level produces norms, often of soft-law character, which are transposed and, if needed, specified and

[5] Büthe and Mattli, 2011. [6] Halliday and Shaffer, 2016.

converted into hard law at the state level, and realised at the local level. In some regimes, national legislation may also delegate the further specification of transnational standards to the local level; to national private or private/ public bodies, which exercise self- or co-regulation. It is perhaps needless to say that in the normative dimension, the three levels do not constitute a hierarchical structure, comparable to Kelsen's *Stufenbau* of a national legal order, where the higher level would authorise and, in case of a conflict, override the lower one.

In a state legal regime, legislative practices constitute a sequential and unified process of drafting, deliberation, and adoption. In transnational law, legislative practices are fragmented into several phases, some of them transpiring at transnational and others at national level; even the local level may be involved. At transnational level, important 'norm entrepreneurs' are operative whose work extends to several transnational legal regimes. In order to become legally binding, the norms they produce need recognition by national or transnational legal regimes, such as the WTO or the EU, which have the power to issue hard law. If transnational norms blur the distinction between soft and hard law, in producing these norms the public or private character of the relevant organisations scarcely matters. In private-law harmonisation, central actors include UNCITRAL and UNIDROIT. Despite the international legal background of these two organisations, the model laws and principles they produce do not fall under international law but are more aptly classified under transnational normativity, the drafters of which act as legal experts rather than representatives of their governments. In particular UNIDROIT presents its principles, not as production of 'new' normativity, but as 'non-binding codification' 'or 'restatement' of existing law and, thus, comparable to the US Restatements of private law by the American Law Institute.[7] The Restatements are private, non-legislative codifications, devoid of formal legal validity. However, they have a played an important role among the sources from which judges draw information on applicable law. US Restatements have served as a source of inspiration for two recent European non-legislative, academic, codifications of private law located in the grey zone between soft and hard law: the Principles of European Contract Law by the Lando Commission, comprising comparative legal scholars, and the Draft Common Frame of Reference by the von Bar group.[8] Codifications by both public and private actors may cross the border into hard law through three passages: incorporation by state legislation, reference by court rulings, and incorporation or reference to as applicable law by contracts.

'Standardisation' connotes a sub-category of 'harmonisation', emphasising the technical character of the enterprise. Such a connotation also facilitates

[7] Jansen, 2010, 68–71. [8] Ibid., 59–66.

a manipulation of terms. To call harmonisation 'standardisation' implies that, as a technical exercise, it should be left to technical experts, unburdened by requirements of transparency, public discourse, or democratic legitimacy. Yet technical standardisation has non-technical consequences, too, and may involve significant non-technical interests, mainly of an economic but potentially even of a political nature. Fights over standards of video equipment, computer hardware and software, or digital networks and equipment recall the non-technical aspects of standardisation. ISO, which is the central actor in transnational standardisation, has extended its activities from technical standards guaranteeing the technical compatibility of components and products to areas remote from its original focus, implying value choices transcending technical expertise, such as occupational health and safety or 'corporate social responsibility'.[9] ISO, in line with CEN as its European counterpart, is a private organisation with national standardisation bodies as its members. If ISO and CEN have stretched the concept of standardisation, even more problematic is its use in transnational financial governance, where a multitude of standard setters - none of them established under international law - are active. In transnational financial governance, economic and political stakes may be high and entail clashes among expert knowledge, 'stakeholder' interests, and value-based ideological and political positions.[10]

In transnational legal regimes, a characteristic hybridity and interplay between diverse levels marks not only the legislative but also the judicial and monitoring function. Some regimes possess distinct bodies for settling disputes or imposing sanctions. These include the EU, with its mixed transnational and national judiciary, and the WTO with its dispute-settlement mechanism, but also the favourite regimes of systems theorists: *lex mercatoria*, *lex digitalis*, and *lex sportiva*. *Lex mercatoria* is applied by international arbitration bodies; *lex sportiva* by associations and arbitration bodies at both national and transnational level; and *lex digitalis* by the ICANN (Internet Corporation for Assigned Names and Numbers) and its panels, and dispute-settlement bodies of service providers, such as eBay. However, the transnational law of global social systems has not been able to shut itself entirely outside national law enforcement. The Convention on the Recognition and Execution of Foreign Arbitration Awards, as well as national arbitration laws, provide for resort to the coercive machinery of the state in the execution of *lex mercatoria*; the Swiss Supreme Court has held the Convention applicable to the decisions of TSA – CAS (*Tribunal Arbitral du Sport* – Court of Arbitration for Sport), the central transnational arbitration body; and the dispute-settlement practices of *lex digitalis* do not usually prevent the parties from taking the issue to a state court.

[9] Büthe and Mattli, 2011. [10] Helleiner, 2016.

The typical three-level structure makes clear how dependent on state law transnational law remains. Transnational law is not only transnational but also national and, we can add, in many cases even local. Transnational law not only responds to the shortcomings of state law; it also works through state law, which it especially needs to turn soft into hard law and to guarantee the realisation of its norms. Whenever transnational law needs support from the sword of Iustitia, it has to turn to the state. Transnational law is not only transnational but also state law.

Despite the hybrid nature of transnational law, and the dispersal of its norms and practices, the distinctions elaborated above with a view to state law seem to find a correspondence. However, due to the prevalence of the expert culture of contemporary specialised practices, most instances of transnational law have probably not developed a particular legal culture which would facilitate a distinction between surface-level and sub-surface cultural layers. Here EU law and, with some qualification, WTO law are exceptions, availing of a transnational corps of legal scholars dedicated to doctrinal elaboration of surface-level normative material. In addition, *lex mercatoria* as *Juristenrecht* assigns legal scholars a prominent role both in codifying the normative reservoir and in applying it as members of arbitration bodies.

Not all instances of transnational law constitute full-blown legal regimes, with an identifiable normative corpus, differentiated legislative and judicial practices, and a representative authority defending its autonomy and identity in post-national plurality. Some are clearly legal regimes in this demanding sense, others as clearly are not. Where we draw the line depends, again, on the context and purpose of our exercise. Thus, for instance, for analysis of what I call fundamental conflicts of authority, only those instances of transnational law are of relevance which in general raise a claim to autonomy and which possess a representative authorised to give voice to that claim. On the other hand, a legal theorist or sociologist may discern a distinct instance of transnational law even where the participants from their first-person singular or plural perspective do not share her insight; where they do not acknowledge any representative authority; and where the putative instance of transnational law does not possess any collective self-identity.

Do transnational legal regimes possess a constitution? The question only makes sense if 'constitution' is understood not in a formal but in a substantive sense. The substantive sense relates to constitutional functions, such as the ones I have proposed above: constitutive, positioning, restrictive, and legitimating. If possessing a constitution requires differentiation and accomplishment of all these functions, few instances of transnational law would qualify; perhaps only the EU legal regime. Yet at least embryos of some constitutional functions can be discerned in other instances of transnational law as well: rules addressing norm-producing or norm-monitoring bodies (constitutive function), or positioning transnational normativity vis-à-vis state and local norms; or *ordre public* principles fulfilling the restrictive function which in state constitutions falls to fundamental rights. What seems to be particularly problematic is the legitimating function. Here the incomplete and parasitic nature of transnational law comes to the fore: even EU law must rely on Member State democratic procedures in order to procure at least an appearance of democratic legitimation. Furthermore, the shift from state to transnational law and from hard to soft law has been accompanied by a shift from government to governance, and various forms of 'experimental democracy' and 'stakeholder' participation, allegedly substituting for state-level democratic procedures.

In the context of transnational law it is more appropriate to speak of constitutionalisation than constitutions. Thus, the extension of fundamental or human rights to transnational law may be considered a sign of constitutionalisation. There is not much sense in discussing whether constitutionalisation has reached a level where the regime at issue can be said to possess a constitution. To debate where, exactly, the boundary between constitution and non-constitution runs is as useless as the search for sharp and universally applicable parameters for demarcating law from non-law. Moreover, related to the problematic legitimating function, if we concluded that a transnational constitution exists, it would not match all the characteristics of the constitution of a democratic *Rechtsstaat.* A state constitution displays both a political and a juridical dimension, and establishes a structural coupling between politics and law. This coupling is crucial for the way a state constitution is supposed to accomplish the legitimating function. But where in transnational law do we find the political dimension and input? This is the question that makes the legitimating function such a vital problem for transnational constitutionalism.

EU Law as Transnational law

Among transnational legal regimes, EU law is in many respects a special case. It is by far the most developed regime of transnational law, measured by such criteria as production of hard law or advancement of the normative and social differentiations that characterise modern state law. It is also a conspicuous example of a legal regime which has largely disconnected itself from its foundation in international law, although from the perspective of the Member States as 'Masters of the Treaty' it still retains some of its international legal character. Primary EU norms derive from international treaty law, but secondary norms, such as regulations and directives, are but artificially classified through international legal doctrine. Furthermore, EU treaty law, when falling under the principle of direct effect, treats even private persons as legal subjects, thus departing from the traditional premise of international law. Ever since the 1960s, the ECJ/CJEU has characterised EC/EU law as an independent legal order, distinct from both Member State legal orders and international law. Nevertheless, as is typical of transnational law, in both the normative and social dimensions EU law is intertwined with Member State legal regimes. It not only reacts to deficiencies of state law, but its remedies harness state law for transnational purposes.

Transnational normativity is often a response to a diversity of state legal regimes that poses obstacles to cross-border practices. Here, too, EU law is a case in point. Legal diversity, recalling the black-box model, was seen as an impediment to a Europe-wide common market for goods, workers, services, and capital. Consequently, combating detrimental diversity has dominated European integration as legal integration. EU law also facilitates distilling techniques which transnational law can employ to overcome adverse legal diversity. These include direct applicability and direct effect of transnational norms; as well as harmonisation, mutual recognition, and coordination of national legislation.

EU legislation as the primary instrument of legal integration ranges from directly effective Treaty provisions to directly applicable regulations and harmonising directives, issued under the powers established by the Treaties. The central constitutional principles, introduced by the ECJ in the 1960s, purport to secure that diversity-fighting EU legislation is realised in Member States. These include EU law's direct effect and primacy, as well as efficacy and uniformity as second-order, justifying principles. These are complemented by the interpretative principle, also established by the ECJ, which obligates national courts to interpret national legislation in conformity with EU law and to treat EU-law concepts as autonomous concepts with autonomous meanings. Harmonisation is driven by directives which call for implementation through national legislation but which may even attain direct effect in case of negligence of a Member State. As distinct from the harmonisation efforts of UNICITRAL or UNIDROIT or private bodies, such as the Lando Commission and the von Bar group, EU directives entail an obligation to adopt implementing national legislation and, thus, restrict the legislative sovereignty of Member States. Another instrument of harmonisation consists of standards produced by European standardisation bodies at the request of the European Commission.

The principle of mutual recognition, introduced by the ECJ in *Cassis de Dijon* (1979), addresses situations where harmonisation or standardisation have not succeeded in abolishing non-tariff barriers to cross-border trade. If a product meets the product safety or other requirements on marketable commodities of 'home-state' legislation, other Member States as 'host states' should not, as a rule, prevent its access to their national markets by divergent requirements. Subsequently, mutual recognition has been extended to the Area of Freedom, Security and Justice, where it supports, for instance, the European Arrest Warrant. Mutual recognition does not aim to abolish diversity but combats its consequences for cross-border activities. Unlike direct applicability, direct effect, or harmonisation, Member States retain sovereignty over national legislation but are obligated to acknowledge the legislative choices of other Member States.

Coordination is a version of techniques used in conflict of laws, or private international law as it is called in civil-law countries. Conflict of laws does not harmonise the substance of state law but determines which law is to be applied to issues with connections to more than one state legal order. It is part of the legal orders of the respective states. Thus it can only resolve problems created by legal diversity if state legal regimes apply identical conflict-of-laws rules. This is exactly what the EU-law method of coordination aims at. In line with mutual recognition, coordination has been especially important in fields where the EU, due to Member States' sovereigntist concerns, does not possess legislative competence but which are still considered vital for European integration. Coordination of national social security legislations has facilitated the free movement of workers and, after Maastricht, European citizens. Subsequently, the technique of coordination has been expanded to healthcare, to benefit mobile patients. The emphasis in the EU-law method of coordination, though, is different from traditional conflict of laws. The objective is not so much to adjudicate between rival claims to jurisdiction, but to guarantee that European mobility is not hindered by non-application of national social security or healthcare legislation. Yet the EU has been active even in the traditional field of private international law. The two Rome Regulations on the law applicable to contractual and non-contractual obligations have raised conflict-of-laws rules in central fields of private law to transnational level and pre-empted Member State legislative competence.

As in transnational law in general, state legal regimes play a crucial role in the implementation of EU law. They have also been made to serve the techniques that EU law employs to fight legal diversity impeding European integration. EU law demonstrates how transnational developments do not lead to sidestepping state law but, rather, to co-opting it. In the normative dimension, even directly applicable and directly effective EU law works as integrated into Member State law. In the dimension of specialised legal practices, national courts also function as courts of EU law. Their cooperation is pivotal for the success of the particular EU techniques for achieving legal integration. At the apex of the EU judicial structure, the CJEU is the main guarantor of the uniformity of European law. The primary procedural device is the preliminary-ruling procedure, which also requires the active involvement of national courts. In both normative and social respects, EU law adheres to the three-level template of transnational law. However, specific for EU law is the strong position of the transnational level, manifest by the range of binding legislation and the key role of the CJEU. What is also exceptional is the contribution of transnational legal scholarship to the gradual emergence of a distinct EU legal culture, supporting surface-level EU law. Finally, differing from other instances of transnational law, the EU legal regime clearly possesses a constitution both in the formal and substantive senses of the term. The formal constitution consists of the

Founding Treaties, which the ECJ has labelled the 'constitutional charter' of the EU.[11]

Hard law and developed second-order practices monitoring its observance are a distinctive feature of the EU legal regime as an instance of transnational law. Still, EU normativity is not only about hard law and judicial monitoring. In Europe, the EU has played a crucial role in the move, not only from national to transnational law, but also from hard to soft law and from governing to governance. Standardisation has prospered under the EU; the Open Method of Coordination, introduced in fields where the EU does not possess legislative competence, is based on benchmarks and peer review; and EU comitology has been portrayed in terms of 'experimental democracy' and 'stakeholder' participation.[12]

Indigenous and Religious Law

As non-state law, indigenous and religious law both share common features and display significant differences. Neither indigenous nor religious law need be non-state. In post-apartheid South Africa, indigenous (customary) law can trace its legal recognition to the 1996 Constitution and, in this sense, can be considered state law on a par with common law, although the indigenous tribes themselves do not perhaps acknowledge such a validity basis. Religious law can also exist as state law, as it does in Islamic states such as Saudi Arabia, Pakistan, and Sudan. As non-state law, indigenous and religious law differ in vital respects from transnational law, so that bringing them all under a common umbrella, that of non-state law, may appear rather artificial. Furthermore, to label indigenous and religious law, as distinct from transnational law, as non-state law below the state is not wholly correct, either. It is true that in secular Western states, religious law, in line with indigenous law, appears as non-state law below the state. Yet the law of the three world religions of the book in particular displays transnational features too. This holds not only for the normative dimension but also for specialised practices: for scholarship, which occupies an important position in all the laws of the religions of the book, and even for adjudicative and legislative functions, especially in canon law. Commonalities exist in the fundamental principles and values of indigenous law, connected to the particular relationship to Nature – Mother Earth – of indigenous peoples, although the extent and significance of these commonalities is controversial. Moreover, transnational networks have been established to defend indigenous cultures, ways of life, and communities. Still, it would be audacious to postulate in indigenous law a transnational level, corresponding to that of the law of the religions of the book.

[11] Tuori, 2015a. [12] Eriksen et al., 2003.

Modern state law is supported by a specialised and differentiated legal culture, which, as I have argued, forms part of the law. Leaving aside public and private restatements of private - especially contract - law, transnational law has but rarely developed a legal culture of its own. Instead, in the field of, say, standardisation, cultural embedding consists of technical expert culture. In contrast, both indigenous and religious law are embedded in the everyday culture, the way of life, of the community. As positive law, modern state law tends to privilege the surface level and to downplay legal-cultural layers. In indigenous and religious law, the order is inversed: the emphasis lies on cultural principles instead of their surface-level expressions.

In contrast to issue-specific transnational law and more in line with multi-purpose state law, indigenous and religious law possess a comprehensive scope. They cover even aspects of life where modern state law does not extend and relationships which individual-centred modern state law does not conceive as legally determinable. The culture with which indigenous law is inseparably interwoven is identical with the way of life of the community, and the central concepts of Jewish and Islamic law - *halakhah* and *shari'a* - translate into 'path of life'. For modern state law, it is impossible to conceive of the relationships of humans to Nature or God in legal terms; by contrast, this relationship stands at the very centre of indigenous and religious law. Indigenous and religious law are not only more inclusive, attending to fields which modern state law reserves for private autonomy or which it is not even able to juridify because of a lack of conceptual tools. They are also more focused. Modern state law serves multiple purposes; consequently, it would be rather contrived to attribute to it an overriding point; the closest one can come is constitutional identity, distilled from fundamental constitutional values and principles. Non-state law is different. The claim to authority of transnational law is defined and circumscribed by policy issues and fields. Instances of transnational law are policy-oriented even in their point. Indigenous and religious law, too, display a paramount normative point, which, however, diverges crucially from the policy orientation of transnational law. Arguably, when an indigenous community in general resorts to law-talk, the focus is on the survival and reproduction of the community and its culture, its particular way of life, including its particular relationship with Nature and the Divinity. Maintenance of the religious culture and community is important for religious law, too, but it is subordinated to the supreme point of salvation.

Because of the prominent role of soft law, drawing the boundary between law and non-law in transnational normativity may be difficult. From the internal perspective of transnational law, the distinction may not even be so important in the first place; it may well be that the distinction only matters for legal theorists looking at transnational law from their meta-perspective. The same goes for indigenous and religious law: ignoring the debate among legal anthropologists, theorists, and comparativists, indigenous or religious communities from their first-person perspective may not be in the least concerned about whether a norm or practice is classifiable as legal or not. It may well be that the legal aspect only enters their field of vision when the normativity or practices of the community collide with state law. For those looking from the outside and through the cultural lenses of modern state law, problems of demarcation arise from the cultural embedding and interwovenness of indigenous and religious law.

In indigenous law, even extracting a normative aspect from social practices may be questionable. This goes not only for first-order practices where the customs – the way of living – of the community are (re)produced. It also goes for second-order practices where the emphasis often lies on reconciliation and reintegration, instead of application of pre-existing normativity. And even if the normative aspect can be detached from practices, a further predicament consists of defining where and when a custom has been transformed into law. Where particular tribal courts have been established – in, say, South Africa – separating law from non-law may be an issue for the courts. For scholars occupying a meta-level position, it is largely useless to debate whether indigenous law really is law or what indigenous law really meets the criteria of law. What matters is to realise, first, that indigenous law is a cultural construct and, secondly, that it is a construct not of indigenous but of Western culture. If the distinction between 'folk' concepts and analytical concepts were to be effaced – as if this were possible! – and the definition of law were left to folk concepts so that law were what the participants say it is,[13] there would be rather little indigenous law. Compared to modern state law, all alleged instances of indigenous law are incomplete or deficient legal regimes. Whether they can be called law depends on who poses the question, in what context, and for what purposes.

In the law of the religions of the book, a distinct normativity undoubtedly exists, yet delineating a legal dimension in this normativity or in second-order monitoring practices can be artificial. The normativity of modern state law is textual, positive, coercive, and ordered. The law of the religions of the book shares the textuality but the backdrop to this important feature is different. Religious written law does not stem from formal legal speech acts issued by human legislators and judges. Religious law is not positive but revealed. The law stems from God, who has revealed it to the intermediaries Moses, Jesus, and Mohammed, whose words were subsequently written down. Commentators have added further layers to the Holy Texts: the Torah, the New Testament, and the Koran. The German Historical School distinguished between law's sources of origin and sources of cognition (*Erkenntnisquellen*). The source of origin of religious law is the Word of God – or God's law – while writings, starting from the Holy Texts, serve merely as sources of cognition. In addition, religious law may even take recourse to legislation, too, either for

[13] Tamanaha, 2001. See also Woodman, 1998; Benda-Beckmann, 2002; Roberts, 2005; Twining, 2009, 89ff.

codifying purposes – a well-known example is the Code of Canon law (1983) – or for filling gaps in religiously relatively indifferent fields of modern society.

In contrast to religious law, indigenous law has retained its primarily oral nature. Written recordings exist, mostly by colonial or post-colonial officials or by legal anthropologists but sometimes by tribal chiefs and elders as well. Still, indigenous communities do not necessarily recognise restatements by outsiders or even by tribal representatives, although state courts, in particular, may take recourse to these. In South Africa, 'official' and 'living' customary law live side by side.[14] Still, as is the case in religious law, too, in indigenous law written records may only function as sources of cognition, while the source of origin lies in the culture and way of life, immersed in customary social practices. With some exceptions among for instance Native Americans, indigenous law does not recognise a distinct legislative function.

Both indigenous and religious law are non-positive, and their deep-cultural embedding deprives even raising the issue of the relationship between law and morals of sense. Law and morals are indistinguishable. As non-positive law, indigenous and religious law can also be approached as natural law, anathema to Legal Positivism. In indigenous law, the natural-law aspect flows from an intimate relationship with Nature, and from understanding this relationship in terms of harmony and custodianship. In Christianity, theologically warranted Natural Law received its great synthesis in Thomas Aquinas' *Summa Theologiae*. Only in early modern individual-focused political philosophy did Western Natural Law cut its connection to divine law as the Word of God. In contemporary Catholic doctrine, a distinction is drawn between revealed and natural divine law, which both derive from the Word of God. Revealed law can be known only through revelation, natural law, in contrast, through reason. Natural divine law is binding on everybody, revealed divine law only on those who have been baptised.[15]

Second-order, specialised, monitoring practices exist in both indigenous and religious law, and even coercive sanctions may be used. However, second-order practices aim at reconciliation and reintegration, rather than retribution. Neither can adjudicative practices in indigenous or religious law be labelled law-application. If indigenous law can in general be said to exist as rules, these constitute a repertoire from which a tribunal or a chief can draw support in an effort at reconciliation, rather than a system of pre-existing rules. In modern state law, the justice that judicial practices pursue is formal and abstract, with the emphasis lying on the similarity between cases. In indigenous and religious law, justice is substantive and concrete, calling for attention to the uniqueness of cases.

In sum, the distinct features that mark off legal normativity under the conditions of modern state law are largely lacking in indigenous and religious

[14] Bennett, 2004. [15] Ferrari, 2002.

law: textuality, positivity, coerciveness, and order. Even distinguishing normativity from sociality is questionable in indigenous law. Second-order monitoring practices exist but their point and relationship to available rules differ from law-application in modern state law. Where a distinct legislative function can be discerned, its declared point is not so much to induce and facilitate legal change but, rather, to clarify and ascertain existing law. Scholarship is important for religious, especially Judaic and Islamic, law, but its religious orientation separates it from the legal scholarship of modern state law.

Transnational law is, to a significant extent, jurists' law (*Juristenrecht*) and even co-opts parts of national law. Although influenced by the technical language of the specialised practices it addresses, the language of transnational law lies close to that of modern state law. Misunderstandings may occur but lack of a common language does not constitute a major source of conflict between national and transnational law. By contrast, the concepts and the underlying distinctions of modern state law travel much more arduously to indigenous and religious law. Even the very concept of law and the demarcation of law from non-law, and, within law, the binary distinction - so dear to systems theorists - between legal and illegal may cause confusion. Before colonial encounters, indigenous peoples did not in general talk law and after these encounters, might experience law-talk as a menace to their culture and way of life. That indigenous peoples have been forced to speak law is not merely a token of Western cultural imperialism; they have also learned to use law-talk for defensive purposes and for exploiting the facilities which national law or transnational human rights law offer for protecting their lands, resources, culture, traditional knowledge, and self-determination.[16] Yet even if they talk law, their idiom may differ significantly from that of modern state law, wanting, for instance, equivalents to the concepts of individual right or individual ownership. In South African customary law, *ubuntu* is a central notion but lacks unequivocal translation in South African common law.[17] As usual, problems of translation are not only linguistic but run deeper: they are rooted in cultural idiosyncrasies and in the limits to our ability to adopt the perspective of another culture. Translation and the possibility of dialogue presuppose deep-cultural commonalities which modern state law and indigenous law and culture do not necessarily display.

Due to commonalities in Jewish-Christian cultural roots, translation issues are probably not equally intricate between modern state law and the laws of the religions of the book, but should not be ignored, either. Canon law of the Roman Catholic Church is an offshoot of Roman law, which brings its language close to that of modern state law. In contrast, both the concepts and the way of reasoning in Islamic law may be strange to a jurist raised in the culture of a Western state legal regime. Thus, instead of the binary code of

[16] Tobin, 2014. [17] Bennett, 2011.

legal/illegal or allowed/prohibited, Islamic law recognises five legal modes of classifying behaviour, and instead of syllogistic deduction, analogical reasoning dominates judicial processes.[18]

From the first-person individual or plural perspective, extracting a distinct legal aspect from religious normativity and practices may be highly problematic. Religions of the book share with modern state law the textuality of normativity. Yet, where religious normativity is supposed to cover the entire life, gleaning from it a distinct legal aspect may contradict the individual or collective self-understanding of believers. As is the case with indigenous law, too, even posing the question of the relationship between law and morality, not to speak of defending the legal positivist separability thesis, would hardly touch a chord. And, often enough, the binary code of (il)legality does not work in religious law, nor is it able to demarcate law from non-law; here, too, indigenous and religious law are similar. Contrary to indigenous law, the religions of the book do possess a legal language but neither the vocabulary nor the grammar of, say, Jewish (Talmudic) or Islamic law coincides with the legal language of modern state law. Analogously to indigenous law's intertwinement with the general culture and way of living of indigenous peoples, religious law cannot be detached from other aspects of religious culture and normativity or social practices supposed to lead to salvation. It would not make much sense to speak of a particular legal culture or to distinguish between surface-level and legal-cultural layers in either indigenous or religious law. Like indigenous law, religious law, too, can be a construct of state law and its legal culture.

Human Rights Law

Human rights law is a species of transnational law, but it is a particular species and a peculiarity among the constituents of contemporary post-national plurality. Human rights law displays pretensions of meta-law, that is, law which is relevant for and can make interventions not only in state legal regimes but also instances of transnational and international law, as well as indigenous and religious law. As distinct from other law, human rights law raises universalist claims to authority. Human rights law is a conspicuous example of transnational law which has detached itself from its international legal background. The main human rights instruments include the two United Nations conventions on civil and political rights, and on economic, social and cultural rights; the European Convention on Human Rights (ECHR) and the Social Charter; as well as the American Convention on Human Rights, and the African Charter on Human and Peoples' Rights. These are international treaties, concluded under international law. However, both further elaboration

[18] Glenn, 2014, 171ff.

of the normative corpus and compliance-monitoring have escaped the control of Signatory States, and thrust the legal regime in a transnational dimension.

In the dimension of specialised legal practices, the distinctive features of transnational law can be attached to either norm-production or compliance-monitoring. Transnational norm-production assumes other forms than bilateral or multilateral treaties among states. In turn, compliance-monitoring which involves bodies outside the control of states suggests the emergence of transnational law. Yet, because of the role that the praxis of the monitoring bodies plays in developing the normative dimension, no impermeable boundary exists between norm-formation and compliance-monitoring. Through its jurisprudence, a monitoring body established by an international treaty and enjoying judicial independence elaborates on and complements the treaty provisions it is supposed to watch over. Treaty provisions are usually formulated in very general terms, and for an understandable reason. Consensus among states is the easier to reach the vaguer the provisions under negotiation are; hence, their specification is left to legal experts charged with monitoring compliance. In human rights law, treaty provisions display perhaps even exceptional vagueness and leave wide room for specification by the monitoring body.

To take a conspicuous example, the rather equivocal provisions of the ECHR have only gained precision through the case-law of the Strasbourg Court. Thus, the mere wording of Article 6 ECHR conveys but a pallid picture of the normative contents of fair trial. European human rights law possesses a treaty basis – the Convention and the Protocols. Nonetheless, it is warranted to speak of a transnational legal regime which has, in both the normative and social dimensions, distanced itself from international law. The Court's case-law exemplifies not only transnational human rights review but, through its erga omnes precedential effects, even transnational law-making. The Court's at least partial breakout from general international law is also manifest by the qualifications it has made to the applicability of the Vienna Convention on the Law of Treaties. The Court has underlined the constitutional character of the Convention and concluded that the Vienna Convention's provisions on reservations and international legal succession are not applicable as such.

Significant overlaps exist among the four main human rights treaties – the African, American, European, and UN ones. These also share a common background in the UN Universal Declaration of Human Rights (1946). Yet important differences can be perceived too. American and African states have opted for a unitary treaty which contains the rights of all three generations: civil and political liberty rights of the first; economic, social, and cultural rights, requiring positive action from states, of the second; and, finally, group rights of the third generation. Opting for a unitary treaty emphasises the interdependence of rights. In the UN and European regimes, first- and second-generation rights are each included in different treaties, while third-generation group rights are either derived from the former rights or – insofar as in general they are recognised – enshrined in more focused instruments, such as the European Convention on the Protection of National Minorities, or the UN Declaration on the Rights of Indigenous Peoples. To a certain extent, the substantive overlap among the human rights treaties can be explained by a common deep culture which has animated their drafters. Human rights instruments, starting with the UN Declaration of 1948, have been written in the language of modern state law, and their contents also reflect the dominance of the individual-focused principles of this particular type of law. Still, the reach of human rights deep culture, which overlaps between human rights instruments reflect, should not be exaggerated. Acceptance of these instruments has not been unanimous, but criticism has been raised from the perspective of both indigenous and religious – particularly Islamic – law. For their part, the deviations of the American and African conventions from the UN and European template – such as the inclusion of second- and third-generation rights in the same treaty with rights of the first generation – respond to this criticism.

Distinct monitoring bodies have been established to oversee compliance with the main human rights instruments. Accordingly, the UN, European, American, and African systems can each be examined as particular transnational legal regimes. Yet significant substantive overlaps and constant institutional dialogue among the monitoring bodies, including cross-references in their rulings, also justify treating global human rights law as one mega-sized transnational legal regime.

In addition to the main treaties, each of the four sub-regimes avails of more specific treaty instruments, as well as soft-law normativity: declarations, recommendations, guidelines and so on. As so often with transnational law, the boundary between hard and soft law is far from clear. In principle, hard law consists of treaties and the precedents of monitoring bodies, especially those with court-like status, such as the regional human rights courts. Yet monitoring bodies, including the human rights courts, may also accord legal relevance to instruments which in principle fall to the soft-law side of the divide. In the Council of Europe framework, for instance, the Strasbourg Court as a hard-law institution and the Venice Commission as a soft-law body stand in a dialogical relationship. In its rulings, the Court includes references to Commission guidelines and country-specific opinions and, respectively, in its guidelines and opinions, the Commission treats the jurisprudence of the Court as a baseline for human rights protection. Furthermore, the courts of the Signatory States may resort to soft-law instruments as interpretative means when specifying human rights or fundamental rights enshrined in national constitutions.

Typically, transnational law displays a three-level structure: transnational, state, and local. In human rights law, too, state legal regimes mediate between transnational normativity and monitoring, and local social practices. The local level may also include instances of indigenous or religious non-state law.

Hard-law normativity primarily addresses states, which are obligated to ensure realisation of the rights within their jurisdiction. If the state does not adhere to the monistic model where international law is directly applicable, human rights treaty law can be implemented through, say, incorporation in a constitutional Bill of Rights, a blanket reference in the constitution or ordinary legislation, or an interpretative principle which obligates national judges to use human rights law as a baseline when interpreting and applying national fundamental-rights law. Corresponding to states' obligation to ensure realisation of human rights, the rulings of the transnational monitoring bodies are addressed to states, which are also obligated to take the appropriate measures to execute them.

The starting point in transnational human rights law is that it only extends to the local level through the intermediary of the state legal regime. From the transnational perspective, national fundamental rights, implementing and specifying transnational human rights, and national rights-based constitutional review form part and parcel of the transnational regime, constituting its middle level. Once again, transnational law co-opts parts of state law, showing its parasitic nature. Yet adopting the perspective of a state legal regime, a different view opens. Now transnational human rights normativity is co-opted by national fundamental-rights law, and used in interpreting and specifying constitutional provisions in national constitutional review. Different perspectives may lead to clashes between transnational human rights and national fundamental-rights review.

Concepts and distinctions elaborated with a view to modern state law seem to be more compatible with human rights law than with many other instances of non-state law. Distinguishing between law and non-law or hard and soft law may, though, be as difficult (and futile) as in transnational law in general. Yet norms can be demarcated from practices, as well as first-order social practices where human rights are realised from second-order legal practices where human rights norms are (re)produced and their realisation monitored. In both social and normative dimensions, further distinctions can be drawn. Among specialised legal practices, norm-producing, compliance-monitoring, and scholarly practices stand out at both transnational and national levels. Moreover, a transnational, closely networked community of human rights lawyers has emerged, occupying crucial positions not only in drafting and monitoring human rights instruments and in scholarship. They are also activists in a transnational civil society and public sphere, where NGOs, such as Amnesty International or Human Rights Watch, have been able to establish themselves as transnational watchdogs and should be included in a portrayal of the transnational human rights regime. In addition to surface-level normativity, a transnational human rights culture has emerged, adding to the potential impact of human rights law. In spite of the starting point that human rights law is formally binding merely on states, through legal-cultural interlegality it may realise its meta-level pretensions even in transnational and international law. At least some transnational legal regimes, such as *lex mercatoria*, *lex digitalis*, and *lex sportiva*, are developing an *ordre public* that fulfils a similar restrictive function as human rights.[19] Human rights principles lie at the core of this *ordre public*.

In the interplay among human rights law, (other) transnational law, and state law, EU law is, again, a special case. The European human rights regime has three prongs: the European Convention, the EU Charter of Fundamental Rights, and national constitutional Bills of Rights, supervised, respectively, by the ECtHR, the CJEU and national constitutional courts. Relations among the three prongs are rather complex and susceptible to perspectival clashes. However, common European human rights culture has facilitated dialogue and prevented conflicts from coming to a head.

[19] Teubner, 2013.

13

From Simple Diversity to Interlegality and Pluralism

Post-National Interlegality

Post-national plurality not only puts items on the global map of law that had no place in the black-box model of Legal Positivism: instances of non-state law, such as transnational, indigenous, and religious law. Post-national law also fundamentally alters the relations among instances of law, and annuls the self-sufficiency and reciprocal closure of the black boxes. The black-box model depicted the plurality of law as simple diversity, as mere coexistence of state legal orders, without any hint of either dialogical or conflictual relations. In contrast, post-national plurality invites us to conceive of the global constellation of law as interlegality where instances of law overlap and communicate in various modes.

Some conceptual clarifications are in order. 'Plurality' should be distinguished from 'pluralism'. 'Plurality' connotes the coexistence of multiple instances of law. Alongside 'simple diversity' and 'interlegality', 'pluralism' invokes a particular possible constellation among these instances. 'Pluralism' connotes a situation where instances of law raise overlapping claims of authority; say, state law and indigenous or religious law, or state law and transnational law, such as EU law. Pluralism comes in two guises: pluralism of normative legal orders and pluralism of legal regimes. In pluralism of legal orders, the same courts apply different sets of norms depending on the persons involved or the substance of the issue. In pluralism of legal orders, some of the four Kelsenian validity spheres coincide – usually the spatial and temporal ones – while some others – usually the personal and substantive ones – diverge. In the 'weak' legal pluralism of colonial states, colonial courts were supposed to apply either received or indigenous law, in accordance with the parties and the issue. In the weak pluralism which colonial states recognised, there was no parity of the legal orders. Applicability of indigenous law was considered a concession – in practice it was a practical, administrative, necessity – which the colonial state was entitled to withdraw whenever it considered this expedient. In a pluralism of legal regimes or 'strong' legal pluralism, pluralism of legal orders is complemented by separate legal practices and institutions. Furthermore, each of the legal regimes claims an independent basis of authority. In a pluralist constellation of overlapping claims of authority, conflicts are all but inevitable. Even fundamental conflicts of authority which turn on the autonomy or identity of at least one of the parties are possible.

Two alternative approaches to fundamental conflicts of authority are conceivable. Interlegality does not negate occurrence of conflicts, not even fundamental conflicts of authority, but draws attention to the potentials of a consensual solution. It constitutes an alternative to radical pluralism which declares the insolubility of fundamental conflicts of authority. 'Interlegality' refers both to existing 'peaceful' contacts and to a particular approach to relations among instances of law. It is an alternative both to legal positivist simple diversity and to contemporary variants of radical pluralism. When 'interlegality' and 'pluralism' are treated as approaches to post-national plurality, the reference is to the meta-level perspective of a legal theorist. A phenomenological account, trying to capture the first-person perspective of social or legal actors, is also possible. First, however, I shall stick to the meta-level viewpoint.

Manifestations of interlegality can be detected in both the normative and social dimensions of law. The most conspicuous epitome of interlegality is interlocking of legal regimes which involves both dimensions. Such interlocking occurs in the relations between transnational and national law. Transnational law may co-opt parts of national legal regimes so that national legislation, as well as legal practices and institutions, obtain a dual domicile. Transnationally produced norms are implemented through national legislation, and compliance with them is monitored by national courts. Again, EU law provides an illustrative - although by the same token an exceptional - example. Not only are EU directives implemented through national legislation but directly applicable and effective EU law is integrated into Member State law without intervention by the national legislator. Consequently, EU law constitutes part of both the EU and Member State legal orders. Moreover, when applying norms originating in EU law, national courts act as courts of the EU legal regime. As a further token of institutional interlocking, the Lisbon Treaty (2009) granted national legislatures a role in EU legislative procedures as guardians of the principle of subsidiarity. Intensive interlocking characterises human rights regimes too. In the normative dimension, the European three-pronged regime synchronises the European Convention, the EU Charter, and national Bills of Rights. In the dimension of legal practices, national constitutional review may be examined as participating in both the Strasbourg and the Luxembourg sub-regimes.

In normative interpenetration, a legal order receives surface-level norms of foreign origin either through implementation, or by force of direct applicability or direct effect. In addition to normative interpenetration, various 'softer' ways exist by which legal-cultural influences travel from one instance of law to another, and which opened breaches even in the black-boxist self-containment of Westphalian state legal regimes. Yet 'soft' normative interlegality is not realised by an internal movement in the realm of Ought but only through the social dimension; that is, through cross-border legal practices and dialogue.

At one extreme, we find hybrid legislative and judicial practices which involve both transnational and national bodies, and assign national bodies a dual, national and transnational, role. In a transnational legal regime such as EU law, the legal discourse where the momentary contents of the normative legal order are determined consists of legal speech acts of both EU and Member State actors. Yet such interlocking of even formal legal speech acts is only the tip of the iceberg. Cross-border, inter-regime, dialogue also takes multiple less conspicuous forms. Actors from diverse - both state and non-state - legal regimes meet in drafting and negotiating transnational soft and hard law. The transnational corps of legal experts channel cultural influences not only from but also into national legal regimes. Despite tendencies of national closure, ever since the reception of Roman law, Western legal scholarship has also possessed a cross-border vocation and in Roman law a common transnational basis. Informal cross-border judicial networks are a more recent phenomenon, to which the internet and the 'free movement of juridical arguments' have probably greatly contributed. Earlier examples of judicial dialogue and cross-references in court decisions can be found from culturally close states, such as the common-law or the Nordic countries. Nordic cooperation in law-drafting also harks back to the nineteenth century.

Cross-border dialogue presupposes deep-cultural commonalities, such as a joint legal language or at least the possibility of intercultural translation. At the transnational level, the limits of intercultural dialogue have been tested in negotiations on human rights instruments, where in recent decades even involvement by indigenous peoples has been allowed. The language of Western state law – the language of the present essay too – is the dominant idiom, with pretensions to a global legal *lingua franca*. Disagreements and misunderstanding, obstructing negotiations, cannot be attributed merely to political causes but possess cultural grounds too. Not only the individual-focused principles advocated by the speakers of the dominant language, but even the very idiom in which these principles are expressed may seem strange to someone raised in indigenous or Islamic culture. In some post-colonial states or other states with significant indigenous populations, indigenous representatives have been involved in constitutional consultations. Negotiations on human rights instruments and state-level constitutional consultations are important vehicles for cross-cultural influences which do not travel merely one-way from dominant to subaltern culture, but may also take the opposite route. Thus, not only have indigenous representatives learned the legal language of the post-colonial or settler state. Examples exist of adoption of concepts and principles of indigenous law at least into surface-level state law: such as the notion of *ubuntu*, invoked in the jurisprudence of the South

African constitutional court, or the rights of *Pacha Mama* (Mother Earth) recognised and the Quechuan notion of *sumac kawsay* or *buen vivir* (right living) invoked by the Ecuadorian constitution.[1] Time will show whether examples like these remain surface-level, condescending lip-service or transplants which are not able – or perhaps even meant – to grow legal-cultural roots, or whether they launch a fruitful process of sedimentation.

It is vital to perceive that the deep culture of Western state law is not universal by its extension; that other deeply rooted legal principles, concepts, and ways of legal reasoning exist. Yet equally important is not to foreclose Western state law a priori any possibility of intercultural dialogue or to reject categorically any prospect of intercultural translation. Legal cultures – or cultures in general – are not static, solid, or closed but dynamic, negotiated, and porous; and in our post-national era more so than ever. The black-box account of surface-level law, embraced by Legal Positivism, should not be replaced by another black-box view, now claiming cultural self-containment.

Interlegality can also be portrayed in phenomenological terms from the first-person perspective of a participant in sociolegal practices. On Boaventura de Sousa Santos' account, typical of interlegality are 'different legal spaces superimposed, interpenetrated and mixed in our minds, as much as in our actions'. He argues that we 'live in a time of porous legality or of legal porosity, multiple networks of legal orders forcing us to constant transitions and trespassing' and that 'our legal life is constituted by an intersection of different legal orders, that is, by interlegality'.[2] Sousa Santos' account runs against Kelsen's depiction of normative pluralism from an actor perspective. As may be recalled, Kelsen contends that, in a situation of overlap, the actor must make an either/or choice between law and morality, and between national and international law. When faced with normative pluralism and contradictory requirements of law and morality or state law and religious law, social actors cross the threshold of consciousness and law stands out from general societal normativity where it is enmeshed in the ordinary course of daily life. The phenomenological understanding of interlegality, such as manifest by Sousa Santos' portrayal, implies that an either/or choice is not the only possible outcome of individual or collective deliberation. A both/and conclusion, a conciliation between normative orders, is also an alternative.

Deliberation in *foro interno* or jointly with other participants of a lifeworld practice can be compared with the way courts in particular cases build up a decision norm – the major premise of the judicial syllogism – from norm fragments stemming from diverse sources; in, say, an environmental-law case from national law, EU law, international environmental law, and human rights

[1] Tobin, 2014. [2] Sousa Santos, 2002, 347.

law. This is a conspicuous form of interlegality as it appears in judicial decision-making from the actor perspective of a judge. Interlegality in constructing the decision norm involves judges' discursive knowledge of the plurality of surface-level law. The same holds for the various procedural and doctrinal devices which have been adopted for preventing, dampening, and resolving inter-regime conflicts; such as, say, the preliminary-ruling procedure in EU law or the margin of appreciation doctrine of the ECtHR. At the same time, the success of these devices is premised on and facilitated by a more profound, legal-cultural, interlegality which mainly functions through the practical knowledge, the *Vorverständnis*, of legal actors.

Positioning in Post-National Plurality

Borders between legal regimes are porous and traversed by cross-border practices and dialogue. Yet porosity does not make borders non-existent, and dialogue is conducted by interlocutors on opposite sides. Interlegality can make borders invisible but cannot efface them. Moments arise when the interlegal shroud is ripped off and borders stand out again. These are moments of conflict.

Legal regimes take account of surrounding plurality and try to accommodate to it. One of the major constitutional functions is positioning. At the core of positioning by a state constitution lies the claim to autonomy: the claim to political and legal sovereignty and to recognition of this by other state polities and legal regimes in full conformity with the black-box model. In the juridical dimension, contemporary state constitutions usually contain provisions that position the national legal regime vis-à-vis international law, adopting either monism, which implies international law's direct applicability in national law, or dualism, where international law's intra-state effects presuppose implementation through national legislation. International law occupies a compartment of its own in the black-box model of Legal Positivism, although the monist alternative sits rather uncomfortably with the black-boxist self-containment of legal regimes. Yet positioning with regard to international law does not disturb the static harmony of the black-box model. Looked at from the perspective of international law, what is pertinent is that state legal regimes fulfil international legal obligations even when these require granting international law intra-state effects, not how they accomplish this.

Things get more complicated when we move to examine the mutual positioning of state and non-state law. Non-state law constitutes a potential threat to state law's claim to universal and exclusive jurisdiction. State legal regimes recognise each other's sovereignty – universal and exclusive territorial jurisdiction – on the basis of reciprocity and non-interference, in accordance with international law as interstate law. By contrast, they are reluctant to recognise instances of non-state law on an equal footing. Instead, they may assign legal relevance to non-state law but, as it were, as a voluntary concession which can be unilaterally cancelled. This concerns not only indigenous and religious but even transnational law, such as EU or human rights law.

The positioning function of the constitutions of EU Member States covers the relationship to EU polity and law, which is addressed by either explicit constitutional provisions or principles confirmed by constitutional courts. Formal constitutions may include provisions authorising transferral of competences to the EU, while reaction to EU law's claims to primacy and direct effect is usually expressed in constitutional precedents. The EU Founding Treaties possess a dual character: for the EU they appear as a 'constitutional charter', for the Member States as international treaties. As Member States from time to time point out, they remain Masters of the Treaties, which even implies the right of withdrawal, as Brexit has so tangibly recalled. Nor have the Member States accepted the primacy and direct effect of EU law without qualifications. Signatory States may also question the authority of human rights regimes, invoking the international legal background of human rights instruments and asserting the supremacy of the state constitution. The argument may be less convincing than when challenging the authority of the EU legal regime. As a counterargument, customary international law can be brought in to back up the authority of human rights instruments and jurisprudence.

Not only do state legal regimes position themselves with regard to EU and human rights law; EU and human rights regimes also position themselves with regard to state law. Among state legal regimes, it is justified to expect that reciprocal positioning principles coincide. In relations between state and non-state law, this is not as self-evident, largely due to states' jealous supervision of their sovereignty. The juridical constitution of the EU positions the EU legal regime with regard to both Member State and international law. In both directions, ever since *Van Gend en Loos* (1963) and *Costa v ENEL* (1964), EU law has claimed autonomy and portrayed itself as an independent legal order. These landmark rulings also introduced the primary constitutional positioning principles that define EU law's effects within Member State law, namely direct effect and primacy. In respect of international law, *Kadi* (2008) confirmed 'qualified monism' as EU law's stance towards international law. In their positioning vis-à-vis national legal orders, human rights regimes follow the general premise of international law and leave it to the discretion of the Signatory States how they fulfil treaty obligations. Moreover, the ECtHR, for instance, has adopted the principle of margin of appreciation, which allows further discretion for both monist and dualist states in the realisation of human rights obligations. Margin of appreciation is a doctrinal device meant to prevent inter-regime collisions; subsidiarity could be considered a kindred EU-law principle. On the side of state law, interpretative principles, such as human rights or EU-law confirmative interpretation, are designed to accomplish a similar task. Still, in spite of precautionary devices on both sides, reciprocal positioning principles may lead to contradictory readings of overlapping competences.

Incompatible positioning principles may cause even graver problems in state law's relations with indigenous and religious law. State law may recognise the autonomy of such developed transnational legal regimes as EU and human rights law, although usually with the Master-of-Treaties qualification. Much more arduous is to recognise indigenous law on an equal footing with state law; here state law confronts a menace to its sovereignty, as it were, from the inside. A post-colonial constitution, such as the South African one, may include an express recognition of the jurisdiction of indigenous (customary) law. Still, it would be only a half-truth to say that, after such recognition, indigenous law derives its validity from the constitution. This can only hold for the state legal regime, not for indigenous law. The South African constitution is a constitution of state law, not of indigenous law. Full recognition of non-state law by state law would require recognition of non-state law's independent, autonomous, validity basis; a recognition of non-state law not as one of us but as other, to put the point in Lindahl's terms.[3] Consultations in Canada and New Zealand with representatives of indigenous peoples have perhaps come closest to such a recognition.

Short of recognition on an equal footing, state legal regimes avail of three main alternatives to grant legal relevance to non-state law: incorporation, delegation, and deference.[4] Through incorporation, non-state norms are transformed into state law. This is the preferred technique in implementing soft-law transnational normativity, such as standards and model laws. Employing this technique, the state legal regime does not recognise non-state norms as law; to the contrary, through incorporation the state reinforces its legislative sovereignty. By contrast, when resorting to delegation the state recognises non-state norms as law. Yet non-state law is not recognised on a par with state law. Delegation qualifies non-state norms as non-autonomous law, dependent on state law. Examples consist of collective agreements on which state law confers legal effects beyond the tariff partners and their individual members, as does the law in, for instance, Finland and Sweden. In three-level transnational law on, say, accountancy or banking, the local level may consist of codified best practices, authorised by state law.

Instead of incorporation and delegation, deference is the preferential technique by which state legal regimes accord partial recognition to indigenous law. By this technique, state law relegates indigenous law to the private sphere, where the state refrains from interfering. Paradoxically, by deference indigenous law is not recognised as law but as non-law. Whenever applying indigenous law becomes an issue in state courts, it is not treated as law but as fact. Yet, as distinct from incorporation and delegation, when deferring to non-state law, state law acknowledges its autonomy. Today, deference to indigenous law can be considered an international legal obligation, established by human

[3] Lindahl, 2013. [4] Michaels, 2005.

rights instruments and, arguably, even customary international law. Reference can be made to second-generation cultural rights enshrined in the main human rights treaties, ILO Convention 169 on Indigenous and Tribal Peoples (1989) and the UN Declaration of the Rights of Indigenous Peoples (2007). Bills of Rights of contemporary state constitutions also include group rights which protect the autonomy of indigenous law. Yet deference to indigenous law is not unqualified. Under weak pluralism, when a colonial state allowed for applying indigenous law to indigenous people, qualifications were expressed by the notorious repugnancy clause. In colonial common-law jurisprudence, this principle excluded 'laws that "inherently impress us with some abhorrence or are obviously immoral in their incidence"', or so outrage 'acceptable standards of ethics as to create a sense of revulsion'.[5] In contemporary international and constitutional law, the place of the repugnancy principle has been taken by individual-focused human rights. For indigenous law, human rights law is a double-edged sword. Through second-generation group rights it protects the autonomy of indigenous law, while through first-generation individual rights it imposes restrictions. The tension between second- and first-generation rights is an intricate issue for which no easy, generalisable solutions exist.

Qualified deference is also the preferred state legal technique for recognising the relevance of religious law. The basis, though, in international and constitutional law is different. Religious law is inseparable from religion and enjoys protection under not only cultural group rights but also the collective dimension of the right to religion. Yet first-generation individual rights qualify the protection similarly as with regard to indigenous law. What our discussion shows is that the way state law positions itself in respect of both indigenous and religious law cannot be discussed without drawing in international law as the third leg in the relationship.

Problems arise from the fact that the positioning principles of indigenous and religious law are not necessarily in harmony with the state legal principle of qualified deference. When the theocratic alternative of converting religious law into state law is not realistic, two basic options remain: accommodationist and quietist or isolationist.[6] The former does not reject state law as such. It recognises state law's claim to authority but with qualifications that relate to preserving indigenous or religious culture and identity. In religious law, the accommodationist position may be provided with a theological justification, familiar from, say, Thomist Natural Law. Humans are frail, weak in their faith, and prone to sin, and positive state law is needed to secure that they keep to the right path. God has authorised human polity and law as divine accommodation to human imperfection. The other obvious justification for the accommodationist position is that certain fields of law are irrelevant for religious or

[5] Tobin, 2014, 89. See also Tuori, 2015b, 188. [6] Stolzenberg, 2015.

indigenous culture and may safely be left to the province of state law. Furthermore, the accommodationist position can point to the protective and facilitating effects of state law. Yet even the accommodationist position perceives the potential threat which dominant state law always poses for subaltern indigenous or religious law, starting from the imposition of a foreign legal language which as such may endanger preservation of cultural distinctiveness. For the quietist or isolationist position, the state legal regime inevitably exercises a corrupting effect on the religious or indigenous community and its culture. Therefore, state law's authority is rejected *in toto* and all contact with it is avoided. The possibility to live up to the quietist or isolationist position in the contemporary world can, though, be doubted, in respect of both religious and indigenous law.

Fundamental Conflicts of Authority

Post-national plurality is essentially pluralist, involving overlapping and rival claims to jurisdiction. In assessing overlaps and rivalries of jurisdictional claims, all four spheres of validity listed by Kelsen are relevant: not only spatial but also personal, material or substantive, and temporal. Legal regimes demarcate their claims of jurisdiction in all four spheres. Yet the emphasis that different types of law put on different spheres varies. Accordingly, we can distinguish between territorial, substantive or functional, and personal principles of authority. State law follows primarily the territorial, transnational law the substantive, and indigenous and religious law the personal principle. Here we see a new source of conflict. Not only are there no guarantees that the positioning principles of legal regimes concur. It may also be that legal regimes adhere to divergent principles of authority and define the scope of their jurisdiction on divergent grounds.

Even advocates of the black-box model reckon with the possibility that legal issues have connections to more than one state legal regime and that consequently disputes over jurisdiction arise. Still, disputes are expected to be exceptional and manageable by private international law (conflict of laws). What facilitates resolving them is that the positioning principles of state legal regimes coincide and that these regimes obey the same territorial principle of authority. However, the intractable perspectivism attached to regime conflicts extends to border skirmishes among state legal regimes and may complicate settling these. Rules of conflict of laws are part of national law, so that if the rules differ, so will the solution to the contested issue. Yet the general trend has been towards harmonisation of conflicts of law, also due to the impact of transnational law. Much of EU law can be conceived of as transnationalisation of conflict-of-laws rules applicable in Member States; say, law on cross-border social security and healthcare, or the principle of mutual recognition in internal market law and within the Area of Freedom, Security and Justice. In addition, the Rome Regulations on the law applicable to contractual and non-contractual obligations have supplanted Member State conflict-of-laws rules in core areas of private law.

Conflicts arising in a pluralist situation are more complex than the border skirmishes between state legal regimes, addressed by conflict of laws. Pluralist situations involve different types of legal regime; typically, state and non-state law. Their positioning principles do not necessarily coincide, and they may obey different principles of authority; state law territorial, transnational law substantive, and indigenous and religious law personal. Pluralist contestations do not turn merely on the exact course of the borderline but also, and even primarily, on the priority of different principles of authority. And, what is more, the contestations may develop into fundamental conflicts of authority. In such conflicts, at least for one of the parties what is at stake is its autonomy or identity. When this is the case, the party also wages a battle for recognition.

What complicates the pluralism of Member State and EU law is not only that full consensus has not been reached on the respective positioning principles. In addition, Member State and EU legal regimes follow different principles of authority. Member State law adheres to the territorial principle, claiming universal and exclusive jurisdiction within its territory. The claim is universal in the sense of covering all substantive fields of law, and it is exclusive in the sense of not acknowledging rival legal authorities. Exclusivity and universality are defining features of the sovereignty of a state legal regime. By contrast, transnational law defines its claim to authority primarily in substantive terms, focusing on distinctive substantive field(s). This is true even of EU law, which, in spite of its ever more conspicuous expansionist tendencies, is bound by the principle of conferral, explicitly enshrined in the Treaty on the European Union (TEU). As a rule, transnational law's claim to authority is not exclusive, either. Exceptions to this rule, though, exist, as is proved by Treaty provisions on exclusive EU legislative competence. Transnational law contests state law's claim to both exclusivity and universality. Clashes deriving from contradictory principles of attribution of legal authority seem inescapable: transnational law's substantively limited claims of jurisdiction confront state law's universal and exclusive claim.

Primacy is a central positioning principle of EU law vis-à-vis Member State law. This principle presupposes that national courts accord a directly effective EU rule primacy over a contradictory rule of national law. Constitutional courts are key actors in positioning national law in respect of EU law. Over the years, ordinary national courts have by and large acknowledged both direct effect and primacy; their jurisprudence represents the ordinary course of affairs in relations between Member State and EU law. A somewhat different story emerges from the jurisprudence of national constitutional courts. Constitutional courts have never accepted the primacy of EU law without reserve. Ordinary courts have not shown major qualms in applying the principle to border disputes of a traditional character. By contrast, when constitutional courts have perceived a menace to constitutional foundations or to their jurisdiction as the supreme guardian of those foundations, they have raised the banner of resistance. Constitutional courts, with the German one as the self-appointed mouthpiece, have contested EU law's claim to primacy in three interrelated issues: *Kompetenz-Kompetenz*, monitoring of fundamental rights, and national constitutional identity. Correspondingly, the German Constitutional Court has held available three types of review for assessing the constitutionality of national measures based on EU law: ultra vires, fundamental rights, and identity review. As the German court has repeatedly emphasised, fundamental-rights protection is a vital part of national constitutional identity. Hence the field of possible contestation with the CJEU narrows down to questions of *Kompetenz-Kompetenz* and identity.

Kompetenz-Kompetenz touches on the power to define the boundaries of the EU's functionally defined competence. Is this an issue of EU law where the CJEU, according to the TEU, possesses exclusive jurisdiction? Or does it turn on the interpretation of national constitutional provisions which allow for transferral of competence to the EU and, consequently, fall under the jurisdiction of Member State constitutional courts? The German court has defended its jurisdiction, arguing that the EU can only exercise powers which Member States, in accordance with their constitutions, have conferred on it through the Treaties. Because of the derivative nature of its powers, the ultimate *Kompetenz-Kompetenz* cannot fall to the CJEU. Member States remain Masters of the Treaties, also in the sense of determining the scope of the powers they have relegated to the EU. Thus, the German court has repeatedly declared its readiness to exert, when needed, ultra vires review of acts adopted by EU institutions, including decisions whereby the CJEU exercises ultra vires review vis-à-vis other EU institutions. The CJEU has been as consequent in asserting its own *Kompetenz-Kompetenz*, invoking the TEU provision which assigns it the task and power to 'ensure that in the interpretation and application of the Treaties the law is observed'. From the perspective of the CJEU, denial of its *Kompetenz-Kompetenz* would amount to a denial of the autonomy of EU law. The situation is ripe for a fundamental conflict of authority.

A legal regime claiming autonomy also tries to defend its identity. As European legal pluralism demonstrates, sovereign legislative rights may be transferred to transnational level, and a transnational court may be granted at least preliminary jurisdiction over interpretation of the reach of such transfers. Still, a fault line exists to a national legal regime's self-limitation of its claim to universal and exclusive authority. If a legal regime compromised on what it defines as its identity, it would also compromise on its claim to autonomy. Several Member State constitutional courts have articulated their reservation to EU law's primacy as inviolability of national constitutional identity. In Maastricht, the European constitutional legislator heeded Member State identity concerns by an explicit Treaty provision calling for respect for national identity, and in Lisbon a constitutional dimension was included in that identity. The Lisbon Treaty provision can be seen as a move in the ongoing constitutional dialogue between the EU and the Member States. Yet it cannot by itself ensure that no future inter-regime conflict will arise over the inviolability of national constitutional identity. This would require an additional guarantee of the identity of constitutional identities as interpreted by the CJEU and national constitutional courts. No such guarantee exists.

What further complicates the pluralist constellation is that not only Member State legal regimes but the EU, too, keeps watch over its constitutional identity. The CJEU seems to consider the principle of primacy, along with unity and effectiveness – the trinity of constitutional principles introduced in *Van Gend en Loos* and *Costa v ENEL* – an essential element of the EU's constitutional identity, such as it is asserted in relation to Member State law. Assertion of the EU's constitutional identity may give rise to a new type of conflict: a clash between EU and Member State constitutional identities. The CJEU may agree with Member State constitutional courts that a particular feature of national fundamental-rights law manifests national constitutional identity and hence is protected by the TEU provision. Yet the Court might conclude that protection of the EU's constitutional identity overrides respect for national constitutional identity, and that for the sake of the primacy, unity, and effectiveness of EU law, EU fundamental rights must be applied instead of national ones. Conflicts where identity stands against identity are particularly hard to resolve. Neither side has much room for yielding: from each perspective, the fault line lies close.

Conflicts of authority are not a peculiarity of relations between EU and Member State law. They can arise – and are almost bound to arise – wherever where substantively defined jurisdictional claims of transnational law confront the universal and exclusive pretensions of national law. Overlaps among the three branches of European human rights review entail the possibility of contestations not only between the CJEU and national constitutional courts but also between the latter and the ECtHR, and, moreover, between the CJEU and the ECtHR. Constitutional courts have been hesitant to acknowledge without qualification the interpretative authority of the Human Rights Court as regards both the party-focused and erga omnes effects of the Court's rulings. Again, hesitancy can be due to concerns about national constitutional identity. Introduction of the EU's own fundamental-rights regime, where the final say lies with the CJEU, has led to an overlap with the jurisdiction of the ECtHR, which holds itself competent to review legal acts of the Signatory States relating to EU law. In the Charter of Fundamental Rights, the EU has, at a general level, acknowledged the interpretative authority of the ECtHR by letting the Convention define the bottom line of the protection offered by EU law. Yet this does not exclude jurisdictional contestations in particular cases.

For its part, the ECtHR has adopted a position akin to the *Solange* doctrine of the German Constitutional Court in respect of EU fundamental-rights law. The ECtHR has suspended reviewing national measures related to EU law. Suspension is conditional, and the Court has reserved to itself the right to reinstate its authority if the EU does not live up to the condition of providing equivalent protection.

EU law and Council of Europe human rights law are examples of transnational legal regimes with substantively limited but partly overlapping jurisdictions. Their relations also show that the reciprocal positioning principles of two transnational legal regimes do not necessarily coincide, either. Other examples of overlapping and potentially clashing transnational legal regimes abound. Thus, the CJEU has rebutted WTO law's claim to direct applicability within the EU. One of the favourite illustrations in international lawyers' fragmentation discussion is the contest about jurisdiction over the whale trade between the WTO and international environmental law.[7] Another contestation engaging the WTO would be the conflict with human rights regimes over the respective weight of intellectual property rights and the right to health. If clashes between EU and WTO law involve two transnational legal regimes with a policy focus, in the contestation between WTO and human rights law an instrumentally oriented regime confronts a principle-oriented one. None of the above examples concerns mere border skirmishes. The stakes are higher.

Transnational law may challenge the authority not only of state law or another instance of transnational law but also general international law. *Van Gend en Loos* and *Costa v. ENEL* should be read as a declaration of independence not only from Member State law but from international law as well. In *Kadi*, the CJEU not only reaffirmed EU law's independence but also questioned the supremacy of UN law. The Court argued that the fact that the EU measures under scrutiny implemented decisions of the UN Security Council did not affect the Court's jurisdiction to assess them by EU fundamental-rights law, nor did Member States' international obligations permit challenges to the foundational principles of EU law, such as fundamental-rights protection. Foundational principles draw a fault line which qualifies EU law's adherence to the monistic principle in its relations with international law. The CJEU defends the constitutional identity of EU law against threats deriving not only from Member State law or another instance of transnational law but (general) international law as well.

The CJEU's assertion of the EU's constitutional identity illustrates an important general point. Constitutional identity is not cast in stone at a distinct historical moment, such as adoption of a formal constitution, but is susceptible to change and ongoing debate and negotiation. In the early

[7] Koskenniemi and Leino, 2002.

decades, the normative point of EC/EU law was clearly instrumental, policy-oriented. Only gradually, along with the evolution of the fundamental-rights dimension, did it acquire principle-related features so that in *Kadi* the CJEU could include protection of fundamental rights in the foundations of EU law. Furthermore, the weight of the constituent features may vary depending on the rival legal regime against which constitutional identity is asserted. In *Kadi*, the emphasis lay on fundamental-rights protection, while towards Member State constitutional courts the CJEU has put the emphasis on the principles of the primacy, unity, and effectiveness of EU law, in other words principles with a policy orientation.

In contestations among regimes of national, transnational, and international law, we can presume that there is always leeway for dialogue. Constitutional identity may be negotiable, at least up to the fault line beyond which concessions are impossible. Clashes between national or transnational and indigenous or religious law can be more difficult to conciliate. If a state legal regime employs the technique of deference and concedes indigenous or religious law a sphere of autonomous jurisdiction, controversies can arise over the exact reach of the concession. Yet such controversies easily develop into fundamental conflicts of authority. State legal regimes have been reluctant to recognise indigenous or religious law on a par with their own sovereignty. What for state law appears as a mundane border dispute over extension of autonomy may from the opposite perspective turn on the very identity and survival of the community. Contestations about authority over traditional hunting grounds and fishing waters or holy sites are not only about defining the reach of two different definitions of ownership; from the point of view of indigenous law, what is at stake is the cultural identity and continuance of the community. In relations among state legal regimes, issues of matrimony or inheritance are typically the stuff of private international law (conflict of laws). Correspondingly, for state law, determining the reach of non-state religious law in such issues can appear as a rather technical exercise, while from the opposite perspective it touches on a fundamental dimension of religious life and the very point of religious law.

Indigenous and religious law are culturally deeply embedded, enmeshed in the daily lifeworld of the indigenous or religious community. All questioning of their jurisdiction has the potential to turn into a fundamental conflict of authority. Finding a consensual solution is more arduous than among regimes of national, transnational, and international law. Lack of a common language and difficulties in translation make themselves felt, and on the side of indigenous and religious law the fault line of no-concessions is promptly hit. In contrast, what should alleviate the predicament is that only one of the parties experiences the controversy as a fundamental conflict of authority, hinging on its autonomy and identity. The constellation is different from, say, the clashes involving the CJEU and the German Constitutional Court where both contestants are anxious about the autonomy and identity of their legal regimes. When this is the case for only one of the parties, the other party should have leeway to adjust its initial position. The message sent to state law from human rights law and the principle of constitutional tolerance is to make use of that leeway.

Radical or Dialogical Pluralism?

Two diverse approaches exist to fundamental conflicts of authority between legal regimes with overlapping and rival jurisdictional claims: radical and dialogical pluralism. Radical pluralists stress the inevitability of conflicts and the lack of an overriding reconciling principle or a neutral third-party arbiter. Radical pluralists are born-again black-boxists. They admit that legal plurality has turned into pluralism, entailing new kinds of jurisdictional conflict. However, for these theorists, legal regimes remain shut in their boxes and approach the contested issue from diverse perspectives, without any common legal ground that would facilitate compatible assessments. Radical pluralism is a corollary to exclusive, extreme, perspectivism. Dialogical pluralists concede the ever-looming possibility of fundamental conflicts of authority and the inevitable perspectivism which complicates their solution. Yet in contrast to their radical colleagues, they point to the resources for dialogue, cooperation, and congruent assessments. They rely on interlegality even at the moment of jurisdictional conflict.

Radical pluralism comes in three main guises: Kelsenian normativist, Koskenniemian strategist, and Luhmannian systems-theoretical. The Neo-Kelsenians among radical pluralists emphasise that each of the conflicting legal regimes is subject to a particular *Grundnorm*, which dictates the perspective from which the contested issue is approached. Thus the CJEU is bound to look at *Kompetenz-Kompetenz* from the perspective dictated by the *Grundnorm* of EU law and the German Constitutional Court from that defined by the *Grundnorm* of German law. Inevitably, the two courts arrive at contradictory conclusions: the CJEU assesses the issue in the light of the Treaties as the constitutional charter of the EU, while the German Constitutional Court relies on the German constitution. No neutral ground exists where the divergent perspectives could fuse, nor any meta-level legal principle which could bridge the gulf separating them.[8]

Kelsenians and 'crits' might seem odd bedfellows. Kelsen labels as solipsism and imperialism the monist doctrine which derives the validity of international law and, by the same token, all other national legal orders from the referential national legal order. Koskenniemi concurs. Still, at the end of the day agreement is perhaps not so surprising, considering that 'solipsism' and

[8] MacCormick, 1999.

'imperialism' are apt descriptions of Koskenniemi's portrayal of the antagonistic relations among international legal regimes as well.[9] But of course, a vast distance – diametrical opposition, one could even say – separates Kelsen's from Koskenniemi's legal-theoretical starting points. Kelsen's is an extreme version of the internal point of view. In contrast, Koskenniemi does not try to probe into the *Vorverständnis* of legal actors but shuns discussing the normative presuppositions and implications of legal speech acts; for him, the grand issues of normatively oriented legal theory – validity or authority and meaning – possess no intrinsic significance. Instead of the illocutionary dimension where the normative credentials of legal speech acts are appraised, Koskenniemi focuses on the perlocutionary, strategic, aspect. He subordinates illocution to the strategic, interest-driven, aims of perlocution. On his view, conflicts of jurisdiction are irresolvable, not because of divergent *Grundnorms*, but because of divergent institutional biases and the irreconcilability of the strategic interests which the institutional actors of different regimes are pursuing; say, the CJEU and national constitutional courts or representatives of the WTO and the international environmental legal regime.

In addition to Neo-Kelsenians and legal strategists of the Koskenniemi stripe, a third group of contemporary radical pluralists exists: theorists drawing from Niklas Luhmann's autopoietic systems theory. These theorists argue that, ultimately, the intractability of inter-regime conflicts originates in the self-contained, autopoietic character of global social sub-systems – say, economy, health, and science – which have given rise to transnational law. Nothing can be done to the very source of the problem: the evolutionary accomplishment of (global) social differentiation. As the Master put it: 'The sin of differentiation cannot be undone. Paradise is lost'.[10] At most, we are entitled to hope that some of the consequences of transnational legal fragmentation can be managed through a new type of conflict of laws where the decisive criterion is the primary functional location of contested issues. However, each regime of transnational law is tied to the particular rationality of the global social sub-system where it is inserted and must produce its own functionally oriented conflict rules and reactions to compatibility issues. The source of the problem remains, and although transnational legal regimes are engaged in mutual observation, nothing can ensure that functionally differentiated and autopoietically closed social sub-systems arrive at congruent appraisals of inter-regime disputes.[11]

The three varieties of radical pluralism condemn legal regimes to their solipsist perspectives, with little or no prospect of border-transcending, cross-perspective contacts. They all end up advocating a new version of the black-box model of legal universe. They define the boxes differently from the legal positivist template and acknowledge the emergence of transnational law

[9] Koskenniemi, 2007. [10] Luhmann, 1994. [11] Teubner and Fischer-Lescano, 2004.

beyond the dichotomy of national and international law. Yet they leave self-contained legal regimes shut in their respective compartments.

The other party to the debate on post-national legal pluralism - dialogical pluralists - invokes doctrinal, procedural, and institutional devices which, especially in Europe, have been developed to prevent and defuse inter-regime conflicts, and which testify to extensive interlegality. Neo-Kelsenians are right in explaining legal perspectivism in terms of the *Vorverständnis* of legal actors. They are also right in relating that *Vorverständnis* to a referential legal order. Yet the Kelsenian explanation provides an impoverished account of the legal culture that impregnates legal *Vorverständnis* and, by the same token, produces an erroneous depiction of legal actors' dependence on a referential legal order. At issue is not merely reliance on surface-level normative material or the doctrine of sources by which that material is identified and which determines its legal significance. The devices construed to neutralise inter-regime conflicts draw on and are supported by legal-cultural resources: overlaps and commonalities on the cultural levels of law where the black-box model of Legal Positivism has never really worked. The doctrinal, procedural, and institutional facilities expressly provided by EU law could never create inter-regime dialogue without the support of a unifying legal deep culture; that is, without basic legal concepts, principles, and methodologies which are by and large shared by both Member State legal regimes and EU law.

Most of the fundamental conflicts of authority which have erupted between the ECJ/CJEU and the German Constitutional Court have come to a peaceful, consensual, solution. Their course attests to the availability of inter-regime dialogue. According to the *Solange* doctrine, the German Constitutional Court refrains from reviewing EU legislation in the light of German fundamental-rights law as long as EU law provides adequate protection. *Solange* is often presented as aiming at safeguarding national fundamental-rights protection from the threat perceived as deriving from European law's claim to primacy even over national constitutional law; a claim which the ECJ had explicitly raised in *Internationale Handelsgesellschaft* (1970). This is a correct depiction in the conflictual framework. However, *Internationale Handelsgesellschaft* and the *Solange* rulings of the German Constitutional Court can also be portrayed as contributions to an ongoing cooperative inter-regime discourse on fundamental-rights protection in Europe. Subsequent moves in this discourse related to developing a fundamental-rights dimension in EU law: confirmation of the status of fundamental rights as general principles of EU law in Maastricht (1992); adoption of the EU Charter of Fundamental Rights (2000); and corroboration of the constitutional status of the Charter in Lisbon (2009).

In the two post–Euro crisis *Kompetenz-Kompetenz* cases, *Gauweiler* (2015-2016) and *Weiss* (2019-2020), turning on European economic policy and in particular the mandate of the European Central Bank, the tone has hardened, especially on the German side. From a dialogical perspective, it is significant that in both cases the German Constitutional Court asked for a preliminary ruling from the CJEU, in *Gauweiler* for the first time ever. In both rulings, it also affirmed the interpretative principle of *Europarechtsfreundlichkeit* (conformity with EU law). Yet in both cases it asserted its ultima ratio power to disagree with and discard the CJEU's assessment of the competence of an EU institution. This is in open defiance of the interpretative supremacy of the CJEU and the autonomy of EU law in general. In *Gauweiler*, a final impasse was avoided by the German court's last-ditch retreat. In *Weiss*, the Court let the restraints fall, and declared the CJEU's interpretation of EU law erroneous and non-binding. This is a reminder that even in Europe we cannot put our trust in the omnipotence of interlegality. Not only is there an ever-present possibility of conflicts of authority between legal regimes with overlapping jurisdictions and adhering to different principles of authority. In addition, their consensual solution cannot be taken for granted. Still, dialogical pluralists are right to point out that impasses are not inexorable and that latitude for concessions and compromises usually exists before either party hits the fault line beyond which its autonomy cannot be compromised or its constitutional identity negotiated.

In contestations involving indigenous or religious law, a common cultural understanding on which dialogue could rely is more difficult to attain. Neither do indigenous or religious law possess much latitude for negotiation when autonomy or identity is at stake. As a counterweight, though, national or transnational law does not usually interpret the conflicts as a menace to autonomy or constitutional identity. This should allow for concessions and compromises, provided that human rights considerations as new repugnancy rules are not seen to raise obstacles.

14

Unity under Post-National Plurality

Internal Unity

Unity of law is a two-level issue. It can – and should – be examined at the level of both particular instances of law and the plurality of those instances, that is, as internal and inter-instance unity. These levels interact, so that, for example, insights into the impact of the post-national condition on the internal unity of state legal regimes are relevant for a discussion of inter-instance unity too. The fracturing of the formal unity supposedly guaranteed by a Kelsenian or Hartian Master Rule also affects the way the unity of the plurality of law can be conceived of.

Because of the increasing porosity of borders and cross-border interlegality, post-national plurality profoundly affects the unity - and consequently the identity - of the constituent instances of law, including state legal regimes. On the other hand, we cannot examine the plurality of law if we have no idea how to identify the instances that make up that plurality. In order to identify the instances, we have to grasp them as unities. As has been perceived by some leading legal positivists – Joseph Raz, for instance – unity and identity are closely linked, so that identity presupposes unity.

Both identity and unity can be understood in a thin, formal, or a thick, substantive, sense. Identity in the thin sense connects to identification: it is sameness that allows us to identify an entity - say, an instance of law. We can pursue identification for two purposes: we can be interested in either the diachronic or the synchronic dimension. Diachronic identity is equivalent to the temporal continuity of an instance of law. In turn, through synchronic identity we single out an instance of law here and now and distinguish it from other contemporaneous instances of law. Identity presupposes unity, at least in a thin, formal, sense. However, unity transcends identity, at least if identity is related to identification. Identity for the purposes of identification presupposes only a minimum of unity, but the unity of an instance of law can be pursued far beyond this minimum. Yet identity can also be detached from identification and understood in a thicker sense, just as a person's or a collective's identity can be understood as consisting of 'deep', constitutive, values and objectives, as well as the personal or collective trajectory which has shaped those values and objectives, and along which they have been pursued; identity not as sameness, but as selfhood, to resort to Ricoeur's conceptual pair.[1] And when adopting a thicker sense of identity, that is, identity as selfhood, a new perspective is invoked: the first-person singular or plural from where values and objectives are defined and personal or collective histories narrated.

Above, I have already questioned whether subsuming the legal order under a Master Rule and assuming its hierarchical structure has ever been able to adequately depict the unity of state law. Post-national plurality accentuates the deficiencies of the positivist account. State legal orders are no longer self-contained, even in their surface-level appearance. The derangement of the Kelsenian *Stufenbau* can be illustrated by the impact of EU law on Member State law. In Kelsen's hierarchy, the supremacy of higher norms involves not merely primacy or *Anwendungsvorrang*, which presupposes setting aside contradictory lower-order norms in single cases. Supremacy also covers *Geltungsvorrang*, which implies invalidation of contradictory lower norms as well. In addition, higher norms not only invalidate – they validate, too, by establishing the competence to issue lower norms. The supremacy of directly effective EU law over national law only signifies *Anwendungsvorrang*. The EU-law principle of supremacy dissects the three effects – *Anwendungsvorrang*, *Geltungsvorrang*, and validation – which in Kelsen's *Stufenbau* go together. A further messing up of the Kelsenian hierarchy ensues from implementation of EU directives. Directives are EU-law instruments which, as a rule, require explicit transposition into state law and are only binding as to their purpose and effect. EU law endows the national legal instrument effectuating transposition – say, a parliamentary statute – with legal consequences which set it apart from 'purely' national instruments of the same hierarchical rank. Whatever its hierarchical level in national law, it enjoys the supremacy (in the sense of *Anwendungsvorrang*) of EU law. Thus, validation and *Geltungsvorrang* follow the hierarchy of national law, while *Anwendungsvorrang* is determined by EU-law criteria. By the same token, precepts that in national law govern relations between norms of one and the same hierarchical level – such as *lex posteriori* and *lex specialis* – are rendered ineffective.

The norm explosion accompanying post-national plurality has shaken whatever formal unity national legal orders may have possessed. As the concept of polycentricity seeks to intimate, norm sources have multiplied and attempts to bring them into a hierarchical order under a single *Grundnorm* or rule of recognition seem more futile and far-fetched than ever. The impact of legal plurality on the formal unity of national law is reinforced by fragmentation of the state. The concept of state, which Kelsen inherited from German late constitutional theory of state law, was based on three elements: state territory, state people, and state power. Yet it implied a fourth

[1] Ricouer, 1992, 31ff. See also Lindahl, 2013, 82–83.

dimension too: state organisation. The state was treated as a unitary legal person, but its will – state power – was expressed by state organs, each within its sphere of competence. The formal unity of the legal order was supported by the unity of state organisation.

Developments in recent decades have contested the assumption of a unitary state will and organisation. Parallel to delegation of legislative powers, public administration has adopted new types of non-hierarchical organisational structure, as well as new types of non-legal management and control mechanisms (New Public Management). Regulatory tasks, including norm-giving, have been outsourced, and public/private regulative bodies have sprung up; 'self-regulation' and 'co-regulation' belong to the staple vocabulary of New Public Management and governance talk. These developments have enhanced the functional independence of administrative and regulative agencies within state organisation, also as regards use of delegated legislative powers. It may be more appropriate to portray agencies as representatives of their respective fields – such as healthcare, education, or economy – rather than as components of a uniform state organisation. In a disaggregated state and segmented administration, the bonds of allegiance to private actors and to peer agencies beyond the border may be stronger than to other agencies in home-state organisation.

Organisational fragmentation is connected to transnationalisation. State agencies – central banks, financial supervisors, finance ministries, competition authorities, regulatory agencies of infrastructure industries – are included in transnational networks where common policies are discussed and peer review exercised. Networking of national authorities with an expert mandate is typical of EU regulatory activities but has even wider, global, significance. Networking of central bankers within the Basel-located Bank of International Settlements has obtained an almost mythical reputation. Such networks, where representatives of the private sector may also be admitted, produce much of current transnational normativity, which is then implemented nationally or enforced by national authorities under transnational monitoring of the peer review type. Transnational networking enhances organisational fragmentation, adds to the polycentricity of sources of law, and weakens the formal unity of the state legal order.[2]

Because of the shaking of formal unity, it would seem natural to look to substantive criteria for re-establishing the lost unity of national legal order. Yet the rise of non-state law has spelled problems also for achieving unity through divisions based on substantive criteria. Already in the first half of the twentieth century, increasing legal interventionism and social engineering complicated comprehensive systematisation of national law. New fields emerged which did

[2] Slaughter, 2004; Sassen, 2008, 222ff.

not possess an unambiguous place in the traditional compartments, such as labour law, economic law, and environment law. By its origin, the regulative welfare state is a nation-state political project, and the new fields unsettling inherited divisions were still attached to the monocentric perspective of the state legislator.

Transnational law has further complicated systematisation through law's divisions. Typical of policy-oriented and issue-focused transnational law is a tunnel vision that ignores more extensive coherence. Although it covers a wider range of regulatory fields, EU law is as heedless of traditional divisions as transnational law in general. Yet interest in increasing coherence through law's divisions and field-specific general doctrines has not abated. Current pretenders to the status of a distinct branch of law throw a more profound challenge to the accustomed classifications than, say, labour or environmental law. They are no longer tied to the point of view of the state legislator but take note of post-national legal plurality, also muddling the boundary between law and non-law, as well as hard and soft law. Medical and bio-law or information and communication law transcend the distinction between private and public law, bringing together norms which, in traditional divisions, are dispersed across several fields. That is not all. Besides norms issued by the national legislator, they also collect norms of international or transnational origin.

Systematisation through divisions of law has changed: it can no longer guarantee the unity and identity of a national legal order, nor facilitate demarcating that order from other national legal orders. Putative new fields of law - say, information law or medical law - are border-crossing rather than border-asserting. They comprise law not only from diverse sources – manifesting a new kind of polycentricity – but even diverse legal orders. The coherence they aim at is local and, at the same time, border-transcending, rather than comprehensive but border-maintaining. Fields of law are not expected to add up to a unified legal order. Furthermore, divisions are not static but constantly shifting. Nor are they excluding but overlapping, so that a set of norms can be examined as belonging to more than one branch of law: for instance, provisions on patient insurance fall under both tort and medical law. Fields of law are openly perspectival: they admit that other classifications, for other purposes and adopting other perspectives, can be conceived and justified.

The division of law into distinct fields does not serve merely, or even primarily, classificatory purposes. Fields of law provide the context for elaborating legal doctrine: legal concepts, principles, theories, and methodologies. Only through field-specific doctrines can divisions inject substantive coherence into law. Post-national law can only acquire substantive unity - substituting for the lost formal unity of national law - from legal-cultural layers, which positivist theorists in their reductive normativism tend to overlook. And legal-cultural layers have always been the privileged site for interlegality where the black-boxist self-containment embraced by positivist theorists has broken down. The unity of law can no longer be understood as entailing sharp delineation of a national legal order.

If formal unity shows signs of rupture, and if putative new fields of law are border-transcending rather that border-asserting, can we still in general talk about the unity of state law, approached as distinct national legal orders? In a tentative identification of a national legal order, formal criteria, akin to positivist Master Rules and related to the institutional structure of national legislatives and judiciaries, still play a role. Even for legal theorists, it is wholly justified to talk about, say, the Finnish legal order and to invoke statutes enacted by the Finnish Parliament, by-laws issued by the Finnish Government and subordinate administrative authorities, as well as precedents of the Supreme Court and the Supreme Administrative Court. Still, as I hope has become clear, such an identification can only be provisory, and cannot be based on unequivocal and clear-cut demarcations. Nor does the hierarchical structure that such a tentative identification implies achieve Kelsenian unambiguity or a unity extending much beyond an agglomerate of surface-level norms. If thicker unity and identity is sought, one must look below the surface, to the legal-cultural layers. Despite all cultural interlegality and the testimony of cross-boundary branches of law and legal scholarship, it is still plausible to presume that national legal cultures, supporting national surface-level law, have retained at least part of their characteristic mixtures and particularities which impregnate the *Vorverständnis* of national legal actors. If this presumption holds, national legal orders may possess a thicker unity, produced by a unifying national legal culture. As Member State legal regimes have asserted in their relations to EU law, this legal culture may also include a distinct constitutional identity; a distinct interpretation of the universalist values and principles allegedly common to the EU and its Member States.

When discussing the unity and identity of law, legal theorists – and not only those of a positivist stripe – usually focus on the normative aspect of law. However, law is not only about normative legal orders. It is also about the first-order social practices where norms realised, and about the second-order legal practices where norms are (re)produced and their realisation is guaranteed. A full-blown legal regime comprises all three modes of existence of law. These also provide alternative perspectives on unity and plurality, including identification of the instances making up the plurality.

Hans Lindahl has engaged in a phenomenologically oriented endeavour to build up the unity and identity of law from its realisation in first-order sociolegal practices, and the concrete orders of behaviour that structure these practices.[3] Savigny's doctrine of legal institutions is an earlier example of an attempt to construct unity starting from law's realisation, actual or anticipated.

[3] Lindahl, 2013.

However, the problem is that in contemporary, differentiated society first-order sociolegal practices, all possessing their particular points, hardly add up to an integrated whole – a meta- or mega-practice, as it were – with a unifying comprehensive point. The unity which can be construed from first-order sociolegal practices is local by its nature. Fragmented local unities do not fuse into the unity of a national legal regime. Furthermore, first-order sociolegal practices are increasingly of a cross-border character; this, as may be recalled, is a central backdrop to the expansion of transnational law.

Second-order legal practices are a more promising candidate for conceiving of this unity. Thus, the unity a modern state legal regime can be reconstructed focusing on the legal speech acts which constitute the final phase of specialised legal practices and which are linked together into an ongoing legal discourse. Due to their institutional ties – the legislative, executive, and judicial branches of the state, and law faculties – specialised legal practices and the legal discourse connecting them provide a more reliable reference for identificatory purposes than diffuse first-order sociolegal practices. Yet the interlegality of post-national plurality affects specialised legal practices, too, and relativises the unity which can be built on their interconnections. Legislators, judges, and scholars are engrossed not only in national but also cross-border discourse with, say, their partners in transnational legal regimes.

The legal positivist understanding of the unity of state law as formal unity of the normative legal order is in increasing difficulty. In non-state law, its insufficiency is even more conspicuous. In transnational law, a normative dimension can be distinguished from the social practices (re)producing and realising it. Yet the dispersion of legislative and adjudicative functions and the blurriness of the boundary between hard and soft law makes it impossible to arrange transnational normativity in anything resembling a Kelsenian *Stufenbau*. As a rule, instances of transnational law do not even possess a constitution which would bring clarity and order to the relationships among normative instruments.

Once more, EU law deserves separate treatment. The EU legal regime possesses a constitution in both the substantive and formal senses of the term. As I have argued elsewhere, the EU constitution displays several dimensions: the framing political and juridical constitutions, as well as the sectoral economic, social, and security constitutions.[4] The juridical constitution addresses the EU legal regime, both as a normative legal order and specialised legal practices. Corresponding to the Kelsenian understanding of material constitution, the juridical constitution enables the EU legal order through Treaty provisions on legislative and judicial competences. What the European juridical constitution has not been able to achieve is Kelsenian clarity in the internal

[4] Tuori, 2015a.

arrangement of that legal order. EU law can hardly be presented as a hierarchical *Stufenbau* where higher norms provide the validity basis for lower norms and prevail over them in conflicts. A degree of uncertainty has always permeated relations among Treaty-based legal instruments. Furthermore, the Treaties as the constitutional charter are silent on the importance of the law-making power of the ECJ or the constitutional role of the general principles the Court has established.

Substantive unity can be due either to policies or to principles in *sensu stricto*, such as fundamental rights. The fact that the Treaty of Rome bypassed formal relations among acts of secondary legislation can be explained by the prevalence of the substantive unity brought about by the policy orientation of the Treaty and the secondary legislation it authorised. All legislative acts were expected to promote establishment of the common market, which was the main objective of the Treaty and the point of the legal regime that gradually emerged. The unity of European law was conceived of as a policy-based coherence. Subsequent developments, though, have complicated the situation. Fundamental rights and reference to universalist values in the TEU have inserted a principle element in the substantive unity of EU law.

The jurisdictional claims of transnational law are substantially circumscribed and related to the point which the regimes are expected to pursue. With the major exception of human rights law, the point is policy- instead of principle-oriented. State legal regimes fulfil multiple purposes; and policies, shifting in accordance with political conjunctures, are a source of disorder rather than order. In contrast, instances of transnational law align themselves around particular policy issues, and policy objectives create unity in the normative and social dimensions, both characterised by dispersion and decentralisation. State borders and territorially defined jurisdiction provide more or less uncontroversial criteria for identifying national legal regimes and demarcating them from each other. Diverse ways exist to delineate policy issues, to specify the point of a distinct instance of transnational law, and to demarcate it from other transnational law. No one right way of mapping transnational legal plurality exists, and the resulting chart is highly dependent on context and perspective.

Dependent as it is on unifying policy orientation, substantive unity of transnational law is usually rather thin and devoid of legal-cultural support. Dominant expertise is not legal but, rather, technical expertise of specialised practices. As a rule, no distinct scholarly practices have emerged which could have elaborated a legal culture supporting – and restricting – surface-level normativity. Exceptions, though, exist, such as EU law and human rights law. In its central fields, EU law has started cultural sedimentation from scratch: no state-law field of free movement exists, and even competition law is a relative newcomer. However, over the decades and due to the joint efforts of Luxembourg judges and a transnational corps of EU legal scholars, distinct EU-law principles, concepts, theories, and methodologies have been elaborated; these constitute the nucleus of an emergent EU legal culture. This enhances the substantive unity of EU law. Diverging from EU law, human rights law has been able to draw from the legal-cultural reservoirs of national constitutional law. Human rights scholars, who have internalised their legal *Vorverständnis* in a national constitutional culture, have contributed to the formation of a transnational culture sustaining human rights instruments.

The primarily oral character of indigenous law has prevented scholarly practices from emerging, so that rules, insofar as they exist, lack order. The order and unity that there is in indigenous law is not a property of an autonomous legal regime but derives from law's cultural embedding and its entanglement with communal social practices. In contrast, in religious law a distinct scholarly function exists and plays an important role, especially in Jewish and Islamic law. Different types of laws and the written sources of their cognition are also arranged hierarchically. Yet the order of religious law is not a quality of distinct legal norms and practices, but these are enmeshed with religious doctrine and practices. Correspondingly, the order and unity of religious law derives from its point, related to salvation of the faithful and preservation of the religious community, and inseparable entanglement with other aspects of religious culture and way of life.

Unity in Plurality?

In his obsession with formal unity, Kelsen was not content with reconstructing the internal unity of national legal orders and international law. His ambitious objective was to demonstrate the unity of all law; to arrive at universal law, consisting of all national legal orders and international law. He argued that, ultimately, international law defines the validity of national law and that, consequently, all law constitutes a unity.

Kelsen rejected as inconsistent the view of the relationship between national and international law, which he dubbed 'pluralist', and which assumes the simultaneous validity of national and international law. Instead, he opted for a monist position that does not deny the plurality of legal orders but views all legal orders joined in total or universal law. This is the ultimate manifestation of unity in Kelsen's Pure Theory; a unity which overcomes plurality by moulding it into universal law, comprising both international law and all national legal orders. Two ways exist to (re)construct the monist edifice of universal law: either one proceeds from international law and derives from there the validity of national legal orders, or one proceeds from one particular national legal order and derives from there the validity not only of international law but all the other national legal orders as well. In the first alternative, international law not only determines the territorial, personal, and temporal spheres of validity of national legal orders. In the principle of efficiency, international law also provides the reason for the validity of national legal orders. Consequently, the ultimate reason for the validity of universal law lies in the *Grundnorm* of international law. This, it may be recalled, obligates states to behave as they have customarily behaved. This is not a very thrilling summation of the foundation of all law to someone versed in, say, Thomist or Kantian philosophy of law.

If one chooses the perspective of national law, reconstructing the structure of universal law is more complicated. First, one must specify the referential national legal order. The next step is to derive the validity of international law from that legal order. Usually, recourse is taken to recognition: international law is explained as owing its validity to explicit or tacit recognition by the national legal order. Kelsen argues that this entails international law being annexed by the referential national legal order. What, then, about other national legal orders? What is the basis of their validity? On Kelsen's account, through the principle of efficiency, international law, even if part of the referential national legal order, provides the reason for the validity of the other national legal orders. Consequently, by first subsuming international law, the referential national legal order ultimately grounds the validity of all the other national legal orders too. It is no wonder that Kelsen, allowing himself politico-ideological remarks rare in his legal-theoretical *oeuvre*, detects in this fictitious argument not only state-solipsist but also nationalist, even imperialist, tones. The true universal law appears to be the referential national legal order, which is superior not only to international law but all other national legal orders as well. Yet the hypothetical nationalist legal theorist has accomplished his epistemological mission: 'the cognitive unity of all valid law' has been achieved.

Kelsen does not hide his preference for the primacy of international law; for internationalism over nationalism and state-solipsism; and for peace through law over imperialism. In disclosing where his sympathies lie, Kelsen acknowledges that he is overstepping the legitimate boundaries of objective scholarship. Yet he shuns the position assuming the primacy of national law also because of the perspectivism of the available referential national legal orders. The monist position attains cognitive unity through universal law at the high price of a new cognitive plurality. Each monist theorist subsumes international law and other national legal orders under her own national legal order which, for her, constitutes the universal legal order. Hence, at the end of the day victory would fall not to unity but to plurality. Of course, this is not a very attractive vision for a legal theorist for whom cognitive unity is a high-ranking epistemological value, if indeed not the highest.

Kelsen's legal-theoretical acrobatics culminates in the claim that, in the monist account, the validity of even the referential national legal order is based on the international legal principle of efficiency. How is this possible? If the validity of international law is based on a particular national legal order and if, in turn, the validity of the latter is – in accordance with all the other national legal orders – based on international law, are we not moving in a circle? Kelsen tries to break out of the circle by suggesting that we speak of the referential national legal order in two senses, wide and narrow. It is the referential national legal order in the wide sense that grounds the validity of international law and which through recognition includes the latter in its system. In turn, it is the referential national legal order in the narrow sense – that is, not including international law – which derives its validity from the international law principle of efficiency. This may not sound very persuasive.[5]

Kelsen's recapitulation of universal law is elegant, although dangerously close to conceptual gymnastics. However, even today his account may still provide international lawyers in particular with valuable insights and inspiration. Yet, in our post-national era, it can hardly convince as a portrayal of the unity of global law. Kelsen's universal law does not recognise non-state law at all, and, as we have seen, national legal orders can no longer – if indeed they ever could – be depicted in terms of a hierarchical normative *Stufenbau*, crowned by a *Grundnorm*, or in the international-law version of universal law, the international-law principle of efficacy and, ultimately, the *Grundnorm* of international law. Although in his discussion of the interdependence of international and national law Kelsen is no hard-core black-boxist, his account is a version of state-sovereigntism, which can no longer serve as the Master Principle bringing order to the disorder of global law. Nevertheless, Kelsen sends an important message even to someone who tackles the unity of post-national plurality from other premises: the perspectival character of all reconstructions of the unity of plurality.

Instead of Kelsenian formal unity, inter-regime unity of post-national law must be conceived of in discursive and cultural terms, keeping in mind that in addition to its normative aspect, law also consists of sociolegal practices, including legal discourse, and that the normative aspect involves sub-surface cultural layers too. What inter-regime unity exists is primarily produced by cross-boundary legal discourse and dialogue which, in turn, would not be possible without legal-cultural overlaps, commonalities, and border-transcending influences. I have found it fruitful to speak of a joint deep culture shared by diverse legal orders and which facilitates inter-regime contacts. Thus, for instance, sufficiently uniform application of EU law or European integration as legal integration in general would hardly have been possible without such a deep culture, common to the national legal orders of the Member States, as well as EU law.

In a globalising world, the legal culture informing legal *Vorverständnis* is globalising too. This also holds for legal language. The concepts, principles, theories, and methodologies of globalising legal culture have originally been developed in Western legal cultures: Continental European Romano-Germanic and Anglo-American common-law cultures. Subsequently, they

[5] Kelsen, 1967, 333–347.

have at least partially severed their ties with their cultural seedbed and undergone a process of formalisation; consequently, they can now be specified and substantiated with diverse culturally determined contents.[6] We could contend that, at its core, globalisation of law amounts to globalisation of a common legal deep culture. This would facilitate inter-regime dialogue and consensual solutions to fundamental conflicts of authority, and be the major cause for what unity the plurality of law can display at the global level. Yet such a contention must be accompanied by at least three vital qualifications.

First, we should be careful with universalist terms and pretensions, and not equate globalisation with universalisation. Universalist claims easily obtain ethnocentric and even neo-colonialist tones, especially when including indigenous and religious law. Because of its often individual-focused emphasis, not even human rights culture can profess universal adherence. How widespread legal deep culture is, is an empirical question. The answer also depends on how thick are the terms we use in defining the contents of this deep culture. The more we enrich the normative contents, the more controversial universalist claims become. This also means that it is possible to speak of legal deep cultures with wider and narrower reaches. Even when abandoning universalist claims, it may still make sense to speak of European legal deep culture. And, to narrow the scope, Nordic legal deep culture, common to the national legal orders of the Nordic countries, may be given a thicker definition than the European one. This entails – and this is my second qualification – the existence of a plurality of unities of plurality, (re)constructed at different levels and with different extensions.

The lesson of perspectivism we can learn from Kelsen leaves us with a similar conclusion; this constitutes my third qualification. For a legal theorist, no Archimedian point exists above and beyond all differentiated legal cultures. Legal theorists always embark on reconstructing both the unity and plurality of law carrying with them the legal-cultural package they have internalised in their *Vorverständnis*. For those of us who have been raised in Western legal culture(s) there is no escape from an imposed Eurocentrism. Among us, too, culturally determined perspectives vary, producing variety in our 'reflexion theories'.

So, plurality of unities there is, and in the dialectic of unity and plurality, it is plurality that finally gains the upper hand.

[6] Günther, 2001.

Epilogue

Incertitude

Abstractions of the Ideal Type

In this essay, my aspiration has been to present a legal-theoretical recapitulation of law; a reflexion theory of law, as Luhmann put it. I have resorted to two main methodological devices, which also imply perspectival choices. First, I have opted for discussing law in the framework of an ideal-typical modern state legal regime. The choice of modern state law as the perspectival premise has been motivated by its high grade of differentiation. This facilitates elaborating analytical distinctions which can then be applied to exploring other types of law too. In modern state law, legal norms have become detached from sociolegal practices and, due to their objectivation and dissemination in writing, embarked on a trajectory of their own, although never losing contact with sociolegal practices as law's social modes of existence. Parallel to the detachment of norms from practices, second-order, specialised, legal practices have emerged. First-order sociolegal practices remain the chief locus of law's realisation, while second-order practices monitor and react to disturbances in that realisation, and assume the tasks of (re)producing the normative legal order. The differentiation within sociolegal practices finds its parallel in the normative dimension in the division of primary and secondary rules, addressing, respectively, first- and second-order sociolegal practices. Differentiation of specialised second-order legal practices enhances the role of legal professionals and the importance for those practices of professional legal *Vorverständnis*, informed by the prevailing legal culture. Legal culture displays normative, conceptual, and methodological components. It also includes a legal language where legal concepts function as the vocabulary and patterns of legal argumentation and reasoning as the grammar.

My second methodological device has been to proceed in my discussion of modern state law by way of a criticism of Legal Positivism. Throughout the essay, my main interlocutors have been Hans Kelsen and, to a somewhat lesser degree, H. L. A. Hart. Arguably, modern state law has been the focus of Legal Positivism, too, although positivist analyses often come with universalist pretensions and are presented as conceptual truths, allegedly capturing the essence and the necessary features of law in general. Yet neither modern state law nor Legal Positivism's depiction of it can be accorded universal status. Modern state law is a particular type of law. It has not existed from the beginning nor will it survive until the end of time or the history of law; indeed, as I shall argue in this Epilogue, there are signs of its having already passed its high point. Neither has it ever been or will ever be the sole inhabitant of the global realm of law. Law is not, has never been, and will never be equivalent to modern state law. This is one of the main lessons of examining plurality in Part III. Still, I have found it rewarding to use modern state law as a general framework even when examining non-state law, such as transnational or religious and indigenous law. Thus, much of the discussion in Part III focused on how non-state law differs from and relates to state law.

In my criticism, I have attacked the universalist pretensions of Legal Positivism. Even as the dominant reflexion theory of modern state law, Legal Positivism has not gone uncontested. Legal positivists, though, have been quite denigrating with their criticisms and have availed themselves rather loosely of the label of Natural Law; for them, no third way exists that keeps clear of the shallows of both Legal Positivism and Natural Law. In a more detailed critique, I have targeted the reductionism of Legal Positivism: reduction of law to its normativity and exclusion of its sociality (Part I); reduction of law's normative substance to its surface level and downplaying its sub-surface, legal-cultural layers (Part II); and, finally, reduction of law's plurality to the simple diversity of state law and neglect of non-state law, as well as legal pluralism and interlegality (Part III).

In my own portrayal of modern state law, arrived at through criticism of Legal Positivism, I emphasise the importance of a relational approach. The three modes of existence of law provide three alternative gates of entry to law: law as a normative legal order; law as first-order sociolegal practices where the norms of the legal order are realised; and law as specialised legal practices where legal norms are (re)produced and which also react to disturbances in norms' realisation in first-order practices. Through whatever gateway one prefers to enter law, the other modes of existence cannot be ignored, either. Legal normativity must be related to sociality, and legal sociality to normativity. I have chosen to address first the sociality of law (Part I) and only then turn to its normativity (Part II), though sticking to the relational approach. The order could as well have been the reverse.

Legal norms are realised as part of the internal normativity of sociolegal practices. These, in turn, provide the basis for gathering legal norms into legal institutions. The main second-order, specialised legal practices of modern state law consist of legislation, adjudication, and legal scholarship. They all accomplish particular legal functions, but they all also participate in (re)producing the normative legal order. Legislative, judicial, and scholarly speech acts are interlinked by legal discourse, where their validity claims are reciprocally assessed and where the contents of the momentary legal order are determined. The normativity of modern state law is labelled by textuality, positivity, coerciveness, and order. Crucial for understanding how legal normativity connects to legal practices is the insight into its multi-layered nature. Legal culture, informing the *Vorverständnis* of legal professionals, forms part and parcel of the legal order. Inclusion of legal culture in law and refocusing discussion of legal validity on validity claims of legal speech acts also sheds new light on the relations of law and morality. The positions I defend are, first, that morally laden principles are integral elements of legal culture and, as such, are resorted to not only in hard but even in easy, routine, cases; and, secondly, that legislative and judicial speech acts always raise a claim to not being unjust. Some of the central legal principles have been enshrined in constitutional provisions on fundamental rights. Institutional support by legislative or judicial speech acts is necessary in order for moral principles to attain legal relevance. My examination of the normativity of modern state law concludes with a discussion of constitution. I treat constitution as the great mediator: it mediates between law and politics, facilitating the influence of law on politics and of politics on law; between *pouvoir constituant* and *pouvoir constitué*; and between deep-cultural principles and surface-level law. Nevertheless, I caution against exaggerating the significance of the constitutional problematic; a tendency common to present-day Kelsenians and theorists who, rather, seek inspiration from Carl Schmitt, Walter Benjamin, Jacques Derrida and Giorgio Agamben. Kelsen's hierarchical *Stufenbau*-view of the normative legal order neglects other than legislative sources of law, as well as law's sub-surface, legal-cultural layers. The same fallacy afflicts the search for the origin of all law in an act of *pouvoir constituant* or foundational violence beyond constitution.

Discussing law in the framework of ideal-typical modern state law has been my conscious perspectival choice. It does not, so I have argued, necessarily imply adopting an evolutionary view where modern state law with all its differentiations would epitomise the endpoint of progressive and cumulative development. In Part III, I survey post-national plurality, which also includes non-state law. Instances of non-state law coexist with but have emerged before (indigenous and religious law) or after (transnational law) modern state law. In this temporal sense, they can be termed instances of pre- and postmodern law, respectively. They are a healthy reminder of the parochiality of modern state law. The three modes of existence are not differentiated in all law with the same clarity, nor does all law share the same principles, concepts, and methods or employ the same language.

The methodological device of ideal types was elaborated by Max Weber and – a fact often ignored – Georg Jellinek. Ideal types are based on abstractions: to arrive at an ideal type of, say, capitalism, bureaucracy, or modern state law, certain prominent features of existing capitalist economies, administrative organisations, or state legal regimes are extracted and accorded a certain relative importance, while other features, considered less important or less representative, are ignored. Ideal types as such do not exist; all the existing tokens – say, existing state legal regimes as tokens of modern state law – deviate to a major or minor extent from the ideal type. Ideal types facilitate classification, identification of deviations, and discussing the backdrop to those deviations. Furthermore, they can be used at least partly as contra-factual premises of normative argumentation. If ideal types are criticised by reference to contradictory 'real-life' examples, the point of ideal-type methodology has been missed. In the ideal type of modern state law I have included respect for the principles of a democratic *Rechtsstaat* - or constitutional democracy, as the term goes in US debates. Of course, not all contemporary, past, or future state legal regimes live up to these principles. We have seen failed states; authoritarian or even dictatorial states, with no deference either to democracy, fundamental rights, or the rule of law; or states whose representatives portray them as an 'illiberal democracy'. And, inevitably, sooner or later in the discussion, extreme and appalling, wicked, state legal regimes pop up; say, Nazi Germany, apartheid South Africa or Stalin's Soviet Union. It is important to examine such deviances from the ideal type, as well as their societal and cultural setting; indeed, to repeat, enabling such an examination is one of the very points of ideal types. Yet the objective of this essay has not been to contribute to that discussion. At an ideal-type level of abstraction, I have, first, explored properties of modern state law which from a relational point of view appear pertinent but which Legal Positivism has tended to ignore or downplay. Secondly, by introducing instances of non-state law, I have wanted to show the historicity and particularity of this distinct type of law.

Common to the above-mentioned deviations is loss of law's autonomy. Autonomy is a central feature of the ideal type I have portrayed in Parts I-II. Autonomy displays multiple dimensions: normative, methodological, procedural, professional, and institutional. Normative autonomy distinguishes law from politics and from non-legal-normative orders, especially morals. Yet in neither direction does normative autonomy amount to isolation; a separability thesis is not warranted in respect of either politics or morals. Politics impacts law mainly but not exclusively at the surface level, while morality exercises its influence primarily through general legal principles, with their domicile in law's sub-surface layers. Law is not only about politics; it is also about morally laden principles. Its vocation is not only to generate order, in a conservative or reformist spirit. It also possesses a moral calling: to do and promote justice. In the methodological dimension, legal reasoning, decision-making, and justification are guided by a particular doctrine of legal sources, particular interpretative principles, and particular patterns of argumentation, which distinguish law from, say, political or economic reasoning, decision-making, and justification. Formal legal speech acts – laws and court decisions – are end products of legally determined procedures; hence the procedural autonomy. Key actor positions in specialised legislative, judicial and scholarly practices are occupied by legal professionals: legislative experts, judges, and legal academics. Legal professionals possess a legal *Vorverständnis*: practical knowledge of the normative, conceptual, and methodological ingredients of legal culture. Consequently, professional autonomy is an integral dimension of the autonomy of modern state law. Finally, institutional autonomy reserves legal practices for particular institutions: legislative ones for parliament, judicial ones for courts, and scholarly ones for universities and their law schools.

In explicit terms, I have said rather little – for some readers probably much too little – about power and interests in law. Yet they are a crucial aspect of all law, which should be included even in an ideal-typical presentation of modern state law; whatever else law is, it is also about power and interests. And, at least implicitly, power and interests have accompanied my survey of the properties of law. Law is not only about *ratio* but also about *voluntas*, and in modern state law the main expression of that *voluntas* is state power, backed up by coercive machinery. In turn, the content of state power is determined by political forces pursuing particular societal interests. Every time I have referred to policy-based legislation, law's use as medium, or its increased instrumentalisation, I have also implicitly referred to power and interests. I have also pointed to law's conservative and reformist potential but, by the same token, intimated that revolutions are not made by or through but against the law; within the domain of a-legality. Revolutionary disorder runs against the ordering vocation of law. Power in society is unevenly distributed and so is power *on*, *in* and *by* the law. Power *on* law is power affecting law; power *in* law power inherent in legal practices; and 'power *by* law' refers to the power effects of law. Through its power effects, law may amplify the uneven distribution of power and chances of interest realisation in society. Law also exercises symbolic power: it reflects, reinforces, and legitimates a particular view of social practices and relationships.

Emphasis on law's normative, methodological, procedural, professional, and institutional autonomy tends to sidetrack power and interests. Indeed, obscuring power and interests is a major symbolic power effect of autonomous law. That is why the implicit needs to be made explicit and the persistence of power *on*, *in*, and *by* law needs to be recalled. Still, equally important is to avoid reducing law to extra-legal power and interests. Law is not only about *voluntas* but also about *ratio*; not only about policies but also about principles; not only about medium but also about institution; not only about regulation but also about facilitation; and not only about perlocution but also about illocution. *Ratio* disciplines *voluntas*; principles filter policies; law as medium is embedded in law as institution; and laws and court decisions cannot engender perlocutionary effects without first obtaining illocutionary force. Power and interests do not enter the law in, as it were, a raw form, but as mediated and filtered through specialised legal practices and multi-layered legal normativity. Consequently, law not only amplifies, reinforces, and legitimates extra-legal power or serves as a vehicle for realising extra-legal interests. Law also constrains power and modifies the interests it is put to serve. Law is not only for the strong and powerful; it also for the weak and powerless.

At least, this is the case when a modern state legal regime approximates its ideal type. Legal practices and multi-layered legal normativity can only accomplish their mediating, filtering, and protective functions if law retains its autonomy. Flagrant aberrations from the ideal type tell about loss of autonomy; about extra-legal power and interests bulldozing an unconstrained entry into the law. Still, to complicate matters again, autonomy is a double-edged sword: it not only constrains but also produces power effects of its own. Autonomy entails uneven distribution of legal knowledge and power which exploits legal knowledge as a resource. It entails disempowerment of legal laymen who are illiterate in legal language; who are granted only subaltern, if any, roles in specialised legal practices; who are, through translation into legal language, deprived of their lifeworld problems; and who do not wield or benefit from but are subject to law's symbolic power. In discussing the autonomy of law, this flipside should not be passed over, either.

Throughout this essay, I have stressed the importance of legal culture, informing the *Vorverständnis* of legal professionals, for the functioning of modern state law. Accordingly, the principles of a democratic *Rechtsstaat* cannot be implemented without backing by an accommodating constitutional culture, animating not only legal but also political actors, as well as the citizenry at large. The existence of a legal and constitutional culture, simultaneously supporting and restricting legal and constitutional practices, cannot be taken for granted. It does not emerge from nothing but results from a process of sedimentation, carried forward by the very practices it is supposed to facilitate and constrain. This process can be lengthy and twisty, replete with controversies and interrupted by backlashes. This is one of the lessons to be learned from recent developments in some of new democracies of Central and Eastern Europe.

The normative, methodological, procedural, professional, and institutional autonomy of ideal-typical modern state law has facilitated my focus on the law's internal workings. Thus, in Part I, I examined law's internal sociality – its social modes of existence; society in law rather than law in society. Still, of course, law exists in society, and, as I have already pointed out in my remarks on power and interests, surrounding society impacts law and law impacts surrounding society. But as I also have already argued, in an ideal-typical, relatively autonomous modern state legal regime societal influences are intermediated through legal practices and filtered through legal culture. Yet law is dependent on society in an even more profound sense. Modern state law has rested on specific societal presuppositions which also have individual-level implications. To a large extent, incertitude about the future of law stems from the shaking of these presuppositions under the impact of the interwoven mega-trends of digitalisation and globalisation.

In the ideal type as a methodological device, 'ideal' does not connote normative preference but, rather, is used as a synonym for 'abstracted' or 'stylised'. But ideal types can never be normatively wholly innocent, either. Normative preferences influence what features a researcher incorporates in her ideal type and what importance she accords them. Inclusion of respect for the principles of a democratic *Rechtsstaat* in the ideal type of modern state law also reflects a normative position and lends 'ideal' a normative flavour too. The incertitude we experience about the future of law is not only cognitive uncertainty. Existing societal trends which seem to have repercussions for law. too. may make the future appear as a threat to the basic values which we have learned to cherish in modern state law - values such as democracy, fundamental rights, and the rule of law - and which together define a democratic *Rechtsstaat*. Transnational law does not relinquish state law but tends to reduce its role to formal transposition and legitimation and, when needed, coercive enforcement of norms drafted and negotiated beyond state borders. If the values of a democratic *Rechtsstaat* are considered worth defending, much depends on how they can be realised in denationalised and, at the same time, digitalised law. In the following, my focus will be on digitalisation, which in the long run may pose an even graver threat to those values than denationalisation as such. A word of caution is needed. Digitalisation is proceeding at such a pace that all depictions of its impact on societal presuppositions of law and on law itself tend to be already outdated by the date of publication. Yet this volatility makes it ever more important to heighten awareness of what is and what will be happening. Both the sociality and the normativity of law are undergoing at least potentially fundamental changes. Yet where, exactly, these changes and the underlying mega-trends are leading law is still uncertain, as indeed is the fate of state law.

The third mega-trend of our time is climate change, which constitutes a menace to human civilisation as a whole, even to the survival of the species. Here I must content myself with a few catchphrases. Taking climate change seriously and combating it by legal means presupposes rethinking the fundamental subject / object relationship between humans and surrounding nature on which modern state law is based. Clearly, this is one of the main issues where state law – as well as international and transnational law, which speak the same language – should learn from indigenous law. Why could not humans be considered custodians rather than proprietors and masters of nature? Why could legal subjectivity not be extended to nature?

Societal Presuppositions

However autonomous law may be, it is not isolated from surrounding society and societal changes, and even autonomy has societal presuppositions. In the decades elapsed since Kelsen's and Hart's recapitulations of modern state law, the societal environment has been undergoing momentous changes.

The ideal-typical modern state law has been the law of an ideal-typical modern national society, characterised by a capitalist market economy, a centralised state and bureaucracy, and the lifeworld as the sphere of everyday sociality. Capitalism there still is but it is not identical with the capitalism which, say, Weber had in mind when examining the affinity of modern, 'formal-rational' state law to capitalist economy and bureaucracy. The capitalism of Weber's time was industrial capitalism. Now steps - perhaps already decisive - have been taken to informational, digitalised, capitalism. Characteristic of the new form of capitalism is not only digitalisation – and, simultaneously, denationalisation – of production and commerce in goods and services but also, increasingly importantly, the emergence of a new, 'dematerialised' factor of production and assets: information or, to be more exact, data. The market economy still exists, too, but a new level mediates relations among sellers and buyers, and the realisation of economic laws of supply and demand: platforms. The market economy is taking the shape of a platform economy. Platforms – such as Amazon, Google, Uber and Airbnb – not only intermediate the functioning of the market economy; they also extract, collect and mine data as an ever more essential asset of informational capitalism. They are crucial players in what has come to be called Big Data and which is rapidly transforming not only capitalist market economy but also the other societal presuppositions of modern state law. For Weber, economy was still largely the national economy, although cross-border trade punctured national isolation. Contemporary corporations and their supply chains are transnational, as are financial institutions and transactions as well.

Present-day state administration bears little resemblance to bureaucracy such as Weber famously portrayed it. Weber's bureaucracy consisted of a centralised, hierarchical, and stable organisation, manned by appointed civil servants and clearly separated from surrounding society, only entitled to intervene in society within legally strictly delineated spheres of competence through legally defined means. Now we are confronted with a disaggregated state and a flexible, fluid, administrative organisation which is in multiple ways networked with not only national, transnational, and international peer units but also societal, primarily economic, corporate actors. In contemporary 'new governance', state administration and economy are connected by co-regulation and other types of partnership, blurring the boundary between public and private which was so unambiguously staked out in Weber's bureaucracy. The means of administrative intervention – 'regulation' as the term goes – have also been revolutionised, not least due to digitalisation and the rise of Big Data.

'Big Data' refers not only to the huge amount of data extracted, collected, and processed but also, and even primarily, to a combination of hardware and software technology, facilitating 'cloud'-computing, and algorithmic 'mining' of digital data for the purposes of pattern recognition and profiling, which, in turn, allow for both algorithmic prediction and pre-emption of human behaviour. Big Data relies on machine learning where algorithms improve automatically through experience. Big Data and machine learning as contemporary manifestations of digitalisation are rapidly bringing about potentially momentous changes in not only economy and administration but also the daily lifeworld, by the same token transforming the social practices where modern state law has been realised and (re)produced. Digitalisation also fundamentally affects what Mireille Hildebrandt has aptly termed 'the information and communication infrastructure of law'.[1] For its part, this infrastructure defines what kind of law is possible and what is not. Here we are not talking of causal determination but 'affordances', as the speedily spreading term goes. Evolutionary traps should be avoided, but still it is evident that oral infrastructure affords a different kind of law than a written one and that the affordances of an infrastructure relying on the printing press differ from those of a digitalised one. Writing has facilitated differentiation of legal norms from practices, and textuality is an integral feature of the normativity of modern state law, entailing the necessity and centrality of interpretation. Digitalisation of the information and communication infrastructure has consequences for all three modes of existence of modern state law: first- and second-order socio-legal practices, as well as legal normativity.

In the late seventies and early eighties, critical discussion of contemporary Western society was dominated by Foucault's genealogies of discipline, bio-politics, and normalisation, and Habermas' analysis of colonisation of *Lebenswelt* by System. Colonisation proceeded through the media of money and administrative power, as well as law also used as medium and closely intertwined with the other two media. At the time, digitalisation was only taking the first groping steps in specialised expert practices, and its future repercussions in the daily social lifeworld could hardly be anticipated. Both Foucault's and Habermas' critiques are still pertinent but they need updating. Digitalisation and Big Data afford new techniques of discipline, bio-politics, and normalisation. They also engender a threat of digital colonisation of the lifeworld. The everyday lifeworld is digitalising, under the impact of, say, the smart phone, home, and city or, to use other terms, the Quantified Self, the Internet of Things, and Ambient Intelligence, relating, respectively, to the digital mediation of our relation to ourselves (the subjective world), things around us (the objective world), and sociality (the social world). In the lifeworld the boundary between online and offline is increasingly blurred. Digitalisation not only affords new means of colonising lifeworld practices and relations by the systemic action fields of economy and administration. Digitalisation itself constitutes a new type of colonisation which affects the subjecthood of social actors and the social relations and practices they engage in.[2]

[1] Hildebrandt, 2015, 2018. [2] See, e.g., Hildebrandt, 2015; Greenfield, 2017; Cohen, 2019.

Modern state law has also relied on a particular view of individuals – the social actors of first-order sociolegal practices and the legal actors of second-order, specialised legal practices – as cognitively and volitionally autonomous persons, capable of deliberating their actions both collectively and individually and assuming responsibility for these. In the ordinary course of things legal norms are unconsciously realised in lifeworld practices, as part of diffuse social normativity. Yet social actors are able to cross the threshold of awareness and become conscious of legal normativity. Manifesting their autonomy, they are also capable of consciously breaking legal norms. The reasons may be interest-based, instrumental, as with the 'bad man' of Oliver Wendell Holmes; moral reasons, as with those engaging in civil disobedience; or ethical, value-related, as with conscientious objectors.

Foucault's and Habermas' critiques hinged on autonomous personhood. In his genealogies, Foucault not only laid bare the non-autonomous basis of modern, autonomous, subjectivity, thus continuing the dethronement of the sovereign subject, initiated by Nietzsche and Freud. The contemporary concern animating his 'histories of the present' consisted in the expansion and intensification of disciplining and normalisation, including harnessing law for these purposes and the intrusion of the 'logic of the norm' inside the law. In turn, what Habermas was worried about was the conversion of autonomous subjects of lifeworld relations into objects of bureaucratic interventions, as well as economic commodification and monetarisation. Digitalisation may constitute an even direr threat to autonomy. Not only is our relationship to the subjective, objective, and social world to a growing extent digitally mediated. Digitalisation facilitates manipulating our behaviour without our awareness, not to speak of control. The Freudian Id is complemented by the digital unconscious of Big Data, to resort again to Hildebrandt's terminology.[3] The next phase following data-extraction, data-mining, and profiling is pre-emption of our autonomous agency. Pre-emptive computing is probably only taking its first steps but already it influences what music we listen to; what movies we watch; what books we read; what advertisements we see and, consequently, what goods and services we acquire; what news we receive; or how we define our friends and enemies. Pre-emptive computing does not target us as autonomous individuals, but as data doubles algorithmically constructed from the traces we have left on the surface of the interconnected digital world and which have been processed as digital data. Pre-emptive computing targets behaviour, instead of actions by meaning-giving and autonomous persons. The crucial question is whether the digital unconscious will keep on growing and conquering space from autonomous personhood, by the same token threatening a central extra-legal presupposition for modern

[3] Hildebrandt, 2015.

state law and for realisation of the values and principles of a democratic *Rechtsstaat.*

In sum, the societal presuppositions of modern state law are shaking: economy and administration, as well as the daily lifeworld, are all caught in a rapidly advancing process of digitalisation and denationalisation: capitalism is turning from industrial into informational; the market economy is assuming the shape of a platform economy; Weberian bureaucracy is being substituted by fluid and networked administration where boundaries between national and transnational, as well as public and private, are becoming increasingly blurred; the information and communication infrastructure dominated by the printing press is being supplanted by a digital one; and even our everyday life is digitalising and, by the same token, denationalising. At the level of individuals, Big Data and pre-emptive computing and data-driven agency are shrinking the space of autonomous personhood and human agency. Foucauldian discipline, bio-politics, and normalisation have been reinforced by digitalisation, and Habermasian colonisation of the lifeworld has assumed digital shapes.

What, then, about law itself? What can we say of law's future and threats to the values of a democratic *Rechtsstaat*, that is, the value element of the 'ideal' of the ideal type of modern state law?

Towards Digitalised Law?

Digitalisation affects law in three ways. First, it alters societal and individual-related presuppositions on which modern state law has rested. Secondly, it creates new kinds of problem which call for legal remedies but where the means of modern state law may prove powerless. The call is for law on digitalisation. Thirdly, digitalisation impacts law itself, in all its three modes of existence: as first- and second-order sociolegal practices and as a normative legal order. Now the issue is not law on digitalisation but digitalisation of law.

Digitalisation raises intricate issues in diverse fields of law, ranging from human rights to intellectual property and competition law. Perhaps the most important concern privacy and data protection, relating to the relentless extracting, collecting, and processing of personal data by both private and public institutions. Problems start from the very definition of privacy and data protection.[4] Not without reason has contemporary society been called a surveillance society and contemporary economy not only informational but also surveillance capitalism.[5] The data we create through our online activities and by entering the focus of the sensors inbuilt in our smart phones, homes, and cities are divided into volunteered and observed. Volunteered are data deliberately posted on a web page - say, a photograph on an Instagram or

[4] Lessig, 2006; Hildebrandt, 2015; Cohen, 2019. [5] Zuboff, 2019.

Facebook account - or submitted to a platform or other service provider - say, credit card details to Amazon or eBay. I would call 'formally volunteered' – a third category between volunteered and observed – data whose collection and processing we formally consent to by a quasi-automatic click as a precondition for entering a web page and gaining access to information or services that may be indispensable for managing in contemporary society. In many - if not most - cases, the 'notice-and-consent' policy of platforms and other service providers makes a mockery of consent and contract, which, under the presuppositions of modern state law, are supposed to imply autonomous deliberation and agency. No policy of notice and consent extends to observed data on our online behaviour or data on our location and mobility collected by the sensors of our smart phones, homes, and cities. Issues of privacy and data protection transcend extraction and collection of data and reach out to subsequent processing: data-mining, pattern recognition and profiling, pre-emptive computing, as well as algorithmic decision-making by public and private institutions.

The European Data Protection Regulation (2018) is an heroic attempt to address a broad array of data-protection issues, from cybersecurity through notice-and-consent requirements to algorithmic decision-making. A detailed analysis of its achievements exceeds the ambition of this essay. Let me only point to a fundamental difficulty which law confronts when trying to cope with societal repercussions and applications of technological development. By its nature, law is reactive, responding to problems which can already be perceived and defined. The proactive potential of law is limited, and law tends to lag behind rather than anticipate technological innovations and their economic or administrative exploitation. And when the pace of technological change is as hectic as it is at present, laws may be outdated by new technologies even before entering into force. It is no wonder that the internet or cyberspace is one of the foremost fields of experimentation of new techniques of regulation; 'regulation 2.0', connected to 'new governance' and facilitated by digitalisation.[6]

The potential consequences of digitalisation on law's realisation are manifold and profound. Advancing digitalisation of both the general lifeworld and specialised expert practices is reducing the space for autonomous human agency and transforming the target of regulation from action to behaviour. Algorithms and computational codes and protocols regulate behaviour and bypass or pre-empt autonomous human agency. By the same token, law is loosening its connection to the internal normativity of social practices. Law crosses the threshold of awareness increasingly rarely, and 'bad men', conscientious objectors, and those engaging in civil disobedience have ever fewer opportunities for conscious, autonomous, violation of rules. Of course, social

[6] Stemler, 2016; Cantero Gamito, 2020.

practices exist - starting from the favourite example of marriage - where thorough-going digitalisation is hard to imagine. Digitalisation has also given rise to new social practices and corresponding collectives, within, say, commerce, the recycling economy, and political activism. These practices possess their own internal normativity and often enough transcend national borders, testifying to a denationalisation not only of the economy and administration but the daily lifeworld as well. Resistance and counter-tendencies to the sapping of autonomic human agency exist. Yet few action fields would be wholly immune to digitalisation; smart phones and homes, for instance, are digitalising family practices, too, thus introducing digital-driven agency into the heart of lifeworld practices.

Digitalisation has a potentially revolutionary impact even on second-order, specialised, legal practices. However, what that impact will, exactly, be is still largely a matter of guesswork. The affordances of a digital information and communication infrastructure differ from those of an infrastructure where the fundamental technology consisted of the printing press. Legal texts, a heritage from an age dominated by the printing press, have largely been converted into digital form, while those which have not are losing their value as legal sources. This has not only made legal texts more easily available. Even more important is their conversion into data; datafication, as one of the myriad neologisms of the digital age would have it. In this case, too, datafication facilitates algorithmic data-mining, pattern recognition, and prediction. American realists adopted the perspective of practising lawyers, and, from Holmes onwards, understood law as consisting of predictions of judicial decisions. Datafication makes prediction more reliable than ever before. Hart, among others, put forth the obvious objection that at least judges themselves, in identifying the law, are not predicting what judges will do. I would no longer be so sure. Maybe datafication of law turns out to be the ultimate, deferred triumph of American Legal Realism! What the realists could not, of course, anticipate is that such a triumph could also spell the end of autonomous legal reasoning and at least a partial replacement of human by data-driven agency even in legal practices; not only in legal counselling but also in adjudication and legal scholarship.

Algorithmic profiling is extensively used in such pre-judicial or pre-legal practices as policing and combating terrorism, where it may lead to preventive measures, even detention, with ensuing rule-of-law issues and at least a tension with the principle of presumption of innocence. Algorithmic decision-making is already in use, not only in private insurance companies or credit institutions, but in public administration too; in Finland, for instance, in taxation, social security, and refugee and immigration administration. No exceptional sibylline abilities are needed to presage that the same techniques will be sooner or later be adopted in judicial practices too; first in easy high-volume, low-cost cases but, subsequently, in a widening field. Even where reliance on algorithms does not extend to data-driven decision-making but space is left for autonomous deliberation, recourse will probably be taken to algorithmic support, for example, in processing legal source material, converted into digitalised data, or in profiling defendants in criminal cases and in general anticipating the perlocutionary effects of judicial decisions.[7] Digitalisation inserts itself into what has been termed the managerial turn in adjudication. This turn is manifest by transfer of high-volume, low-cost cases from ordinary courts to specialised tribunals, which in their composition, procedure, and decision-making often stand closer to administration than the ideal-typical courts of legal theorists, among them the present author.[8] As boilerplate clauses including waivers become increasingly common in contemporary - especially online - contracting and as, in the remit of *lex mercatoria*, hard cases are directed to arbitration, judicial practices appear to be losing much of the significance and the characteristics that legal theorists – among them, again, the present author – have accorded them in their reflexion theories.

Parliamentary legislative practices will probably formally retain the central position granted to them by the constitution of a democratic *Rechtsstaat*. Yet in transnational law the contribution of state legislation tends to shrink into sanctioning, transposing, and legitimating norms stemming from public and, increasingly, private transnational sources, such as transnational standard-setting bodies. In this constellation, parliamentary legislative procedure is relegated to a mere formality and disconnected from the discourses of deliberative democracy. Standardising practices stem from the age of industrial capitalism. The aim of industrial standardisation was to secure compatibility of industrial products and facilitate cross-border trade, to which, subsequently, were added considerations of occupational health and consumer protection. Francois Ewald, Foucault's disciple and assistant in Collége de France, discerned in standardisation an important token of Foucauldian normalisation.[9] Standards are formulated by technical experts and expressed in technical, instead of legal, language; in this respect, they are a conspicuous manifestation of technolegality. Yet alternative ways exist to achieve technical compatibility, enable cross-border trade through harmonisation of national standards, and define the criteria of occupational safety and consumer protection. At stake are not only 'objective' technical requirements but economic and even political interests as well. Standard-setting does not result unambiguously from application of technical expertise but is mediated by negotiations among affected interests; or, to be more exact, interests recognised as being affected and granted a 'stakeholder' position. Negotiations, conducted mainly behind closed doors, follow the logic of bargaining rather than the argumentative and public discourses of deliberative democracy. Interests and stakeholder positions may be far from equal. Behind the veil of technolegality, both economic and political power have their say.[10]

[7] Yeung, 2018, 2019. [8] Cohen, 2019, 143ff. [9] Ewald, 1990.
[10] Büthe and Mattli, 2011.

In the age of informational capitalism and digitalised communication and information infrastructure, standardisation is ever more crucial. Informational capitalism and Big Data not only thrive on but would be impossible without standard-produced interconnectivity – 'hyperconnectivity', as it is also called – among devices, networks, and data bases. These standards, too, result from standard-setting involving both technical expertise and interest assertion and bargaining. Yet the technolegality they embody displays novel features as well. They rarely pass the intermediary of state legislation but constitute a conspicuous example of self-regulation. They do not need the coercive machinery of the state and can therefore dispense with conversion into hard state law. Formulated as computational codes and protocols, they are self-executing, allowing for no contestation or deviation. The internal regulation of the internet is a prime example of two central features of regulation 2.0: self-regulation and self-executing technolegality.

Existing trends intimate that computational technolegality will label the future of both the sociality and normativity of law to an ever-widening and ever-intensifying extent. Its repercussions will probably transcend legislation which merely sanctions, transposes, and legitimates technolegality and where the inherent political choices have been made elsewhere than in a democratic legislative process worthy of a democratic *Rechtsstaat*. The textuality of legislation in general will probably not remain the same. Even if laws will not be expressed in the digital language of the novel communication and information infrastructure, they will probably be written in a way that facilitates translation into algorithms, enabling algorithmic administrative and judicial decision-making or at least algorithmic support for decision-making that still retains the appearance of autonomous deliberation and discretion. The targets of algorithmic regulation and decision-making are not treated as autonomous and individual human agents, but as data doubles, constructed from the data traces of individuals. The objective is not to provide reasons for action but to influence behaviour; not to pre-empt reasons but autonomous agency in general.

One of the binary distinctions which have structured my examination of the properties of law is law as institution and medium. Digitalisation and new-type technolegality have enhanced the position of law as medium at the expense of law as institution and, by the same token, aggravated the threat of colonisation of the lifeworld. Law as medium is a tool of social engineering and, as such, replaceable, if expedient, by another tool, another medium. Or, at least, this is the view of social engineering. From a legal perspective, this view ignores an important feature of modern state law, respecting the principles of a democratic *Rechtsstaat*. Specialised administrative law as perhaps the main token of law as medium is embedded in – and constrained by – normative principles and procedural safeguards of constitutional law and general administrative law: fundamental rights; judicial review, and contestability of administrative decisions; principles of *détournement de pouvoir* (France) or reasonability (the United Kingdom), *audiatur et altera pars* and other principles of 'natural justice'. These are principles and procedural safeguards of a democratic *Rechtsstaat*, which manifest law as institution rather than medium. Opting out of the legal alternative of social engineering entails opting out of rule-of-law principles and safeguards too.[11]

A tendency exists to approach law in general under the conceptual umbrella of regulation and to let efficacy determine the regulatory choice. In regulation studies, the standard definition is the following, formulated by Julia Black:

> Regulation is the sustained and focused attempt to alter the behaviour of others according to defined standards or purposes with the intention of producing a broadly identified outcome or outcomes, which may involve mechanisms of standard-setting, information-gathering and behaviour modification.[12]

The definition makes clear that regulation targets behaviour instead of reasoned actions. Under the regulatory approach, all law is treated as a medium which may have to retreat from the way of, say, more efficient technological regulation. If that happens, not only is law as medium freed from the tethers of law as institution; law as institution is simply ignored. If this is the direction where digitalised and denationalised law is heading, rule *of* law would come to an end; what, at the most, would remain would be rule *by* law. And if technological regulation through codes, protocols, and self-executing algorithms expands and substitutes for legal regulation, even the province of law as medium and rule *by* law will shrink. In the 1980s, critique of colonisation of the lifeworld and the disempowering repercussions of the welfare state involved a critique of juridification.[13] In contrast, critique of digital colonisation may involve a critique of dejuridification!

Digitalisation and the novel communication and information infrastructure display potential repercussions with regard to all the central characteristics of the normativity of modern state law: coerciveness, textuality, positivity, layeredness, and order. Self-executing regulation or self-executing, 'smart' contracts can take leave of coercive enforcement. With advancing digitalisation and transformation of legal source material - including laws - into data, textuality is dethroned from its key position. And if textuality goes, the need for interpretation goes as well. Data and algorithms not only require no interpretation; they do not even allow for interpretation and meaning-giving. This would alter the nature of legal practices, where interpretation has played such an integral role. Interpretation has been guided by legal professionals' practical knowledge, their *Vorverständnis*. What space digitalised law will leave for legal culture and *Vorverständnis*, and how digitalisation will affect these, remains to be seen. If the written repositories of legal cultures are digitalised, too, can we any longer talk of legal culture as a sub-surface layer of law, with both enabling and restricting consequences? Are we heading

[11] Hildebrandt, 2018. [12] Black, 2002. [13] See, e.g., Teubner, 1987.

towards a uni-level, cultureless law, towards a pure epistemological positivity where law, in line with other information converted into data, is reduced to its surface? What could be the principle of order of digitalised law? Networking and hyper-connectivity?

Only technological determinists would consider the scenarios and developmental paths sketched above as inevitable and exclusive of any alternatives. An appropriate reaction requires, first, specifying the legal issues engendered by digitalisation and accompanying denationalisation, extending from, say, intellectual property and competition law to the fundamental values and principles of a democratic *Rechtsstaat*. Secondly, the points should be identified where development and application of technology involve value-related, political, choices, related, for instance, to the information to be converted into digitalised data, as well as to extraction, collecting, mining, and processing of data. These are also the main points where legal reactions should set in.

Farewell to the Democratic *Rechtsstaat*?

The interwoven mega-trends of digitalisation and denationalisation put pressure on all three principal constitutional values of a democratic *Rechtsstaat*: democracy, human rights, and the rule of law. Democratic legislative processes, with their main institutional locus in parliament but interacting with free media and a robust civil society, have been crucial for democracy. Transnational law does not negate state law nor the legislative procedures prescribed by a state constitution. But it tends to reduce the role of these procedures to formal sanctioning and legitimation of contents drawn up beyond state borders, thus draining much of their deliberative and discursive substance. This is particularly conspicuous with transnational law manifesting tendencies of standardisation and expansion of technolegality.[14]

Law's digitalisation and denationalisation are closely connected to the regulatory approach: 'new governance' and 'regulation 2.0'. In institutional respect, the regulatory approach has led, not only in the USA, but also in the EU and individual European states, to proliferation of independent regulatory authorities: a third type of independent bodies, adding to courts and central banks. Independent regulatory authorities constitute an integral aspect of the disaggregation of the state. They work at arm's length from the political arena and are exempted from guidance by the political branches of government. Independent bodies are not supposed to either take or receive instructions from political institutions, such as parliament or government. Consequently, they lack the democratic legitimation which the legislative and the executive receive through elections, either directly or indirectly. The main rationales

[14] As a demolition of the concept of governance, see Christodoulidis, 2020.

behind independent regulatory authorities are, first, time consistency and credibility; second, expertise and professionalism; and, third, avoidance of conflicts of interest.[15] Yet, in a democratic *Rechtsstaat*, disconnect from democratic legitimation should be justifiable by other constitutional values. Judicial independence is warranted by both protection of fundamental rights and the rule of law. In contrast, constitutional justifiability of independent regulatory authorities is more questionable.

Legal remedies to the manifest democratic deficit, with its background in digitalisation, denationalisation, and the regulatory turn, have been sought in administrative legal principles and procedures – with the US Administration Procedure Act (1946) as an early trailblazer – and so-called stakeholder democracy. Despite all the innovativeness of theorising within Global Administrative Law, it is doubtful whether administrative legal means – such as hearings, reason-giving, and judicial review – can guarantee realisation of the constitutional value of democracy. The affordances of administrative procedure relate to the rule of law rather than democracy. In turn, 'stakeholder democracy' comes dangerously close to corporatism, with its bargaining processes and strained relationship with parliamentary, deliberative, democracy. 'Stakeholder democracy' should also be able to grapple with defining the relevant interests and guaranteeing them a level playing field. Even if, say, consumer and environmentalist interests are formally included in standard-setting, they may lack the technical expertise and the economic means needed for a real say in the process.

Originally, human rights have targeted state-level public authorities. Both theory and practice have changed, and the clear tendency is to extend their application to other institutional power holders at both state and transnational level. With the major exception of the EU, transnational legal regimes do not possess a constitution in the formal sense of the term. Still, they may display distinct constitutional functions, and fundamental rights may be part of the *ordre public* of the regime; say, *lex mercatoria* or instances of *lex digitalis.*[16] However, defining and protecting the right to privacy, as well as data protection as a human right on its own, in a digitalised, online world remains one of the most important tasks confronting legal and computing professionals; not to forget more traditional rights which call for redefinition in the digital context, such as freedoms of speech and religion.

The rule of law requires, among other things, legibility, clarity, and stability of laws, and transparency, accountability, and contestability of their execution. Laws which transpose technical standards into hard law or otherwise manifest a novel type of technolegality are largely illegible, not only to legal laymen but legal professionals too. They are written not in legal but in technical language, and not by legal professionals for other legal professionals but by technical experts for other technical experts. If laws which as such could be legible at

[15] Majone, 1994. [16] See, e.g., Teubner, 2020.

least to legal professionals are translated into digital, algorithmic language, they too are moved to the domain of illegibility. The algorithmic mode of expression enhances volatility of regulation, especially where machine learning is applied: machine-learning algorithms are constantly correcting themselves. Instability (and simultaneity) rather than stability (and linearity) marks the temporality of digital law. As acute observers have remarked, digitalisation reverses the constellation of institutional and individual transparency and opacity from what the rule of law implies: the more transparent individuals are rendered to power-wielding public and private institutions the more opaque these institutions become to the individuals subject to their power. Machine learning raises the opacity of algorithmic regulation and decision-making to a new level. Machine learning 'improves' algorithms and decision-making based on them without human intervention and in a way which may remain a mystery even to the designer of the original algorithm. Breaking institutional opacity and controlling and contesting algorithmic regulation and decision-making become crucial rule-of-law issues.[17] Questions keep piling up: how can decisions arrived at through algorithmic means be legally and factually justified; how can the human agents accountable for the decisions and the underlying algorithms be identified; how can algorithmic accountability in general be realised: and how can the decisions and the underlying algorithms be contested and subjected to judicial review?

The Owl of Minerva

Our contemporary age is replete with technological utopias and dystopias. We should be wary of both. Societal and legal development are not technologically determined. Technology provides affordances but the choices – or non-choices! – how to exploit these are made by human agents.

Every age is inclined to exaggerate its significance, so they say. Still, it is possible, even probable, that law is facing profound changes in all its three modes of existence. This essay may turn out to be one of the numerous aspiring owls of Minerva, struggling to take flight in the twilight of a fading historical epoch.

[17] Hildebrandt, 2018; Yeung, 2018; Cohen, 2019, 238ff.

References

Aarnio, A. (1979). *Denkweisen der Rechtswissenschaft*, Vienna: Springer.

(1987). *The Rational as Reasonable*, Dordrecht: Kluwer.

Alexy, R. (1989). *A Theory of Legal Argumentation*, Oxford: Clarendon Press.

(2002). *A Theory of Constitutional Rights*, translated by J. Rivers, Oxford: Oxford University Press.

(2003). *The Argument from Injustice: A Reply to Legal Positivism*, translated by B. L. Paulsen and S. L. Paulsen, Oxford: Oxford University Press.

Austin, J. L. (1984). *How to Do Things with Words*, Oxford: Clarendon Press.

Benda-Beckmann, F. von (2002). Who's Afraid of Legal Pluralism. *Journal of Legal Pluralism and Unofficial Law*, 34(47), 37–82.

Bennett, T. W. (2004). *Customary Law in South Africa*, Cape Town: Juta.

(2011). An African Doctrine of Equity in South African Public Law. *Loyola Law Review*, 57(4), 709–726.

Berger, P. L., and Luckman, T. (1967). *The Social Construction of Reality: A Treatise in the Sociology of Knowledge*, New York: Doubleday.

Black, J. (2002). Critical Reflections on Regulation. *Australian Journal of Legal Philosophy*, 27(1), 1–35.

Bourdieu, P. (1977). *Outline of a Theory of Practice*, Cambridge: Cambridge University Press.

Brennan, G., Eriksson, L., Goodin, R. E., and Southwood, N. (2013). *Explaining Norms*, Oxford: Oxford University Press.

Büthe, T., and Mattli, W. (2011). *The New Global Rulers: The Privatization of Regulation in the World Economy*, Princeton: Princeton University Press.

Cantero Gamito, M. (2020). The Role of the EU in the Transnational Governance of Standards, Contracts and Codes, in M. Cantero Gamito and H.-W. Micklitz, eds., *The Role of the EU in Transnational Legal Ordering: Standards, Contracts and Codes*, Cheltenham: Edward Elgar, 2–26.

Christodoulidis, E. (2020). The Myth of Democratic Governance, in P. F. Kjaer, ed., *The Law of Political Economy: Transformation in the Function of Law*, Cambridge: Cambridge University Press, 62–88.

Cohen, J. E. (2019). *Between Truth and Power: The Legal Constructions of Informational Capitalism*, New York: Oxford University Press.

Cover, R. M. (1986). Violence of the Word. *Yale Law Journal*, 95, 1601–1629.

Dawson, J. P. (1968). *The Oracles of Law*, Westport: Greenwood Press.

Durkheim, E. ([1893] 1984). *The Division of Labour in Society*, translated by W. D. Halls, with an introduction by Lewis Coser, Basingstoke: Macmillan.

Dworkin, R. (1978). *Taking Rights Seriously*, London: Duckworth.

(1986). *Law's Empire*, London: Fontana.

(2001). Thirty Years On. *Harvard Law Review*, 115, 1655–1687.

Eriksen, E. O., Joerges, C., and Neyer, J., eds. (2003). *European Governance, Deliberation and the Quest for Democratisation*, Oslo: Arena.

Ewald, F. (1990). Norms, Discipline, and the Law. *Representations*, 30, 138–161.

Ferrari, S. (2002). Canon Law as a Religious Legal System, in A. Huxley, ed., *Religion, Law and Tradition: Comparative Studies in Religious Law*, London: Routledge, 49–60.

Foucault, M. (1974). *The Order of Things*, London: Tavistock.

(1979). *Discipline and Punish: The Birth of the Prison*, Harmondsworth: Penguin.

Fuller, L. L. (1969). *The Morality of Law*, New Haven: Yale University Press.

Gardner, J. (2012). *Law as a Leap of Faith: Essays on Law in General*, Oxford: Oxford University Press.

Glenn, H. P. (2014). *Legal Traditions of the World*, 3rd ed., Oxford: Oxford University Press.

Goyard-Fabre, S. (1972). *Essai de critique phénoménologique du droit*. Klinckbeck: Paris.

Greenfield, A. (2017). *Radical Technologies: The Design of Everyday Life*, Brooklyn: Verso Books.

Günther, K. (1993). *The Sense of Appropriateness*, Albany: State University of New York Press.

(2001). Rechtspluralismus und universaler Code der Legalität: Globalisierung als rechtstheoretischer Problem, in L. Wingert and K. Günther, eds., *Die Öffentlichkeit der Vernunft und die Vernunft der Öffentlichkeit*, Frankfurt: Suhrkamp, 539–567.

Habermas, J. (1984). *The Theory of Communicative Action*, vol. 1, translated by T. McCarthy, London: Heinemann.

(1989a). *The Theory of Communicative Action*, vol. 2, translated by T. McCarthy, Cambridge: Polity Press.

(1989b). Towards a Communication-Concept of Rational Collective Will-Formation. *Ratio Juris*, 2(2), 144–154.

(1996). *Between Facts and Norms*, translated by W. Rehg, Cambridge: Polity Press.

Haeyk, F. A. (1982). *Law, Legislation, and Liberty*, vol. 1, London: Routledge and Kegan Paul.

Halliday, T., and Shaffer, G., eds. (2016). *Transnational Legal Orders*, Cambridge: Cambridge University Press.

Hart, H. L. A. (1959). Scandinavian Realism. *Cambridge Law Journal*, 17(2), 233–240.

(1961). *The Concept of Law*, Oxford: Clarendon Press.

(2012). Postscript, in *The Concept of Law*, 3rd ed., Oxford: Clarendon Press, 238–275.

Hartney, M. (1991). Introduction: The Final Form of the Pure Theory of Law, in H. Kelsen, *General Theory of Norms*, translated by M. Hartney, Oxford: Clarendon Press, ix–liii.

Hattenhauer, H., ed. (2002). *Thibaut und Savigny: Ihre programmatischen Schriften*, 2nd ed., Munich: Vahlen.

Helleiner, E. (2016). Regulating the Regulators: The Emergence and Limits of the Transnational Financial Legal Order, in T. Halliday and G. Shaffer, eds., *Transnational Legal Orders*, Cambridge: Cambridge University Press, 231–257.

Hildebrandt, M. (2015). *Smart Technologies and the End(s) of Law: Novel Entanglements of Law and Technology*, Cheltenham: Edward Elgar.

(2018). Algorithmic Regulation and the Rule of Law. *Philosophical Transactions of the Royal Society of London, Series A*, 376(2128), 20170355.

Hohfeld, W. N. (1919). *Fundamental Legal Conceptions as Applied in Judicial Reasoning and Other Legal Essays*, New Haven: Yale University Press.

Hurri, S. (2014). *Birth of the European Individual: Law, Security, Economy*, London: Routledge.

Jansen, N. (2010). *The Making of Legal Authority: Non-Legislative Codifications in Historical and Comparative Perspective*, Oxford: Oxford University Press.

Kelsen, H. (1911). *Hauptprobleme der Staatsrechtslehre entwickelt aus der Lehre vom Rechtssatze*, Tübingen: J. C. B. Mohr.

(1929). Wesen und Entwicklung der Staatsgerichtsbarkeit, in *Veröffentlichungen der Vereinigung der deutschen Staatsrechtslehrer 5*, Berlin: De Gruyter, 30–123.

(1945). *General Theory of Law and State*, translated by Anders Wedberg, Cambridge: Harvard University Press.

(1957). *What Is Justice? Justice, Law and Politics in the Mirror of Science*, Collected Essays, Berkeley: University of California Press.

(1967). *The Pure Theory of Law*, translation from the 2nd German ed. by M. Knight, Berkeley: University of California Press.

(1991). *General Theory of Norms*, translated by M. Hartney, Oxford: Clarendon Press.

(2008). *Reine Rechtslehre. Studienausgabe der 1. Auflage 1934, herausgegeben von Matthias Jestaedt*. Tûbingen: Mohr Siebeck.

Klabbers, J. (1996). The Redundancy of Soft Law. *Nordic Yearbook of International Law*, 65, 156–182.

Koskenniemi, M. (2007). International Law: Constitutionalism, Managerialism and the Ethos of Legal Education. *European Journal of Legal Studies*, 1, 1–18.

Koskenniemi, M., and P. Leino. (2002). Fragmentation of International Law? Postmodern Anxieties. *Leiden Journal of International Law*, 15(3), 553–557.

Kramer, M. H. (2008). *Where Law and Morality Meet*, Oxford: Oxford University Press.

Lagerspetz, E. (1995). *The Opposite Mirrors: An Essay on the Conventionalist Theory of Institutions*, Dordrecht: Kluwer.

Lessig, L. (2006). *Code: And Other Laws of Cyberspace, Version 2.0*, 2nd rev. ed., New York: Basic Books.

Lindahl, H. (2013). *Fault Lines of Globalization: Legal Order and the Politics of A-legality*, Oxford: Oxford University Press.

Luhmann, N. (1994). *Die Wirtschaft der Gesellschaft*, Frankfurt: Suhrkamp.

(2004). *Law as a Social System*, translated by K. A. Ziegert, Oxford: Oxford University Press.

MacCormick, N. D. (1981). *H. L. A. Hart*, London: Edward Arnold.

(1986). Law as an Institutional Fact, in N. D. MacCormick and O. Weinberger, eds., *An Institutional Theory of Law*, Dordrecht: Kluwer, 49–76.

(1999). *Questioning Sovereignty*, Oxford: Oxford University Press.

(2008). *Institutions of Law*, Oxford: Oxford University Press.

Majone, G. (1994). The Rise of the Regulatory State. *West European Politics*, 17(3), 77–101.

Makkonen, K. (1965). *Zur Problematik der juridischen Entscheidung*, Turku: Turun yliopisto.

Mataija, M. (2020). Private Standard Setting in the TBT Agreement: Control and Recognition. In M. Cantero Gamito and H.-W. Micklitz, eds., *The Role of the EU in Transnational Legal Ordering: Standards, Contracts and Codes*, Cheltenham: Edward Elgar, 135–154.

Maus, I. (1989). Die Trennung von Recht und Moral als Begrenzung des Rechts. *Rechtstheorie*, 20(2), 191–210.

Michaels, R. (2005). The Re-State-Ment of Non-State Law: The State, Choice of Law, and the Challenge from Global Legal Pluralism. *Wayne Law Review*, 51, 1209–1259.

Micklitz, H.-W. (2011). Introduction, in H.-W. Micklitz, ed., *The Many Concepts of Social Justice in Private Law*, London: Edward Elgar.

Pashukanis, E. B. ([1929] 1978). *Law and Marxism: A General Theory*, translated by B. Einhorn, edited and introduced by C. Arthur, London: Pluto Press.

Pound, R. (1939). Public and Private Law. *Cornell Law Quarterly*, 24(4), 469–482.

Prewo, R. (1979). *Max Webers Wissenchaftsprogramm*, Frankfurt: Suhrkamp.

Raz, J. (1979). *The Authority of Law: Essays in Law and Morality*, Oxford: Oxford University Press.

Reckwitz, A. (2002). Toward a Theory of Social Practices: A Development in Culturalist Theorizing. *European Journal of Social Theory*, 5(2), 243–263.

Reinach, A. ([1913] 2013). *The Apriori Foundations of the Civil Law*, Heusenstamm: Ontos.

Ricoeur, P. (1992). *Oneself as Another*, translated by K. Blamely, Chicago: Chicago University Press.

Roberts, S. (2005). After Government? On Representing Law without the State. *The Modern Law Review*, 68(1), 1–24.

Rosa, H. (2013). *Social Acceleration: A New Theory of Modernity*, translated by J. Trejo-Mathys, New York: Columbia University Press.

Sassen, S. (2008). *Territory, Authority, Rights: From Medieval to Global Assemblages*, Princeton: Princeton University Press.

Savigny, K. F. von ([1814] 2002). Vom Beruf unsrer Zeit für Gesetzgebung und Rechtswissenschaft, in H. Hattenhauer, ed., *Thibaut und Savigny: Ihre programmatischen Schriften*, Munich: Vahlen, 42–87.

([1840] 1981). *System des heutigen römischen Rechts*, vols. 1–2, Aalen: Scientia. (System I–II)

Schatzki, T. R. (1997). *Social Practices: A Wittgensteinian Approach to Human Activity and the Social*, Cambridge: Cambridge University Press.

Schepel, H. (2005). *The Constitution of Private Governance: Product Standards in the Regulation of Integrating Markets*, Oxford: Hart.

(2013). The New Approach to the New Approach. *Maastricht Journal of European and Comparative Law*, 20(4), 521–533.

Schmitt, C. ([1921] 2014). *Dictatorship: From the Origin of the Modern Concept of Sovereignty to Proletarian Class Struggle*, translated by M. Hoelzl and G. Ward, Cambridge: Polity.

([1928] 2008). *Constitutional Theory*, translated and edited by J. Seitzer, with a foreword by E. Kennedy, Durham: Duke University Press.

Schroer, M. (2006). *Räume, Orte, Grenzen: Auf dem Weg zu einer Soziologie des Raums*, Frankfurt: Suhrkamp.

Schutz, A. (1962). Common-Sense and Scientific Interpretation of Human Action, in M. Natanson, eds., *Collected Papers I. The Problem of Social Reality*, introduced by M. Natanson, with a preface by H. L. van Breda, The Hague: Martinus Nijhoff.

Searle, J. R. (1988). *Speech* Acts, Cambridge: Cambridge University Press.

(1995). *The Construction of Social Reality*, Harmondsworth: Allen Lane.

(2010). *Making the Social World: The Structure of Human Civilization*, New York: Oxford University Press.

Shapiro, S. J. (2011). *Legality*, Cambridge: Belknap Press.

Skinner, Q. (1989). The state, in T. Ball, J. Farr, and R. L. Hanson, eds., *Political Innovation and Conceptual Change*, Cambridge: Cambridge University Press, 90–131.

Slaughter, A.-M. (2004). *A New World Order*, Princeton: Princeton University Press.

Sousa Santos, B. de (2002). *Toward a New Legal Commonsense: Law, Globalization and Emancipation*, 2nd ed., Toronto: Butterworths.

Stemler, A. (2016). Regulation 2.0: The Marriage of New Governance and Lex Informatica. *Vanderbilt Journal of Entertainment and Technology Law*, 19(1), 87–132.

Stolzenberg, N. M. (2015). Is There Such a Thing as Non-State Law? Lessons from Kiryas Joel, in M. A. Helfand, ed., *Negotiating State and Non-state Law: The Challenge of Global and Local Legal Pluralism*, Cambridge: Cambridge University Press, 261–307.

Summers, R. S. (1982). *Instrumentalism and American Legal Theory*, Ithaca: Cornell University Press.

Tamanaha, B. Z. (2001). *A General Jurisprudence of Law and Society*, Oxford: Oxford University Press.

Teubner, G., ed. (1987). *Juridification of Social Spheres*, Berlin: De Gruyter.

(2004a). Global Private Regimes: Neo-Spontaneous Law and Dual Constitution of Autonomous Sectors?, in K.-H. Ladeur, ed., *Public Governance in the Age of Globalization*, Aldershot: Ashgate, 71–87.

(2004b). Societal Constitutionalism: Alternatives to State-Centred Constitutional Theory?, in C. Joerges, I. J. Sand, and G. Teubner, eds., *Constitutionalism and Transnational Governance*, Oxford: Hart, 3–28.

(2013). *Constitutional Fragments: Societal Constitutionalism and Globalization*, Oxford: Oxford University Press.

(2020). Counter-Rights, in P. F. Kjaer, ed., *The Law of Political Economy: Transformation in the Function of Law*, Cambridge: Cambridge University Press, 372–393.

Teubner, G., and Fischer-Lescano, A. (2004). Regime Collisions: The Vain Search for Legal Unity in the Fragmentation of Global Law. *Michigan Journal of International Law*, 25, 999–1017.

Tobin, B. (2014). *Indigenous Peoples, Customary Law and Human Rights: Why Living Law Matters*, London: Routledge.

Tuomela, R. (2002). *The Philosophy of Social Practices: A Collective Acceptance View*, Cambridge: Cambridge University Press.

Tuori, K. (2011). *Ratio and Voluntas: The Tension between Reason and Will in Law*, Aldershot: Ashgate.

(2015a). *European Constitutionalism*, Cambridge: Cambridge University Press.

(2015b). *Lawyers and Savages: Ancient History and Legal Realism in the Making of Legal Anthropology*, London: Routledge.

Twining, W. (2000). *Globalization and Legal Theory*, Evanston: Northwest University Press.

(2009). *General Jurisprudence: Understanding Law from a Global Perspective*, Cambridge: Cambridge University Press.

Weber, M. ([1922] 1978). *Economy and Society*, edited by G. Roth and C. Wittich, translated by E. Fischoff et al., Berkeley: University of California Press.

Wintgens, L. (2012). *Legisprudence: Practical Reason in Legislation*, Farnham: Ashgate.

Woodman, G. R. (1998). Ideological Combat and Social Observation: Recent Debate about Legal Pluralism. *The Journal of Legal Pluralism*, 30(42), 21–59.

Wróblewski, J. (1979). Verification and Justification in the Legal Sciences. *Rechtstheorie*, 1, 195–213.

Yeung, K. (2018). Algorithmic Regulation: A Critical Interrogation. *Regulation and Governance*, 12(4), 505–523.

Yeung, K., & Lodge, M. (2019). *Algorithmic Regulation*, Oxford: Oxford University Press.

Zuboff, S. (2019). *The Age of Surveillance Capitalism: The Fight for the Future at the New Frontier of Power*, London: Profile Books.

Index

Other Books in the Series (*continued from page iv*)

Lewis: *Choice and the Legal Order: Rising above Politics*
Likosky: *Law, Infrastructure and Human Rights*
Likosky: *Transnational Legal Processes: Globalisation and Power Disparities*
Lixinski: *Legalized Identities*
Loughnan: *Self, Others and the State: Relations of Criminal Responsibility*
Lunney: *A History of Australian Tort Law 1901-1945: England's Obedient Servant?*
Maughan & Webb: *Lawyering Skills and the Legal Process, 2nd Edition*
McGlynn: *Families and the European Union: Law, Politics and Pluralism*
Mertens: *A Philosophical Introduction to Human Rights*
Moffat: *Trusts Law: Text and Materials*
Monti: *EC Competition Law*
Morgan: *Contract Law Minimalism: A Formalist Restatement of Commercial Contract Law*
Morgan & Yeung: *An Introduction to Law and Regulation: Text and Materials*
Nicola & Davies: *EU Law Stories: Contextual and Critical Histories of European Jurisprudence*
Norrie: *Crime, Reason and History: A Critical Introduction to Criminal Law, 3rd Edition*
O'Dair: *Legal Ethics: Text and Materials*
Oliver: *Common Values and the Public–Private Divide*
Oliver & Drewry: *The Law and Parliament*
Palmer & Roberts: *Dispute Processes: ADR and the Primary Forms of Decision-Making, 1st Edition*
Palmer & Roberts: *Dispute Processes: ADR and the Primary Forms of Decision-Making, 3rd Edition*
Picciotto: *International Business Taxation*
Probert: *The Changing Legal Regulation of Cohabitation, 1600-2010: From Fornicators to Family, 1600-2010*
Radi: *Rules and Practices of International Investment Law and Arbitration*
Reed: Internet Law: Text and Materials
Richardson: *Law, Process and Custody*
Roberts & Palmer: *Dispute Processes: ADR and the Primary Forms of Decision-Making, 2nd Edition*
Rowbottom: *Democracy Distorted: Wealth, Influence and Democratic Politics*
Sauter: *Public Services in EU Law*
Scott & Black: *Cranston's Consumers and the Law*
Seneviratne: *Ombudsmen: Public Services and Administrative Justice*
Seppänen: *Ideological Conflict and the Rule of Law in Contemporary China: Useful Paradoxes*
Siems: *Comparative Law, 2nd Edition*
Stapleton: *Product Liability*
Stewart: *Gender, Law and Justice in a Global Market*
Tamanaha: *Law as a Means to an End: Threat to the Rule of Law*
Tuori: *Properties of Law*
Turpin & Tomkins: *British Government and the Constitution: Text and Materials, 7th Edition*

Twining: *General Jurisprudence: Understanding Law from a Global Perspective*
Twining: *Globalisation and Legal Theory*
Twining: *Human Rights, Southern Voices: Francis Deng, Abdullahi An-Na'im, Yash Ghai and Upendra Baxi*
Twining: *Jurist in Context: A Memoir*
Twining: *Karl Llewellyn and the Realist Movement, 2nd Edition*
Twining: *Rethinking Evidence: Exploratory Essays, 2nd Edition*
Twining & Miers: *How to Do Things with Rules, 5th Edition*
Wan: *Film and Constitutional Controversy*
Ward: *A Critical Introduction to European Law, 3rd Edition*
Ward: *Law, Text, Terror*
Ward: *Shakespeare and Legal Imagination*
Wells & Quick: *Lacey, Wells and Quick: Reconstructing Criminal Law: Text and Materials, 4th Edition*
Zander: *Cases and Materials on the English Legal System, 10th Edition*
Zander: *The Law-Making Process, 6th Edition*

International Journal of Law in Context: A Global Forum for Interdisciplinary Legal Studies

The *International Journal of Law in Context* is the companion journal to the Law in Context book series and provides a forum for interdisciplinary legal studies and offers intellectual space for ground-breaking critical research. It publishes contextual work about law and its relationship with other disciplines including but not limited to science, literature, humanities, philosophy, sociology, psychology, ethics, history and geography. More information about the journal and how to submit an article can be found at http://journals.cambridge.org/ijc

For EU product safety concerns, contact us at Calle de José Abascal, 56–1°,
28003 Madrid, Spain or eugpsr@cambridge.org.

www.ingramcontent.com/pod-product-compliance
Lightning Source LLC
LaVergne TN
LVHW062207200926
848484LV00006B/1344

* 9 7 8 1 1 0 8 8 4 4 7 2 7 *